Message From
RICHARD LAUBSCHER,
NEDBANK MANAGING DIRECTOR

Drum for many years played a significant role in mirroring the experiences of South Africans — capturing the good and the bad times visually and in the written form.

As a bank that is committed to 'the healing process' through reconstruction and development, it is apt that we should be associated with Jürgen Schadeberg's *Sof'town Blues* — a book that presents its readers with an insight into black cultural, social, sporting and musical life back in the swinging 1950s.

Jürgen has for many years photographed and filmed the lives of black South Africans and by supporting his work in a book such as *Sof'town Blues*, we believe we are creating an opportunity for all South Africans to share in the rich cultural heritage that many may previously not have experienced.

We believe that the book has a positive contribution to make, bringing about one nation. It draws on, among other things, the surge of optimism and creativity that prevailed in the 1950s prior to the repressive apartheid years that followed that era.

Our sincere congratulations to Jürgen and all who had the insight and vision to produce this book which shares with all South Africans an history that brings with it a message of hope and promise.

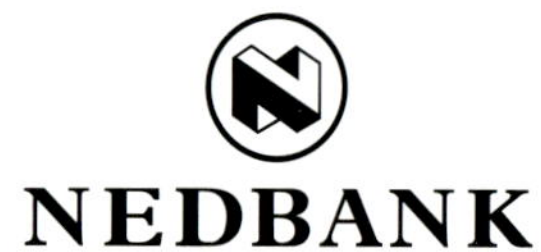

Sof'town Blues
Images from the black '50s

Jürgen Schadeberg

First Published in German.... in Germany in 1991 under the title
DRUM.
Rogner & Bernhardt Gmbh & Co. Verlags KG, Hamburg

Edited & compiled by Jürgen Schadeberg & Klaus Humann

First Published in English in South Africa by
Jürgen Schadeberg, 1994
19 Kangnussie Road
Pinegowrie 2123
South Africa

ISBN O 9583980 1 1

Editor:	*Ingrid Obery*
Cover Design:	*Ingrid Obery*
DTP:	*Centre Court Studio*
Printed by:	*Creda Press, Cape Town*
Distributed by:	*African Book Centre*
	PO Box 15302
	Hurlyvale, 1611
	South Africa

Permission to use Robert Gosani's photographs kindly given by his widow, Tilly Gosani.

The Authors

ANTHONY SAMPSON: Was born in 1926 and studied in Oxford. From 1951 to 1954 he was editor of *Drum*. When he returned to London, he worked for *The Observer*. In the early 1960s he published *The Essential Anatomy of the British Democracy*, an analysis of the British working class system, and a book which made him famous. He has continued to write and has published widely on issues ranging from the American oil industry to the international arms trade.

JÜRGEN SCHADEBERG: Born in Berlin, West Germany in 1931. After the war, he studied photographic theory at the School for Optic and Phototechnic, Berlin. He then went on to work as an apprentice photographer for the German Press Agency in Hamburg. During the 1950s he came to South Africa where he worked as the chief photographer on *Drum* magazine. In the early 1960s he went to London where he edited the magazine *Creative Camera* and freelanced as a photojournalist around Europe and the United States. In the 1970s he taught photography at the New School in New York and film making and photography at the Central School of Art and Design in London. He was also involved in devising and organising an exhibition called the 'Quality of Life' which showcased the opening of the National Theatre in London. He also made documentaries for British and German television. In the 1980s he retuned to South Africa and has since been directing and co-producing documentaries, such as: *Have you seen Drum recently, ANC —War and Peace, The Seven Ages of Music, Drumbeats* and, more recently, *Voices from Robben Island*.

Schadeberg has also had numerous photographic exhibitions and has compiled and edited many books. He is presently working on proposals for television documentaries and drama's.

Foreword

For a brief time there was a new monthly magazine called *African Drum*. The first word in the title indicated it was intended for Africans in a country where race and colouring determined everybody's position in society. It was also a time of the emergence of an Afrikaner government that had vowed to put everybody firmly in their place, political and social, through legislation that went under the umbrella of a concocted Afrikaans name, apartheid — which soon attempted to hide its sinister purpose by claiming to be 'separate development'.

Neither the *African Drum* nor apartheid was popular with Africans, now insistently called Natives by the Nationalist Party government, which claimed African-ness for its own race, the Afrikaners. But it in time realised that it was abdicating its proclaimed native status to black people, and so called them Bantu — which, alas, only means 'people'. The black magazine also dropped 'African' from its title and became, simply, *Drum* — a publication that was to interest people of all colours, and not only in South Africa, by indirectly opposing a government that was to change apartheid's official names for decades in its attempt to make the ideology palatable to the country and the world.

Drum could not confront apartheid head-on because it would be banned — as other publications were to be over the following years. The strategy it developed, starting in its first birthday issue, was to expose the evils of the racist system without actually condemning official policy. That first exposé was of a convict labour system which won the government votes among Afrikaner farmers in the Eastern Transvaal. Africans convicted of minor offenses were hired out to farmers as cheap labour for the duration of their sentences. But many never came back — beaten to death for unsatisfactory work or simply retained beyond the end of their sentences because they were productive workers. Or the farmer didn't want to give up such cheap — almost free — labour in a country where all black labour was so cheap that mechanisation was not necessary.

The bravest journalist ever to pound a typewriter in South Africa had himself arrested and, with some difficulty, convicted: friends around the courts were too willing to pay the fines he pretended he could not afford. Henry Nxumalo came back from the potato farms around Bethal haggard and dirty — but ready to joke about the brutal experiences from which he had finally escaped when he had enough information. And Henry was willing to return to Bethal for Jürgen Schadeberg to take photographs that would be be incontrovertible proof of the exposé he would write.

The cover picture for the birthday issue showed a man on horseback holding a long whip overseeing rows of lesser men wearing only sacks — holes for head and arms — digging up potatoes with their bare hands. There was world-wide shock, questions were asked in the South African parliament, the government could not deny the evidence and appointed a commission of enquiry whose finding did not change anything.

For another *Drum* birthday, Henry Nxumalo had himself arrested to give a first-hand account of the routine breaching of regulations at The Fort, a former military base that had become a prison, which loomed over the centre of Johannesburg and was known by its black inmates as 'Number Four'. But we had to obtain photographic evidence of something, almost anything!, illegal done by warders. The editor, Anthony Sampson, scouted around Hospital Hill and found that the prison yard was in clear view from the roof of the nearby nurses quarters. Deborah Duncan, another white Drummer, posed as a landscape photographer and was given permission to take her unwieldy cameras onto the roof for panoramic shots of the City of Gold in the late afternoon.

The camera was a home-made Big Bertha of the days before telephoto lenses. Of course Deborah had to have black 'boys' to manhandle it, and she chivvied them with proper South African impatience in the presence of the matron. But after the matron's departure, I helped Bob Gosani line up the four-foot long wooden camera as the prison yard filled up with men at the end of their day outside the cells.

The scene Bob Gosani photographed — while Deborah modestly turned away — was as Henry Nxumalo had said it would be. Lines of naked men sitting on the ground and, in turn, rising, approaching the warders and clapping their hands — not holding anything, Baas! — and then leaping in the air to show their bare buttocks: nothing hidden up my arse, Baas...!

That was the central photograph of our birthday issue — and, again, it caused outrage and was published around the world. And again the government was unable to deny the humiliation visited on Africans by white authorities disregarding its own prison regulations.

There were other exposés of the evils of apartheid which made *Drum* an international byword for investigative journalism. But the magazine was far from a simple vehicle for protest. Most of the time, it was a fun publication and so popular with apolitical Africans and any outsiders curious about life in the slum townships. They were amazed to find townships were vibrant and fun-loving — despite a poverty instigated by politics which in turn resulted in often random black-on-black crime.

Photographs and extracts in this book reflect that life which, on my return after three decades in exile, I find is still looked back on with fondness and nostalgia.

Arthur Maimane, 1994

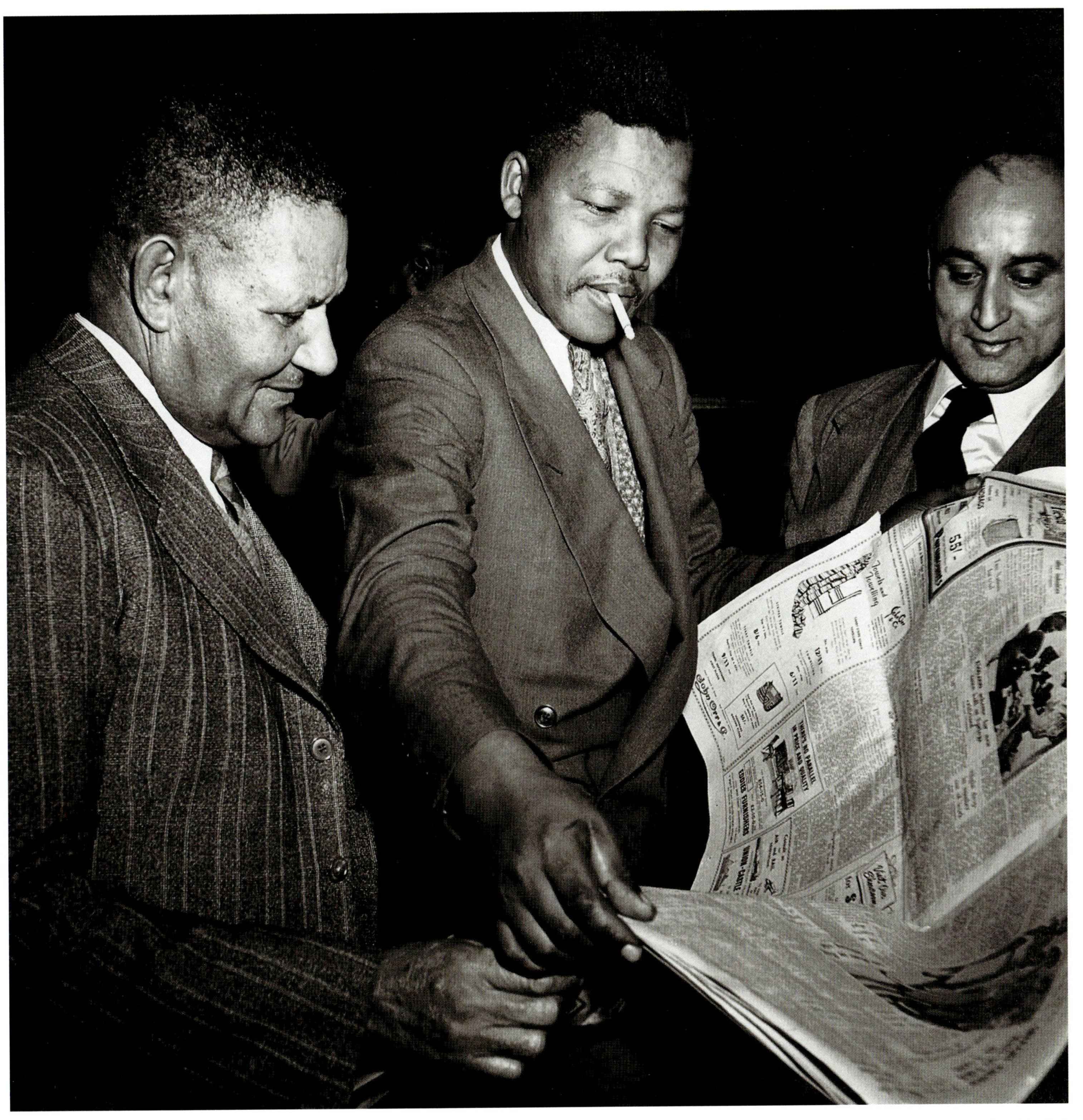

JOHANNESBURG 1952
ANC President J S Moroka, leader of the ANC
Youth League Nelson Mandela and Yusuf Dadoo,
president of the South African Indian Congress,
meet outside a Johannesburg courtroom during
the Defiance Campaign trial. The trial ended with
a verdict of guilty, but the leaders were given a
nine month suspended sentence.

JÜRGEN SCHADEBERG

The Golden Age of Black Journalism

Terms like renaissance or awakening do not do justice to it. It was a period of unequalled black fulfillment and achievement, succeeded by an upsurge of political rebellion which saw the rich and colourful tapestry of arts and culture unravel. Of course brutal repression was soon to follow.

The 1920s to the 'roaring' 1940s in South Africa saw an emergent black society of mimics who followed their 'master's voice' in all spheres of culture and the arts. They dutifully did the Charleston, and copied other whitemen's traits. Even in dress, the slave mentality was evident — they mimicked the Oxford suit styles, Batersby hats and white mannerisms. But the 1940s showed a slight shift towards American influences.

Then like a bolt of lightening, the 1950s came, and only the Creator himself knows what strange chemistry went on among black people. As if injected with a new 'life serum' black people underwent changes for the good that surpassed anything in their history so far. Even the oppressors looked up in surprise.

The period could, in my opinion, be described as one of miracles. These miracles were reflected in the writing, politics, trade, fashion, sport and other activities. And there were talented writers who recorded all this glory and triumph.

In the forefront of the recorders of this historic period were the *Drum* school of writers.

But there was also the serious side to this enlightened period. Politically, we witnessed the emergence of characters like Oliver Tambo, Nelson Mandela, Walter Sisulu, Duma Nokwe, Robert Sobukwe and many more with outstanding leadership traits. Trade unions and other economic aspects of black endeavour increased in size and productivity. There grew an 'awareness to become activists and participants rather than servants'.

In an escape from the drudgery of oppression and repressive laws, the people formulated their own amusements and entertainment. Paramount among these was the shebeen, an institution unique to the cultural, writing and artistic fraternity of black society. It was more than just a beerhall or watering hole. It was more like a home from home.

All of these things were written about, recorded, photographed, during this 'Golden Age of black journalism.

'Doc' Bikitsha, 1994

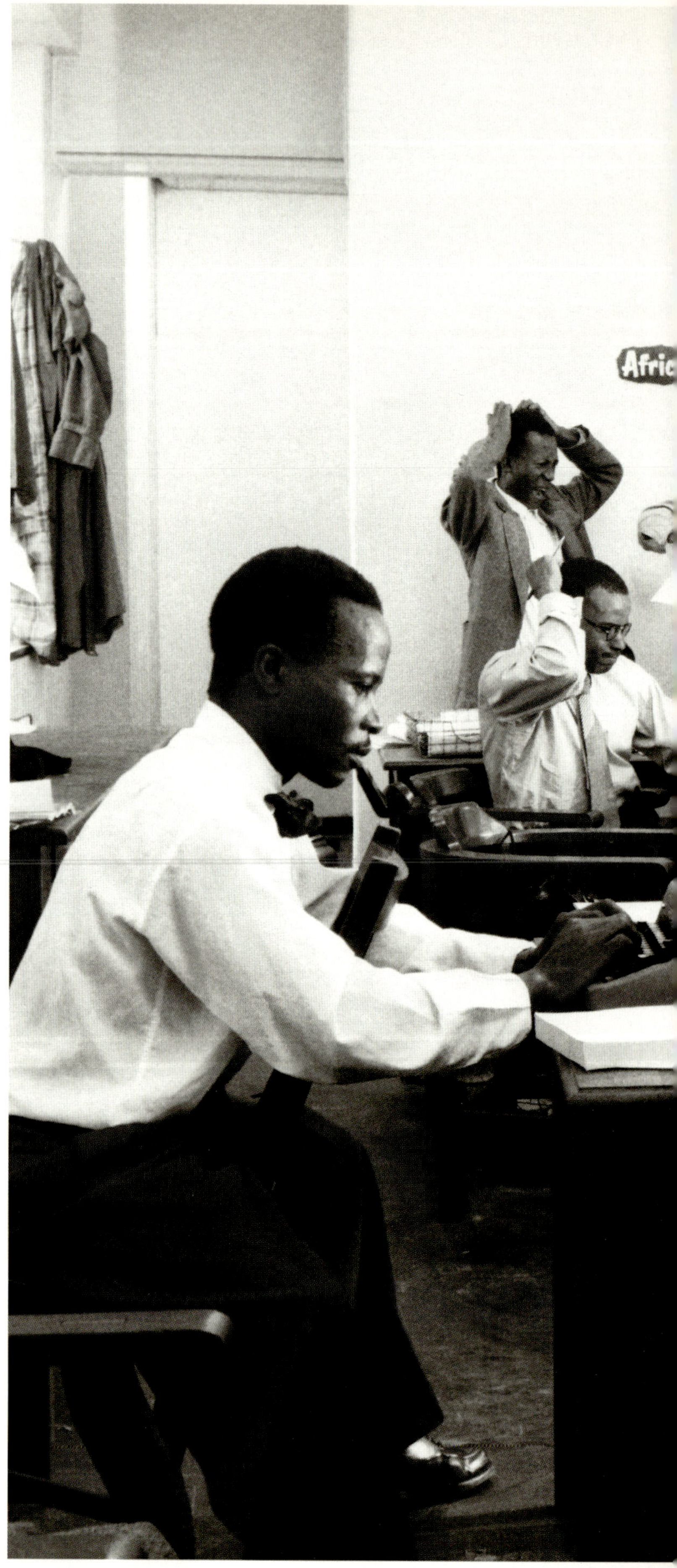

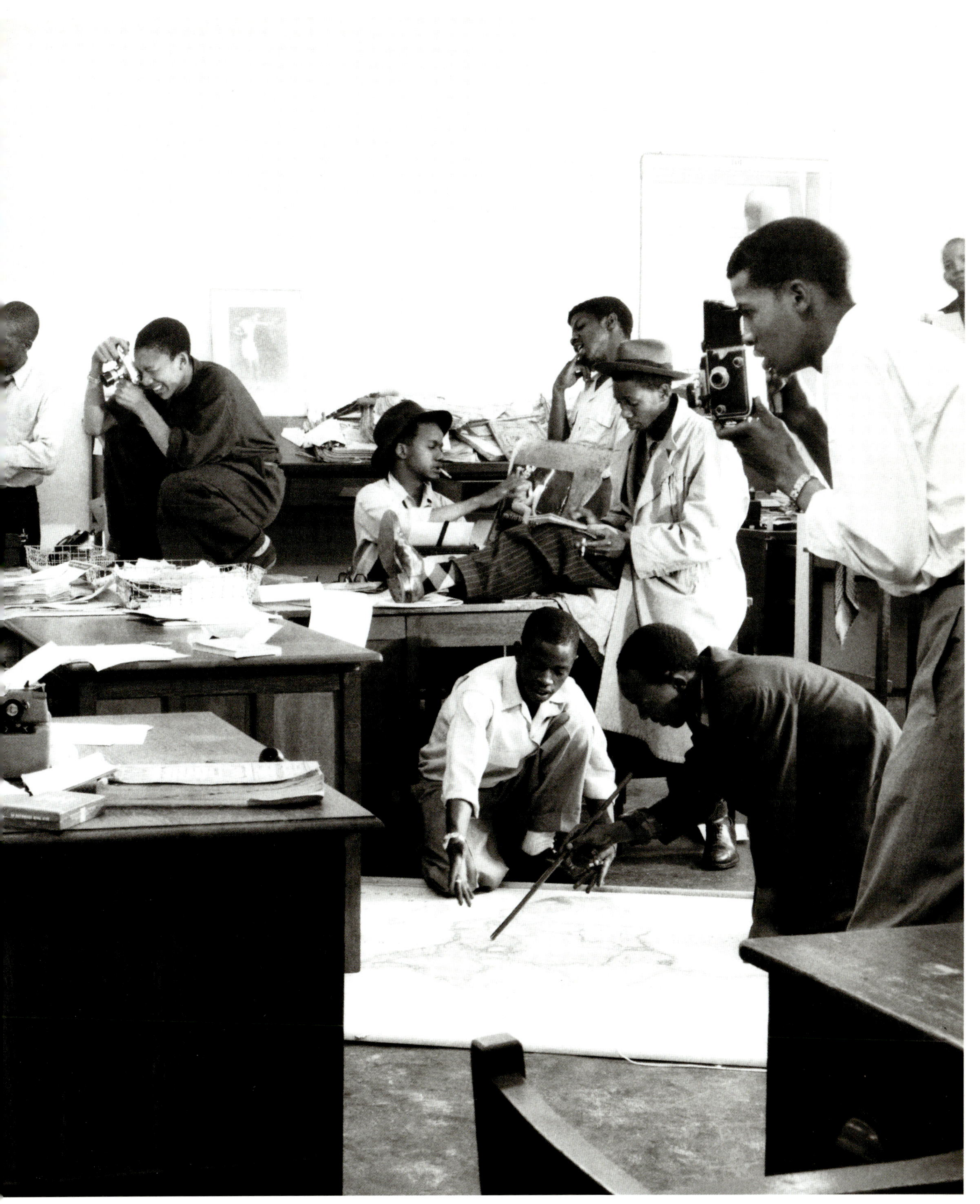

*JOHANNESBURG 1954 The **Drum** office with Henry Nxumalo, Ezekial Mphahlele, Casey Motsisi, Can Themba, Arthur Maimane (wearing hat with cigarette), Victor Xashimba, Dan Chocho and Bob Gosani (right, with camera)*

Black Johannesburg in the 1950s

ANTHONY SAMPSON, 1990

The early 1950's — black Johannesburg! I had the good luck to find myself in the midst of this exciting world when I was invited to South Africa to become editor of *Drum*. *Drum* was a hugely circulating magazine which provided an outlet for black writing and journalism. And it brought me into close contact with many of the most talented black writers and photographers of that time.

Can Themba, Ezekiel Mphahlele, Henry Nxumalo, Arthur Maimane, Casey Motsisi, and Bob Gosani. Now their names are the stuff of legend. Then, they represented young and irrepressible talent.

It was an era when creative young blacks, despite the hardships and constraints, could still express their own aspirations and self-awareness, with an energy and optimism which, during the later decades of oppression, appeared

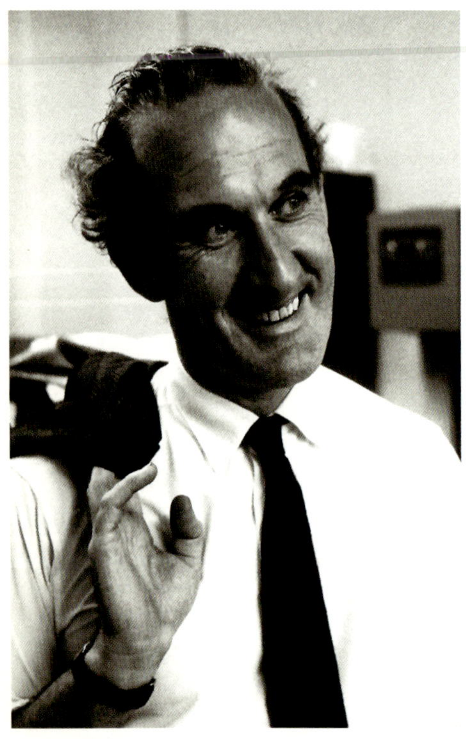

Anthony Sampson started as a journalist with **Drum** in 1951.

JÜRGEN SCHADEBERG

full of both courage and irony. And now in the 1990s, with the relaxing of police restraints and the unbanning of black political organisations, a new generation looks back on the 1950s as a golden age of writers, artists and musicians.

What struck me most in the early 1950s was the irreconcilable contrast between the vigour with which black people at all levels were adapting themselves to city life, and the determination of the apartheid government to prevent them from becoming part of it.

At the simplest level young black workers were recruited from the impoverished rural areas to work the gold mines: they knew of the hardships, but they were still attracted the the excitement of 'The Golden City'. At another level, black writers and intellectuals were cutting their links with their country roots and embracing the complexities, dangers and tensions of urban life.

I arrived in Johannesburg fresh from Oxford, where I had been studying Elizabethan literature, seemingly a world away from the black urban buzz. Not so, however. The vibrating life of the shebeens in the black townships of Johannesburg seemed far closer to the Shakespearean world, and particularly to Falstaff's world, than anything I had encountered in Britain. There was the same sense of constant danger and uncertainty, the pressing together of intellectuals, gangsters and ordinary workers, the excitement with city life, of newcomers from the country, and above all the discovery of language and ideas with a freshness which the English themselves had lost.

The *Drum* office in Johannesburg was a scene of almost continual activity and confusion. It was, as far as I could discover, the only office at the time where blacks and whites sat next to each other, sharing the same typewriters or drinking out of the same tea-cups. To many white secretaries or messengers who visited this multi-racial enclave, it

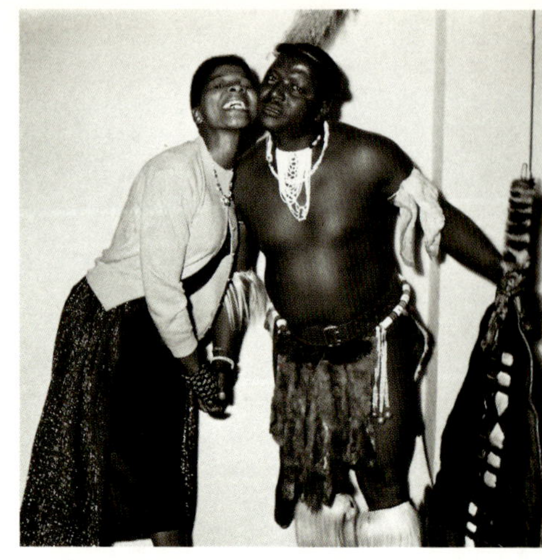

The **Drum** office, never boring... a tribal chief poses with one of the journalists.

BOB GOSANI

was an astonishing revelation that black men were able to type, to operate a telephone exchange, to take photographs — and even to engage visitors in lively repartee.

The office had no visible order, no hierarchy, no division; and it looked all the more chaotic because the reporters did not need to go outside the door to find the news; the news came to them. Gangsters would come into that big shabby room to offer their life stories. Pin-up girls came to be photographed against an improvised back-drop. Politicians came to explain their new campaigns. One day I was told there were seven witch-doctors waiting to see me, and there they were, in their full regalia of beads, complaining that they had been libeled in the last month's issue.

The early 1950s was also the time when the African National Congress was beginning to flex its political muscles, when it organised the 'Defiance Campaign' of passive resistance against the apartheid system. And together with other *Drum* reporters I soon came into close contact with the President of the ANC, Chief Albert Luthuli, and with the younger leaders who were organising the campaign. The most prominent of these was the young lawyer, Nelson Mandela, who had his own law firm with his friend Oliver

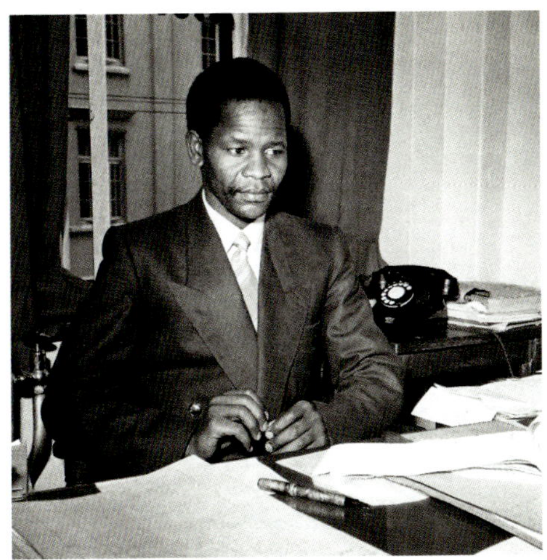

JOHANNESBURG 1952
Oliver Tambo, Nelson Mandela's partner, in their law office.

JÜRGEN SCHADEBERG

Tambo, quite near the center of Johannesburg. Their office was an important centre of news and activity. Mandela organised the volunteers for the Defiance Campaign, and watched as his recruits deliberately broke apartheid laws by walking illegally into townships. He was an important friend and ally to *Drum*.

By the 1950s South Africa already had many more urbanised black communities than existed in most other parts of Africa. Since the end of the last century black townships had grown up around the gold and diamond mines. These were now producing a third and fourth generation of urban black people. The second world war had brought a new boom to Johannesburg and had encouraged a new optimism among black people in South Africa: an expectation that they would become part of a larger western world, in keeping with wartime idealism and anti-racism.

Against this optimism the Afrikaner apartheid government was elected in 1948. The ruling National Party was determined to pursue an opposite course of intensified segregation and removal of black rights — and ultimately the removal of the majority of black people from the 'white' urban areas. Ironically blacks were already becoming more thoroughly urbanised than the Afrikaners themselves, who were much keener to maintain the rural roots from which most of their confidence and culture had sprung.

The Afrikaners still had their own fantasy of a feudal life: themselves as paternal farmers and blacks as grateful serfs — a fantasy which helped them to justify the ruthless forced removals of apartheid. But black people had no such romantic idea of the countryside; to them it meant grinding poverty, over-farmed land and impossible obligations to their families. In the cities, and above all in Johannesburg, they found an escape from those constraints, and from the tribal traditions and hierarchies within which the Afrikaners were so keen to maintain them.

Of all South Africa's cities, Johannesburg was the chief magnet. The gold mines below and around the city absorbed hundreds of thousands of contract workers. They arrived from the rural areas to be kept in bachelor compounds. Then, months later they were sent back to their homes when their contracts expired. This world existed alongside a much more sophisticated black Johannesburg — a Johannesburg of shebeens, dancehalls, snappy dressers — where life was lived fast, and on the streets. And it was this world which provided much of the creative talent in the magazine *Drum*.

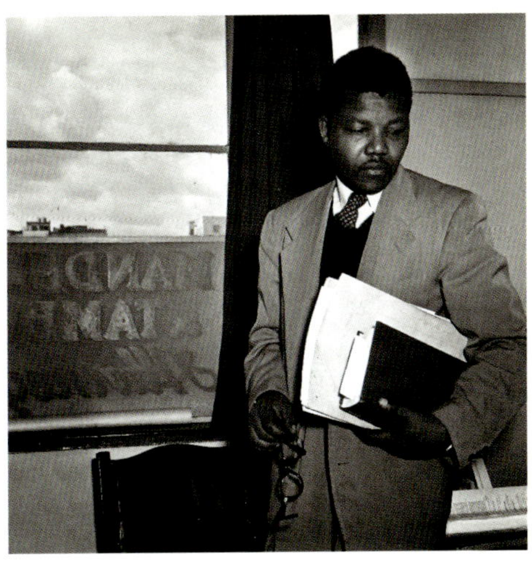

JOHANNESBURG 1952
Nelson Mandela in his law office.

JÜRGEN SCHADEBERG

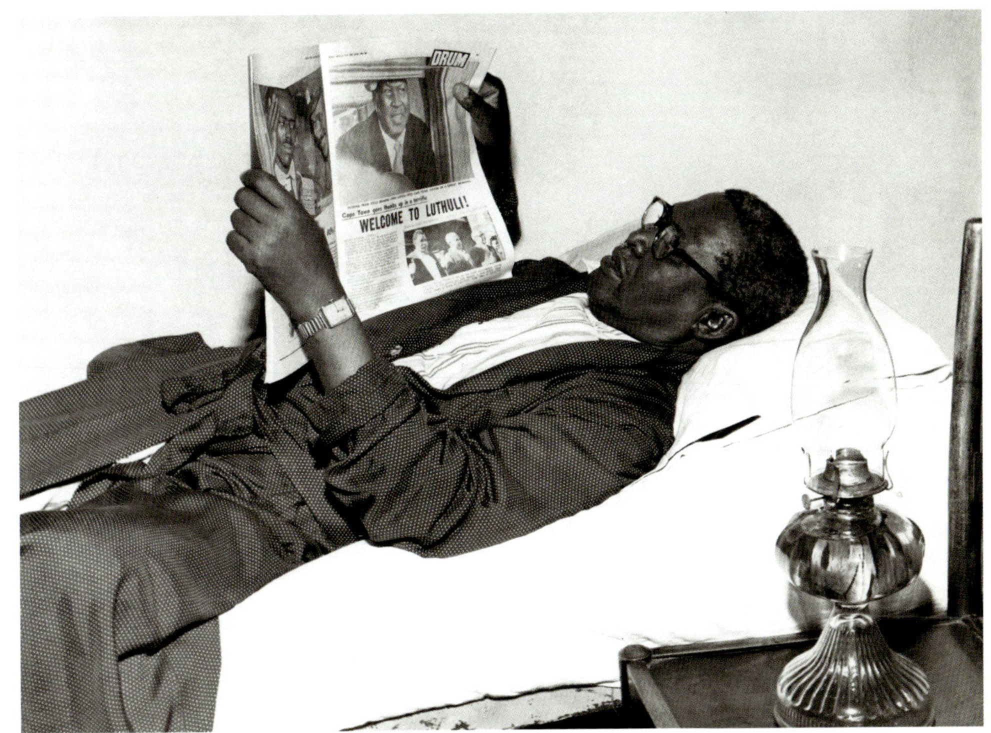

DURBAN 1959
Chief Albert Luthuli, leader of the ANC, reading a article about his recent lecture tour to Cape Town

RANJYTH KALLY

The creative energy of black Johannesburg at that time had an importance beyond the purely cultural field. For it revealed — more clearly than any statistical evidence — that black people had become an essential part of urban South Africa, and would never give up their demands for political rights.

The black talent that was emerging in the 1950s was almost totally neglected by white South Africa — and by the rest of the world. The white press and radio paid hardly any attention to what was happening in Sophiatown, which later became part of the country's mythology. Superb songs would be sold outright to record companies for a few pounds. The short stories and reporting by black writers never found their way into the white press — much was lost forever.

But whites could not fail to notice the vibrancy of this black life, however much it was rendered separate by the apartheid system. Young black children in the streets of Johannesburg played their own tunes on penny-whistles with passionate originality, dancing as they played, while middle-aged whites watched them baffled, worried, yet as fascinated as if they were following pied pipers, by the talent that sprang from these strange outcasts.

Much of the most creative activity in black Johannesburg centered on Sophiatown. It has since often been portrayed with loving nostalgia, for instance in the musical *Sophiatown*, or in the paintings by the black artist Gerald Sekoto. In fact Sophiatown — a slum suburb five miles from Johannesburg's city centre — teemed with criminals, drunks and prostitutes. It was filthy, overcrowded and it stank, and it had a very high murder rate. But it became a heartland of developing urban black culture — it vibrated with activity, talk and excitement. It was full of shebeens or speakeasies like the 'Thirty-nine Steps' or 'Back O' The Moon' — where I spend many an evening in the 1950s — where black teachers, jazz-players or city workers could drink illegally together, and where whites were still welcome de-

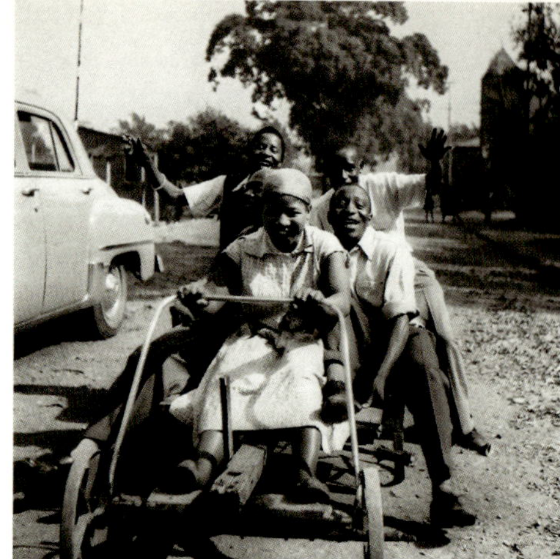

GEORGE GOCH TOWNSHIP, 1958
Jazz queen Thoko 'Skukuma' Thomo and four of her group 'Lo-Six'.

PETER MAGUBANE

spite the incursions of apartheid and the police.

Most of the writers, musicians and artists in black Johannesburg gravitated towards Sophiatown. Two of its most remarkable residents in the 1950s were Bloke Modisane and Can Themba, who were both closely involved with *Drum*. Bloke (who later wrote a vivid autobiography called *Blame Me on History*) was a short-story writer who lived in a squalid backyard, where he had furnished his single room with fastidious taste, complete with a collection of classical records, and champagne waiting in the 'fridge, as if it were part of an apartment in a fashionable white suburb.

Can was the most electric talker of his time, and probably the most brilliant of the writers I worked with on *Drum*. In his Sophiatown base, which he called 'The House of Truth', he always relished argument, drink and seduction. This vibrancy always placed him centre-stage, jerking his wiry body and licking his lips as he talked. More than anyone else, Can expressed both the excitement and the desperation of that place and time. He liked to quote

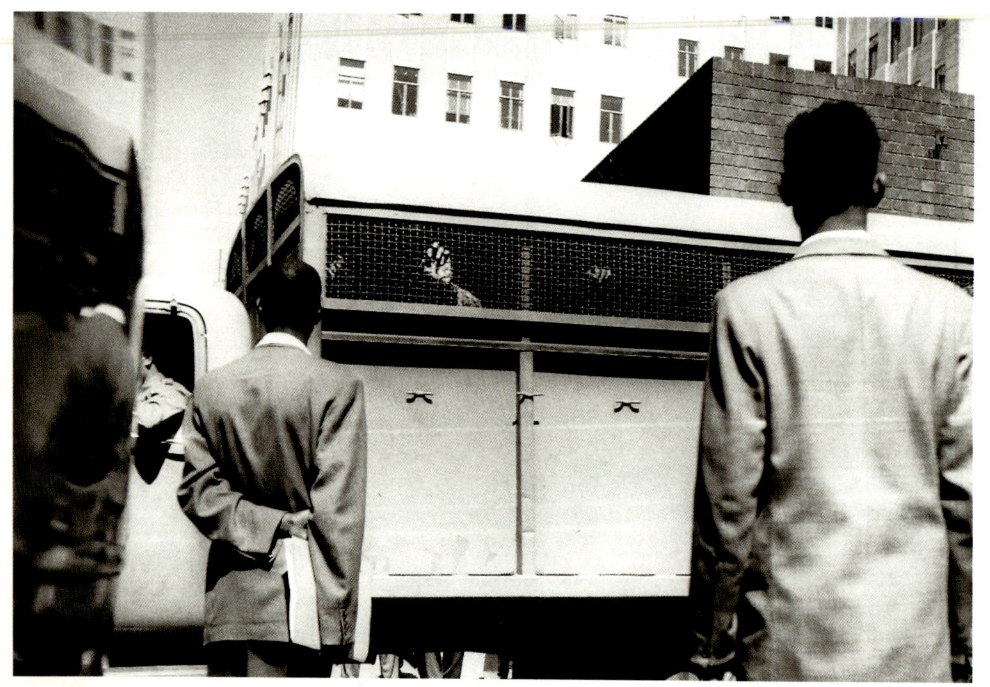

JOHANNESBURG 1956
Treason Trial. Prisoners on their way to court in a prison van.

PETER MAGUBANE

Dickens — '...it was the best of times, it was the worst of times...', and he knew he was escaping from the frustrations of his intelligence into growing alcoholism.

And so it was, for Sophiatown itself was already doomed in the mid-1950s, when the government began forcibly moving its inhabitants out to a bleak settlement called Meadowlands on the outer edge of the city: a prim new Afrikaner suburb called Triompf took its place. The destruction of Sophiatown meant the end of the easy contacts between black and white, and the hopes of a more multiracial society.

But the real end of the era of hope came at the beginning of the 1960s, when a wave of black demonstrations and protests was met by the massacre at Sharpeville. The government soon imposed much more drastic restrictions and penalties on any black political expression, including the banning of the African National Congress and the Pan Africanist Congress. The new police powers, including virtually unlimited detention, systematic torture and networks of informers, forced political activity deep underground, while even the mildest political comment or criticism in magazines and newspapers was dangerous.

The wryly humorous and easy style of black writing and journalism of the 1950s, which Can Themba and Bloke Modisane so well represented, had little place in the 1960s, when the writers who stayed inside South Africa felt compelled to become much more seriously committed to the struggle for change. Many of the best black writers of the 1950s, including Modisane, went into exile. Bloke, after living many years in London, died in West Germany. Can Themba stayed in South Africa, but became increasingly alcoholic and unable to write, until he retreated to Swaziland where he died.

The frustrations of black writers and artists during the decades of oppression were agonising. But black people were not totally demoralised and despairing, or eternally servile — as the white government had hoped — by the persecution and degradation of their lives. Twenty years after Sharpeville, the National Party government was forced to put much of their creaking apartheid machinery into reverse. Today, as any visitor to Johannesburg can see, black people from the surrounding townships have spilt back into the centre of the white city, bringing with them a street life of markets, performers, hawkers or beggars which makes Johannesburg look much more like a vibrant third world city.

While the police and apartheid legislation were able to stamp out political opposition and revolt for most of the 1960s and 1970s, they were never able to obliterate that creative energy and self-expression which provided the surest sign that black people would still demand their rights and their self-respect in the cities which they had made their own.

After the apartheid system was at last abandoned by the National Party government in the late 1980s, and black political organisations were unbanned in 1990, the cost of the repression of the preceding decades was all too evident. Militant young black leaders had emerged in the townships, who rejected any compromise with the government or the white minority. But the leaders of the African National Congress who came out of jail, led by Nelson Mandela and Walter Sisulu, were old enough to look back on the comparative freedom of the 1950s, and to demand once again a multi-racial democracy which took no note of differences of colour.

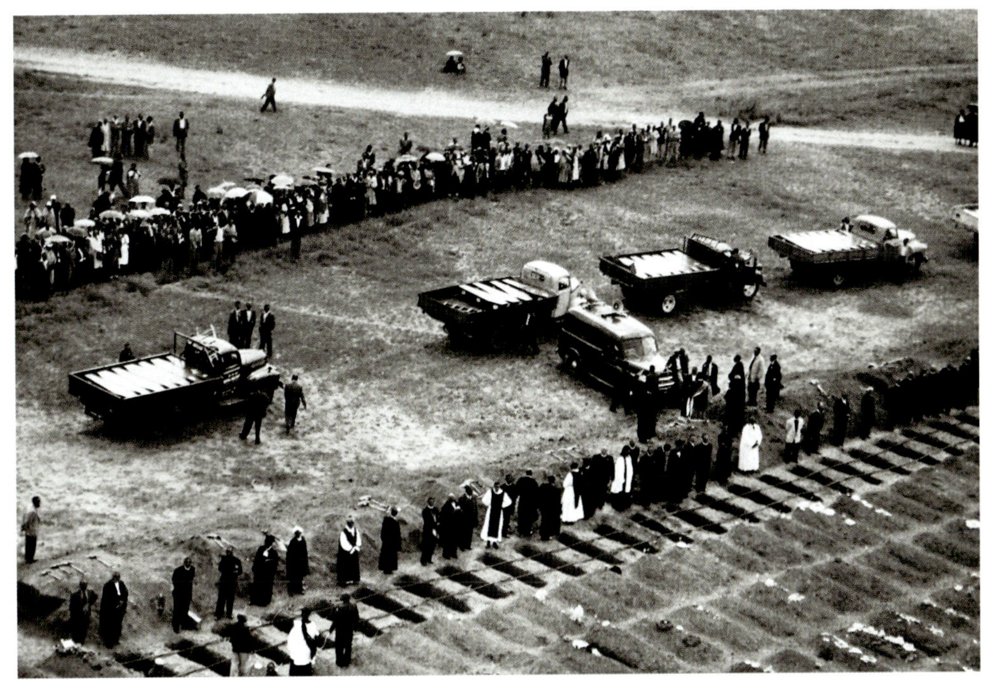

SHARPEVILLE, MARCH 1960
During a demonstration against the Pass Laws at the Sharpeville Police Station 67 people were killed —
shot in the back by police. 186 people were wounded.

JÜRGEN SCHADEBERG

Taking Pictures in the 1950s

JÜRGEN SCHADEBERG, 1990

In 1950, at the age of nineteen, I left Germany for distant and unknown South Africa.

Behind me I left a world that I had learnt to loathe and despise. I was of that generation, often called 'the lost generation', which was too young to have been dragged into the political madhouse and into the war, but old enough to see with clear eyes the monstrous and insane behavior of the whole German nation.

Naively I believed I was going to a country that was all good.

Johannesburg and *Drum*

I stepped off the Union Castle passenger liner in Cape Town a very young photojournalist. Since the age of fifteen I had studied photography — first in Berlin and later in Hamburg at the Deutsche Presse Argentur.

Because my English was very poor, I was initially surprised and delighted to find that my travelling companion on the long train journey to Johannesburg spoke fluent German. My delight soon faded as he began to sing the praises of the Nazi movement, insisting that Hitler was on a par with Caesar and Napoleon. His name was Dr Van Rensburg and he was, as I later discovered, the leader of the Ossewa Brandwag, an extreme rightwing organisation that believed in the superiority of the white race. During the war they actively supported Nazi Germany by sabotaging the South African war effort. With some of its members in the South African cabinet, the organisation had a strong influence on the new National Party government which was actively promoting racist policies.

Thirty-six hours later, at the end of the train journey, on that crisp, dry, winter morning, I stood on the platform at Johannesburg station, quite baffled. I had come to the other end of the world only to find that here racial hatred still flourished, despite the fact that millions of people had just been slaughtered in a bloody World War.

No jobs were to be had on newspapers in Johannesburg, but eventually, in 1951, I was told by a photographer from a leading newspaper group that there was a job going on a magazine '...you know you wouldn't really like it ... it's for Natives'.

I jumped at the chance. The magazine was called *The African Drum*. Robert Crisp, a well known cricketer was the editor and co-founder of *Drum*. He interviewed me and I was taken on to become the fourth member of the *Drum* staff. There was Robert Crisp and Henry Nxumalo, who had the combined functions of writer, associate editor and sports editor, and a young Italian secretary called Mrs Thomas.

Henry lived in Orlando, now part of Soweto's sprawl. Not far from Baragwanath Hospital was a clump of brown buildings perched on a hill — the state's idea of a model location. Known to residents as 'Dark City' or 'New York', Orlando had no electricity.

Henry's two-roomed home was in Orlando East. The houses were tiny, box-like, and their stark brick faces and iron roofs gave the impression of military barracks. In winter the cement floors and hessian ceilings were paltry protection from the cold; in summer the houses were stifling. Water was obtained from communal taps in the street.

Orlando bred a murky world of large-scale and petty crime, of gang warfare and domestic violence. But Orlando also fostered a spirit of solidarity amongst many of its residents. In the location's shebeens, musicians, gangsters, schoolteachers and boxers rubbed shoulders.

In the 1950s, vast numbers of blacks moved from the overcrowded rural 'homelands' to the towns in search of work and a less bitter existence. As a result, squatter camps and shanty towns proliferated in Johannesburg, Cape Town and Durban. Shanty-

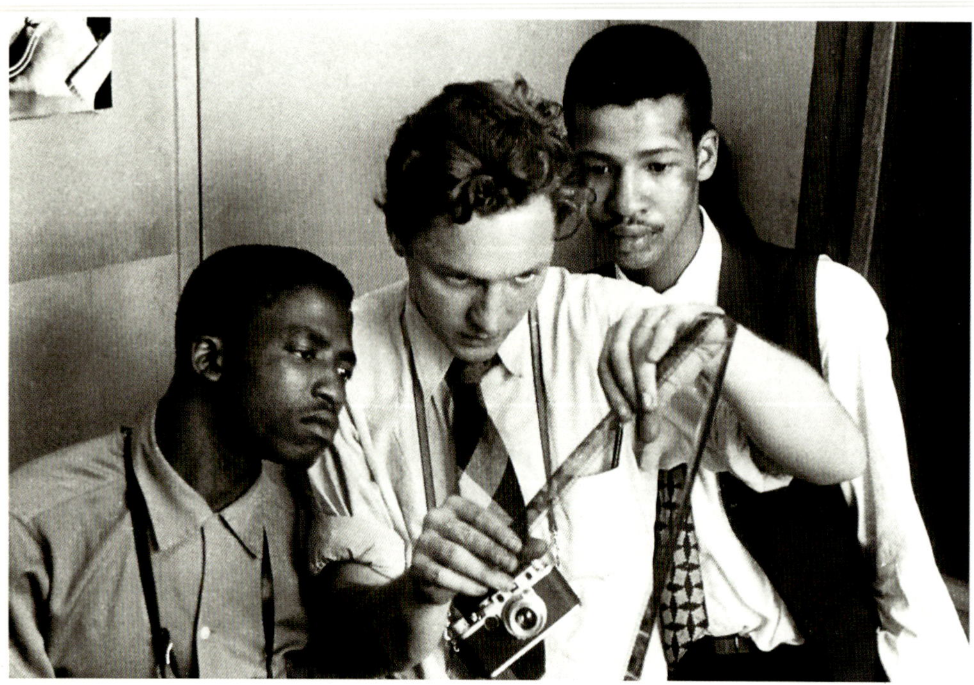

Drum's chief photographer Jürgen Schadeberg with two of his photographers, Peter Magubane (left) and Bob Gosani.

JÜRGEN SCHADEBERG

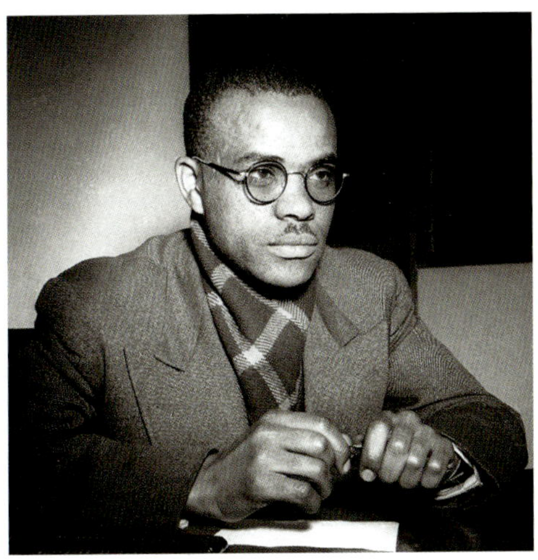

Ezekiel Mphahlele, literary editor of **Drum**. He later became Professor of African Literature at Wits University. He retired in 1991.

JÜRGEN SCHADEBERG

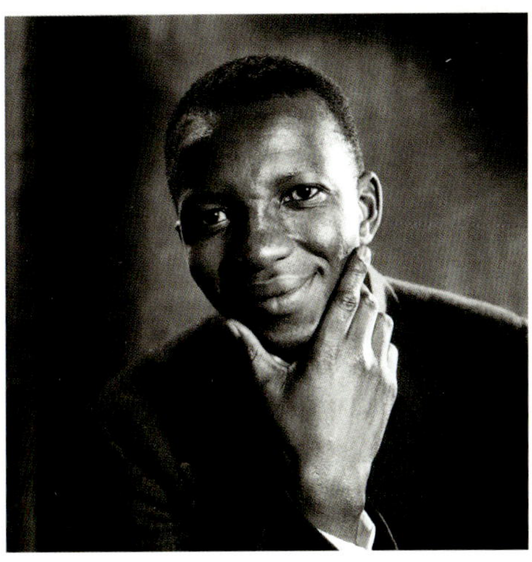

Bloke Modisane . His first short story, 'The Dignity of Begging', was published in 1951. Bloke then joined **Drum**. In the 1980s he settled in Germany where he died in 1989.

JÜRGEN SCHADEBERG

dwellers were plagued by squatter clearances, when municipality officials would raze to the ground homes constructed from iron, grass, mud, a few planks, bits and pieces from some disused house, or salvaged from a refuse dump. Many pass-less migrants, with no official right to live in the towns, were repeatedly sent back to these impoverished 'homelands'.

Henry Nxumalo and I teamed up and travelled around the country, covering sports events and interviewing politicians and socialites, filling *Drum* from cover to cover.

Then one day Jim Bailey appeared. He was by then the sole proprietor of *Drum*. Soon after that Bob Crisp mysteriously disappeared. It seemed that Jim and Bob disagreed about the overall concept of the magazine. Bob wanted *Drum* to be paternalistic and tribal whereas Jim's aim was to produce a modern, city-orientated investigative magazine. Bailey's ideas won out.

In December 1951, not long after Bailey's takeover, Anthony Sampson, who had been a mate of Jim's at Oxford, came over from England. He was twenty five, and took over the editorship of the magazine.

Anthony often came along with Henry and myself on stories. Shortly after Sampson's arrival, he, Henry and I went to a farm in the Free State to interview Dr Moroka, the ANC President. Then we visited Patrick Duncan in Maseru and from there we travelled to Bloemfontein to cover the ANC Congress. At the beginning of 1952 Henry and I went to Bethal to do the first 'Mr *Drum*' story, investigating appalling labour conditions on the potato farms. In April of that year we covered the first Defiance Campaign meetings.

One of my assignments was to take a cover picture of glamorous film star and blues singer Dolly Rathebe. We climbed up a mine dump on the edge of Johannesburg. The dump consisted of fine whitish sand and Dolly, in her bikini, posed against this beach-like background. Suddenly, we were set upon by a number of policemen. They ordered us to stand still and excitedly inspected the sandy ground for marks and prints. We were taken to the police station under suspicion of contravening the Immorality Act — the law which made it illegal for non-whites and whites to have sexual relations. Punishment for this crime was nine months imprisonment. Several weary hours and many phone calls later, we were finally released.

One day Henry brought his nephew, Bob Gosani, into the office. Bob was a lanky, inarticulate seventeen year old who began his sentences with the words 'the thing is...' He seemed unsuitable for switchboard work or journalism, so Anthony Sampson passed him on to me and I took him on as a photographic apprentice. After he'd

Shanty Town

If, one of these days, while you and your loved one forget everything else on the earth's surface to admire the glorious setting sun, you suddenly discover that you are in Orlando Township and what you are gazing at is no longer the sunset but a growing smoke cloud, don't dear reader, call in the fire brigade. The chances are that you are approaching Orlando's shanty towns at their busiest hour!

The majority of the squatters are workers, like you and me. The fire starts burning when they reach home — for the evening meal, for baby's washing, for hot water. In fact, for everything. The only difference is that the squatters do not use stoves.

At the present time, some 63 000 Africans are living under such conditions on the Rand. Owing to the acute housing shortage, they can do nothing but squat, despite the danger that this entails to the health of the community.

Recently, I spent a night in a squatter camp and believe me, I can see nothing in heaven, hell or the Atlantic Charter worse than that night.

Henry Nxumalo, *Drum*, 1953

been helping me for some time in the darkroom, I organised a camera for him and took him with me on assignments. He soon learnt the skills of picture taking and after a few years became one of *Drum's* most outstanding photographers.

During the early 1950s there were virtually no photographers reporting or recording events in the so-called non-white world. Consequently people accepted and welcomed without suspicion the lone photographer. Even the authorities, courts and police, let me get on with it. They were puzzled as to why this crazy man bothered to photograph blacks. Only later, in the mid-1950s, did it become more difficult to record political events. Then, when police were present the photographers, especially black photographers, were often beaten up and arrested.

At the end of 1953, *Drum* publications started its sister magazine *Africa,* and later the Sunday paper *The Golden City Post. Drum* branched out to produce East and West African editions. It was then that I found myself more and more occupied with picture editing, teaching photography, and building up a photographic department with half a dozen or so photographers and darkroom assistants.

Later, in 1955, we employed the streetwise and tough Peter Magubane who joined us as a driver and messenger. He came with us on stories, assisting the photographers. His interest in picture-taking grew and he soon transferred to the photographic department. Ernest Cole, Alf Kumalo, Victor Xashimba, Gopal Naransamy and many others later joined the department. Although none of these photographers had any formal training, the pictures they produced for the magazine were unusual and outstanding in their excellence.

1950s Fashion

The early 1950s, despite the political situation and the hardships it imposed on the people, saw a cultural explosion in the black community of South Africa. It was the post-war period. Inspired by music and the cinema, the American way of life was imitated and emulated in every possible way. For the fist time ever for the black community Fashion had arrived — hairstyles, clothes, jazz, fast city life and city trends.

We started using colour photos of young ladies on the cover of *Drum* in the mid 1950s. We often had to improvise with their clothes since the models did not own anything suitable and clothing manufacturers were indifferent to black fashion. However advertisers soon became very interested in using our cover pictures to promote their products.

Influenced by Humphrey Bogart, wide brimmed hats and fast-talk, Satchmo's jazz and Peter Cheyney's raciness, creativity and inventiveness flourished. Everything was a novelty, everything was new. The models were the first ever models, the covergirls the first ever covergirls, and the modern city musicians and writers were also the first ever. There was no limit, there were no restrictions; they set their own pace, initiated their own rhythms and style.

Blacks, rejected socially by the whites of South Africa, looked up to the black American as their model. They admired the snazzily dressed members of the young 'Americans' — a gang that roamed Sophiatown. The tough guys of the day had names like 'Boston', 'Styles' and 'Homicide Hank'. The aping of black America also resulted in a vibrant jazz scene producing giants like Kippy Moeketsi, Mackay Davashe, Peter Rezant, Miriam Makeba and many others.

The new 'City Black' adopted status symbols like big cars, battleship Cadillacs, Buicks, Lincolns, Chryslers etc ... gangsters preferred the black limousines used by Al Capone, Lucky Luciano and Legs Diamond.

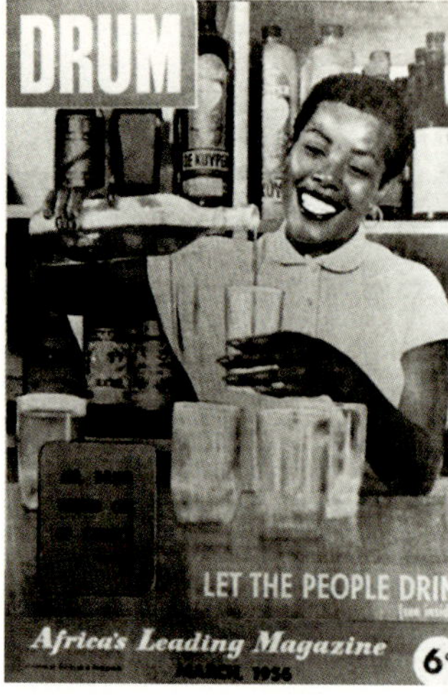

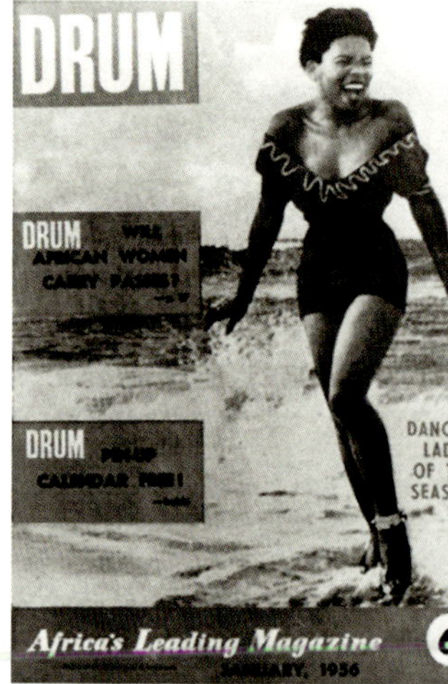

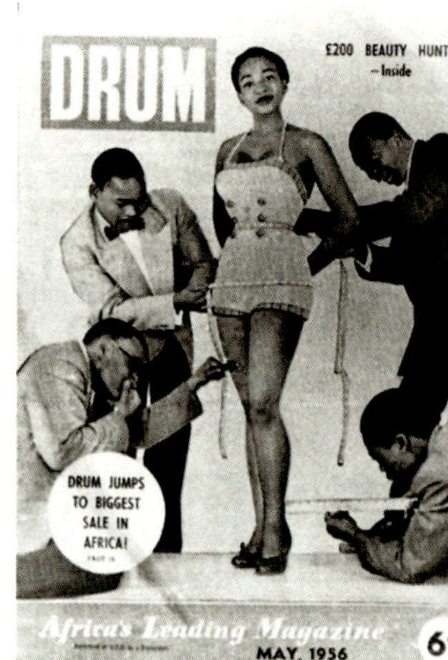

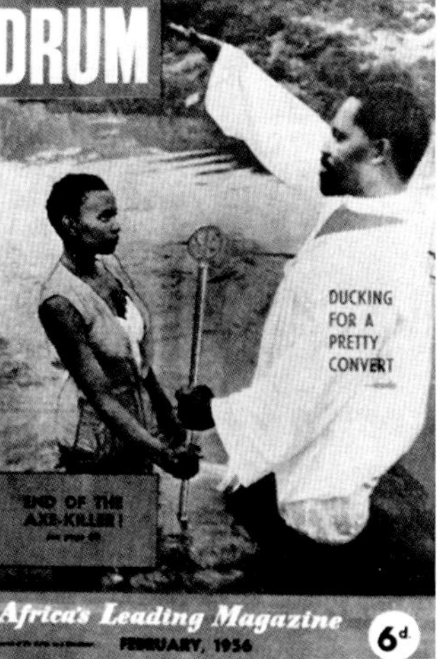

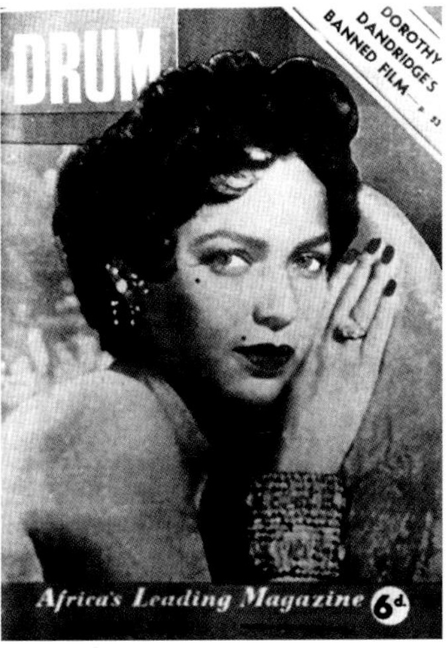

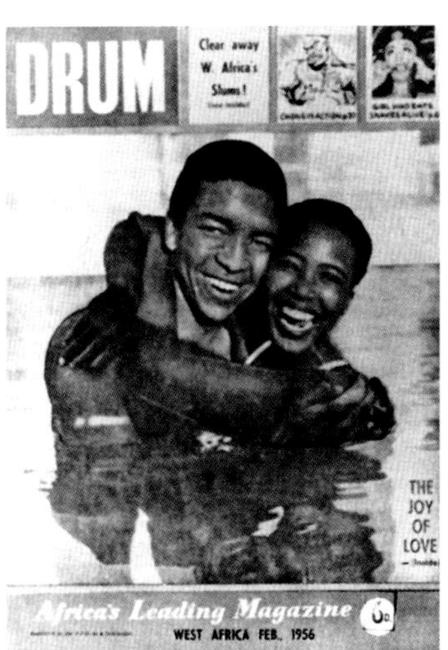

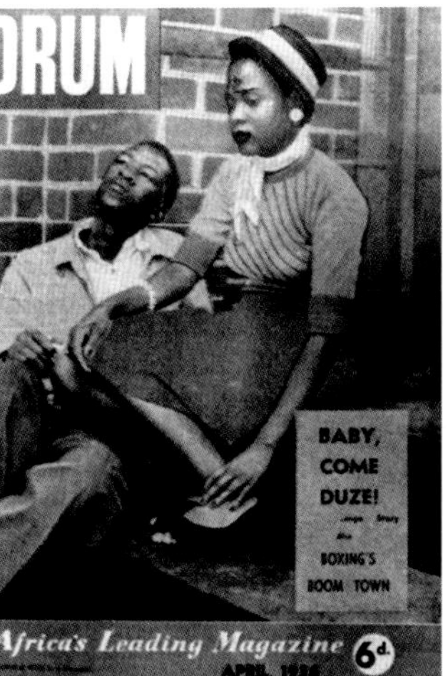

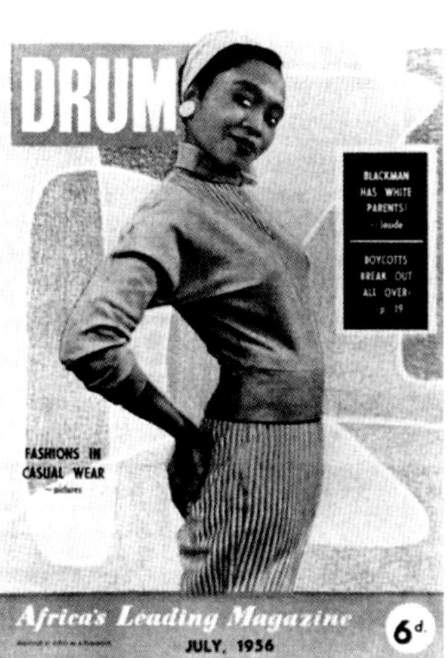

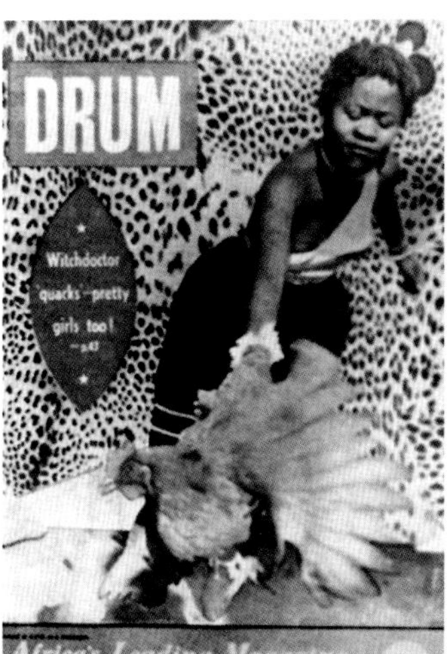

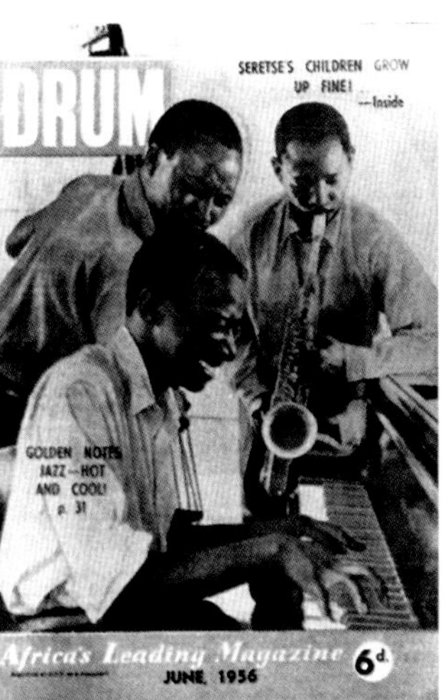

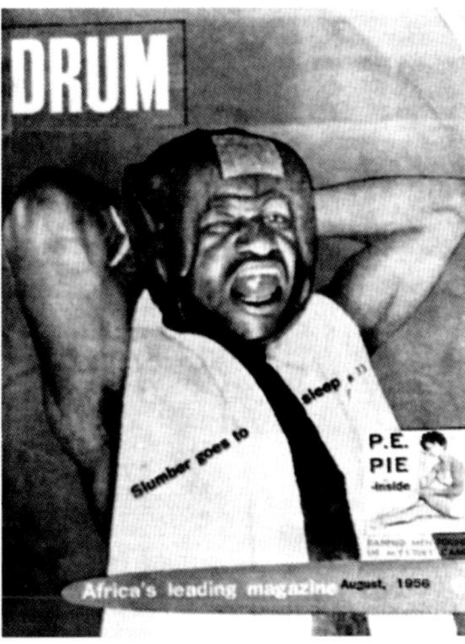

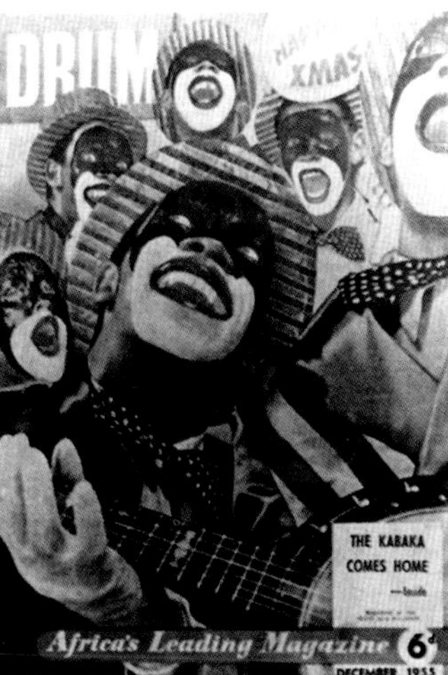

Drum was first published in Cape Town in March 1951 under the title The African Drum, by famous cricketer Bob Crisp. However, Drum was not successful and moved to Johannesburg in September 1951. Under the new publisher, Jim Bailey, Drum flourished, eventually achieving a circulation of 400,000 with wide distribution not only in South Africa, but in Ghana, Nigeria and East Africa.

Just as prohibition brought about speakeasies in America, in South Africa it gave birth to a new township institution — the shebeen — patronised by poor labourers and rich tycoons, by teachers, school dropouts, hoodlums and journalists.

Hats were the in-thing. They gave the wearer a special status. A school teacher would be seen in a Christy Rollaway... a gangster would not be seen without a Borsalino, a Woodrow or a Stetson. A playboy or a sports-minded person would not step out into the street without his straw-Dobbs, snow-white, cream-white or brown. Hats gave males a respectability which made them stand out in public. A Churchman would visit his congregation with a Homburg or Churchill hat. The bowler hat was the favourite of con-men and swindlers.

For the first time, black women were judged according to the 'beauty queen' concept. But apart from her vital statistics the 'beauty queen' was most often judged by the tone and hue of her skin — the lighter, the better. This use of colour as a measure of valuation was the cornerstone of the Population Registration Act. Often, if they were light-skinned, Africans were able to pass as coloured. This meant they avoided carrying the much detested dompass, and as coloureds were entitled to earn higher wages. In their turn, many fair-skinned coloureds passed as whites and enjoyed the advantages of the privileged.

1950s Gangsters and crime

In Johannesburg during the 1950s crime was a day to day reality. But a black man could land in jail just because he was not carrying his pass... so to be called a criminal was no great insult. The opportunities for an ambitious black man were small and the rewards of crime were big. Gangsters had big money, big cars and the best girls. They ruled the streets and the dance floors at night. If you crossed them they beat you up. If you took them to court they beat up the witnesses or they killed you.

The *tsotsis*, on the other hand, were small time criminals. They often had 'respectable' jobs during the day but at nights and on weekends they would 'supplement' their income. A young *tsotsi* could easily earn as much as £5 a day, which was really big money. With that he could look after his girlfriends, keep his parents and gamble away the rest.

During the war, Hitler was a kind of hero to the *tsotsis* because he reminded them of Shaka. They called him *Mlize* or *uDhlumini*. As a result the two main gangs of the early years were called the 'Berliners' and the 'Gestapo'.

A group of brothers, cousins and friends formed a clique of small-time pick-pockets and bagsnatchers. They paraded the Sophiatown streets over weekends, dressed in expensive American clothes — elegant cardigans, brown and white shoes and narrow blue trousers called Bogarts. Because of their clothing they became known as the 'Americans'. They became highly sought after as escorts by the 'nice-time' girls. They even had a resident 'BA' to write their love-letters. They always had the 'sharp' girls — and so there were inevitable confrontations with the 'Berliners' and the 'Gestapo'. Slim, the biggest of the brothers, mobilised the 'Americans' into a gang and it was not long before they effectively ruled Sophiatown. They took what they wanted when they wanted it.

On working days, the 'Americans' travelled to town in cloth caps and dust coats, looking like any other black workers. In this disguise they stole goods from shops and railway sidings, often under the eyes of the white 'baas'. They were known by many as the 'African Robin Hoods' because they robbed goods from the rich white men and sold them in the locations very cheaply.

Being the lone white in a black world, where I spent most of my time, gangsters and *tsotsis* did not bother me at all. When I photographed a gang battle of the 'Msomi Gang' in Alexandra I felt afterwards that I must have been invisible. What worried me greatly, however, was the sight of a police car because I was not supposed to be in a black area.

1950s Music and Jive

Big band jazz was popular with the black public in the 1950s. There sprung up orchestras in the mould of Glenn Miller, Harry James, Ray Anthony, Lawrence Welk, Benny Goodman, Duke Ellington, Elite Swingsters and City Jazz Nine. When it came to singing, there were quartets a la The Inkspots and the Mills Brothers. Hence local groups — the Manhattan Brothers under Nathan Dambuza Mdledle, the Inkspots under Sibanyoni, and the Woody Wood Peckers under Boy Masango. The Ladybird Singers too made a complete break from the tribal modes of entertainment. Dolly Rathebe, Miriam Makeba, Dorothy Masuka and Letty Mbulu sang the blues in nightclubs and dance halls and in township jazz musicals.

Music was everywhere — on street corners, or in front of the City Hall, where groups of teenagers played the penny whistle. Music was heard at bus terminals and on buses and trains... the penny whistle, the harmonica, the guitar or some homemade string instrument, often a tin container attached to a long piece of wood with a few strings. These were the popular and cheap ways of making music. The more sophisticated musicians played the trumpet, saxophone, trombone and clarinet at parties and in dance halls. They blew their horns at birthday parties and funerals. At wakes (where families and friends sit watching over the deceased by candle light) they sounded through the night. Then there was the piano in the high dive shebeens... it was jazz from morning till night.

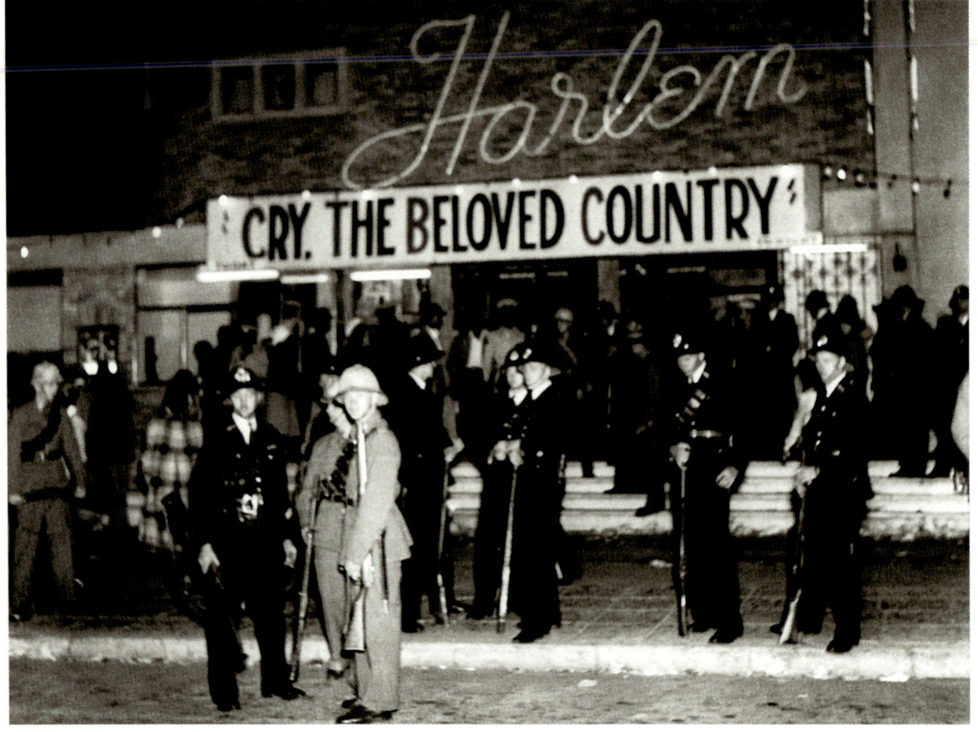

JOHANNESBURG 1951

The film Cry the Beloved Country, based on Alan Paton's book of the same name, was shown in several South African cinemas. The film was an attack on the extreme injustices caused by racism in South Africa.

JÜRGEN SCHADEBERG

Every weekend, from Friday night to Sunday morning, the dance halls in and around Johannesburg were full until four each morning. Often flashily dressed gangsters — the 'Berliners' from the Western Township, the 'Americans' from Sophiatown or the 'Spoilers' from Alexandra Township — would turn up. They would grab the beautiful girls and dance, with guns and knives in their hands. Gambling, shooting and stabbing was the norm. If they were not happy with the band, or if they wanted the band to play a particular song, they would flash their knives and guns. Musicians had to be fit in those days.

I think it was in December 1951 that I photographed a dance and variety show at the Ritz dance-hall at the bottom of Polly Street. The Manhattan Brothers were crooning on stage, people were dancing and drunks were passing in and out through the swing doors at the main entrance. Then Dolly Rathebe and the African Inkspots sang their famous songs *Kalamazoo*, *Carolina Wam* and *Ddinjay*. Suddenly a fire broke out. The story goes that some *tsotsis* who supported a rival group felt that the Inkspots were getting too much applause and started the fire.

Another 1950s folklore music story goes like this ... Nathan 'Dam-Dam' Mdladle, the composer and leader of the Manhattan Brothers, South Africa's most popular singing quartet, was singing on stage in Johannesburg with Miriam Makeba, when a man walked up to the stage telling her that he intended to 'skep' her that night (take her to his hideout). After the show the same man, followed by a few side-kicks, went backstage and pulled a gun, pointing it at Miriam. He told her that if she was ready, he was ready. Nathan jumped between the gunman and his 'nut brown' baby, Miriam, saying 'Over my dead body!'. During the scuffle Miriam managed to escape. Guns were fired and a woman reporter was hit in the leg.

The 1950s were exciting years. The ideas, the ideals, and the achievements of that time should not be forgotten.

The photographs and text of this book are testimony to one of the most dynamic and magical decades of South African history.

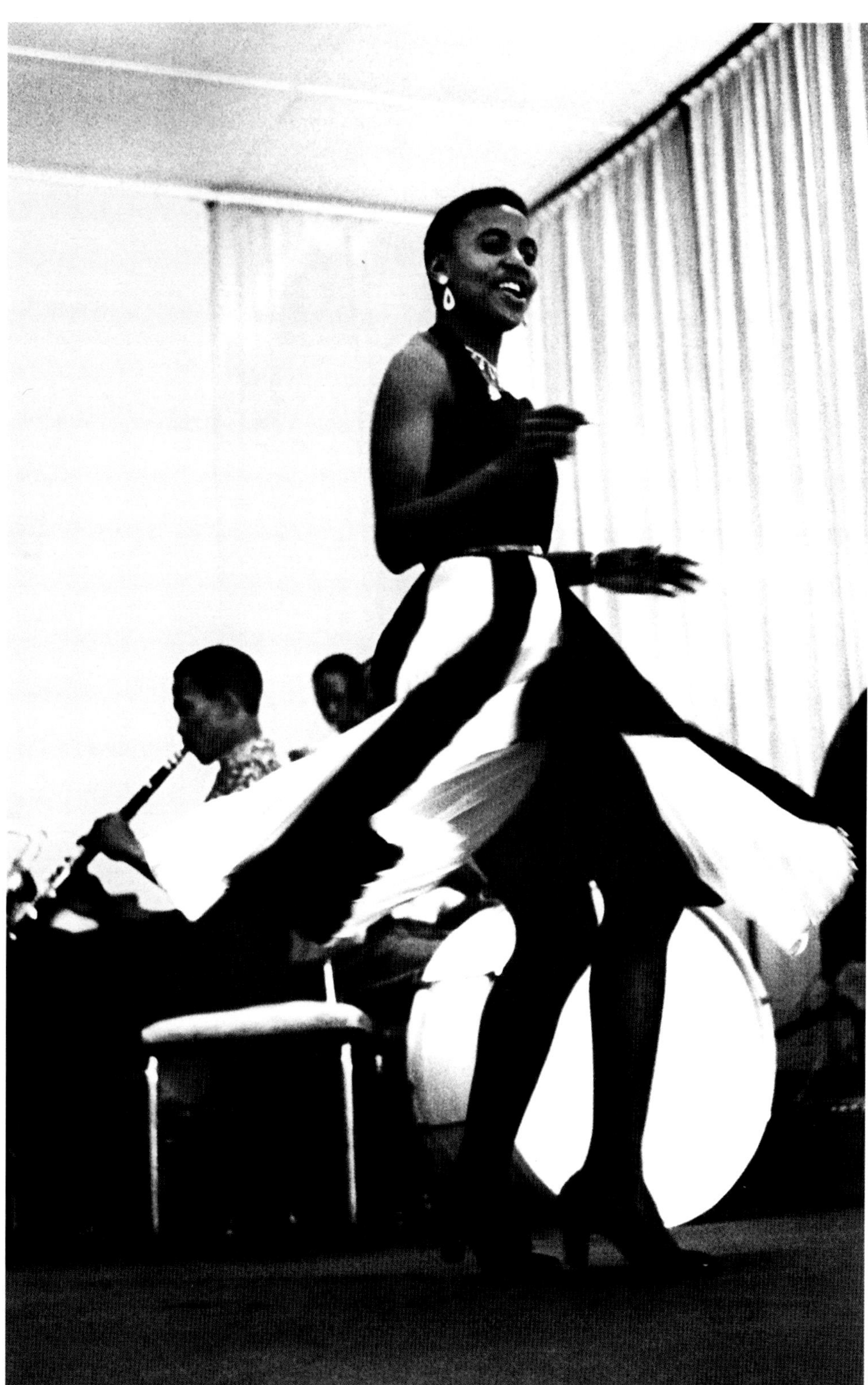

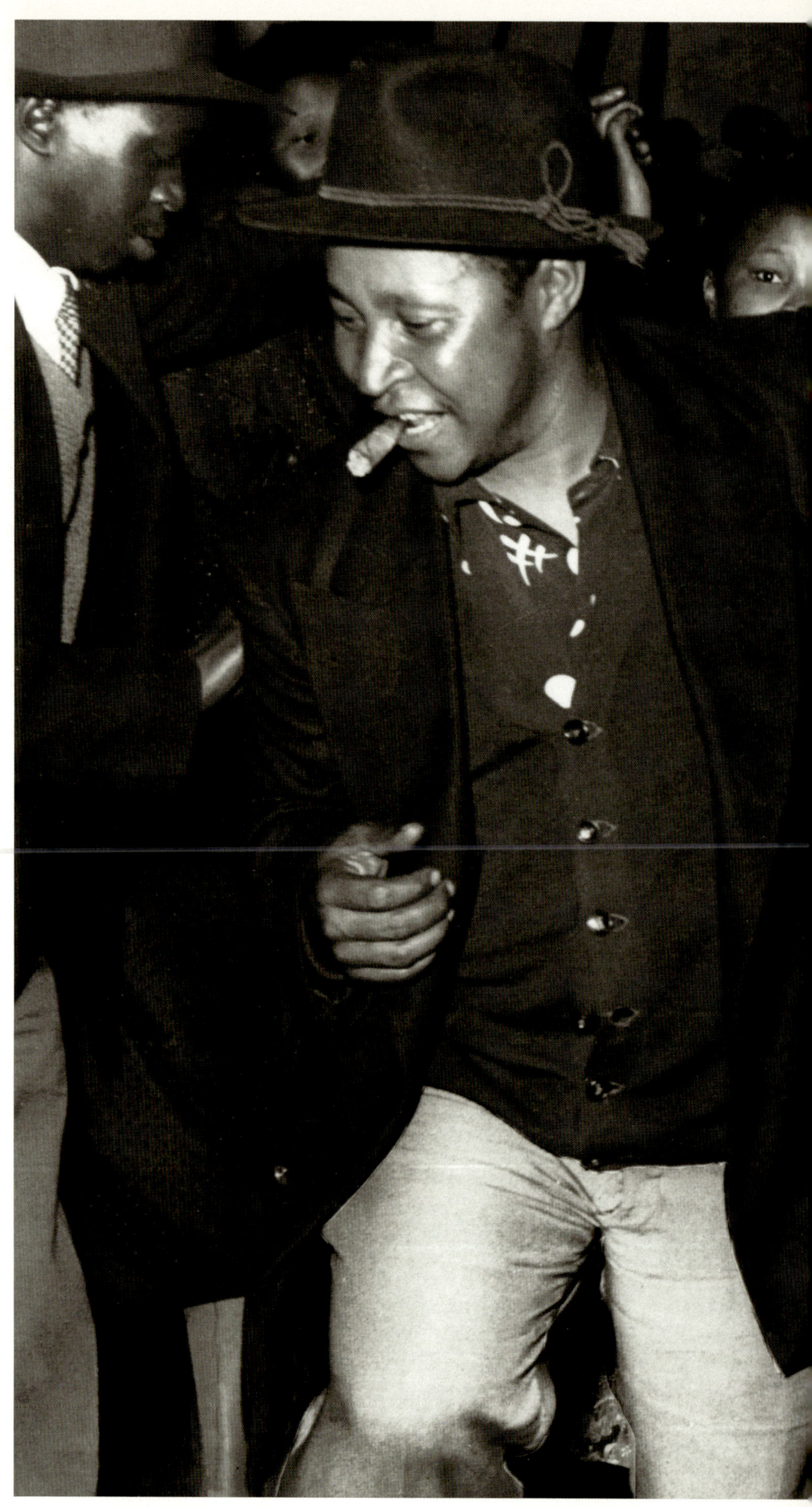

JOHANNESBURG 1956
The dance-halls were packed from Friday night
till Sunday morning. Everyone was jiving and
twisting to the sounds of the big bands.

GOPAL NARANSAMY

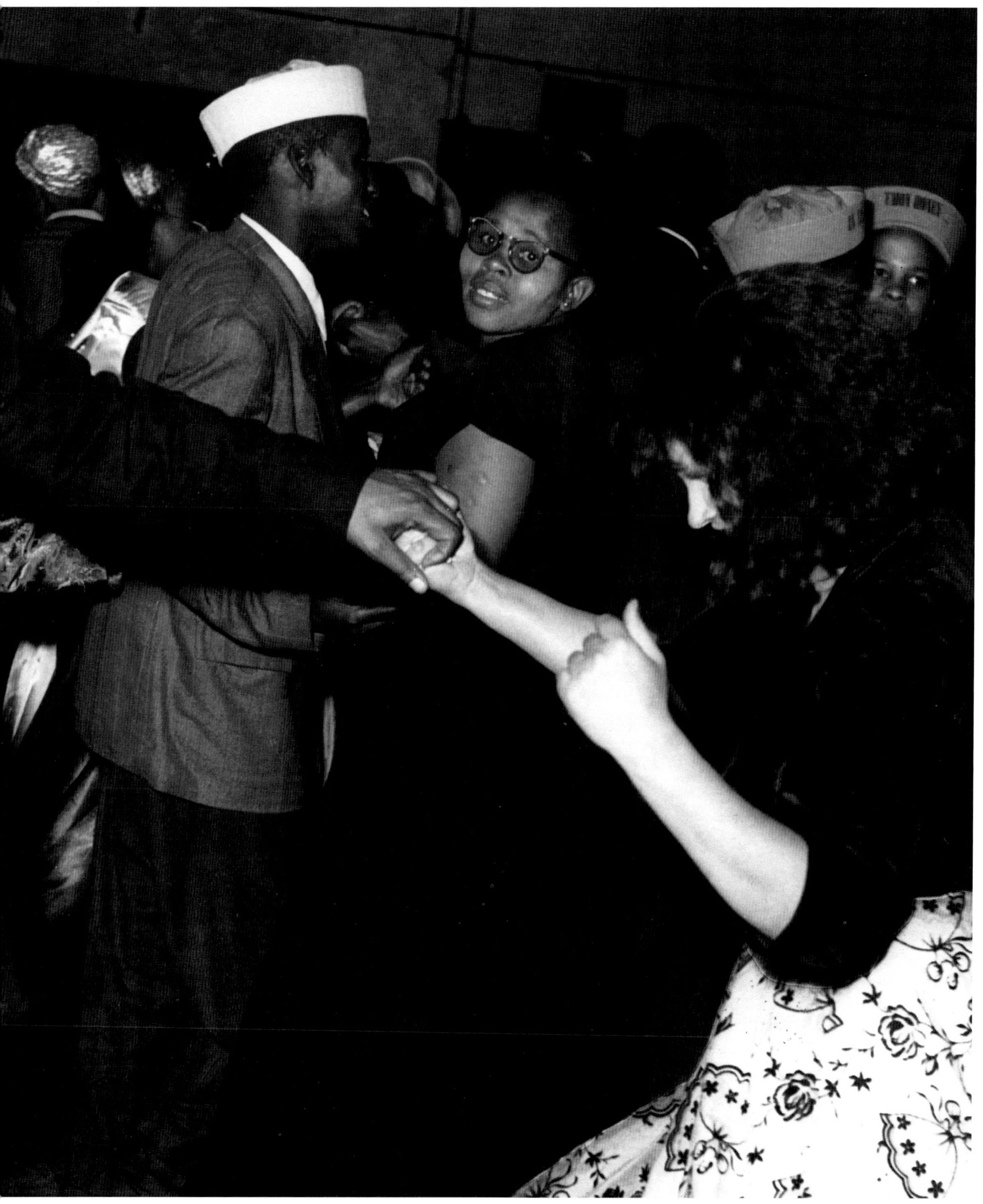

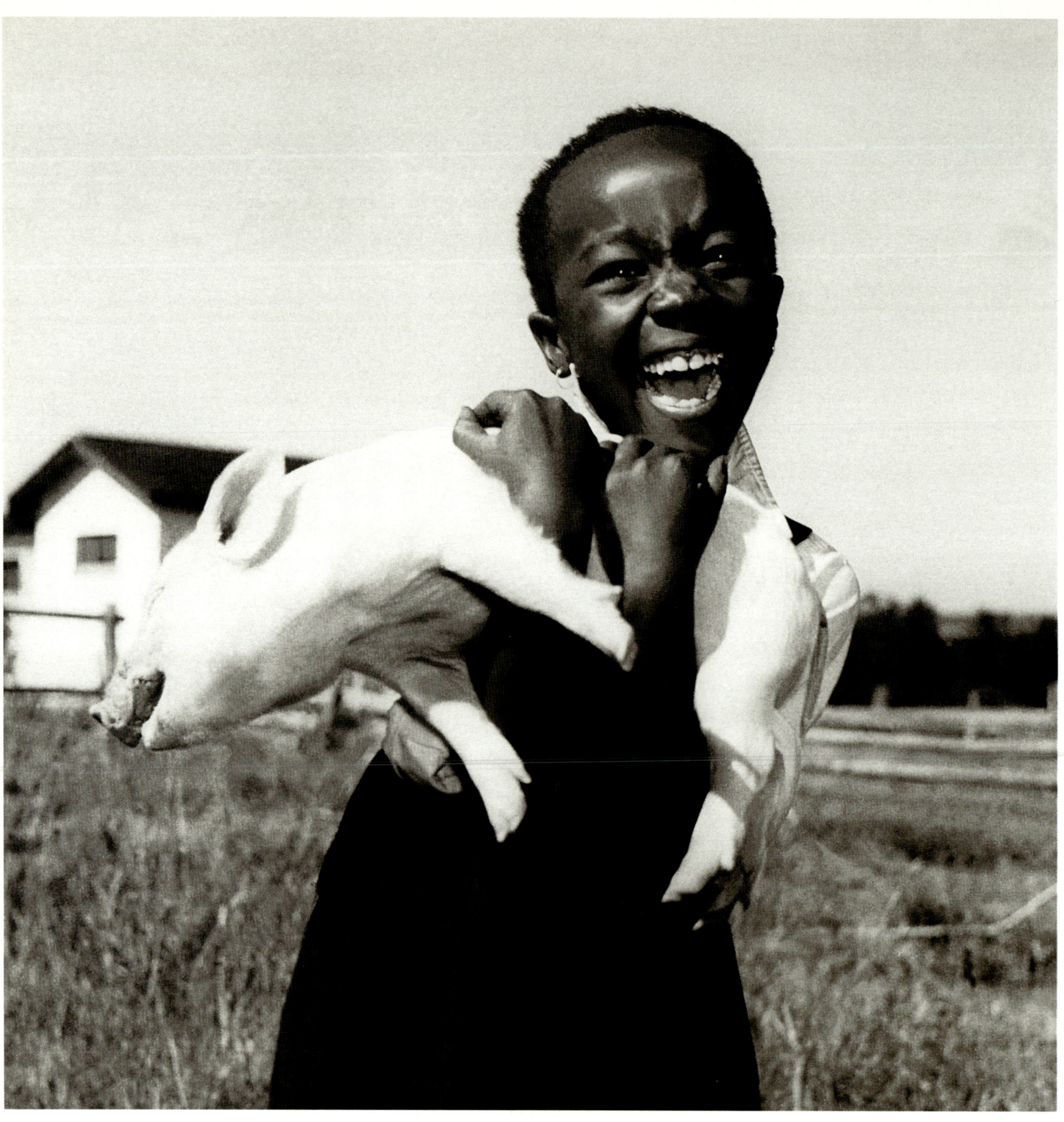

MULDERSDRIFT 1952
A visit to a farm.

JÜRGEN SCHADEBERG

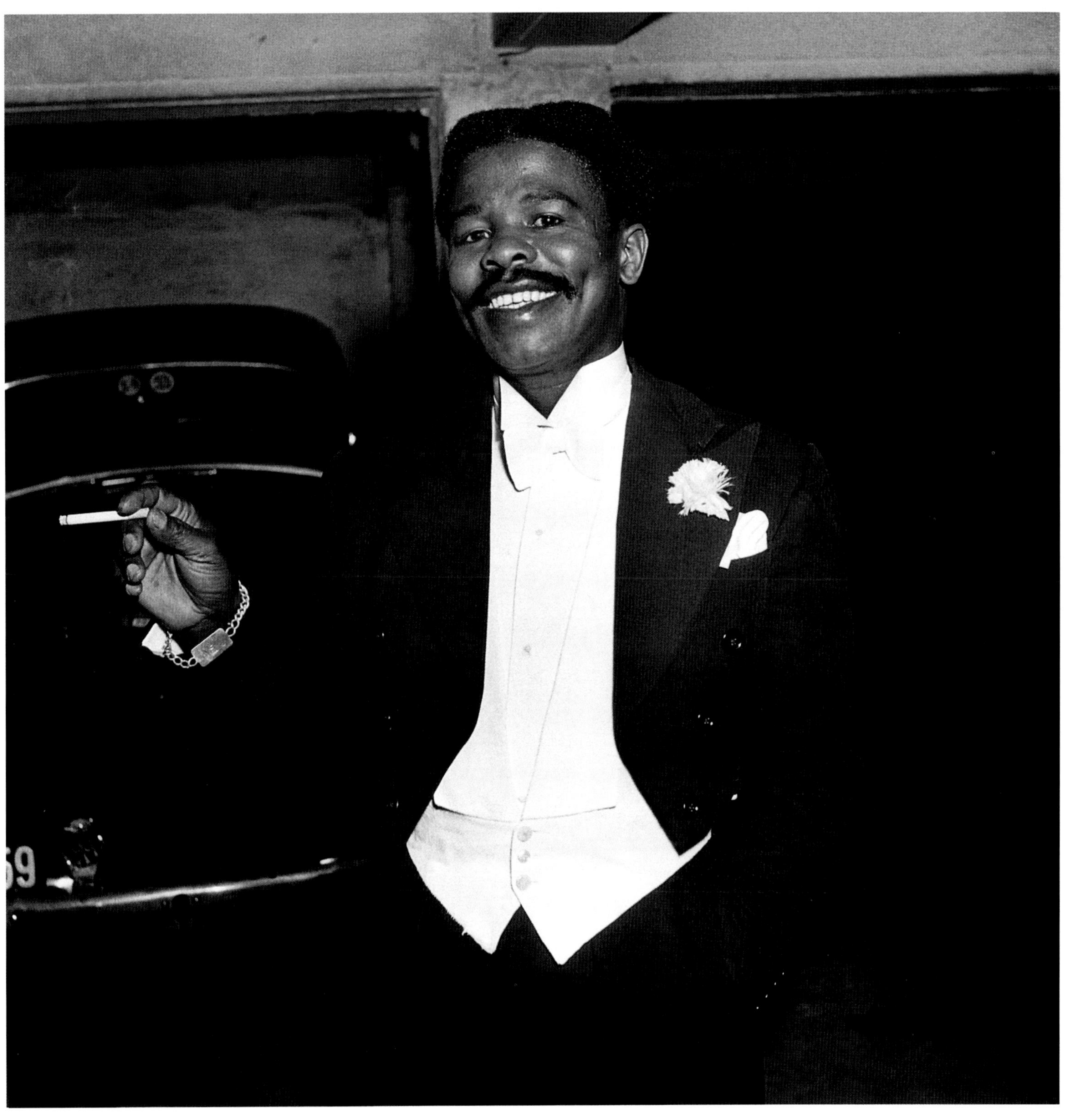

JOHANNESBURG 1954
Ballroom champ Nelson Gordon: 'If you're a ballroom dancer, one of the
people that count one, two, three... one, two, three... don't choose the
dame that's two feet taller and two hips broader than you, 'cause then
you can't see where you're goin' an' you're not allowed to look under
her arm to see the way. An' she's more likely to damage your corns than
you can damage hers. Moreover, it looks silly to dance with a dame
that's tall enough to be yer mom'.

BOB GOSANI

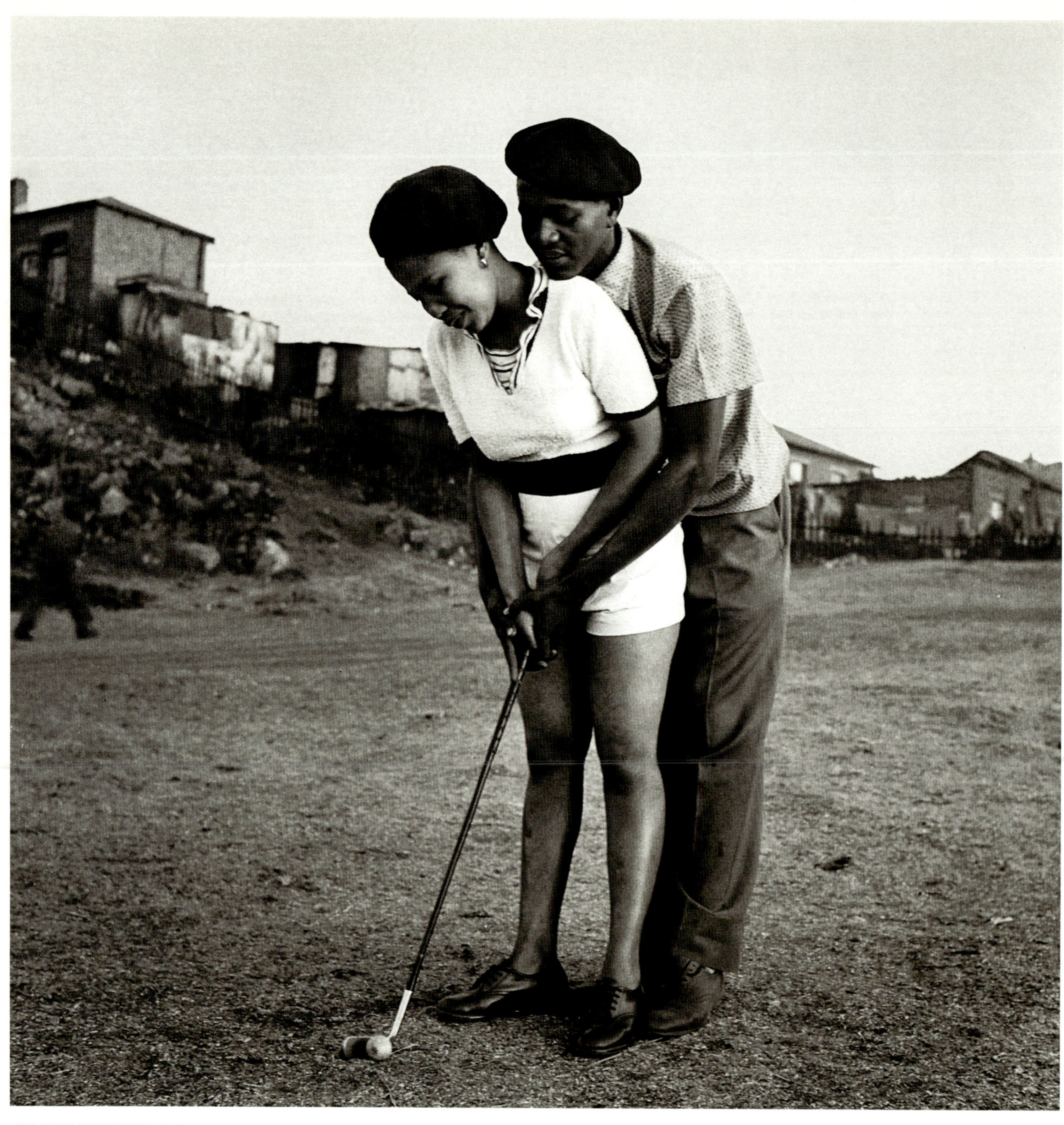

ORLANDO TOWNSHIP 1952
Private golf lessons.

JÜRGEN SCHADEBERG

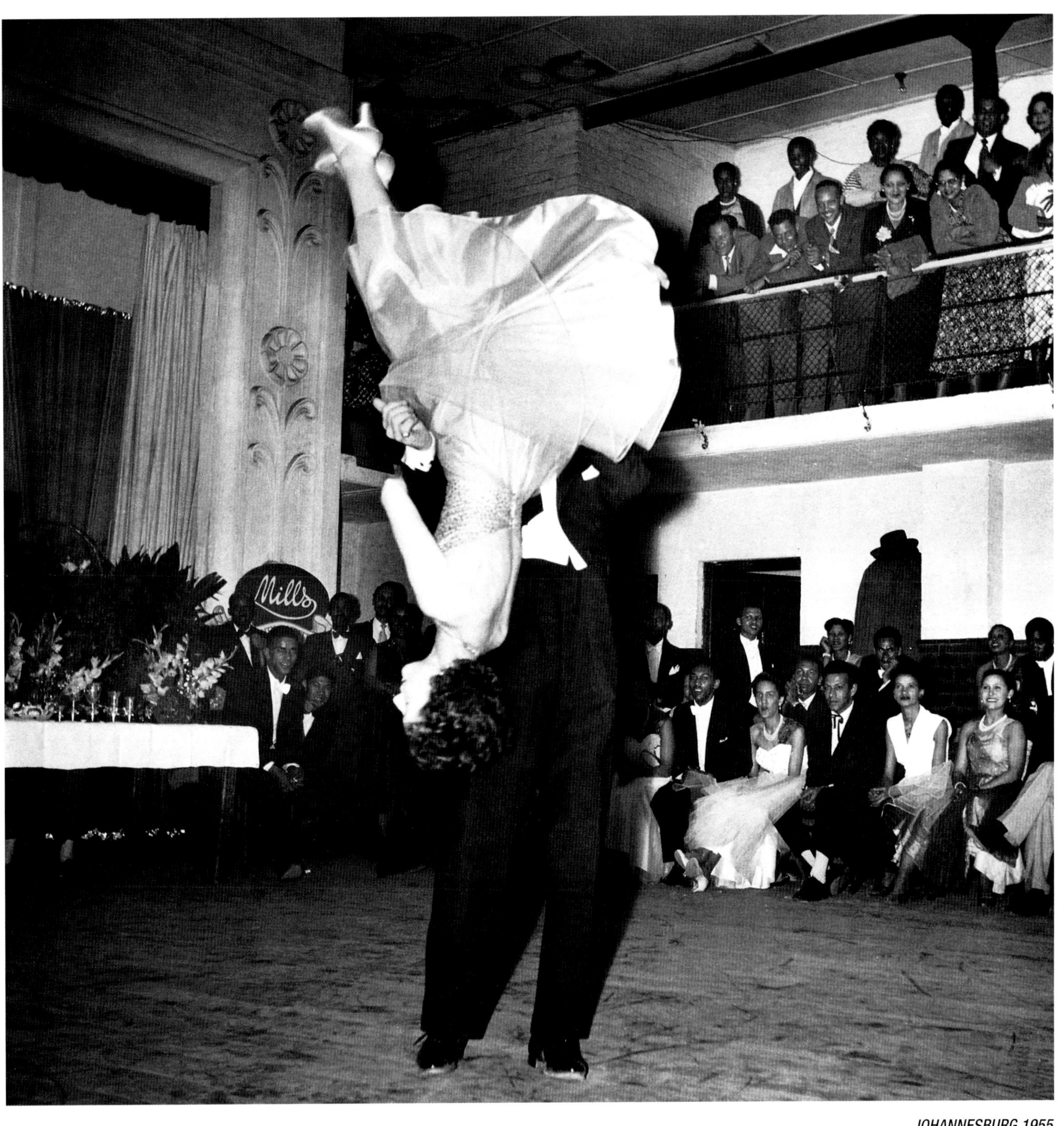

JOHANNESBURG 1955
Ballroom acrobatics.

JÜRGEN SCHADEBERG

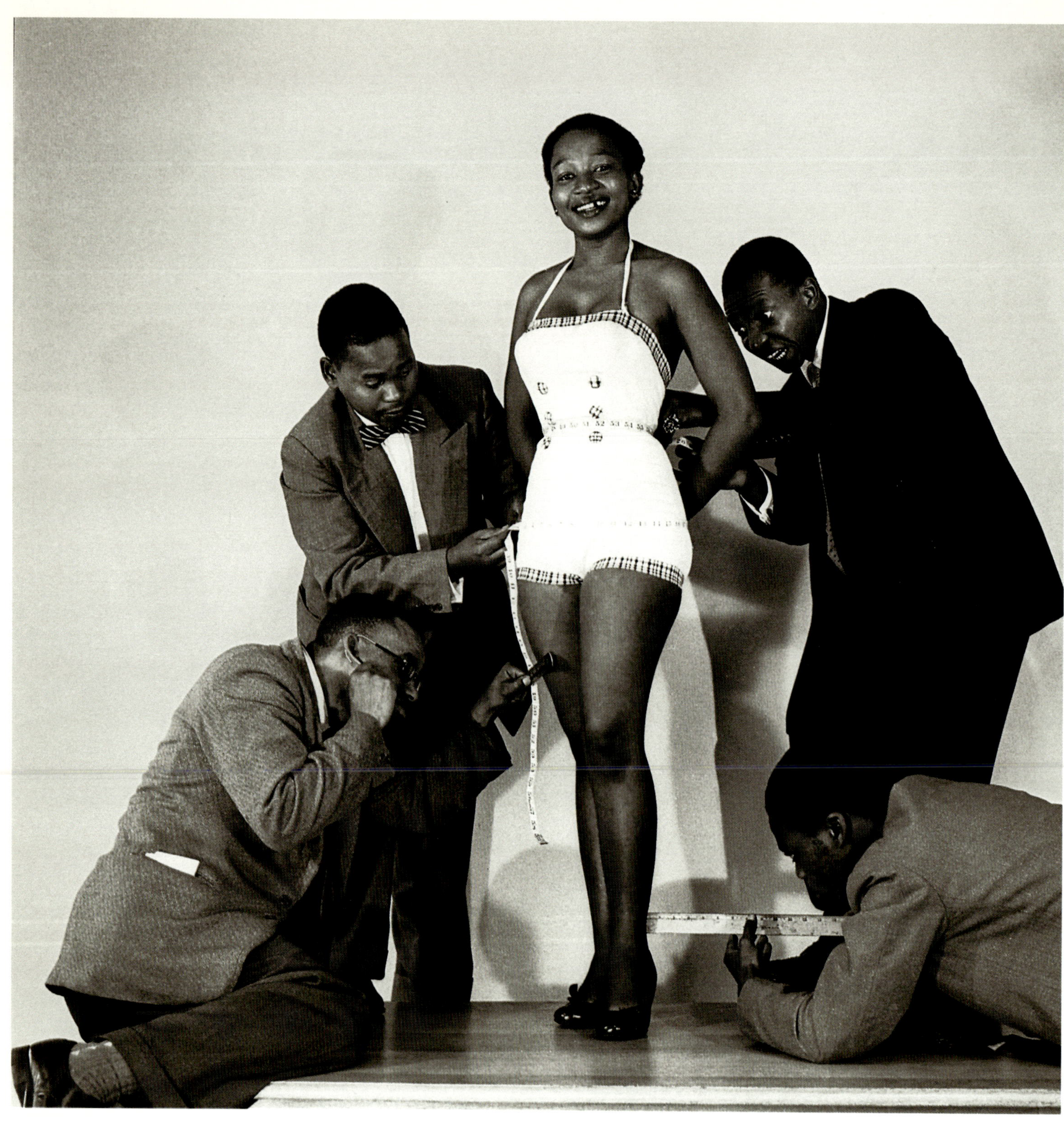

JOHANNESBURG 1954
Drum *cover girl being measured by* **Drum** *staff.*
Ezekiel Mphahlele (bottom left), Bloke Modisane
(standing on right).

JÜRGEN SCHADEBERG

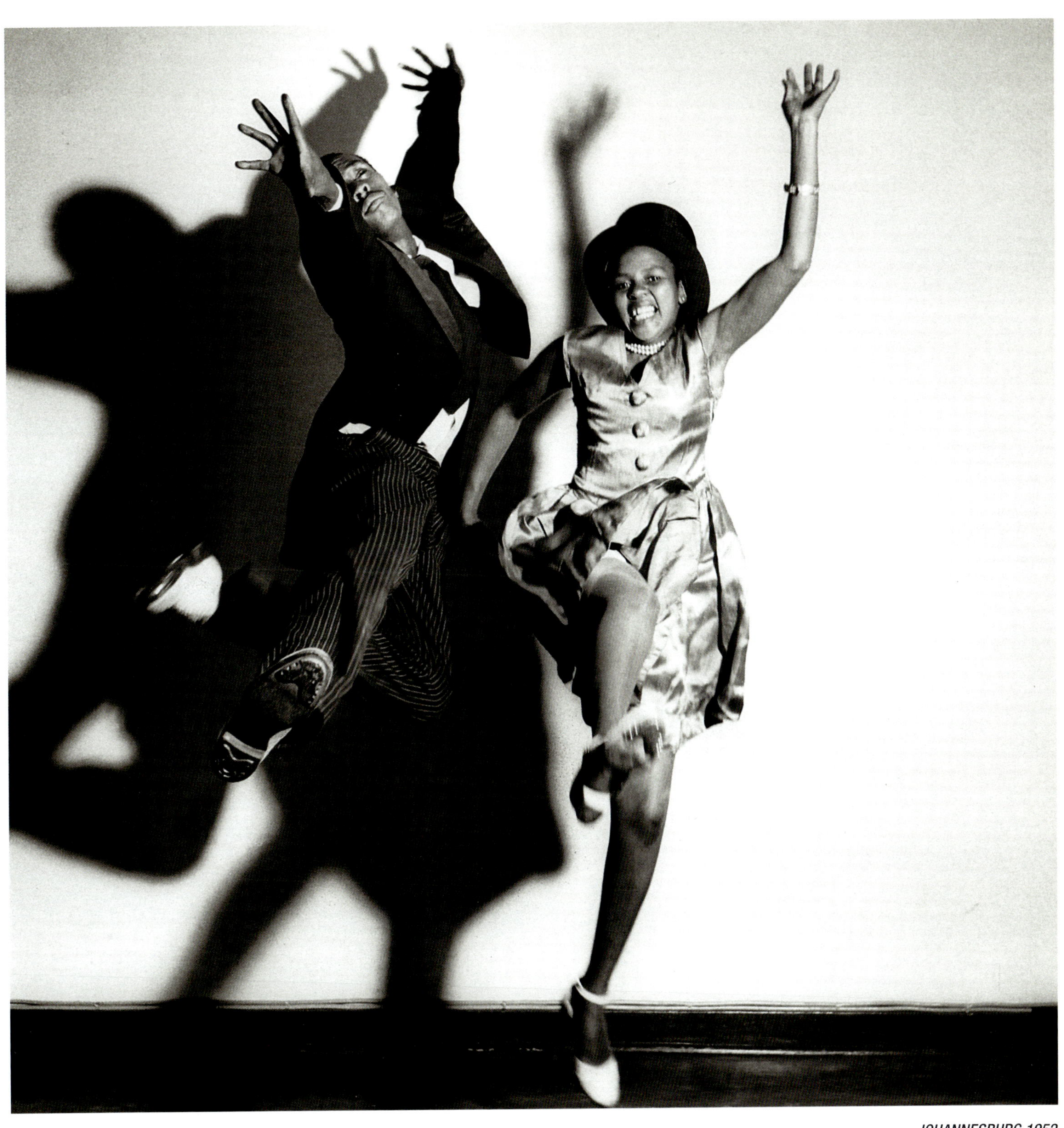

JOHANNESBURG 1952
Dancing at the Ritz.

JÜRGEN SCHADEBERG

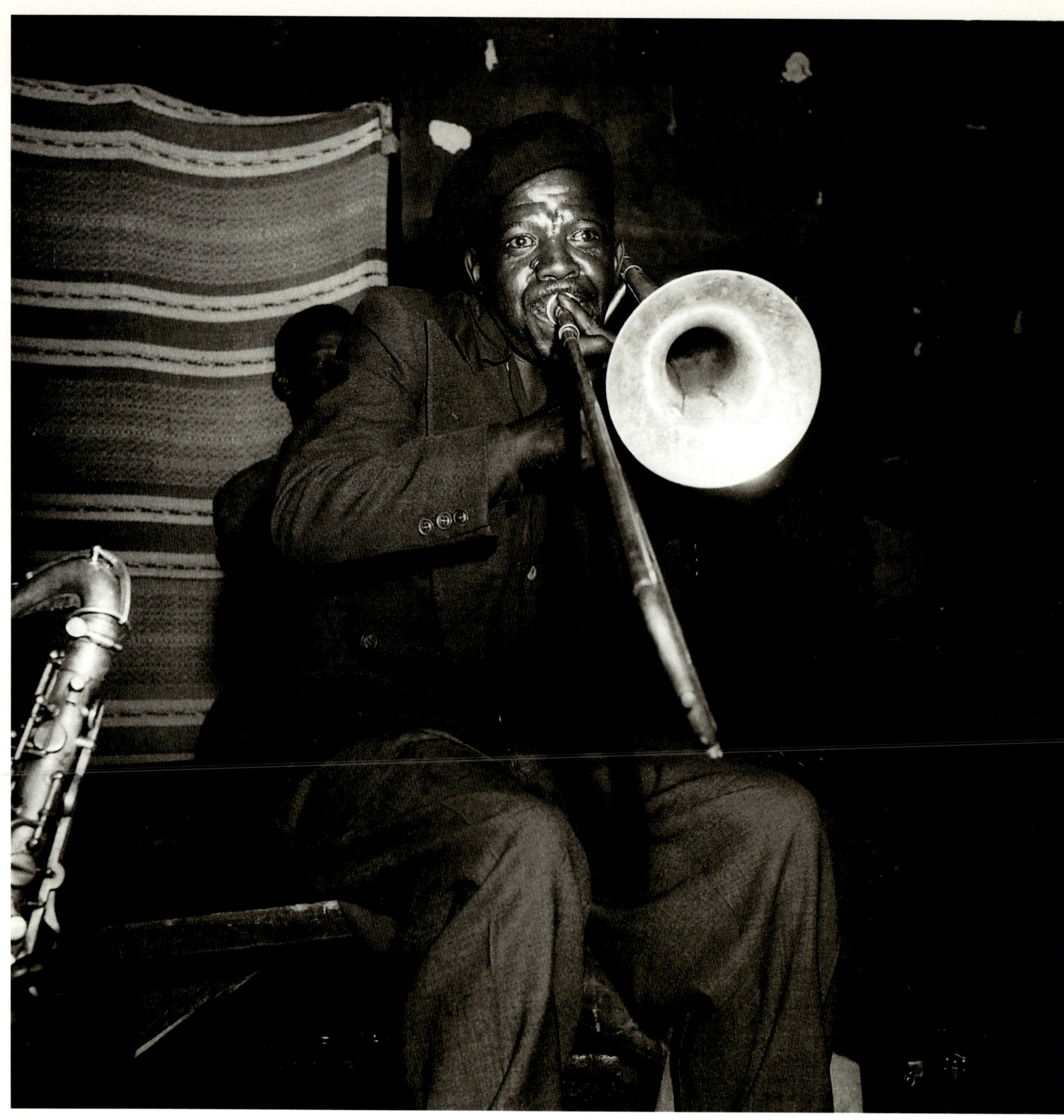

JOHANNESBURG 1952
*In the mood — Vy Nkosi, well known trombonist,
kept the great Jazz Maniacs together for a long
while. His trombone rocked tremors into the
bowels of the earth.*

JÜRGEN SCHADEBERG

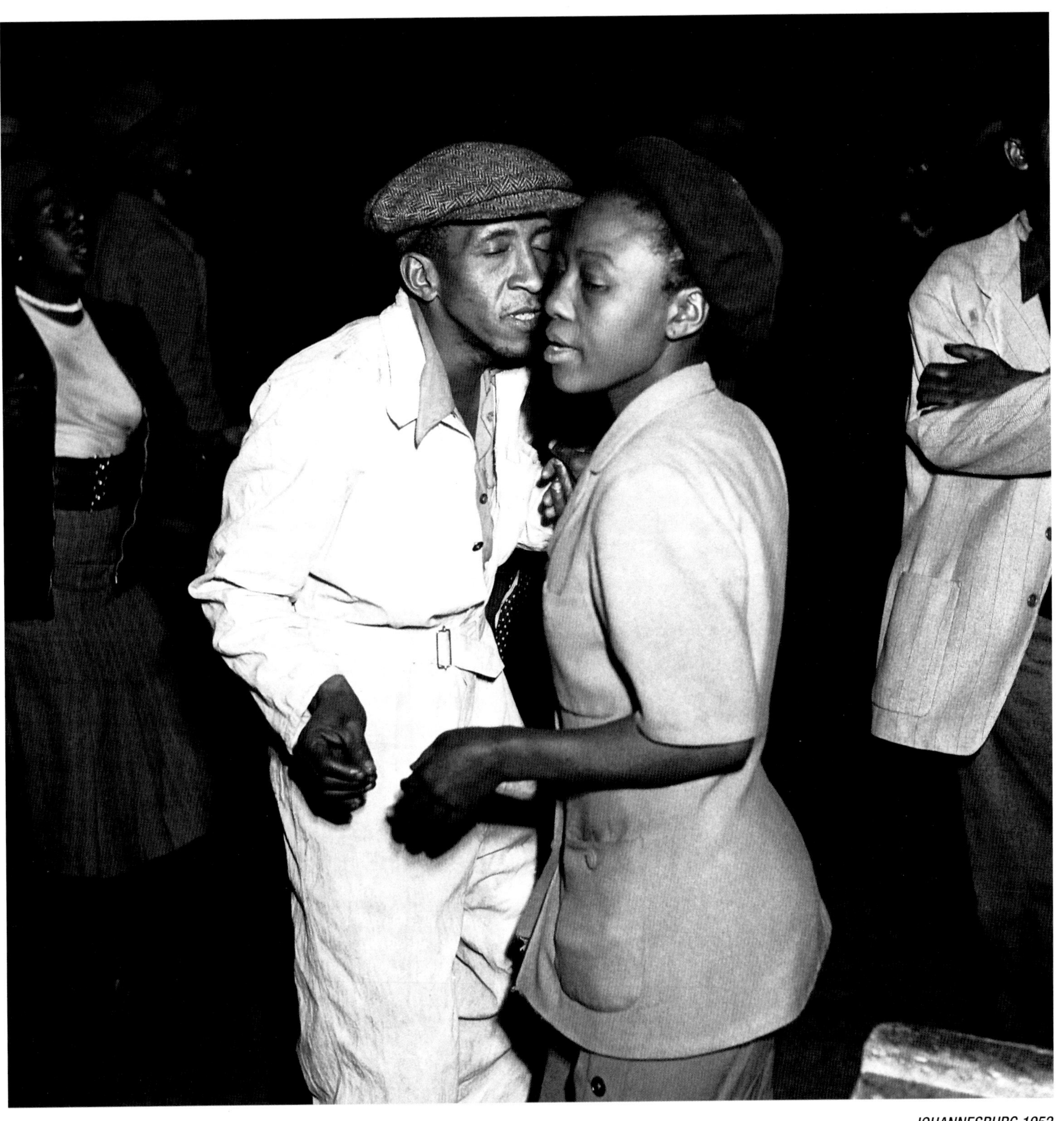

JOHANNESBURG 1952
Township shuffle. We jive, come Friday nights.
The bands are good and the halls are jam-packed
with people.

JÜRGEN SCHADEBERG

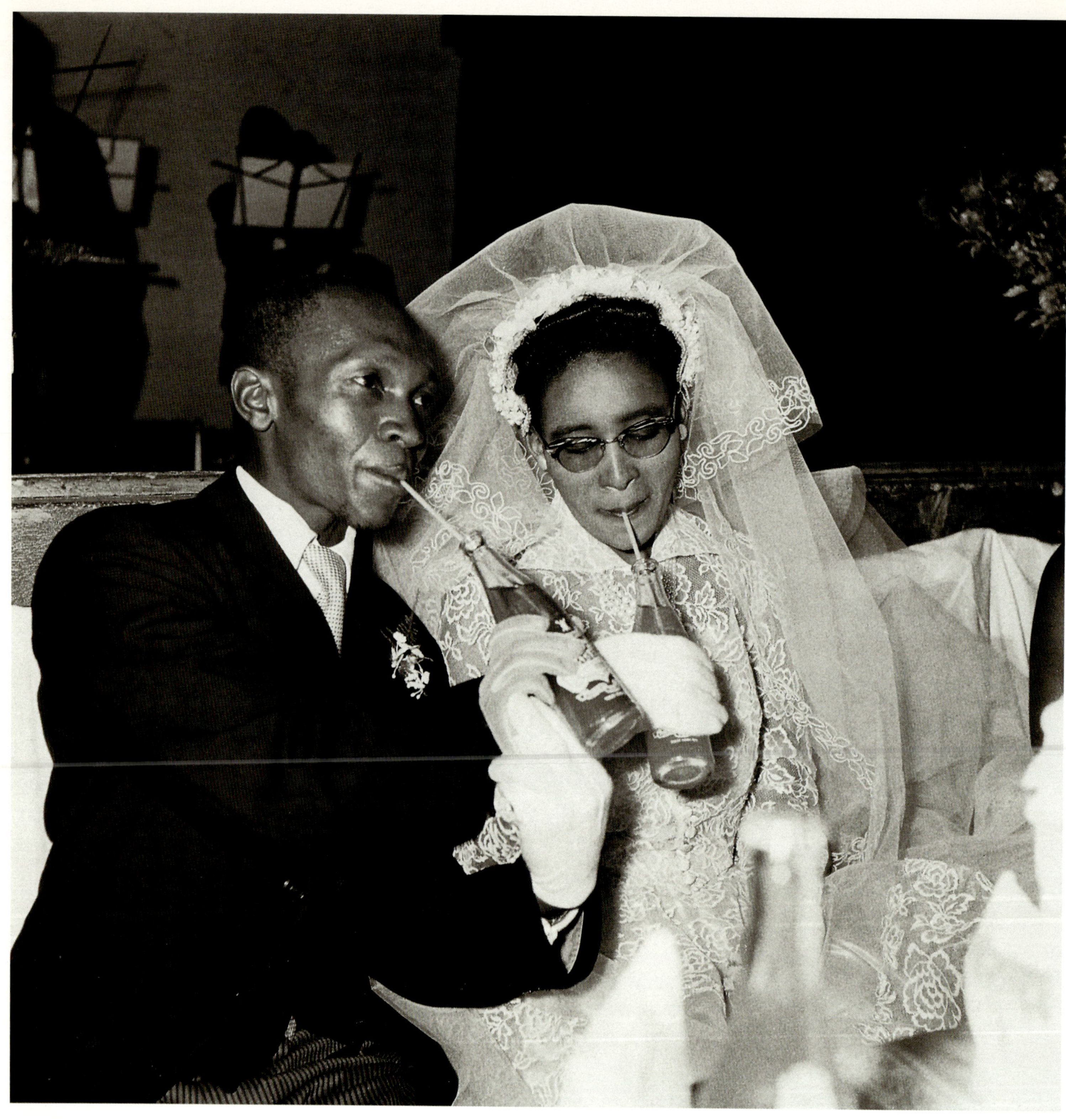

JOHANNESBURG 1957
During prohibition one had to be inventive. Here,
the bridal couple drink their brandy out of
cooldrink bottles.

PETER MAGUBANE

30

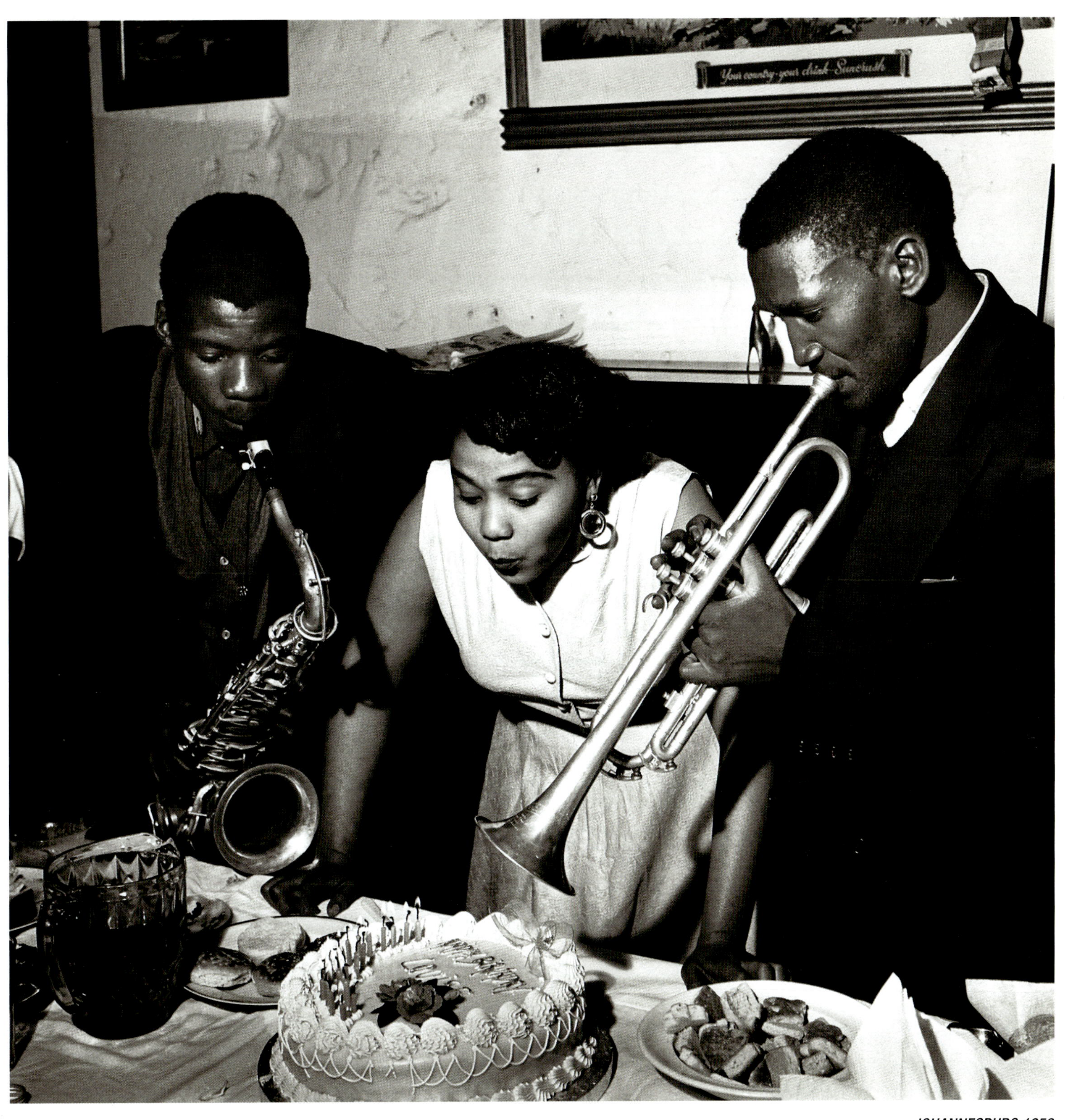

JOHANNESBURG 1956
Louisa Emanuel, famous jazz singer, turns 21. Her
most popular song was Basin Street Blues, in
1954.

GOPAL NARANSAMY

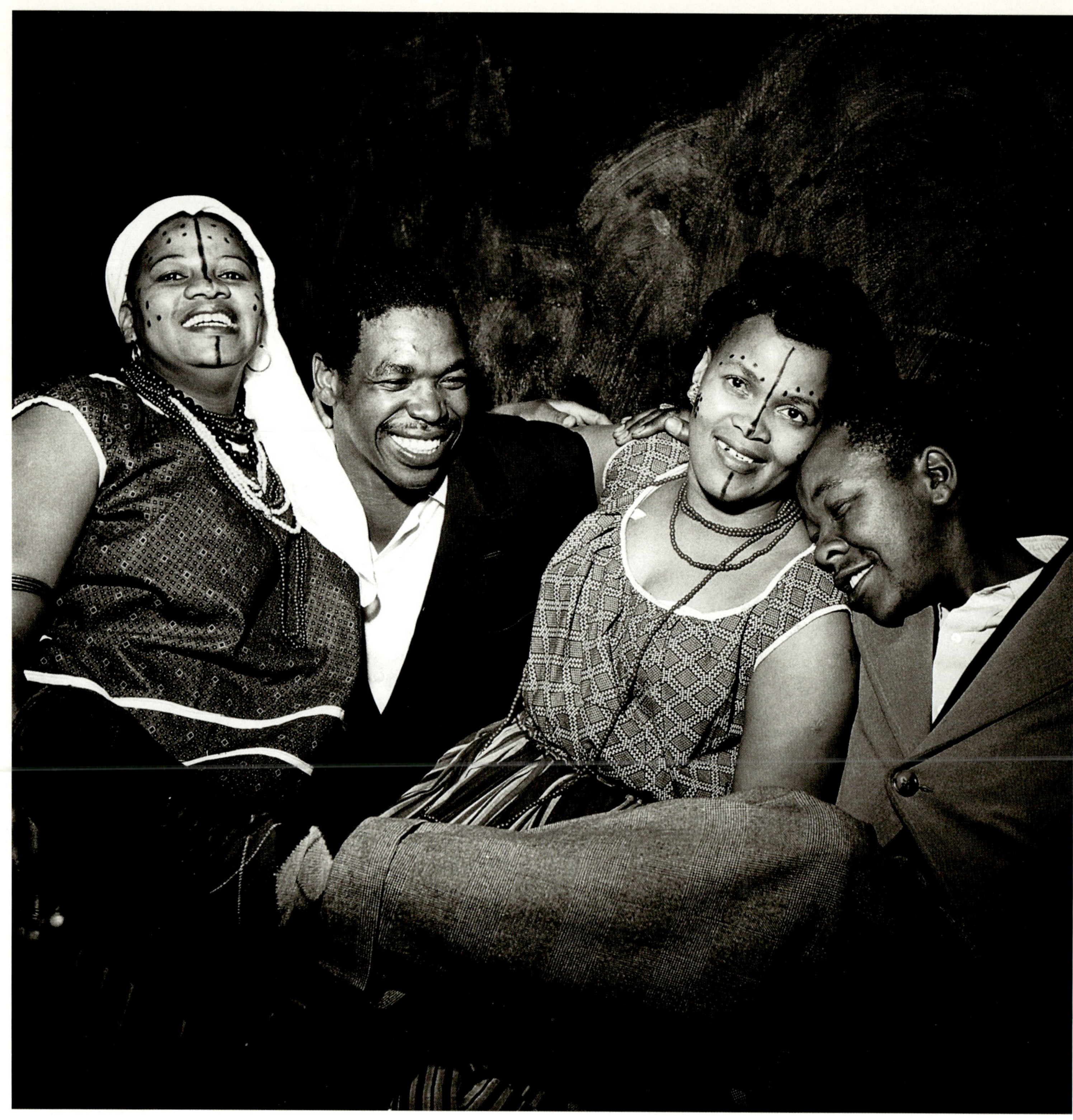

JOHANNESBURG 1955
Ladies with painted faces, flowing scarves,
dangling earrings and gypsy dresses... men in
'jazzy' outfits... under the dingy lights of the
Bantu Mens Social Centre at an April Fools' Day
fancy dress party.

BOB GOSANI

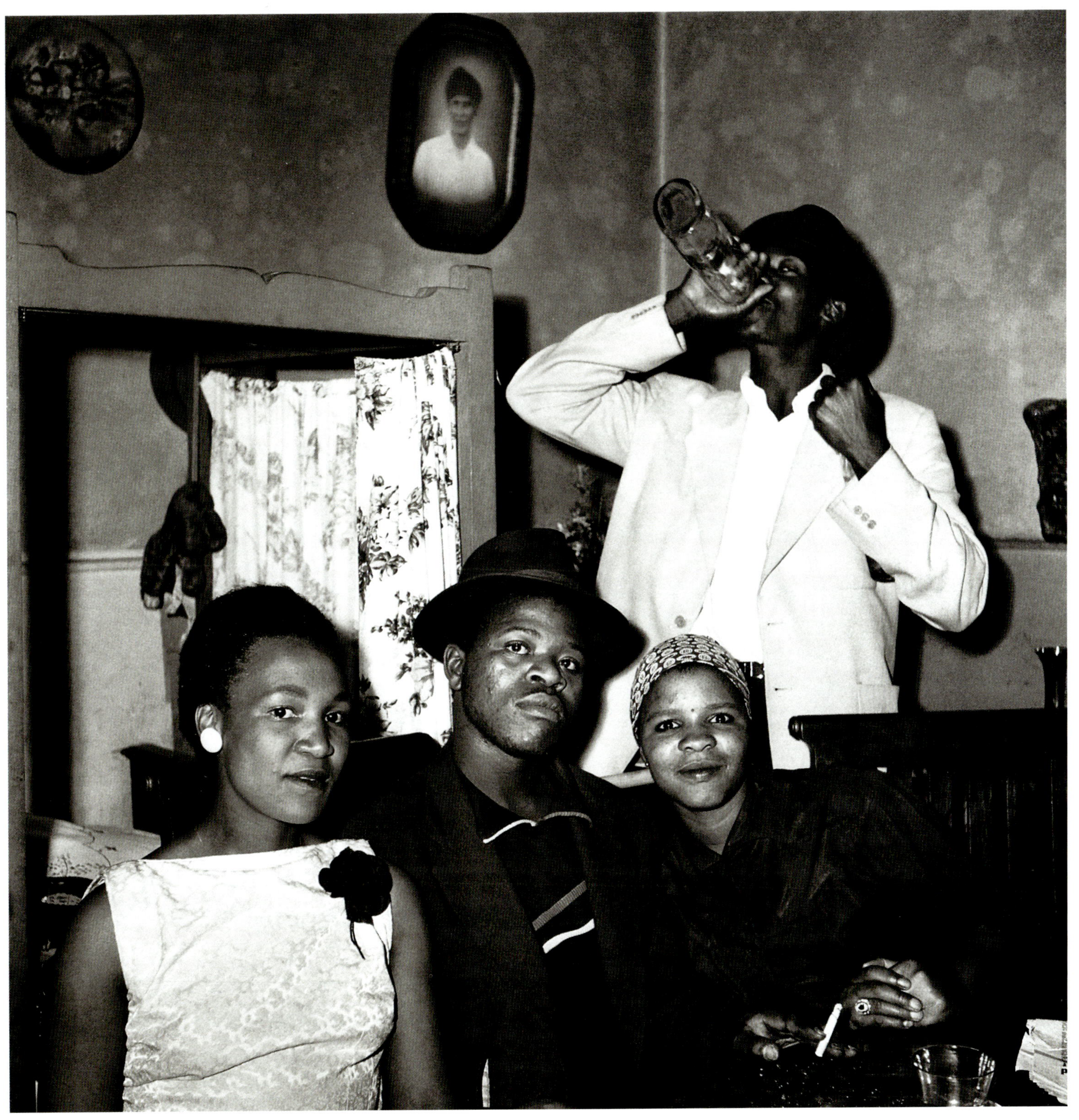

JOHANNESBURG 1956
'There are an unlimited number of shebeens
where you can get brandy, gin and a lotta other
stuff that makes my flesh creep. If you are keen
on brandy, watch out! Don't get drunk on Korea...
this is brandy fortified with spirits of alcohol or
carbide and is calculated to kick the jaws of a
crocodile'.

BOB GOSANI

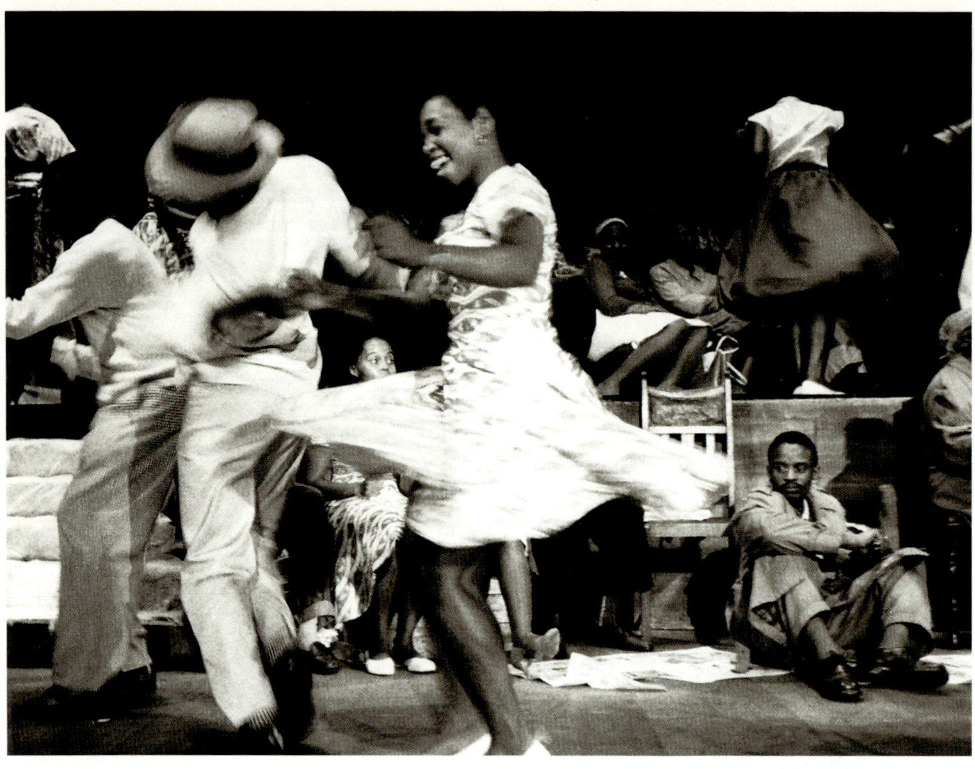

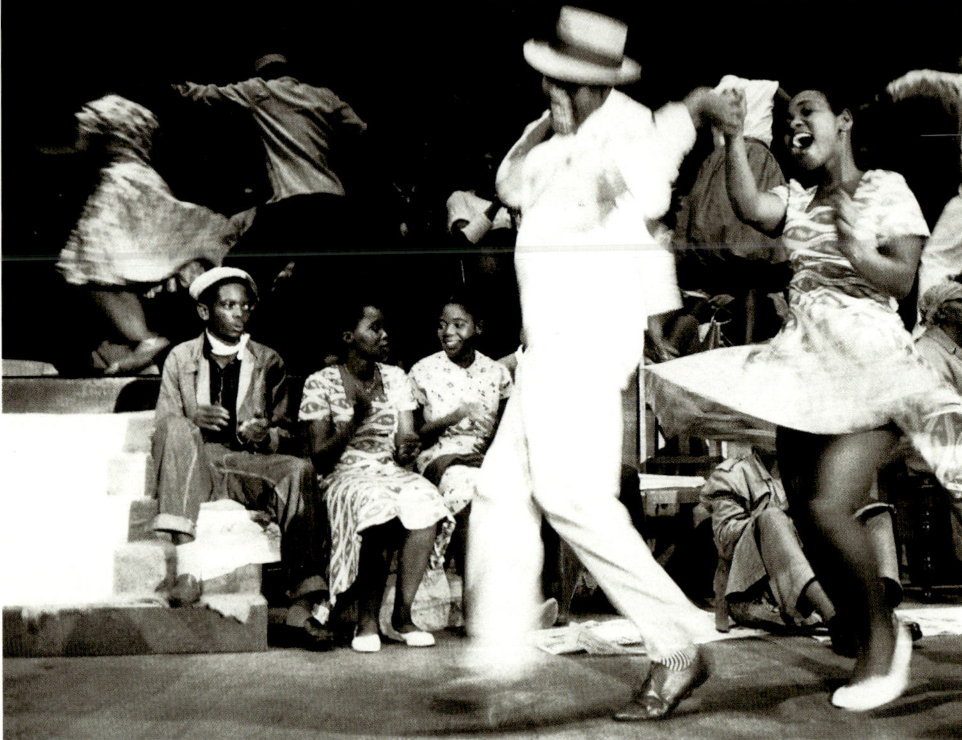

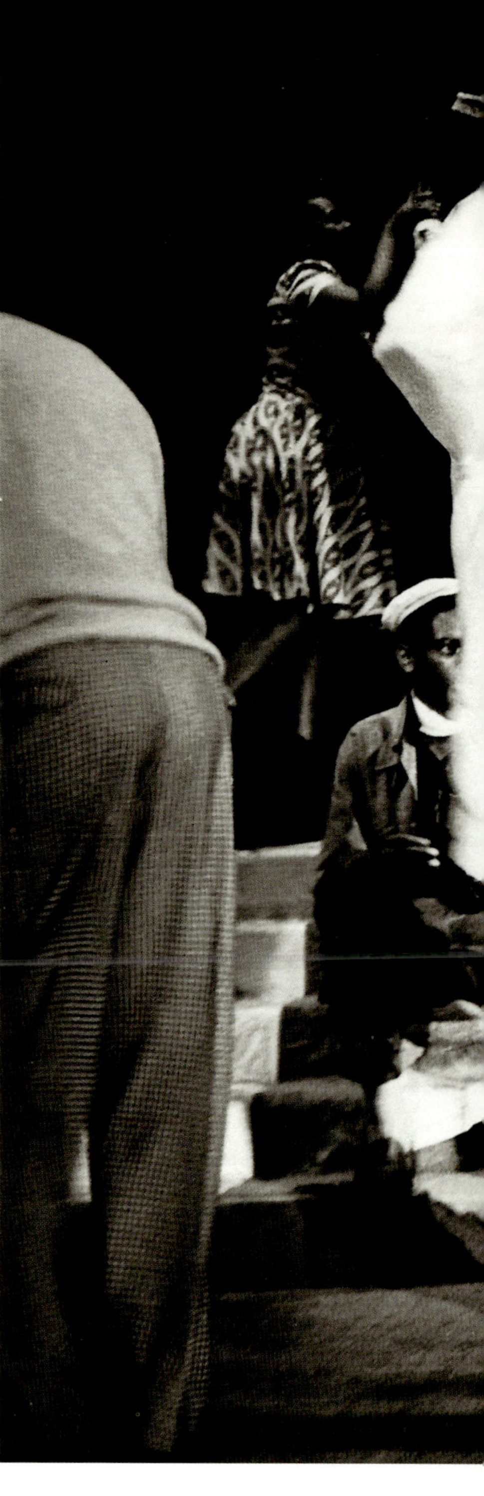

DURBAN 1960 - DIG THIS MUSICAL

The audience is silent. Then the music starts and the players sing:
See how dark it is, how quiet.
Hardly anything is moving.
Only some early person,
Only some early buses in the street
Taking early persons to the town
From Mkhumbane.

*That is part of the haunting prologue to the Alan Paton/Todd Matshikiza musical **Mkhumbane**, or 'Cato Manor', which showed to full houses in Durban in the midst of the disturbances and the emergency. It is a show filled with joy and with sadness, two hours of tuneful, deep-down pleasure.*

Todd Matshikiza, the ebullient and irrepressible composer, was at this best in his musical arrangements, which consisted of a choir of almost 100 voices which supplied the music for the entire show. Todd's ballads, folk songs and jazz arrangements reflected a variety of moods.

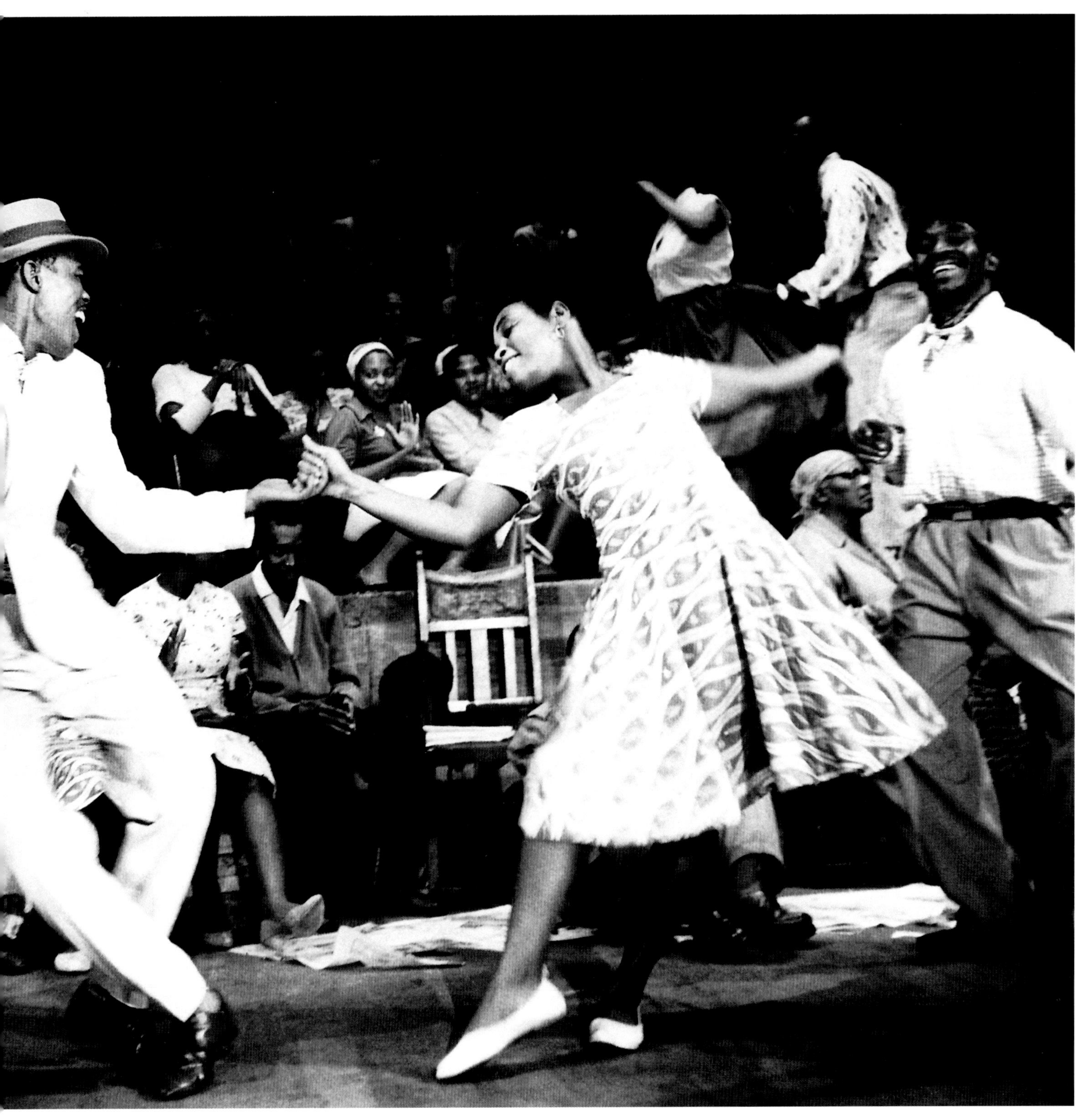

Alan Paton, the man who wrote **Cry the Beloved Country**, did the story for the show. The story of **Mkhumbane** itself is simple. Buthelezi, the 'Bull of Mkhumbane', lives in the slums in Cato Manor. He skimps and saves so that his son can become a doctor. But one day he is assaulted at the bus rank and robbed of his savings. Young John must then obtain the necessary papers to procure his reference book and earn a living. He is buffeted from department to department in his quest. There is plenty of action, partying and delirious dancing and music.

GR NAIDOO

The Birth of a Tsotsi

Every Saturday morning Johannesburg is thronged with a number of well-dressed African youths in Palm Beach suits, straw hats and white shoes, who walk about the streets looking for their victims. Women who carry handbags in the tightly congested streets are their favourite prey; and with the *tsotsis* are the *noasisas*. They wear broad skirts and carry large handbags. Their trick is to enter a shop with a tsotsi and while he engages the shopkeeper in talk the *noasisa* helps herself to any articles lying on the unwatched counter.

On the Reef the crook starts young. No education, no work, or no pass — that means that a young man must live by night and not by day — and that makes criminals. Able men are frustrated by the lack of opportunity in their lives: soon they find that they can make more money by crime than by honest means, and they turn their talents to sinful and degraded ends.

But it's on the streets where the youngster first gets the wrong ideas. Among kids the 'big shot' is the tough guy who uses a knife, and the real big shot is the killer: he's the 'Big Guy'. 'We are educated in the streets,' says one of our correspondents, 'and we graduate in the reformatories.'

Young Sibanibani was a case in point. He was illegitimate. His father had picked up his mother and a house on a forged 'lobola' certificate. But they didn't marry, his father's interest wandered and he went elsewhere. Sibanibani's mother may have been a gentle girl — but at the time of his birth she brewed liquor and passed the day with other doubtful activities. To help her, Sibanibani kept a watch for the police, and so his mother was never caught. He liked it, and that started his career of crime.

The *tsotsi* gangs are classed according to age. The boys of twelve to sixteen specialise in pick-pocketing and handbag-snatching: from seventeen to twenty five or so they go in for payroll-robbing, housebreaking and stabbing. Revolvers, we learn, can now be bought for as little as a fiver, and the studded 'Three Star' knives can be got in shops for 3s. 6d. Knuckledusters are made from anything from a bicycle chain to a studded belt and everyone knows why *tsotsis* wear gloves. The latest and most cowardly tool is a short sharp-pointed bayonet, the victim feels it pressing in his side, and unless he gives up his money he feels it pressing harder through his side.

Tsotsis are divided into different gangs operating in different ways. There are the 'Malume', the railway thieves, who off-load goods trains in the dead of night. 'We mark down a goods train,' one informant tells us, 'and find out what it is carrying in each truck; then we drive in a car to a slope we know, grease the lines with oil for a stretch which slows up the train, jump on the truck and throw down what we want.'

The 'Matsisi' (Sesotho for bugs) are the pickpockets and the men who do the hold-ups are the 'Joavas'. *Tsotsis* often retire at thirty or fifty, if they survive. They marry and set up as respectable citizens on their gains, much like some Johannesburg financiers we could name.

Both *tsotsis* and *noasisas* live a very glamorous type of life. They make a lot of money, but very few save it. They buy swanky clothes and go to the cinemas almost every day and entertain each other lavishly. They go to parties on Sunday, where they are able to impress the shebeen queens with their enormous wealth. For business reasons as well as for fear of reprisals, the shebeens welcome the *tsotsis* and fear them. Other *tsotsis* gamble on high card stakes and lose their money as fast as they get it.

Henry Nxumalo
Drum 1953

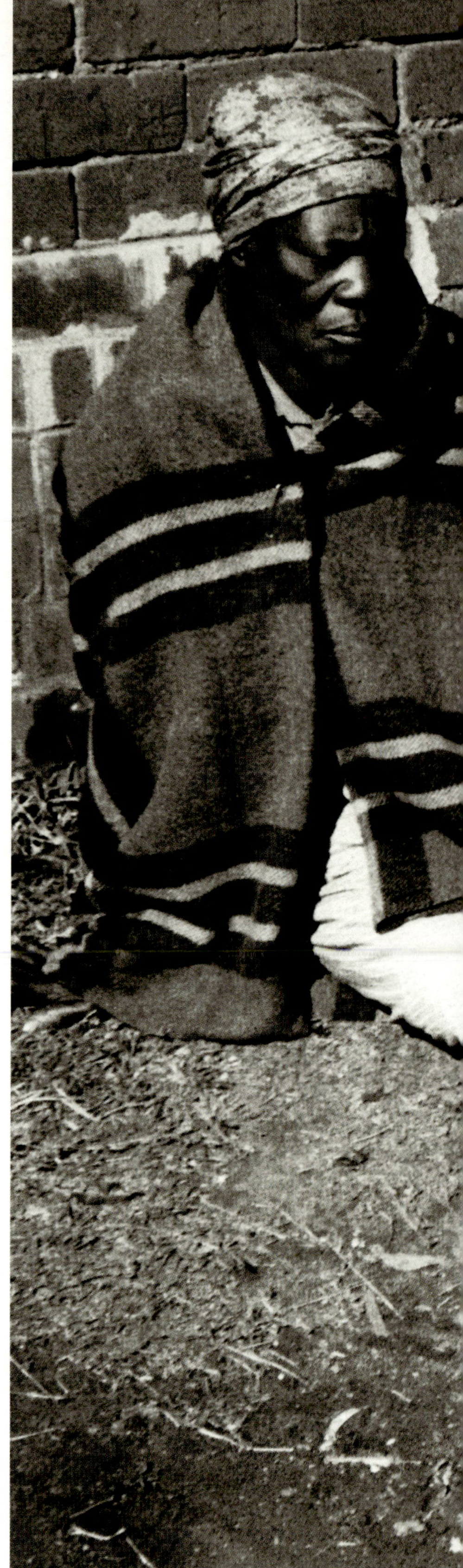

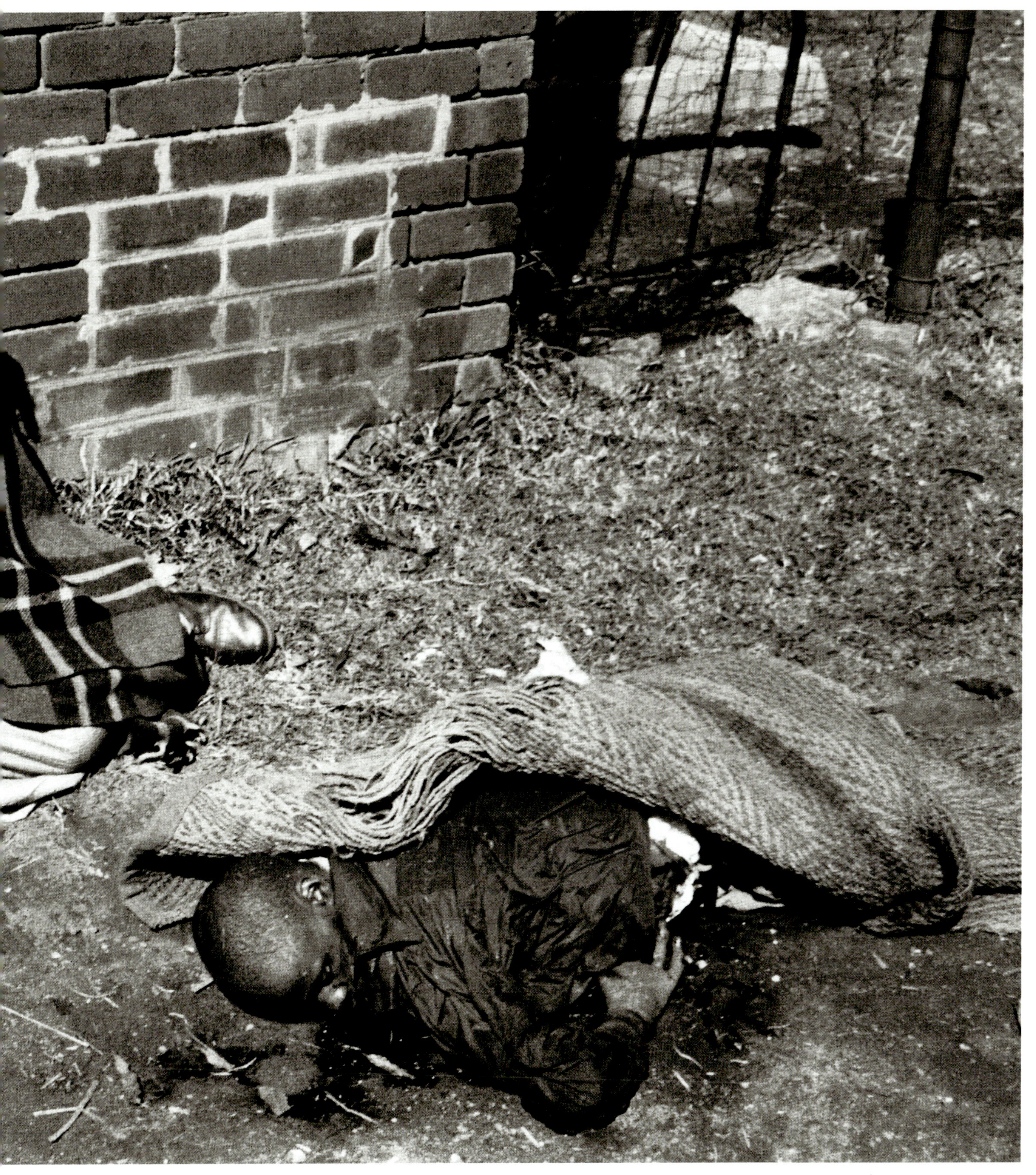

ALEXANDRA TOWNSHIP 1958
The victim of a knife fight.

BOB GOSANI

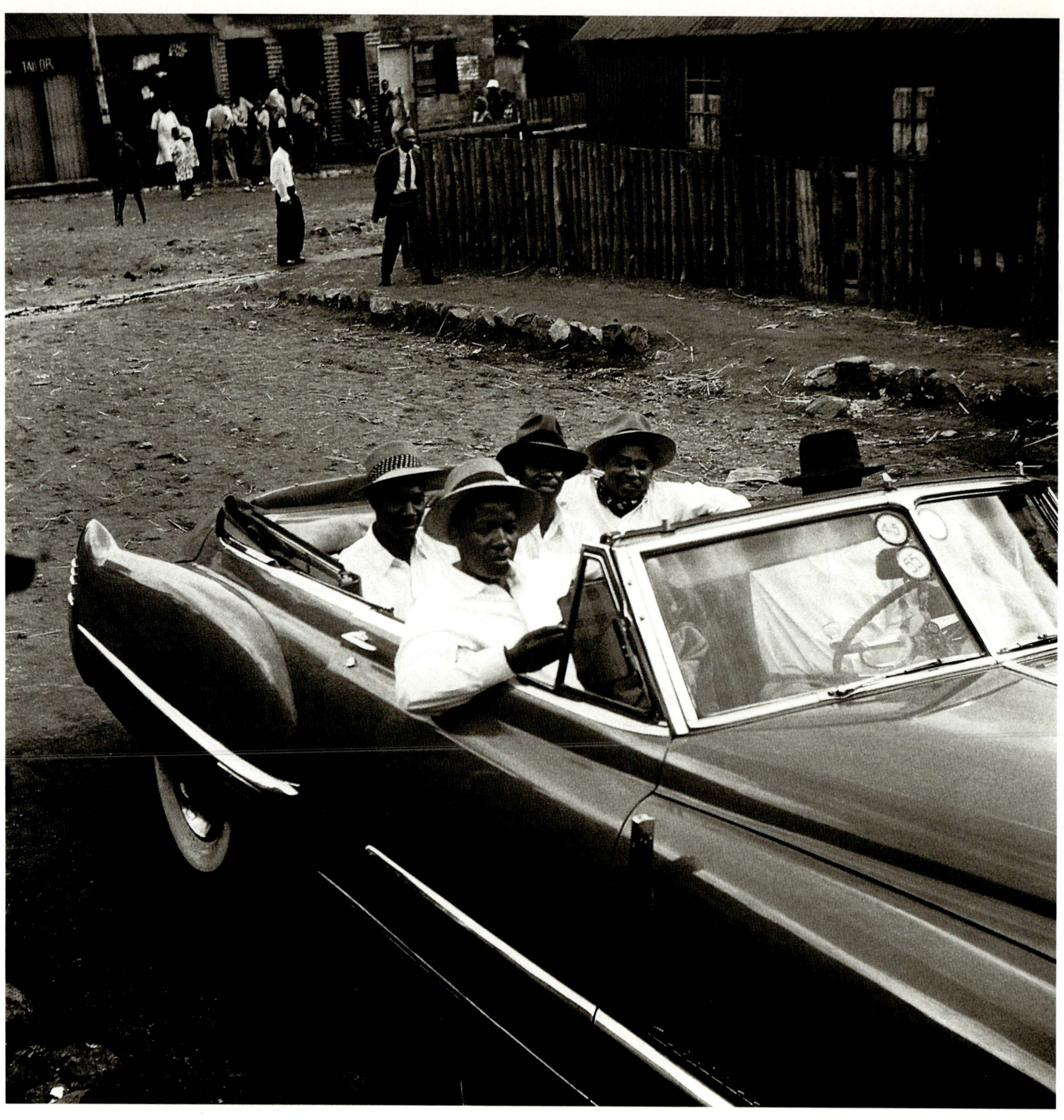

SOPHIATOWN 1954
The 'American' gang in their flashy outfits and
flashy car, claiming Sophiatown.

BOB GOSANI

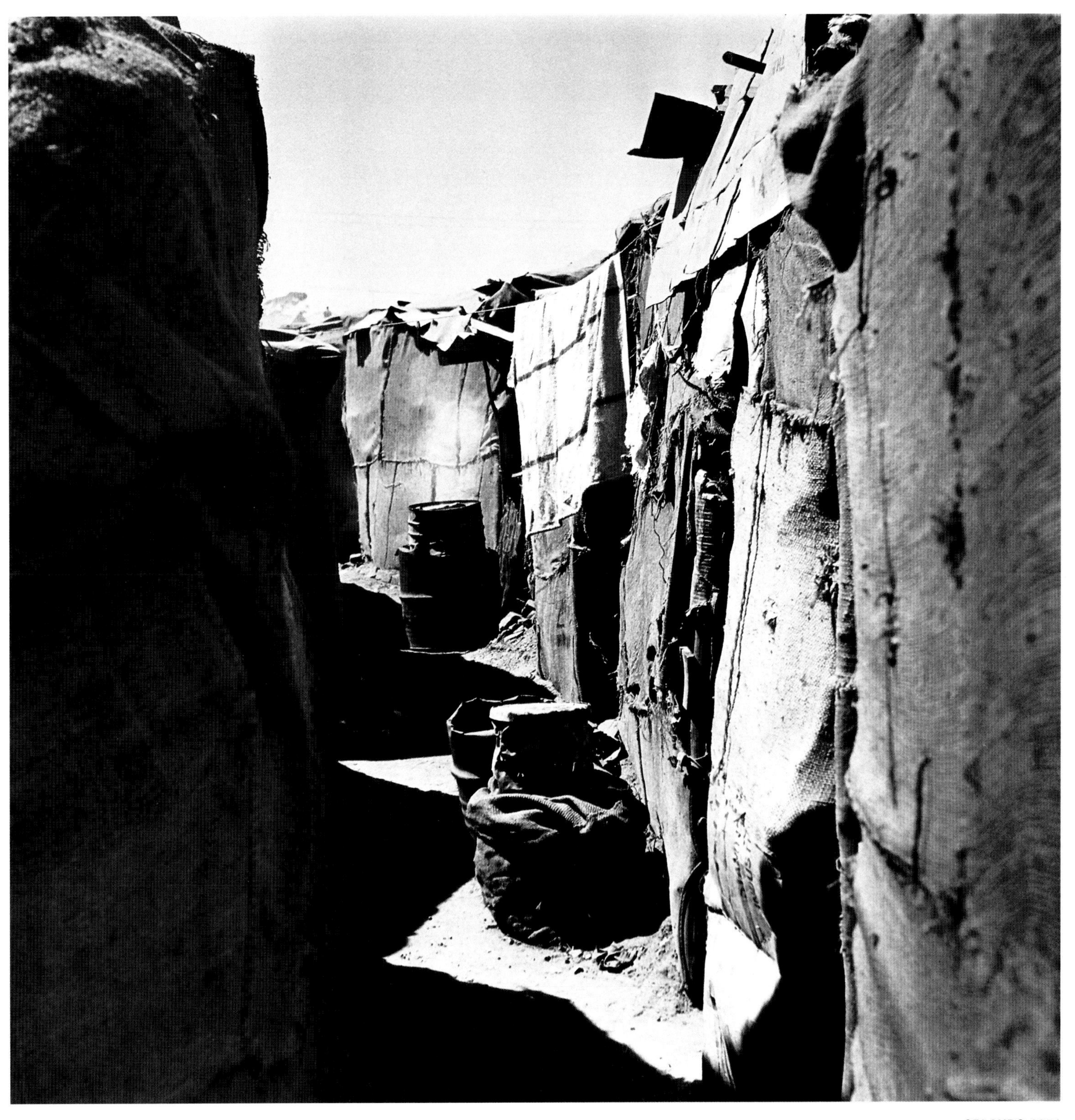

ORLANDO 1951
Shanty town shacks, many made from sacking,
mushroomed around Orlando Township. James
Mpanza fought for the squatters, leading them on
to vacant municipal land.

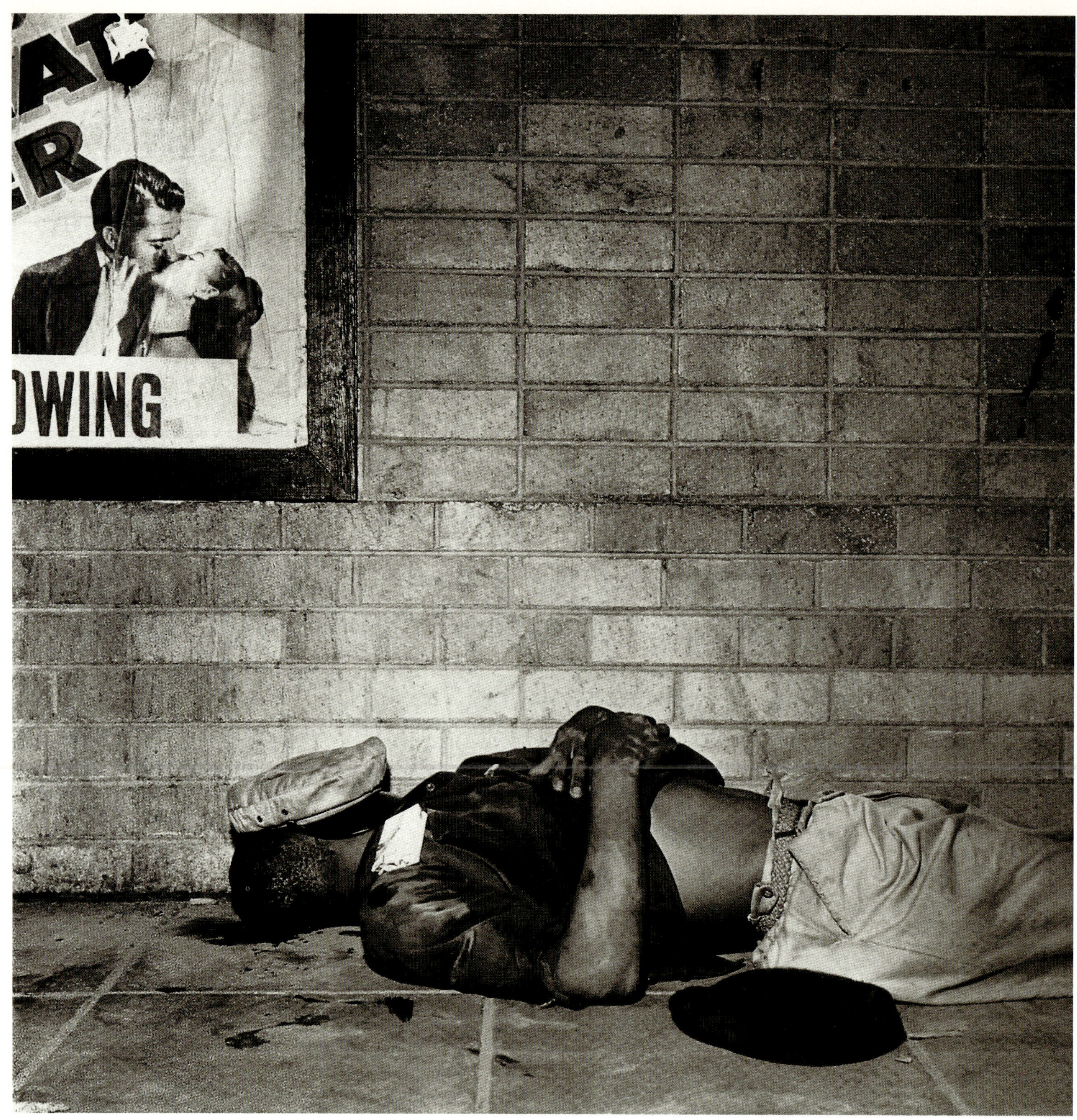

ALEXANDRA TOWNSHIP 1958
Boy Mangena lies dead. The whole reef wants to
know who killed this thug, knifeman and bully.
Now just a lonely corpse, Boy was shot outside a
theatre in Alexandra Township, Johannesburg.

PETER MAGUBANE

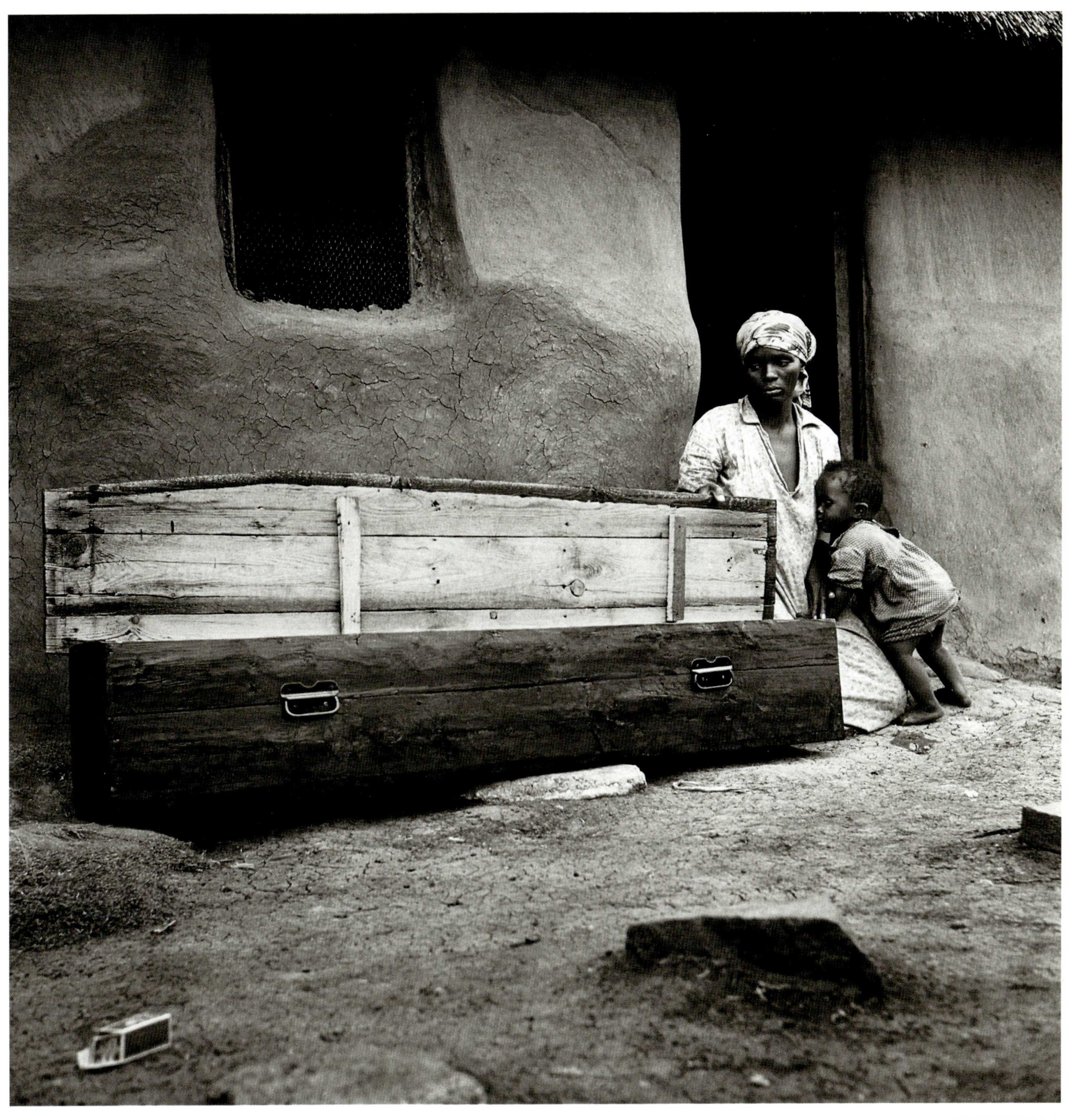

NEWCASTLE 1958
'Watching the Dead'. There are urine pools and stools all over the courtyard. The walls tell the murky story of degenerate backyard lives. Giant cockroaches glide merrily up, over and into the coffin. There is nothing else, except death.

GOPAL NARANSAMY

The Dube Train

The Dube Station, with the prospect of congested trains filled with sour-smelling humanity. Despairing thoughts of every kind darted through my mind: the lateness of the trains, the shoving savagery of the crowds, the grey aspect around me. Even the announcer over the loudspeaker gave confusing directions.

I hopped into the Third Class carriage. As the train moved off, I leaned out of the paneless window and looked onto the leaden, lack-lustre platform churning away beneath me like a fast conveyor belt.

Two or three yards away, a door had been broken and repaired with masonite so that it could no longer be opened. Moreover, near the door a seat was missing which transformed the area into a kind of hall.

Phefeni Station rushed at us, with human faces blurring past. When the train stopped, in stepped a girl. She must have been a mere child. Yet her manner was all adult as if she knew all about 'this sorry scheme of things entire' and with a scornful toss relegated it.

The train slid into Phomolong. Against the red-brick waiting-room I saw a *tsotsi* lounging, for all the world not a damn interested in taking the train, but I knew the type, so I watched him in grim anticipation. When the train started sailing out of the platform, he turned round nonchantly and trippled along backwards towards an open door. It amazes me no end how these boys know exactly where the edge of the platform comes when they run like that, backwards. Just at the drop he caught the ledge of the train and heaved himself in gracefully.

He noticed the girl and started teasing her. All township love-making is rough. She looked round in panic; 'Ah, *Au-boetie*, I don't even know you'.

Mzimhlope, the dry-white station. The *tsotsi* turned round and looked out of the window on to the platform. He recognized some of his friends there and hailed them.

'O, Zigzagza, it's how there?'

'It's jewish!'

'*Hela*, Tholo, my ma hears me, I want that ten-'n-six!'

'Go get it in hell!'

'Weh, my sister, don't listen to that guy. Tell him Shakespeare nev'r said so!'

The gibberish exchange was all in exuberant superlatives.

The train left the platform in the echoes of its stridency.

As the train approached New Canada, and the confluence of the Orlando and the Dube train lines, I looked over the head of the girl next to me. It must have been a crazy engineer who had designed this crossing. The Orlando train comes from the right. It crosses the Dube train overhead just before we reach New Canada. But when it reaches the station it is on the right again, for the Johannesburg train enters at extreme left. It is a curious kind of game.

Moreover, it has necessitated cutting the hill and building a bridge. But just this quirk of an engineer's imagination has left a spectacularly beautiful scene. After the drab, chocolate-box houses of the township, monotonously identical row upon row, this gash of man's imposition upon nature never fails to intrigue me.

Our caveman lover was still at the girl while people were changing from our train to the Westgate train in New Canada. The girl wanted to get off, but the *tsotsi* would not let her.

He ploughed through the humanity of the train, after the girl. Men gave way shamelessly, but one woman would not take it. She burst into a spitfire tirade that whiplashed at the men.

The men winced. They said nothing, merely looked round at each other in shy embarrassment. But those barbed words had brought the little thug to a stop. He turned round, scowled at the woman, and with cold calculation cursed her anatomically, twisting his lips to give the word the full measure of its horror.

'*Hela*, you street urchin, that woman is your mother,' came the shrill voice of the big hulk of a man, who had all the time been sitting quietly opposite me.

Suddenly, the woman shrieked and men scampered on to seats. The *tsotsi* had drawn a sheath-knife, and he faced the big man.

Croesus Cemetery flashed past.

The *tsotsi* lifted the blade and plunged it obliquely. Like an instinctive, predatory beast, he seemed to know exactly where the vulnerable jugular was and he aimed for it. The jerk of the train deflected his stroke though, and the blade slit a long cleavage down the big man's open chest.

With a demoniacal scream, the big man reached out for the boy crudely. He caught the boy by the upper arm with the left hand, and between the legs with the right and lifted him bodily. Then he hurled him towards me. The flight went clean through the paneless window, and only a long cry trailed in the wake of the rushing train.

The big man, bespattered with blood, got off at Langlaagte Station.

Only after we had left the station did the stunned passengers break out into a cacophony of chattering.

No one expressed sympathy for the boy or the man. They were just greedily relishing the thrilling episode of the morning.

Can Themba

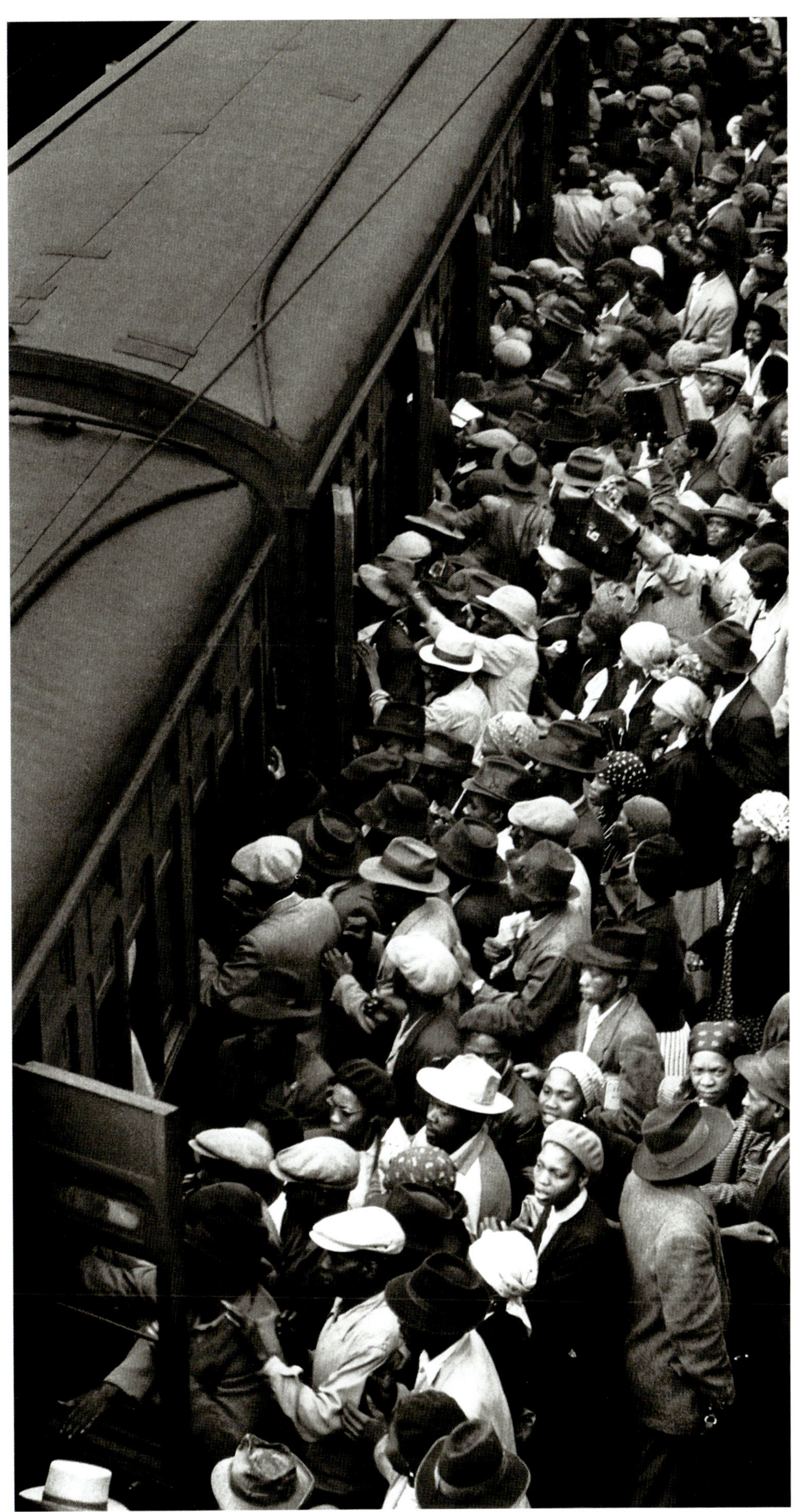

JOHANNESBURG 1956
The weekend was around again to bottle up the
people's weariness, their anxieties, their pains.
Men and women came out of the trains like live
vomit of some monster in a folk tale. They came
out the same way they had boarded the trains in
the morning; savagely, without heed to woman or
weakling; through windows as well as through
doors. 'Forced to live like beasts.'

PETER MAGUBANE

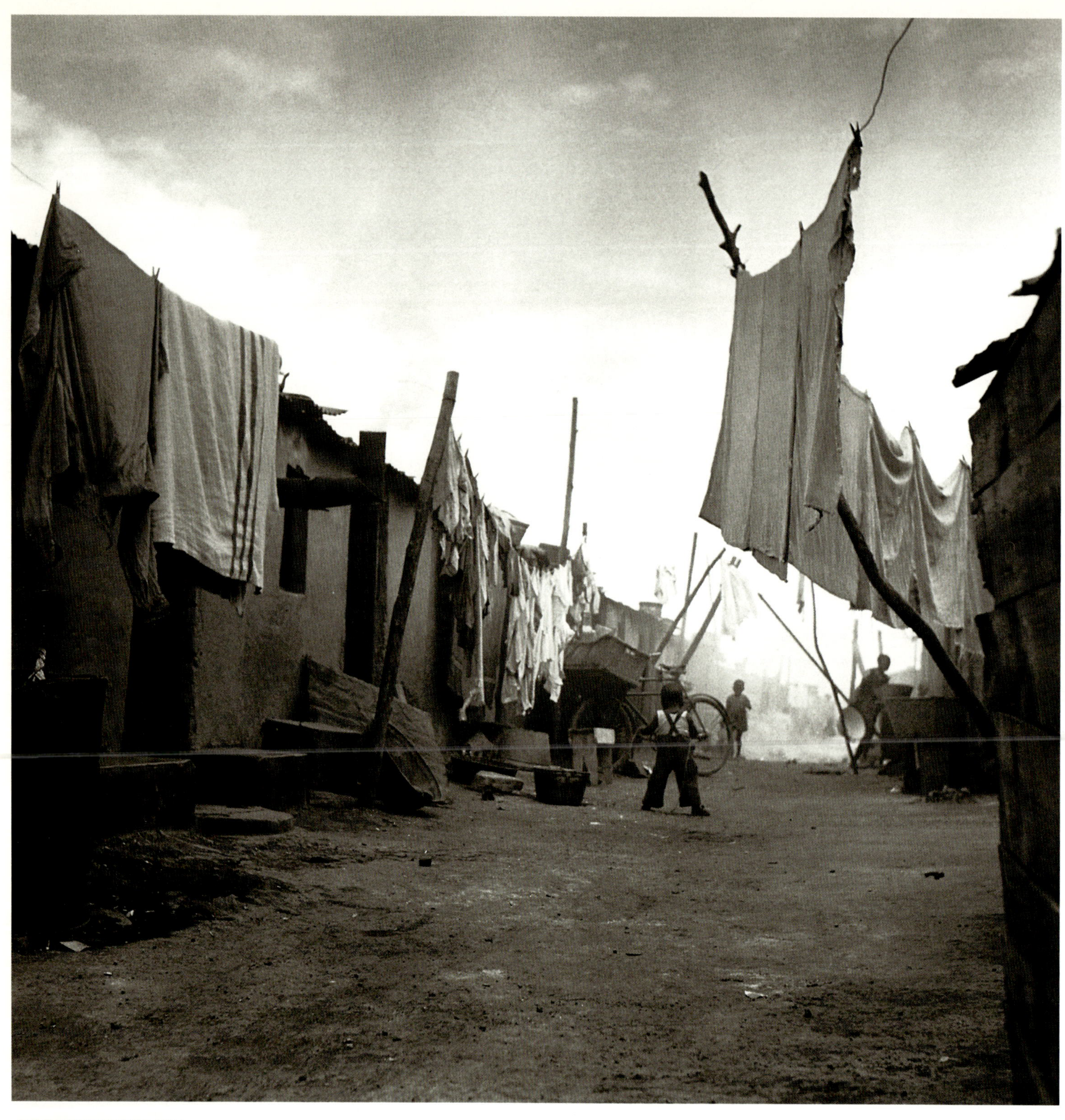

ORLANDO TOWNSHIP 1951
Illegal homes on the edge of Orlando. Many hope
in vain for work in Johannesburg.

JÜRGEN SCHADEBERG

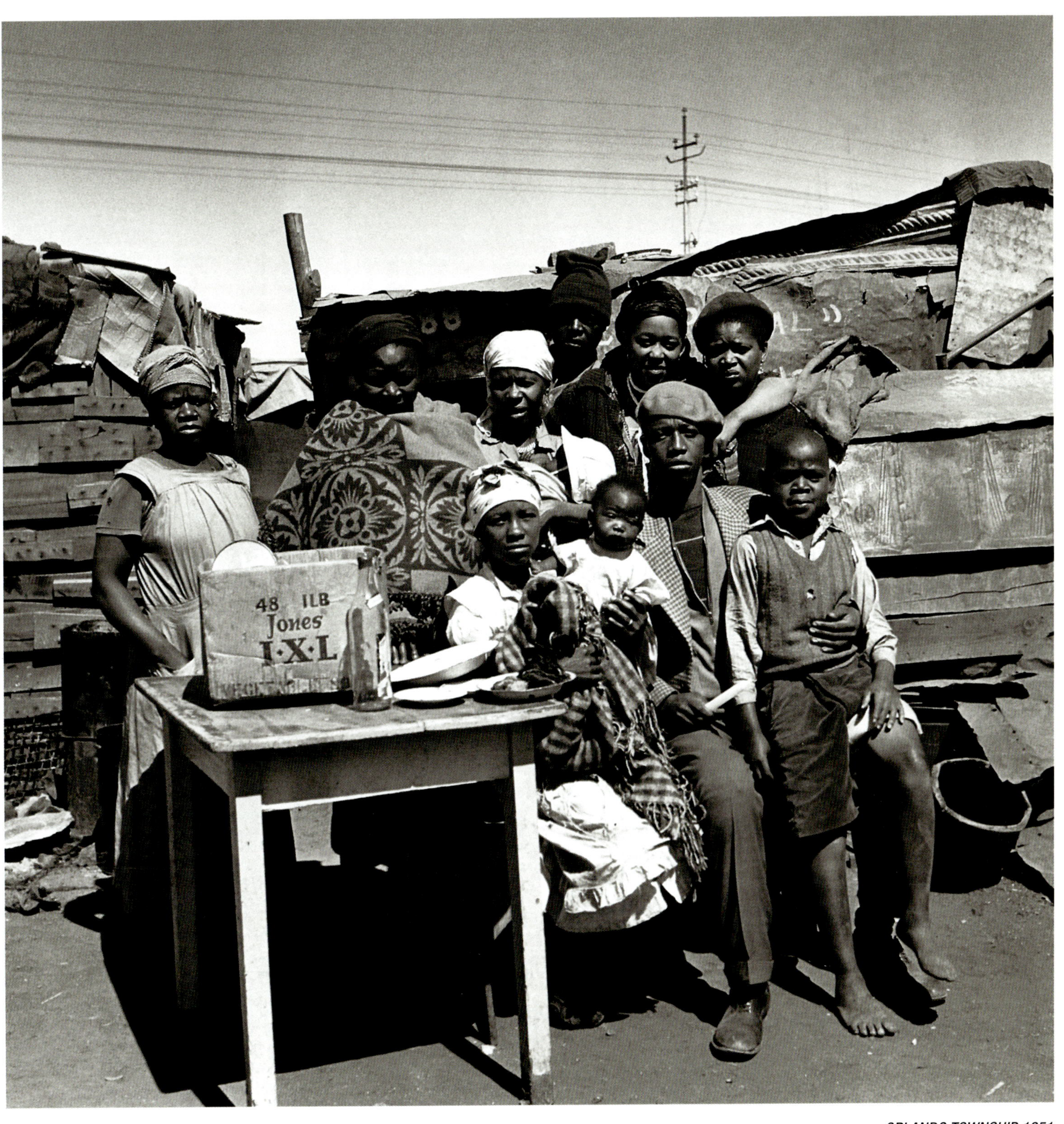

ORLANDO TOWNSHIP 1951
The homes are just put together with bits of
wood, cardboard boxes, rusty bits of tin and cut
up sacks.

JÜRGEN SCHADEBERG

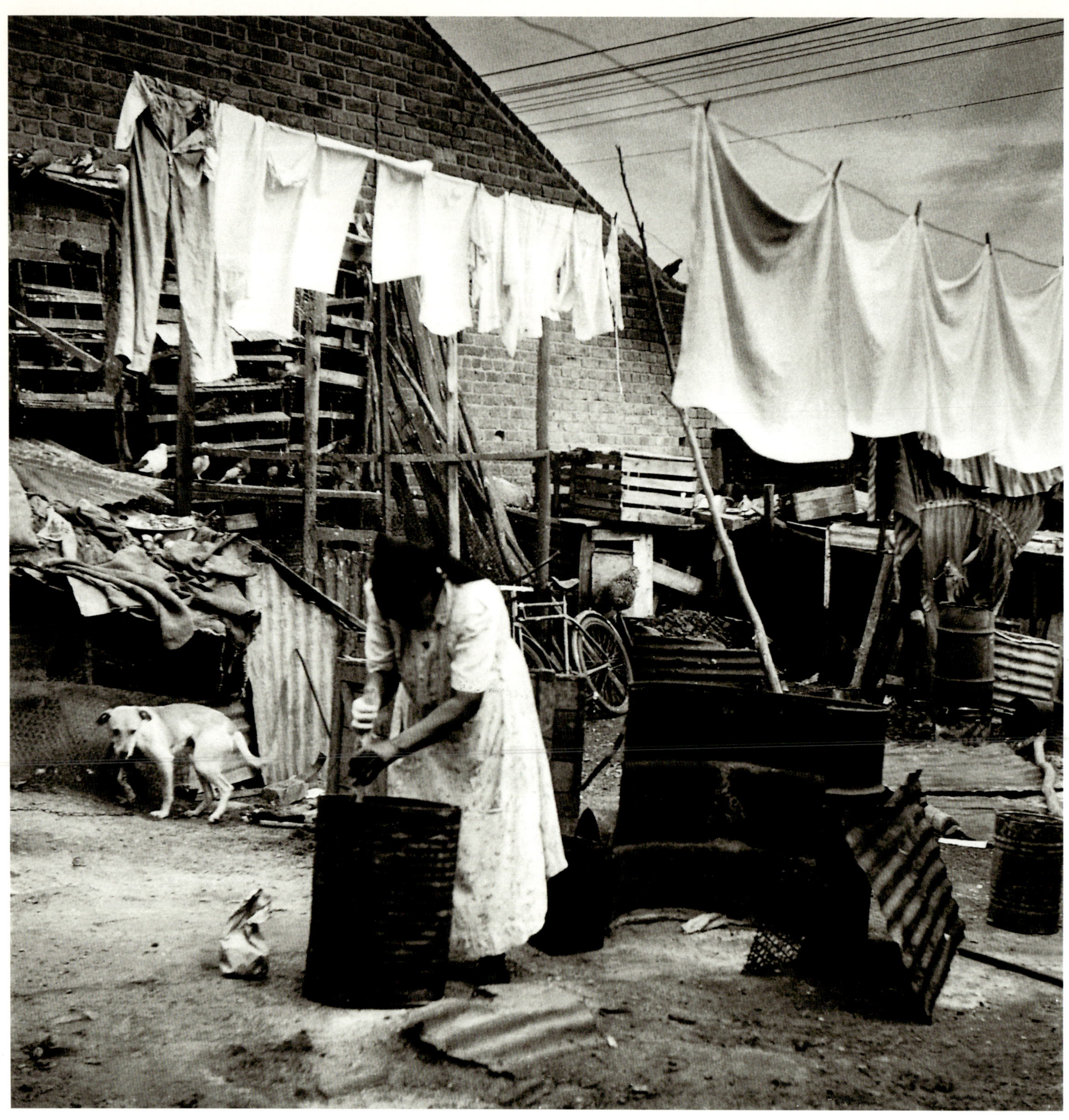

SOPHIATOWN 1954
Brewing 'Skokiaan' in the backyard. Some
claimed that the home-made cocktail could make
you blind.

JÜRGEN SCHADEBERG

46

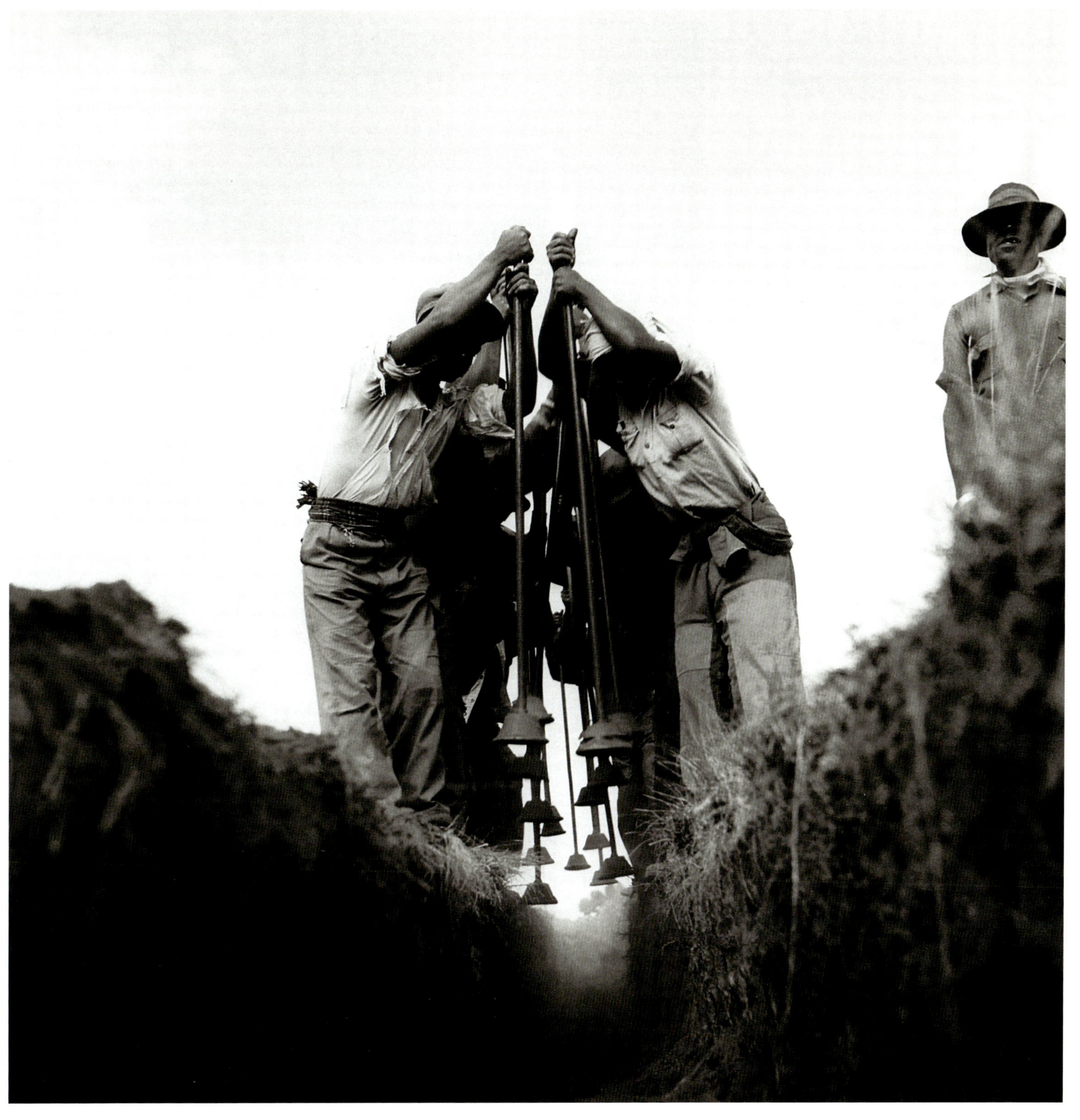

JOHANNESBURG 1951
The ditchworkers stamp in rhythmic unison,
singing their worksong... up and down, up and
down they stamp the freshly dug earth.

JÜRGEN SCHADEBERG

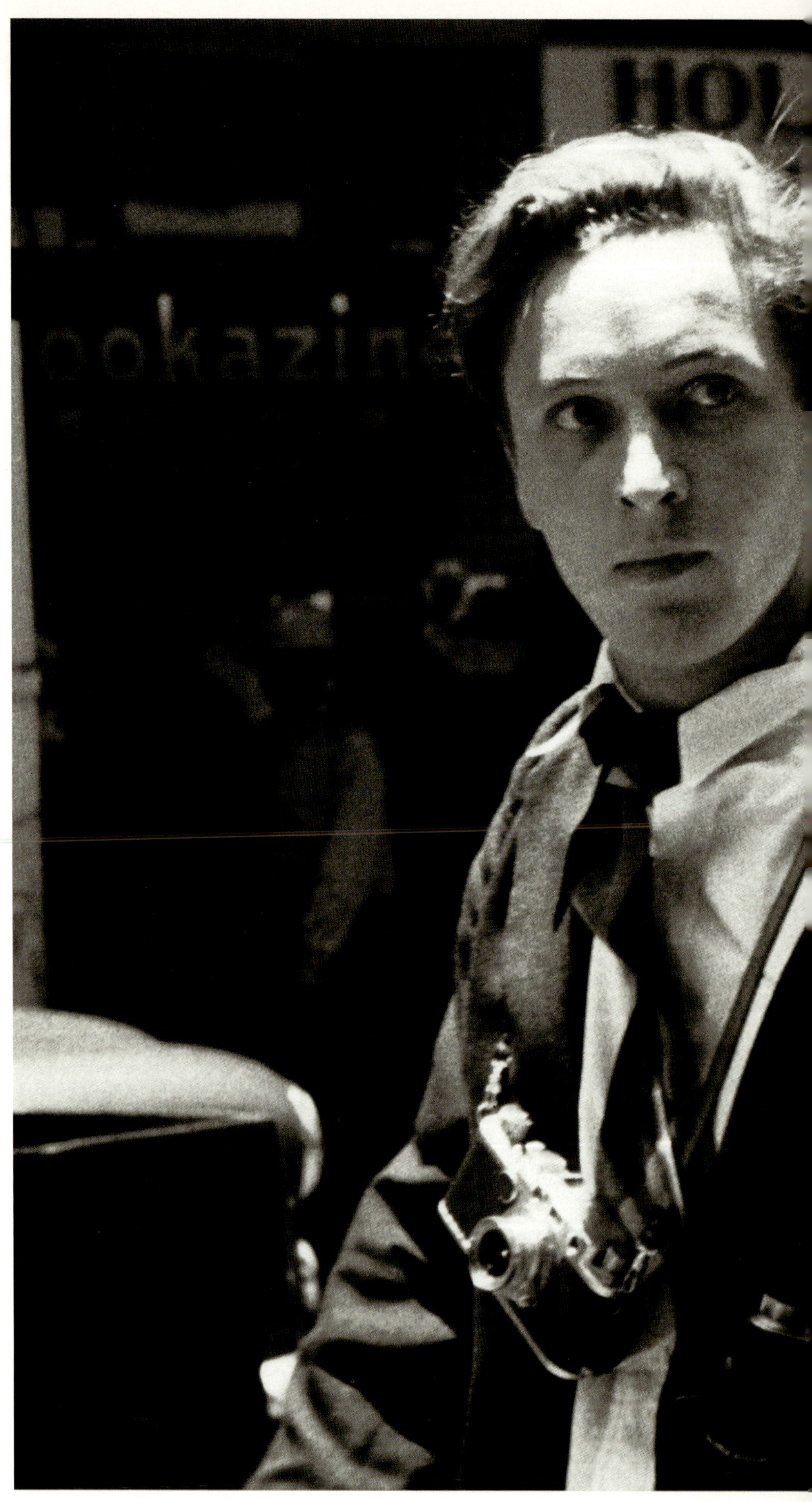

JOHANNESBURG 1956
Drum *photographer Jürgen Schadeberg arrested
during a demonstration at the Treason Trial.*

IAN BERRY

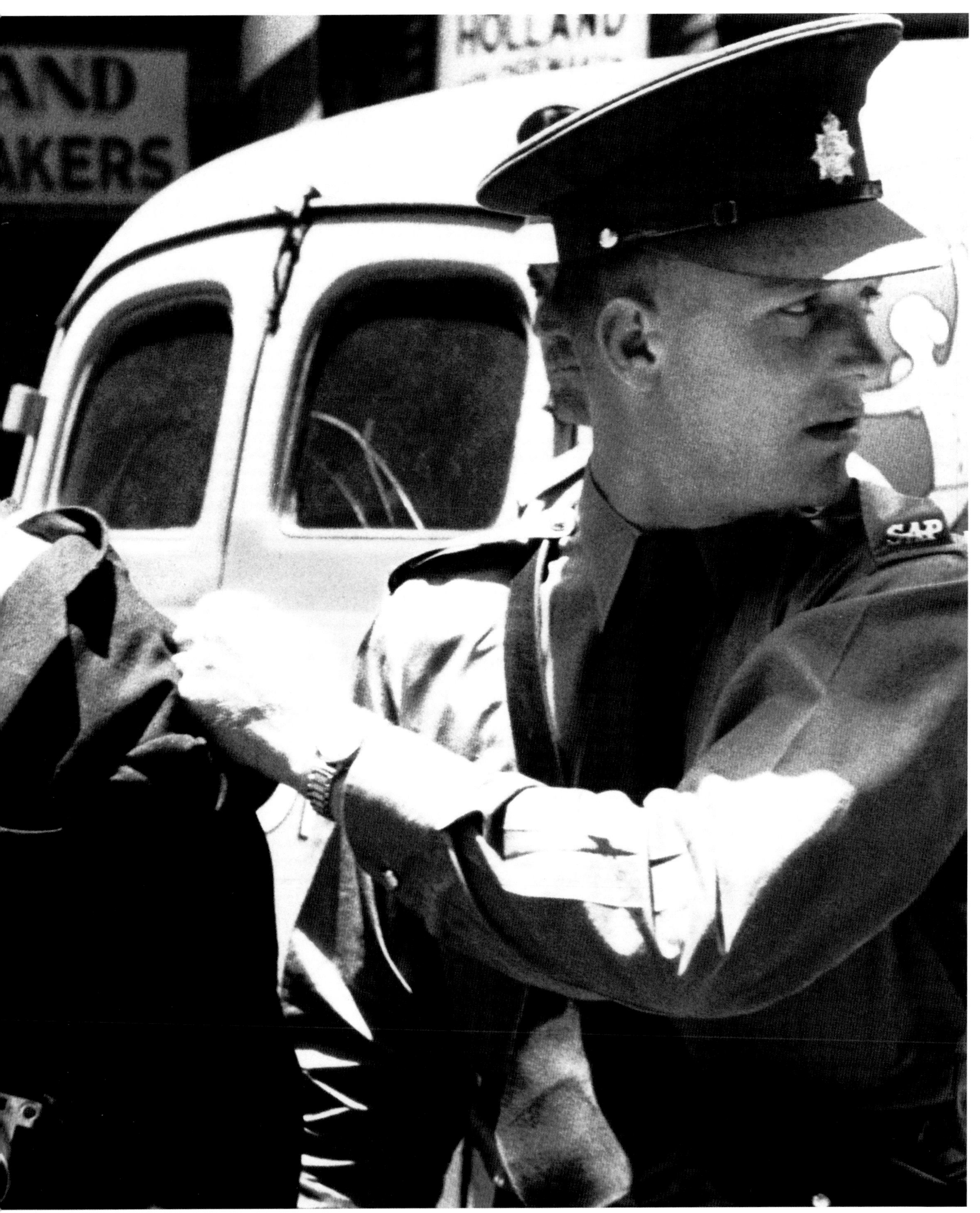
HOLLAND
AND
AKERS
SAP

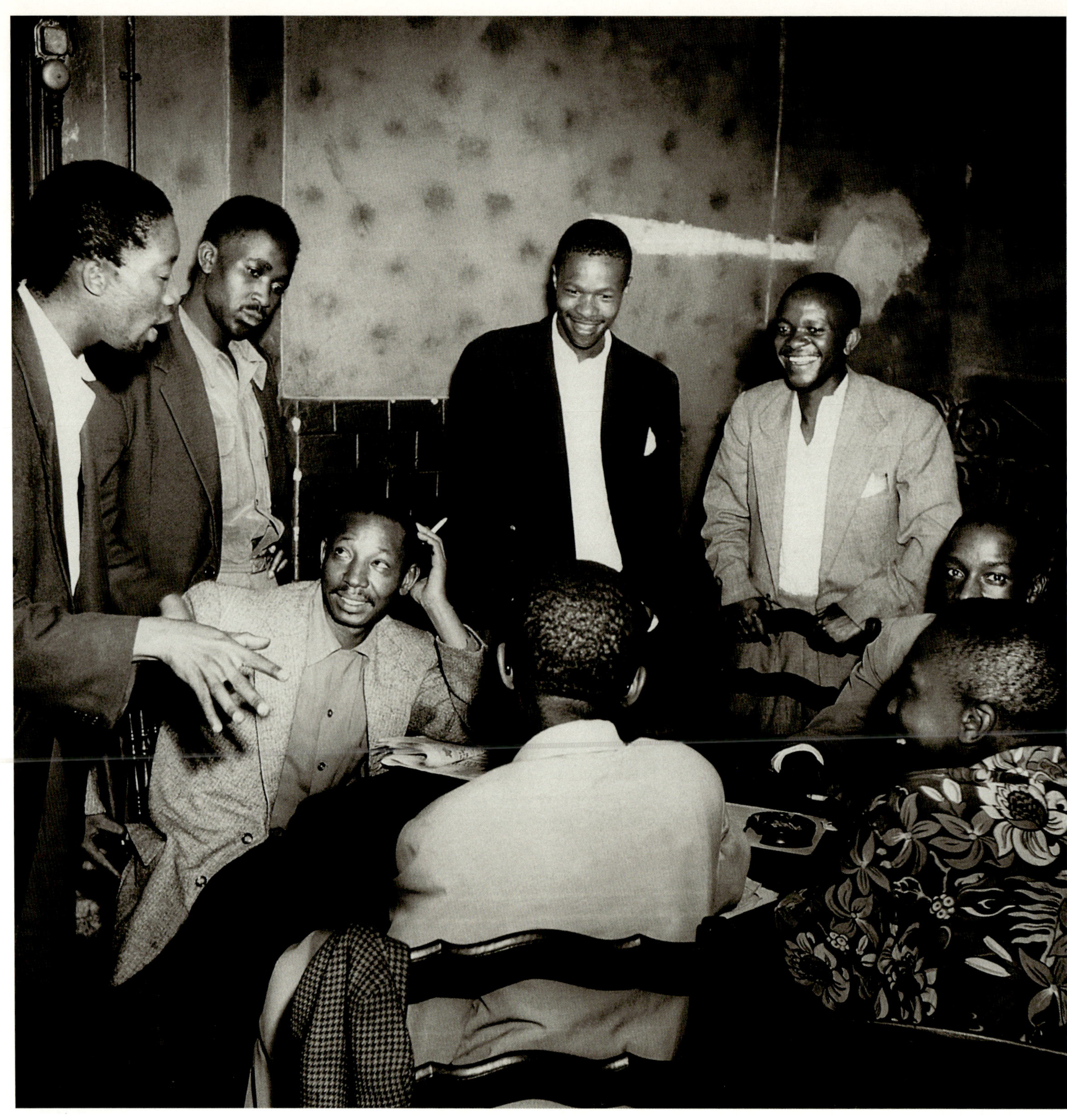

SOPHIATOWN 1956
Can Themba holding court in 'The House of Truth'.
Can Themba (left) Ben Mrwebi, (standing), Sy
Magapi (sitting on right) half covered by David
Sibeko (profile).

BOB GOSANI

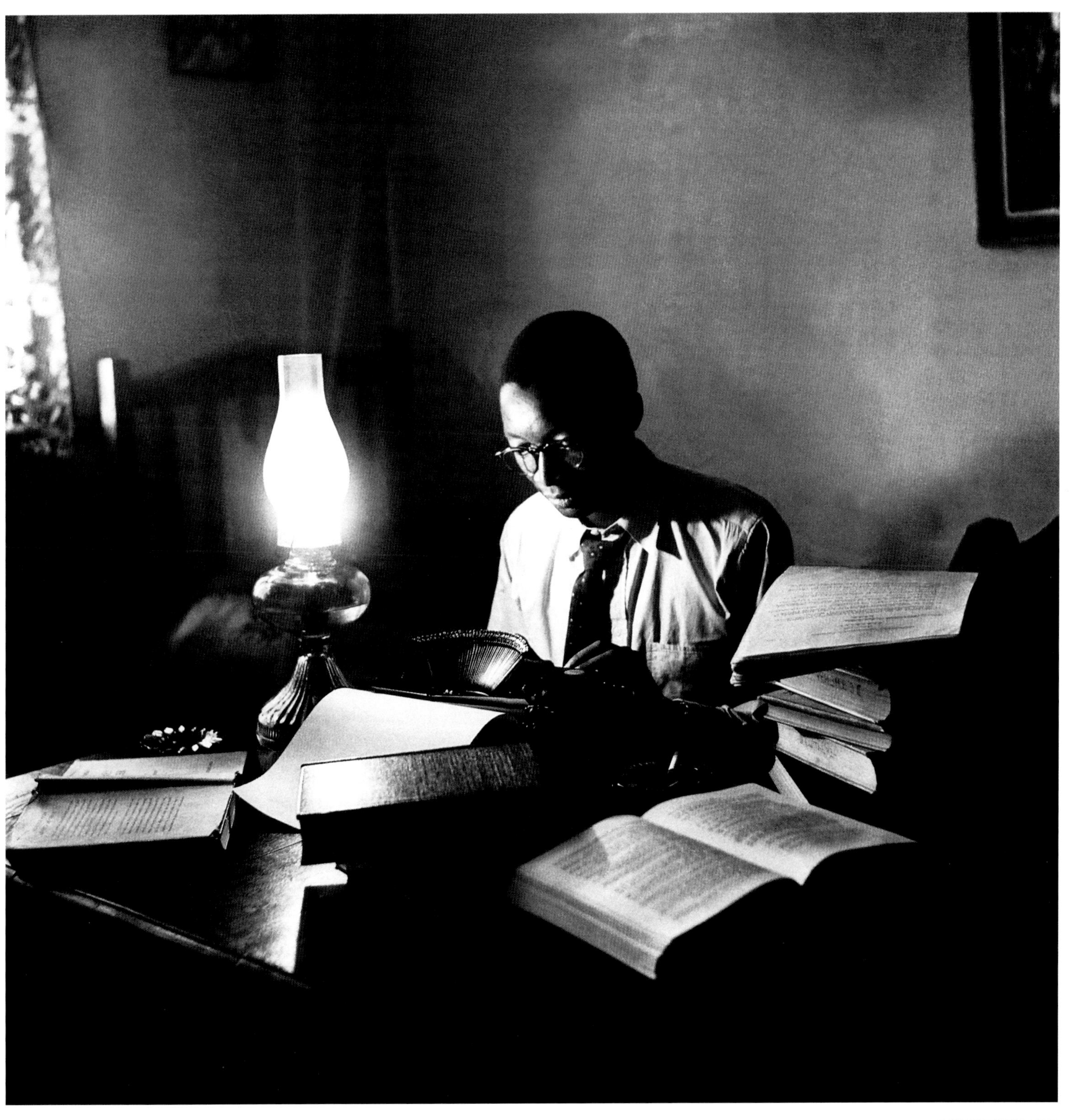

SOPHIATOWN 1952
Can Themba in his room in Sophiatown. Can
Themba was launched into journalism when he
won a short story competition in **Drum**. He soon
stopped teaching English and then went to work
on the magazine.

JÜRGEN SCHADEBERG

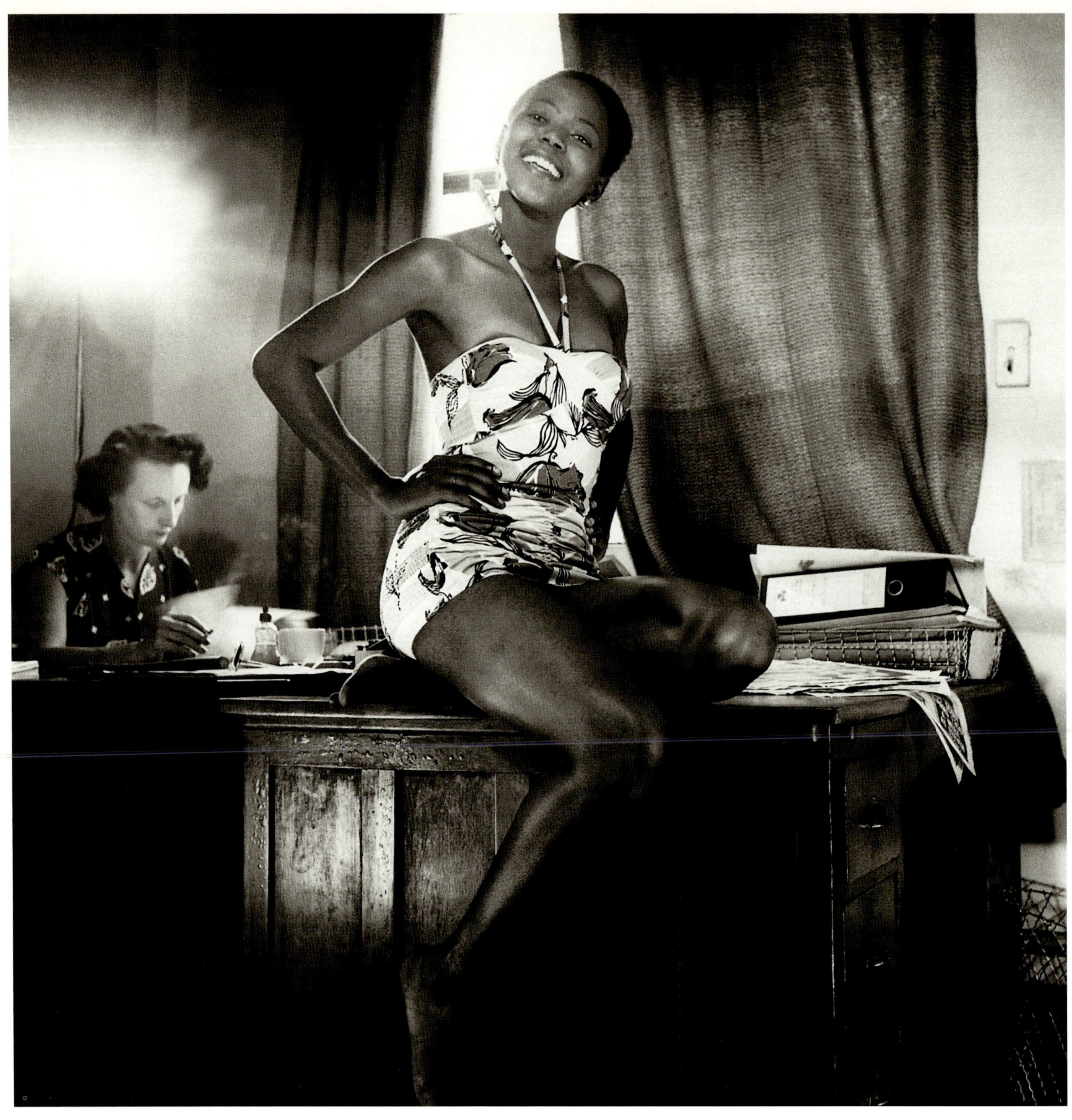

JOHANNESBURG 1951
*In the early **Drum** days there was a shortage of space in the office, so Francina Monarens posed for photographer Jürgen Schadeberg on a secretary's desk.*

JÜRGEN SCHADEBERG

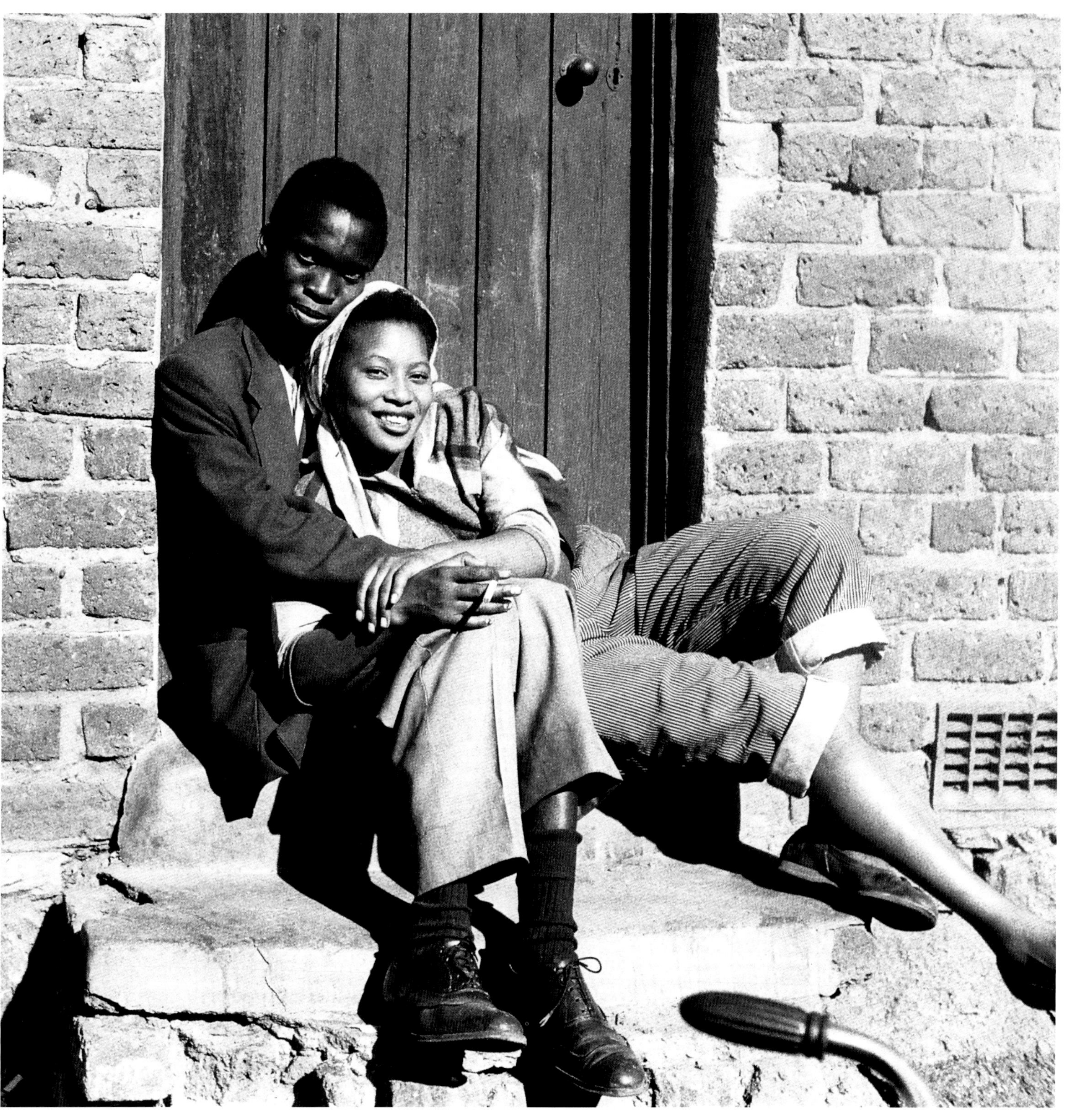

SOPHIATOWN 1958
*Zulu journalist Lewis Nkosi came to **Drum** from*
*the Durban paper, **Llanga Lasa Natal**. He later*
became a Professor of Literature, lecturing at
various American, European and African
universities.

BOB GOSANI

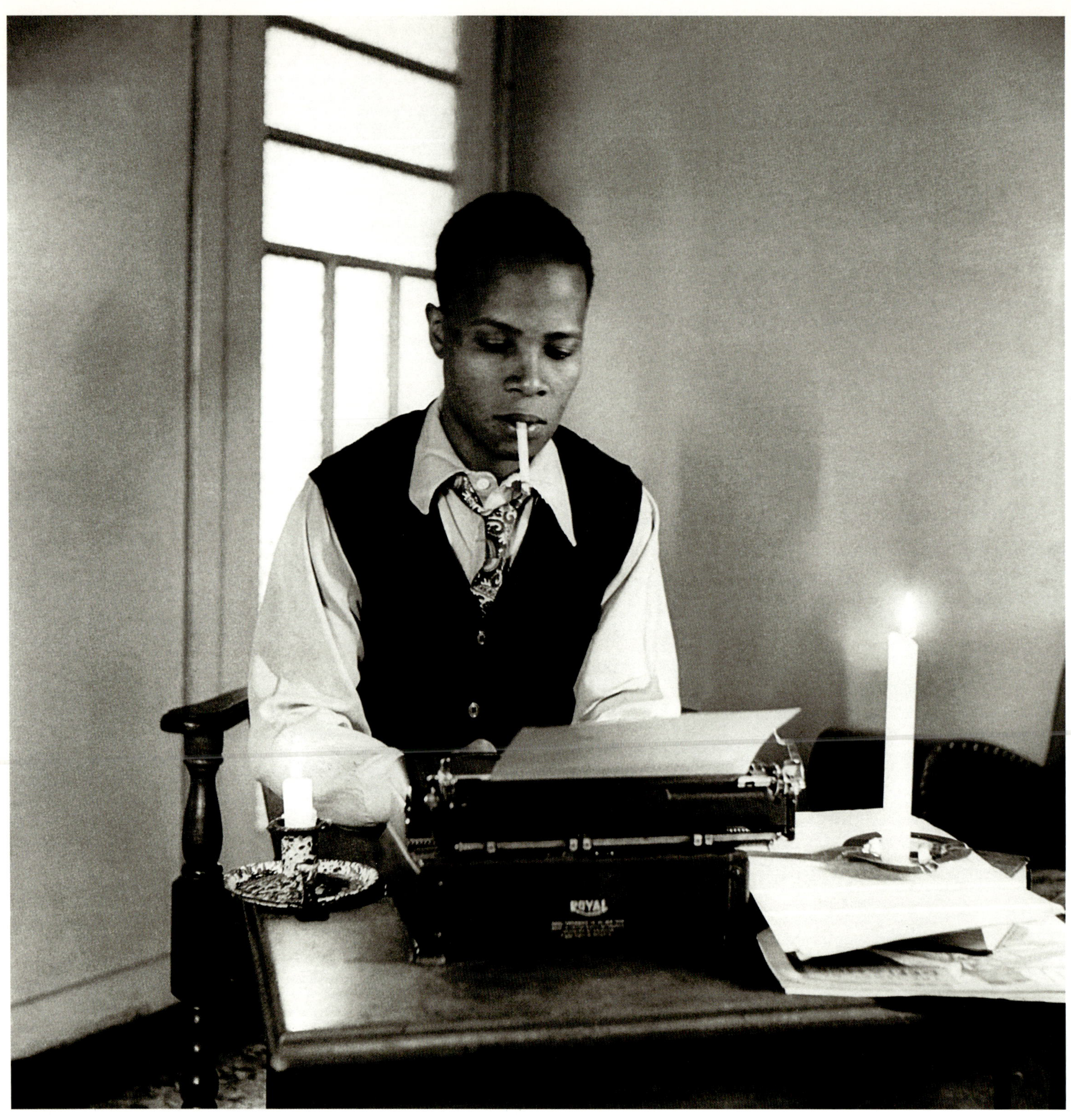

ORLANDO TOWNSHIP 1952
The most courageous journalist, 'Mr Drum', as
Henry Nxumalo was known. For many years
Nxumalo was assistant editor and chief reporter
*of **Drum**. His investigative explorations helped to*
*make **Drum** the successful magazine it soon*
became.

JÜRGEN SCHADEBERG

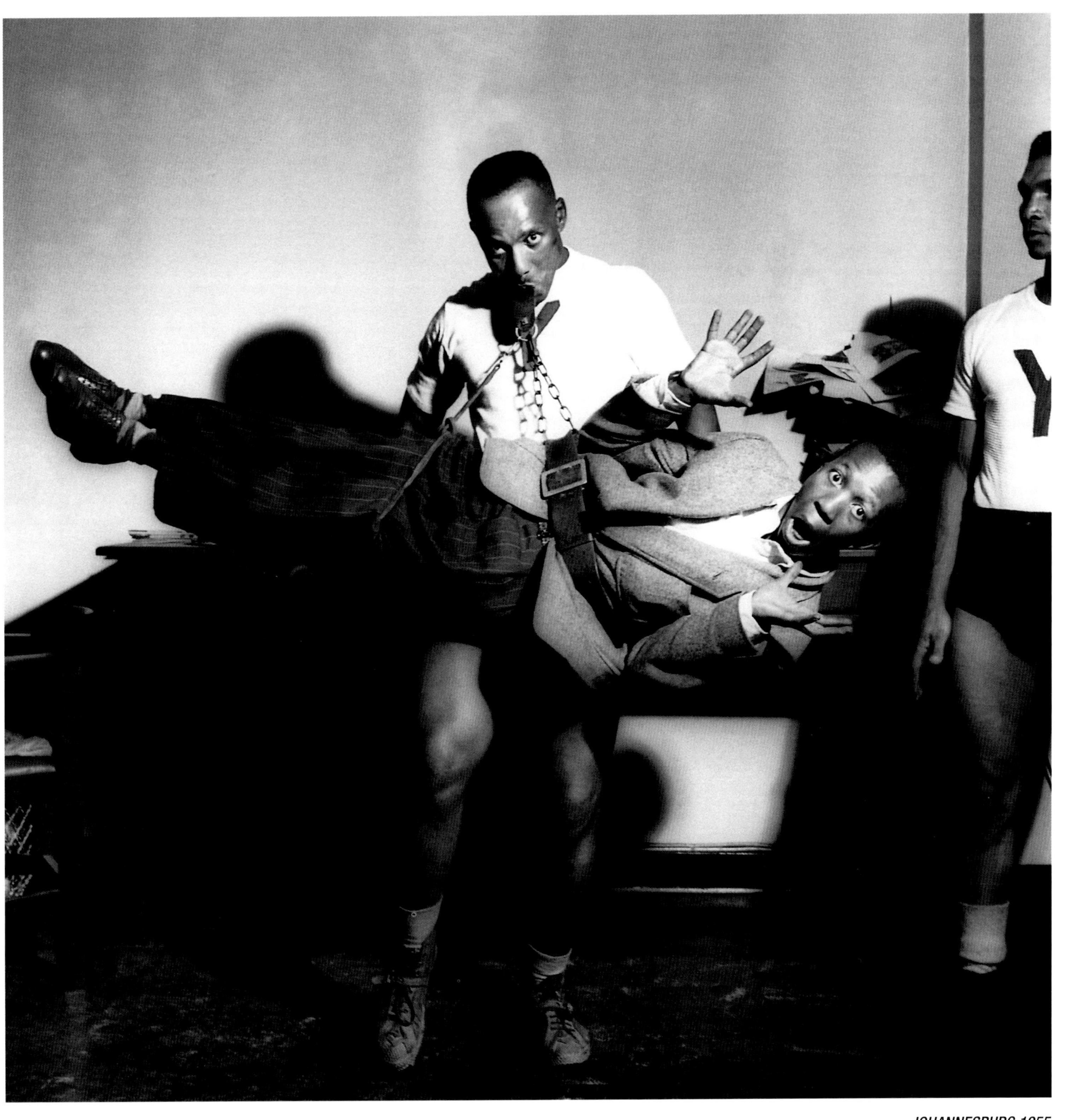

JOHANNESBURG 1955
Casey Motsisi wrote about Johannesburg's
shebeen life for over twenty years. Casey's pen
recorded the humour, pathos and irony of these
venues. 'No nooze is good nooze, but no booze is
sad nooze indeed'.

BOB GOSANI

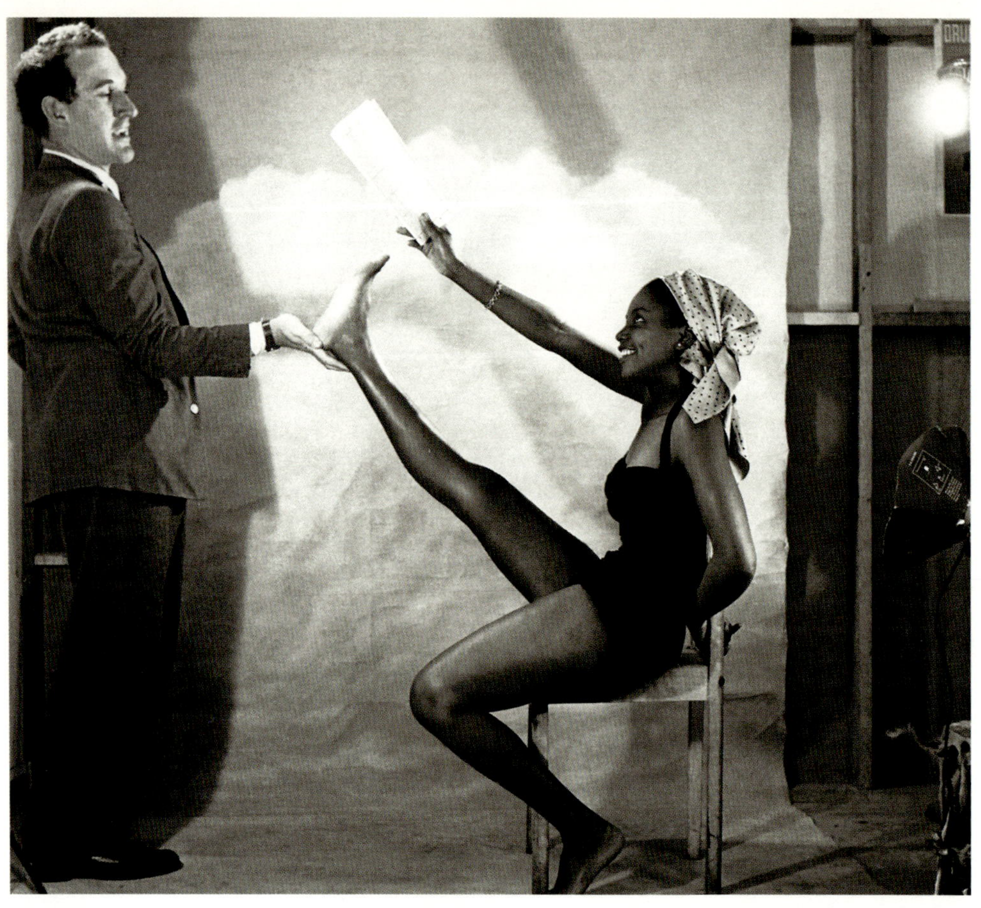

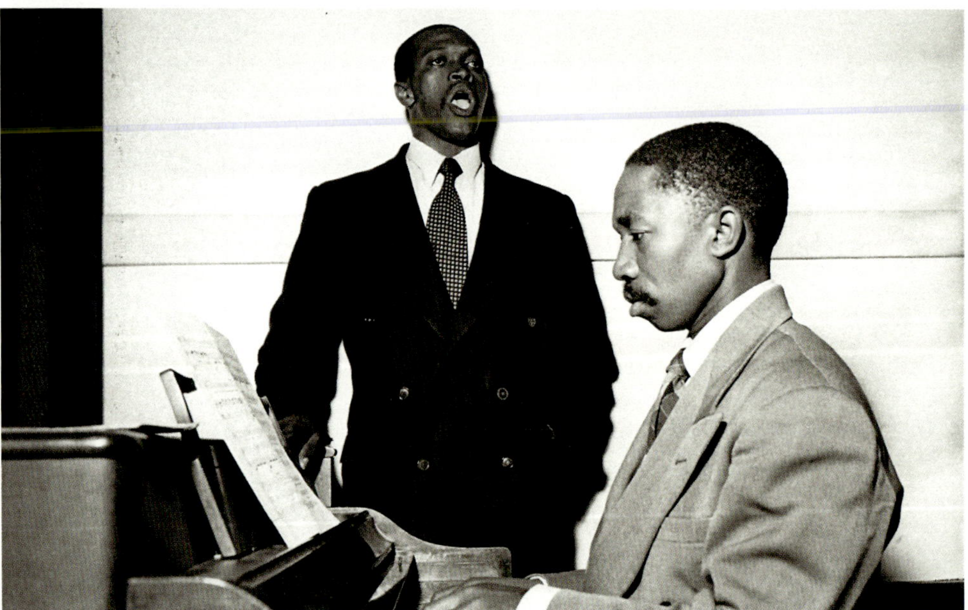

JOHANNESBURG 1952
Lending a hand for the cover pictures. Anthony Sampson was **Drum** editor for four years. Todd Matshikiza (below) was **Drum's** music editor. He developed a great style of reporting while also writing the music for two shows that hit Broadway. He played the English language as he played the piano.

JÜRGEN SCHADEBERG

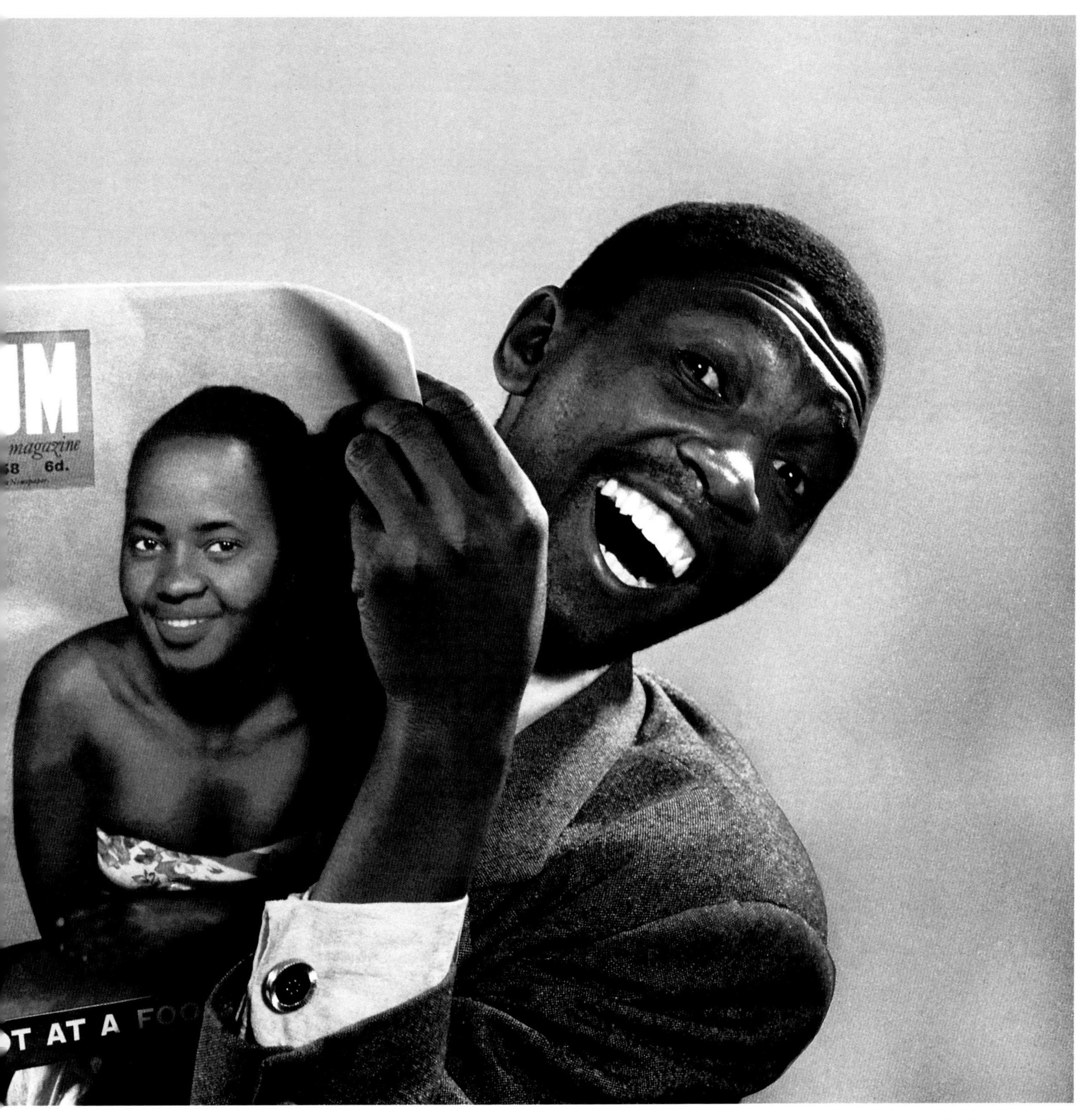

JOHANNESBURG 1958
Sol Rashilo posing for a promotional pamphlet.
***Drum** was the first magazine in South Africa that*
had black beauties on its cover.

JÜRGEN SCHADEBERG

For Freedom

On 26 June 1955, 3 000 delegates from all over the country gathered near the coloured township of Kliptown to discuss the Freedom Charter. The Kliptown football ground was a field of bright black, green and yellow colours in flags and uniform ties. Congress 'freedom' songs were sung at every pause in the proceedings.

Many speakers noted that the day might not be far off when the demands of the Freedom Charter would be met; the road might be long, but a united democratic front was the only solution. ANC President Albert Luthuli, in his message read to the congress, said among other things that 'it should have been plain to the architects of the Union that by excluding from the orbit of democracy, the majority of the population, the non-whites, they were laying a false foundation for the new state, and making a mockery of democracy to call such a state democratic'.

When the armed police arrived and came forward to the grandstand to conduct a search, a leading speaker was introducing the item of the Charter that says 'There shall be peace and friendship'. The police took down the names and addresses of everyone present and confiscated many documents

Ezekiel Mphahlele
Drum, August 1955.

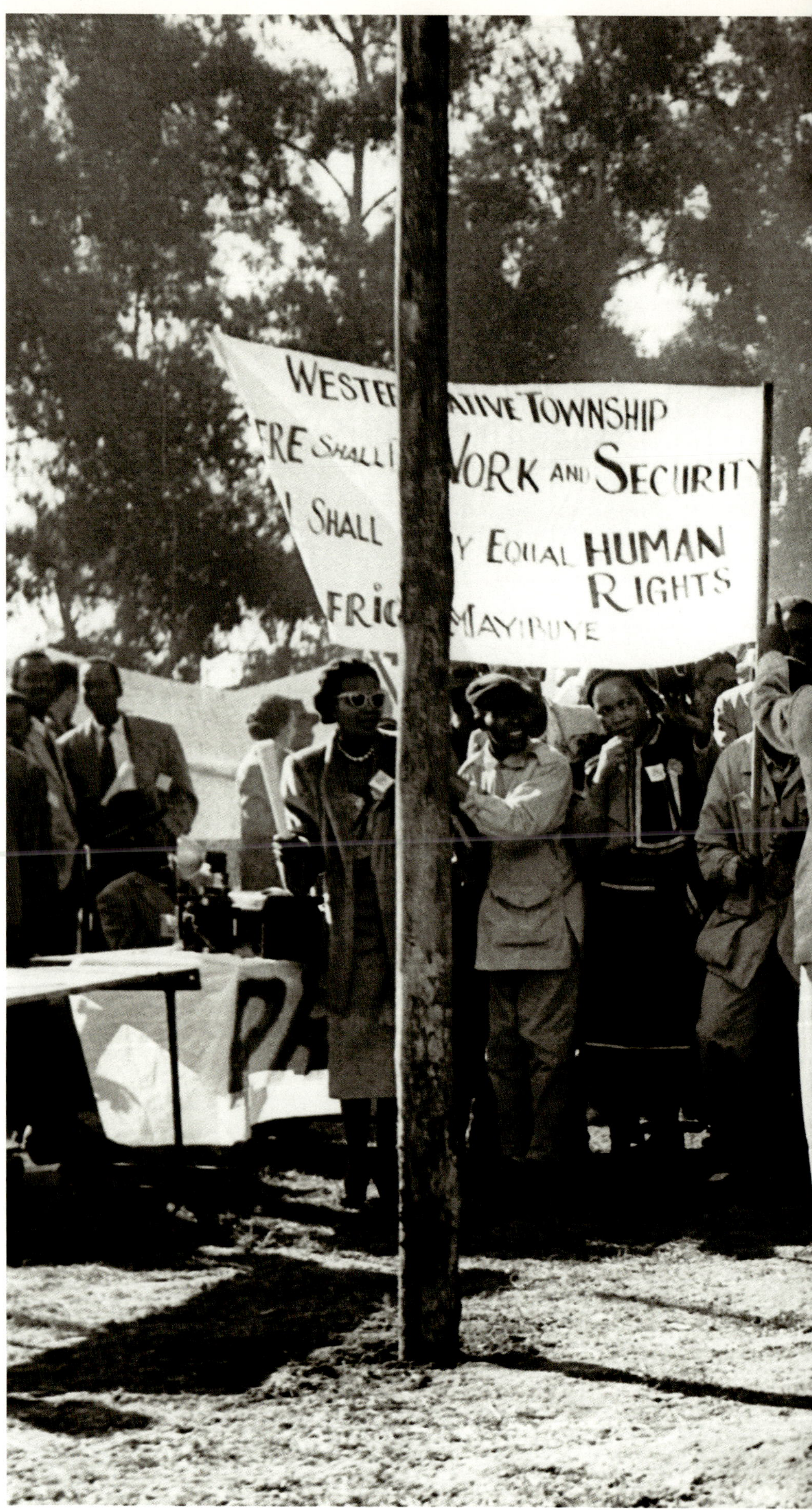

KLIPTOWN 1955
Three thousand delegates arrived at the Congress of the People from all over the country. 'South Africa belongs to all who live in it, black and white .. and we pledge ourselves to strive together, sparing neither strength nor courage, until its democratic changes set out here have been won'.

PETER MAGUBANE

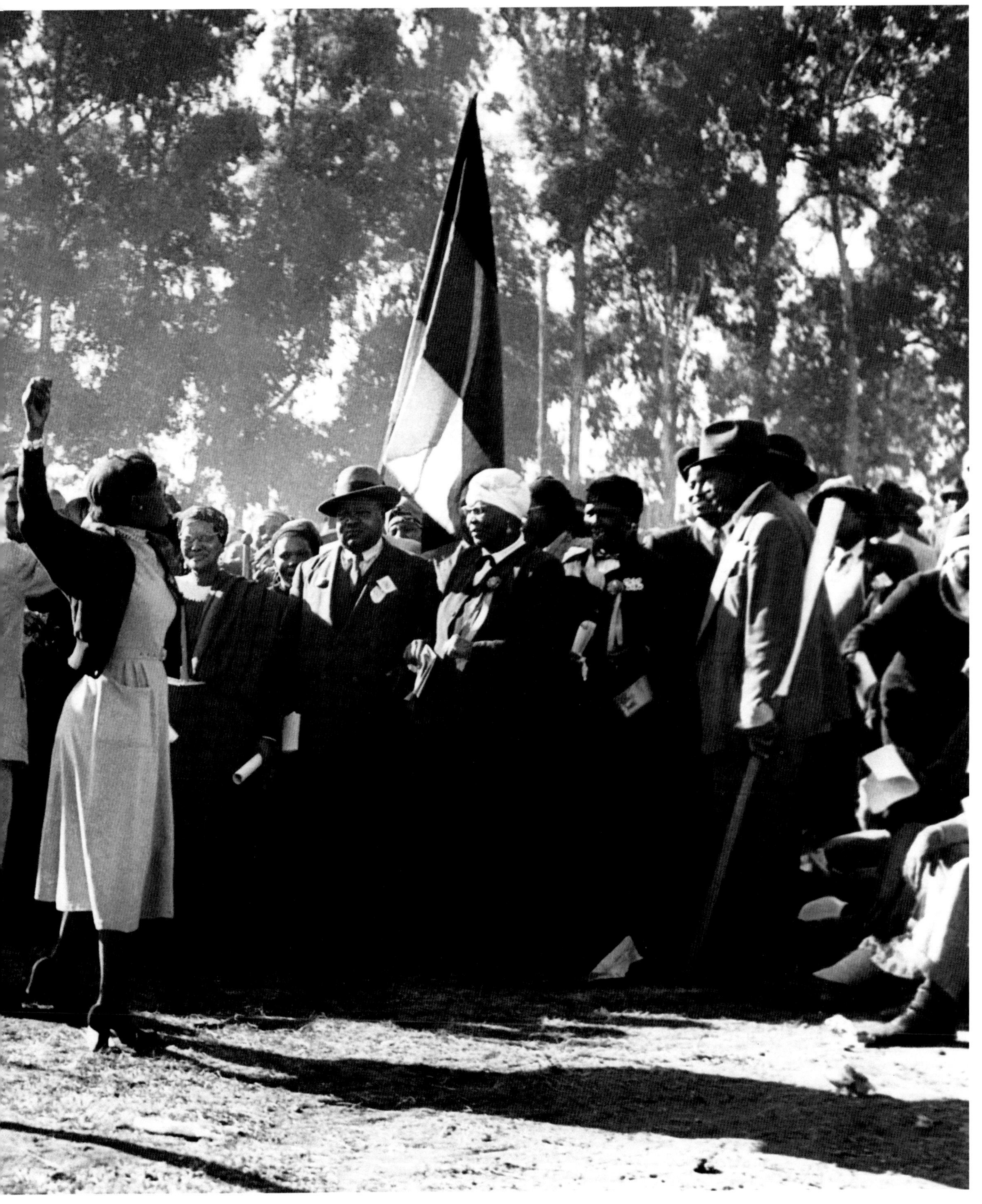

The Defiance Campaign

Our Defiance of Unjust Laws Campaign began on 26 June. It is going smoothly and according to plan; though there have been minor setbacks, like the arrest of Y Cachalia, South African Indian Congress General Secretary, and myself.

The support we have received from the masses has been most encouraging, although I cannot disclose how they are helping the Joint Planning Organisation and its sub-committees to care for the dependents of those volunteers already arrested.

I would like to emphasise the aims of our Campaign. We are not in opposition to any government or class of people. We are opposing a system which has for years kept a vast section of the non-European people in bondage. Though it takes us years, we are prepared to continue the Campaign until the six unjust laws we have chosen for the present phase are done away with. Even then we shall not stop. The struggle for the freedom and national independence of the non-European peoples shall continue as the National Planning Council sees fit.

We welcome true-hearted volunteers from all walks of life without consideration of colour, race or creed. Europeans can also join our ranks to defy these unjust laws — some of which are as unjust to them as they are to us. At the moment the Campaign is still in its first stage: defiance in Johannesburg and Port Elizabeth. Soon it will move onto the next stage, which will be defiance of the laws in all the big centres of the Union. And then lastly it will assume a mass character with defiance spread all over the country.

Nelson Mandela
Drum, August 1952

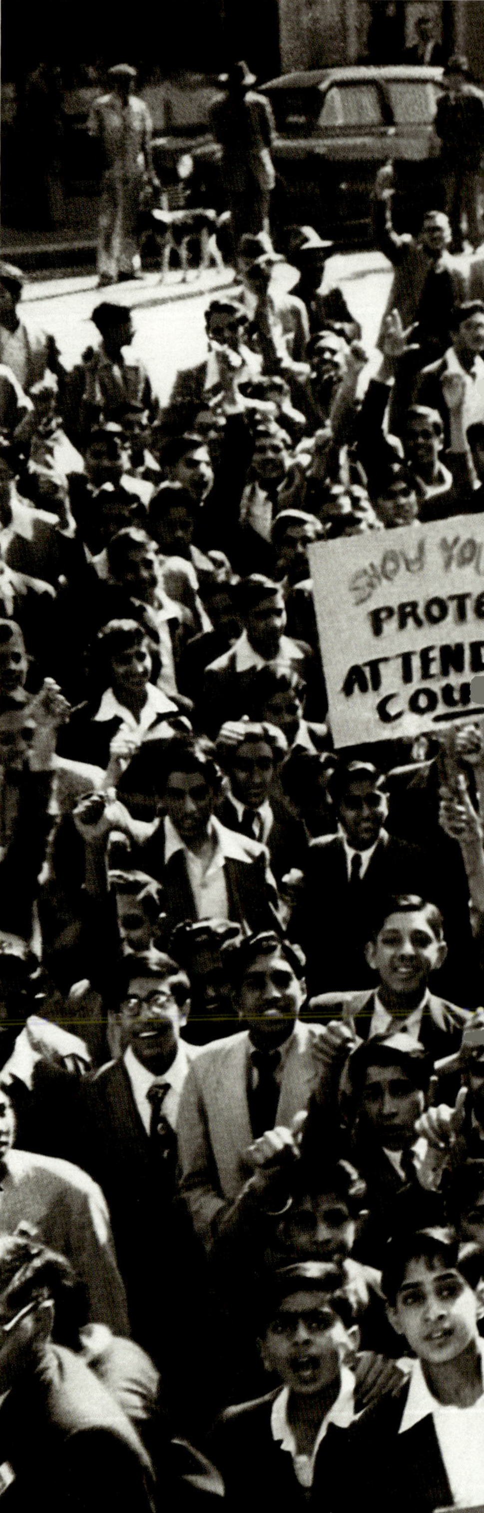

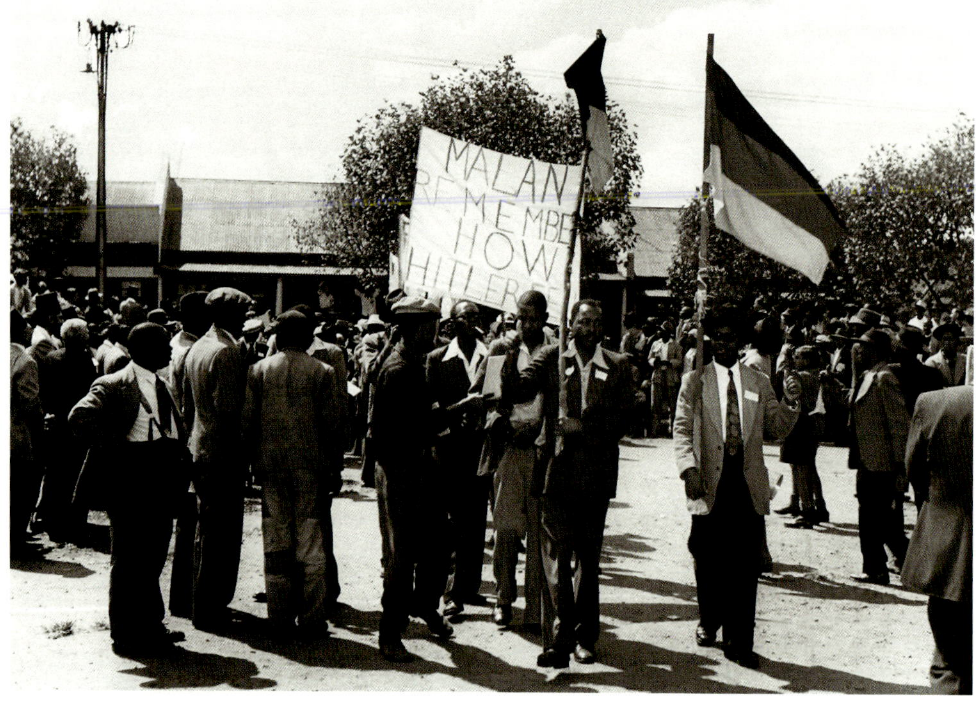

JOHANNESBURG 1952
On 6 April 1952 a mass meeting was held in 'Freedom Square' in Fordsburg. Dr Moroka, president of the ANC, and Dr Dadoo of the Indian Congress, spoke from the platform calling for volunteers for the Defiance Campaign.

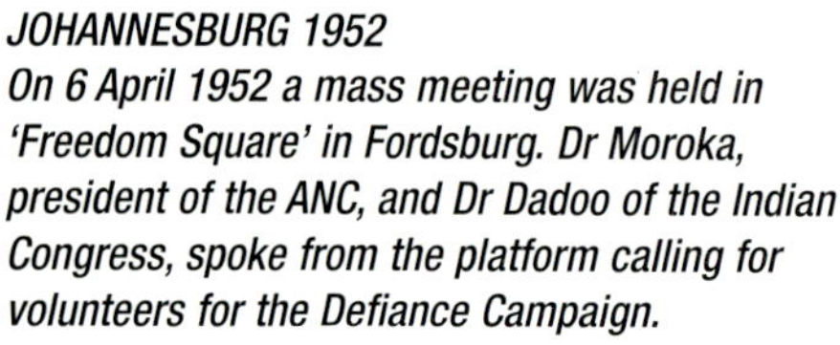

JÜRGEN SCHADEBERG

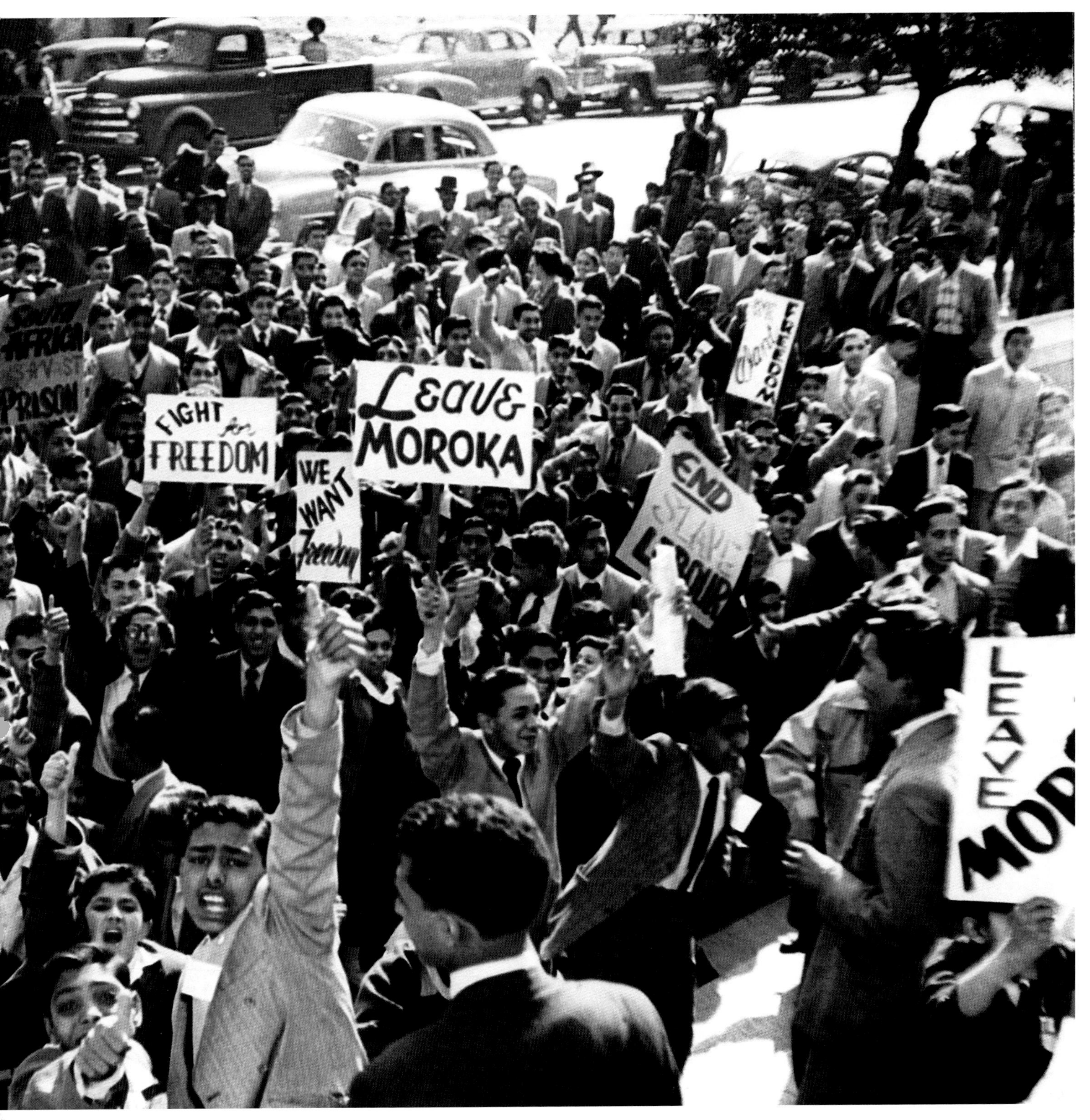

JOHANNESBURG 1952
The crowd of hundreds assembled outside the
courts, including 800 Indian schoolchildren,
protesting against the arrest of their leaders
during the Defiance Campaign.

JÜRGEN SCHADEBERG

61

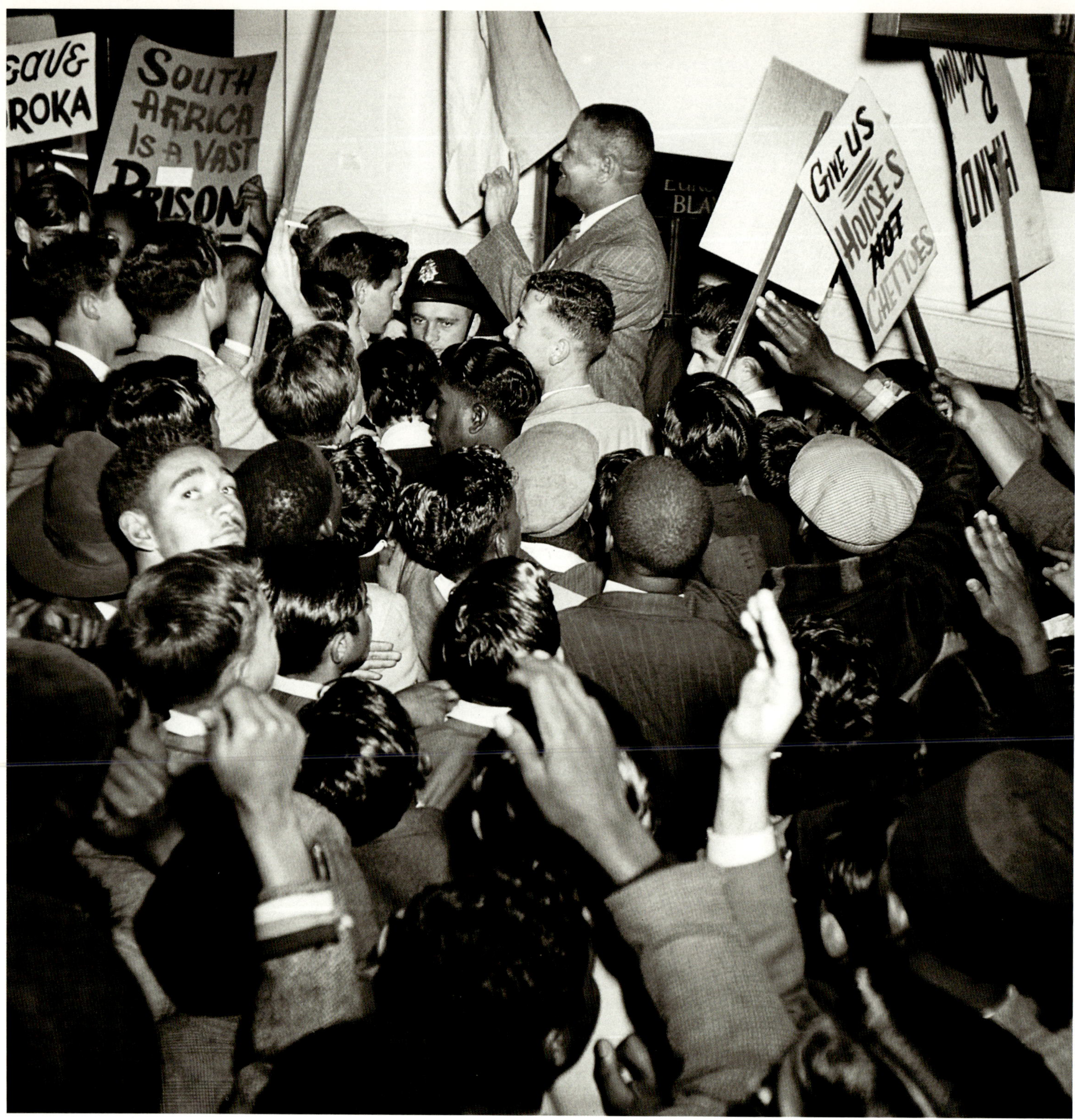

JOHANNESBURG 1952

*'Be quiet, my people, and go in peace', Dr Moroka
says to the crowd that packed the court corridors
during the preparatory examination of the twenty
leaders of the Defiance Campaign. After cheering,
the crowd filed quietly out of the building to an
empty plot and held meetings for the rest of the
day.*

JÜRGEN SCHADEBERG

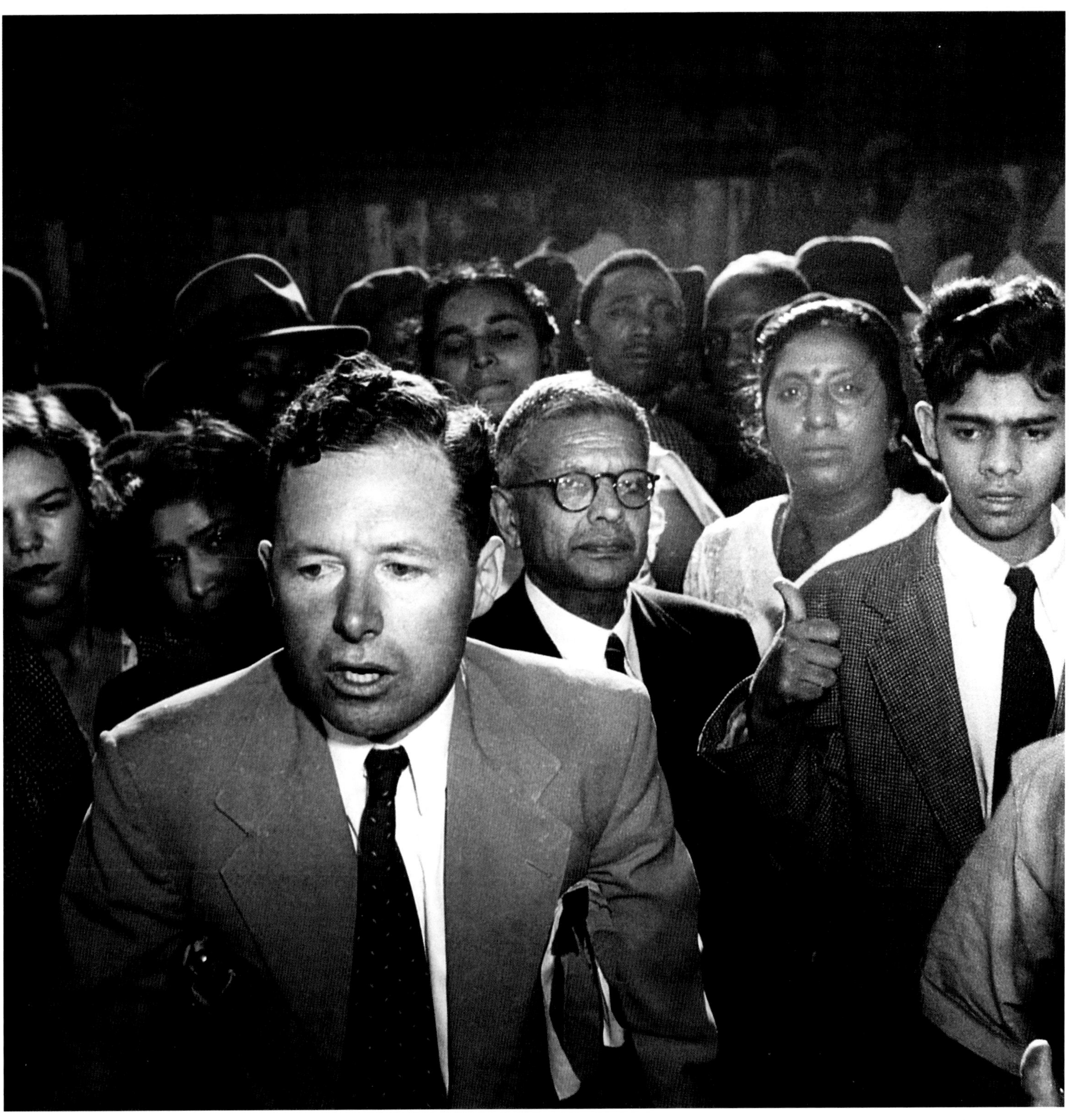

GERMISTON TOWNSHIP 1952
Manilal Gandhi, son of the Mahatma, and Patrick
Duncan (front), son of the war time Governor,
General Sir Patrick Duncan, joined others in
defying the permit regulations.

JÜRGEN SCHADEBERG

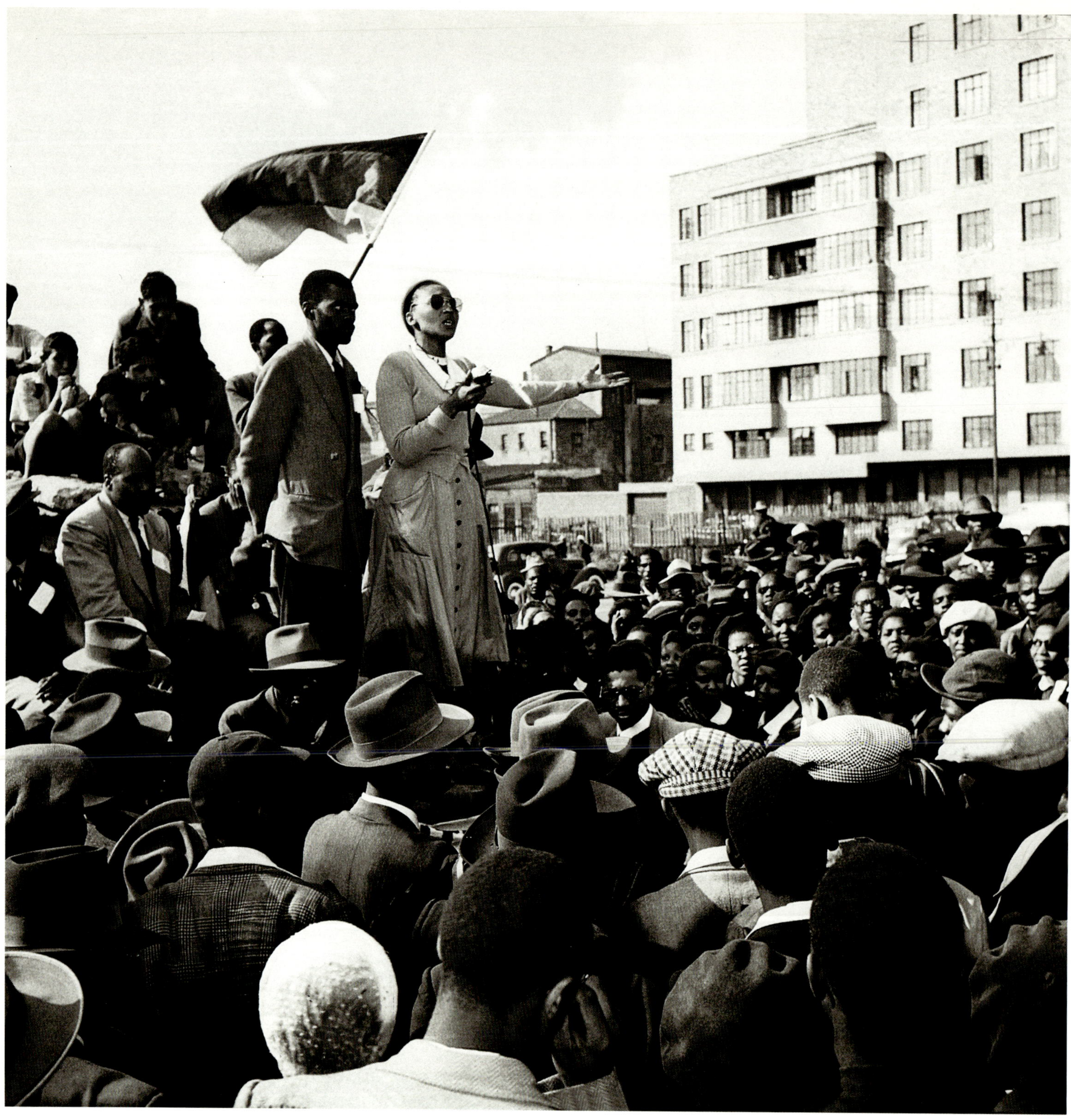

JOHANNESBURG 1952
Violet Hashe, trade union leader, calls out to the
people at 'Freedom Square' in Fordsburg to defy
the unjust laws introduced by the apartheid
regime.

JÜRGEN SCHADEBERG

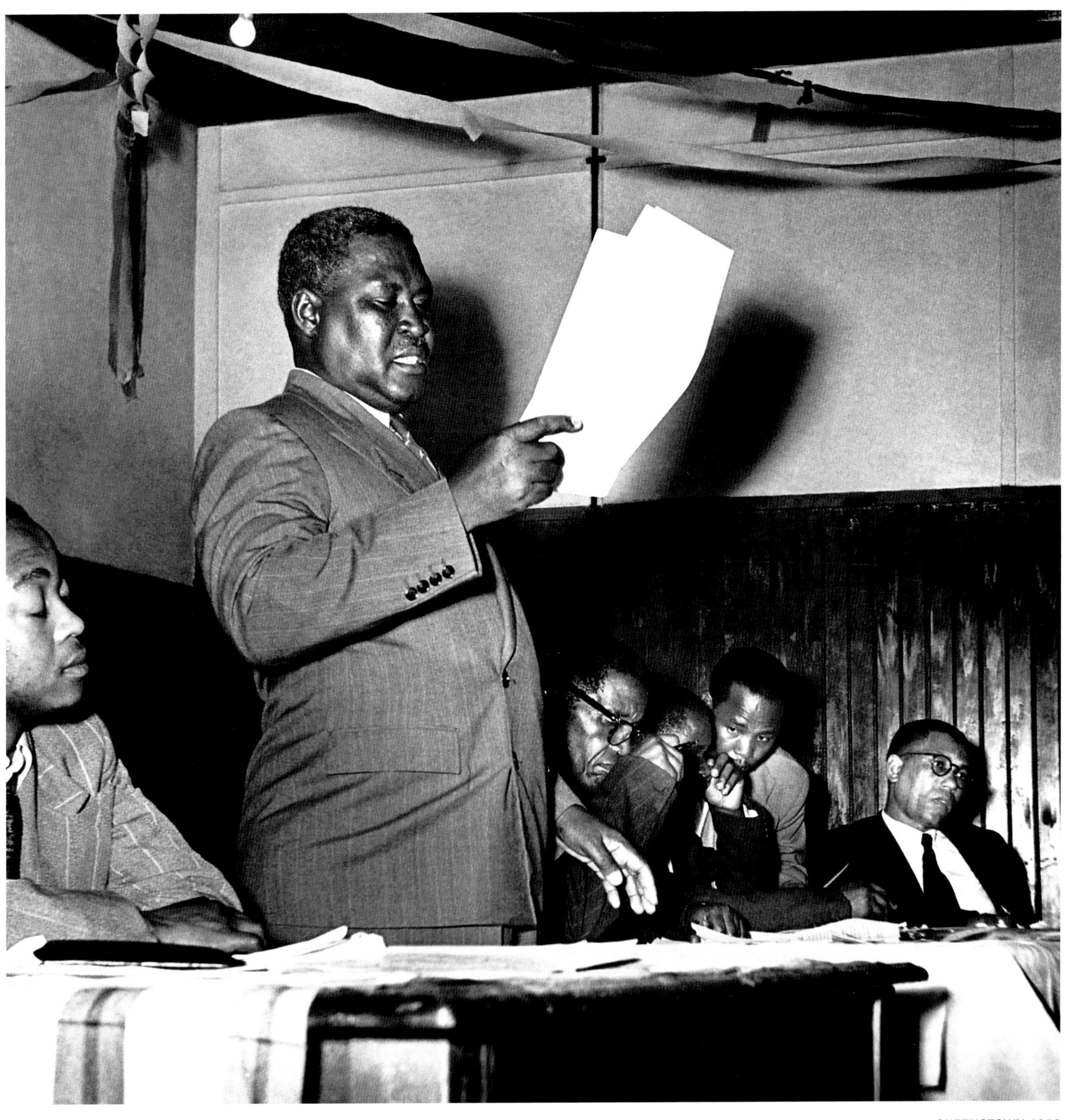

QUEENSTOWN 1953
At the 41st Annual Conference of the ANC, Chief
Albert Luthuli said in his presidential address:
'We can assure the world it is our intention to
keep on the non-violent plane'. From left to right
Duma Nokwe, Chief Albert Luthuli, James Calata,
Oliver Tambo (covered by hand), Robert Resha
and Walter Sisulu.

BOB GOSANI

65

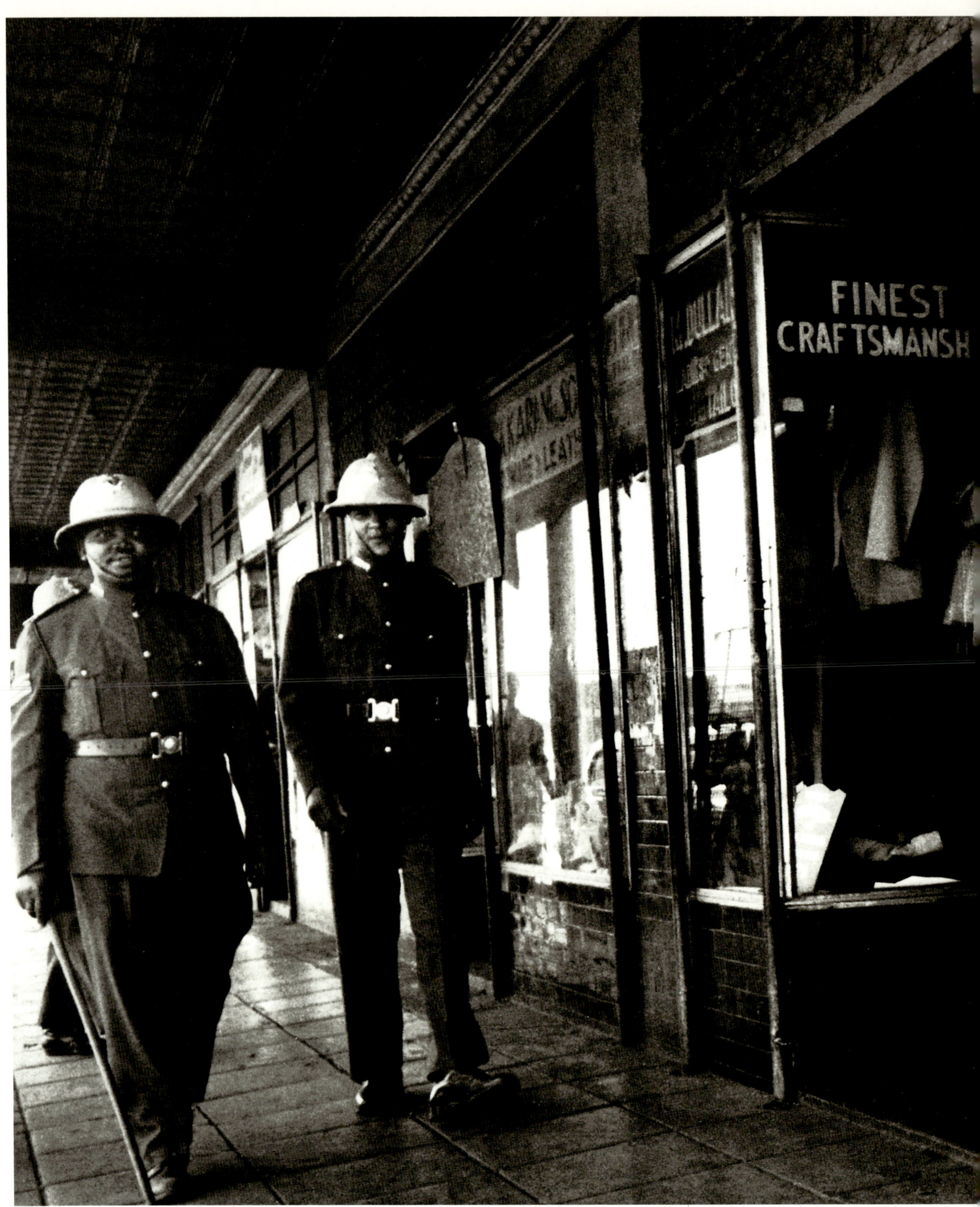

JOHANNESBURG 1955 Blacks had to carry passes. If they were caught in the city without a pass they would be thrown into jail. JÜRGEN SCHADEBERG

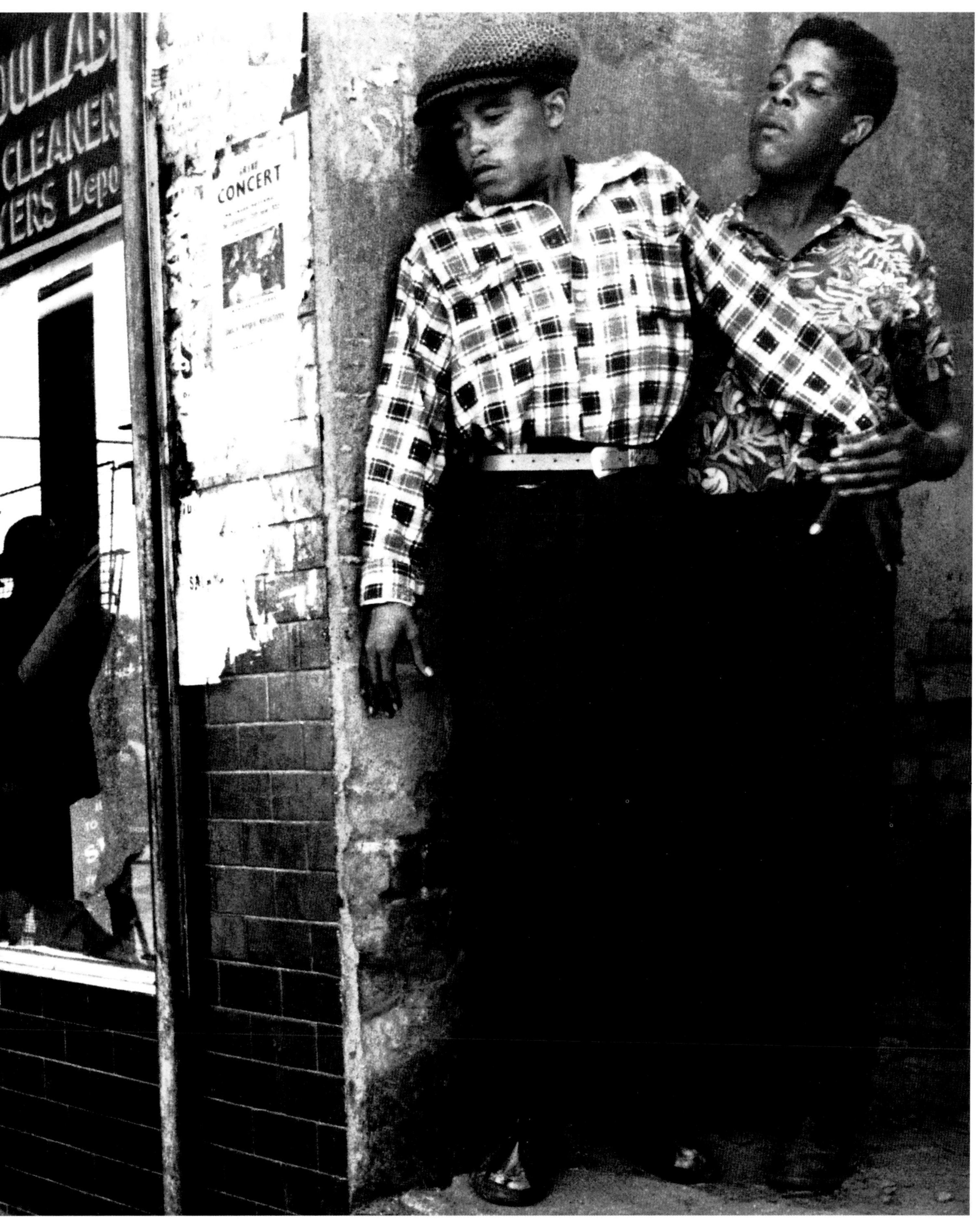
CLEANER
YERS Depo
CONCERT

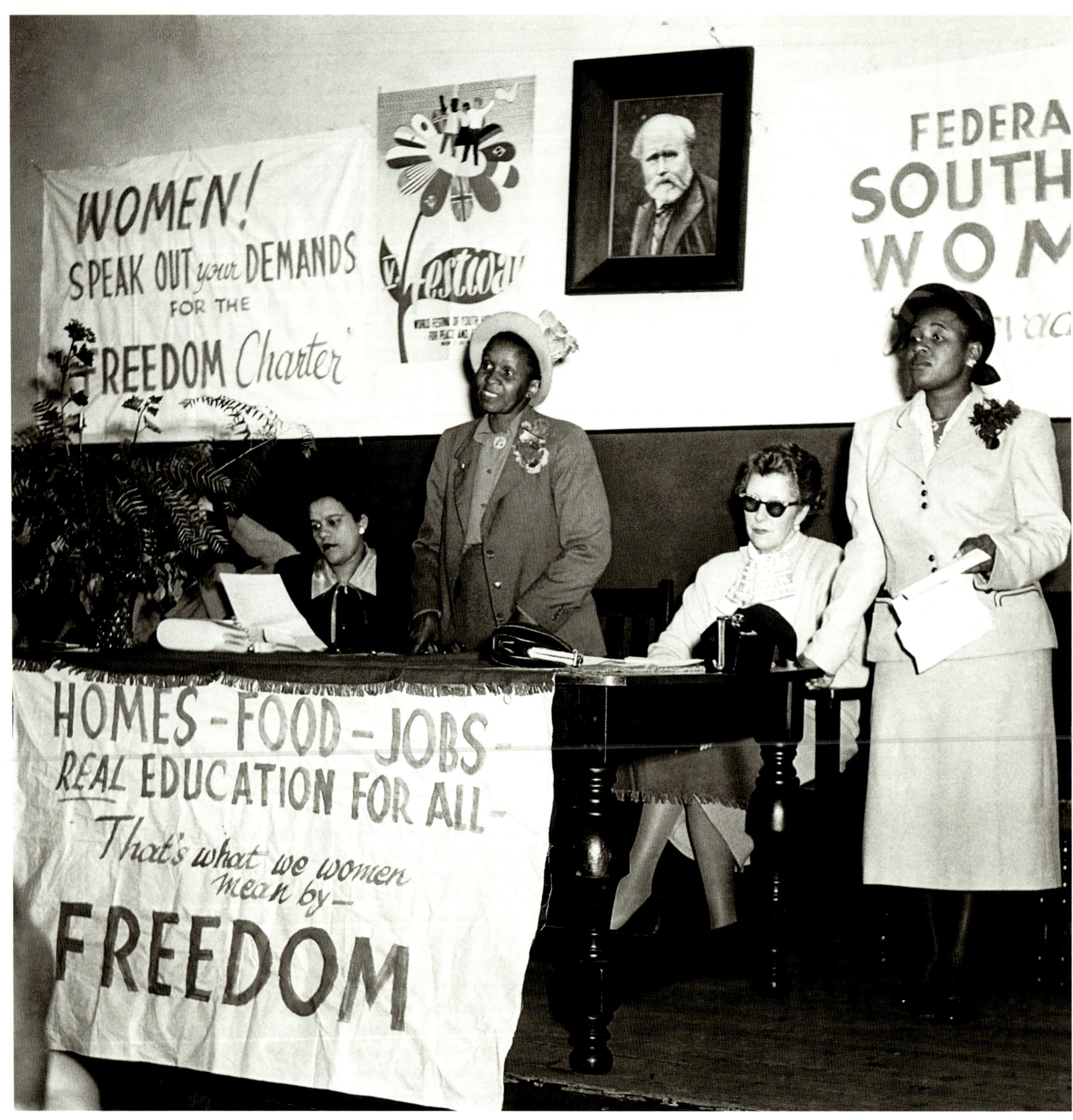

WESTERN NATIVE TOWNSHIP 1955
After months of campaigning on the issue of
passes, the Transvaal branch of the Federation of
South African Women decided to mount a
demonstration in Pretoria against unjust laws.
Rahima Moosa (sitting left), Josie Palmer and
Helen Joseph (dark glasses).

BOB GOSANI

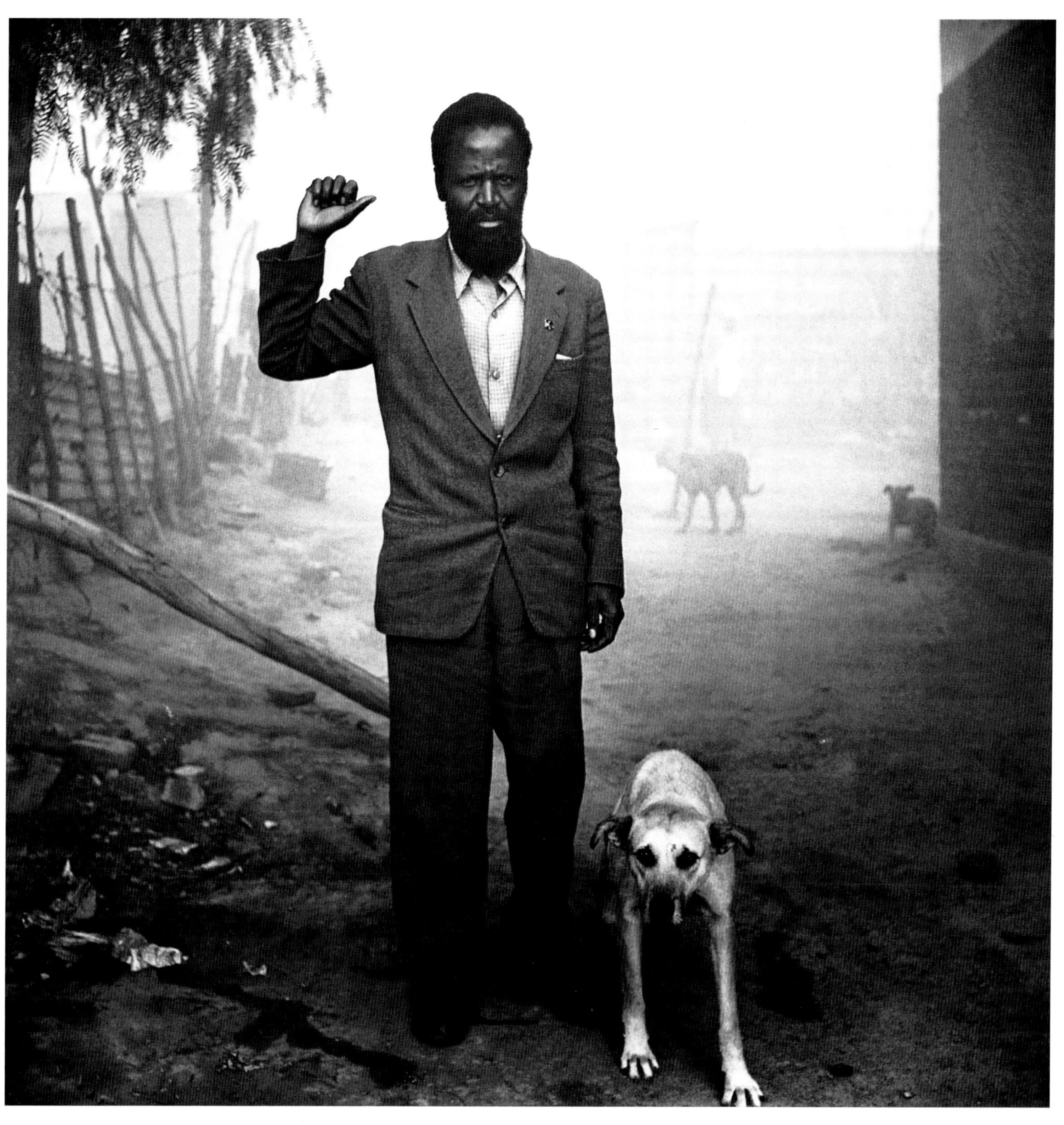

ALEXANDRA TOWNSHIP 1957
Josiah Madzunya was one of the leaders of the
newly formed Pan Africanist Congress. In 1960
he was in the thick of the launch of the PAC's
Anti-Pass Campaign.

BOB GOSANI

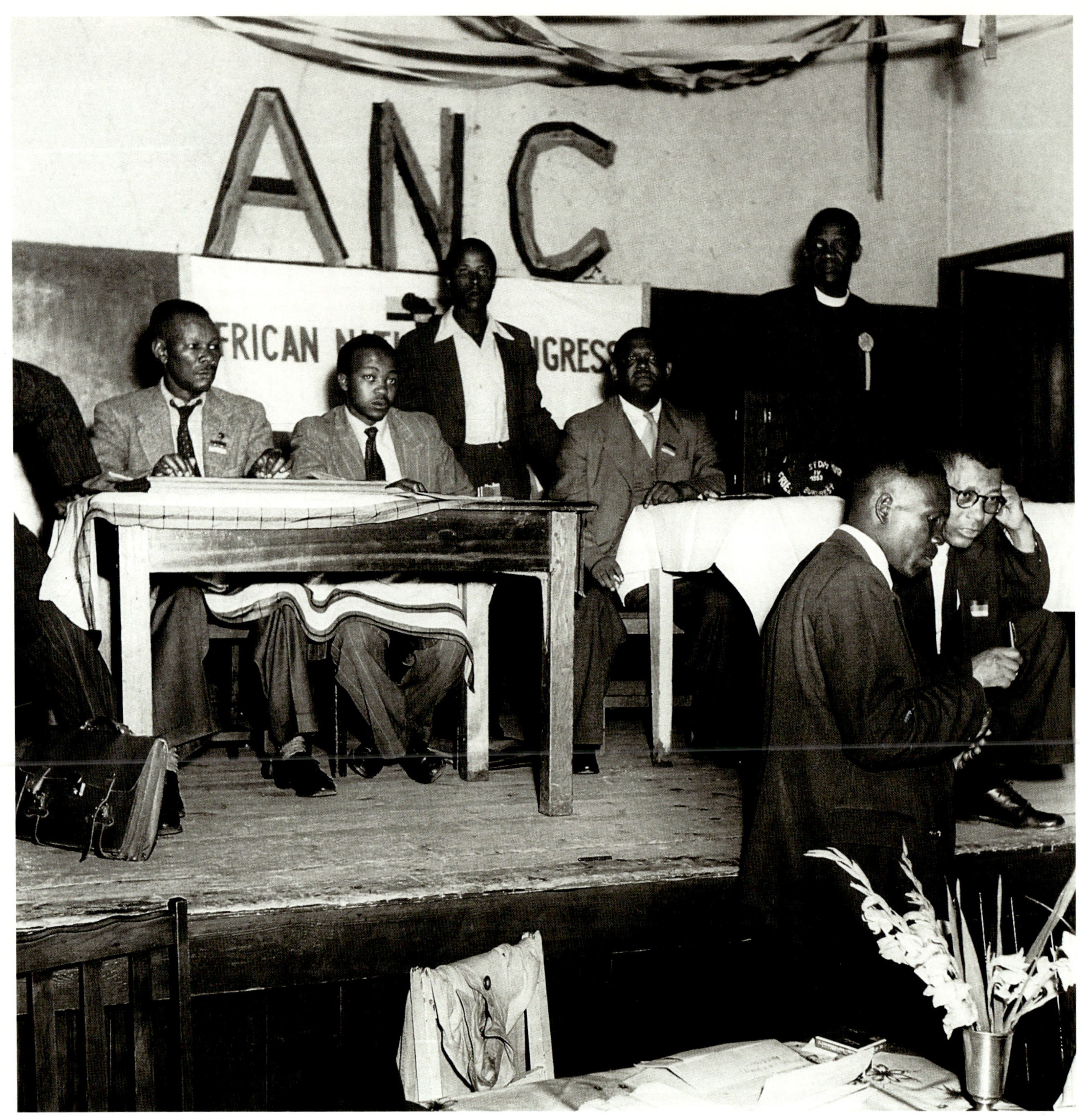

QUEENSTOWN, DECEMBER 1953
ANC Annual Conference. Executive members
listening to views from the floor. Philip Vundla
(left), Duma Nokwe, Professor ZK Matthews,
Reverend James Calata and Walter Sisulu (right,
with glasses).

BOB GOSANI

70

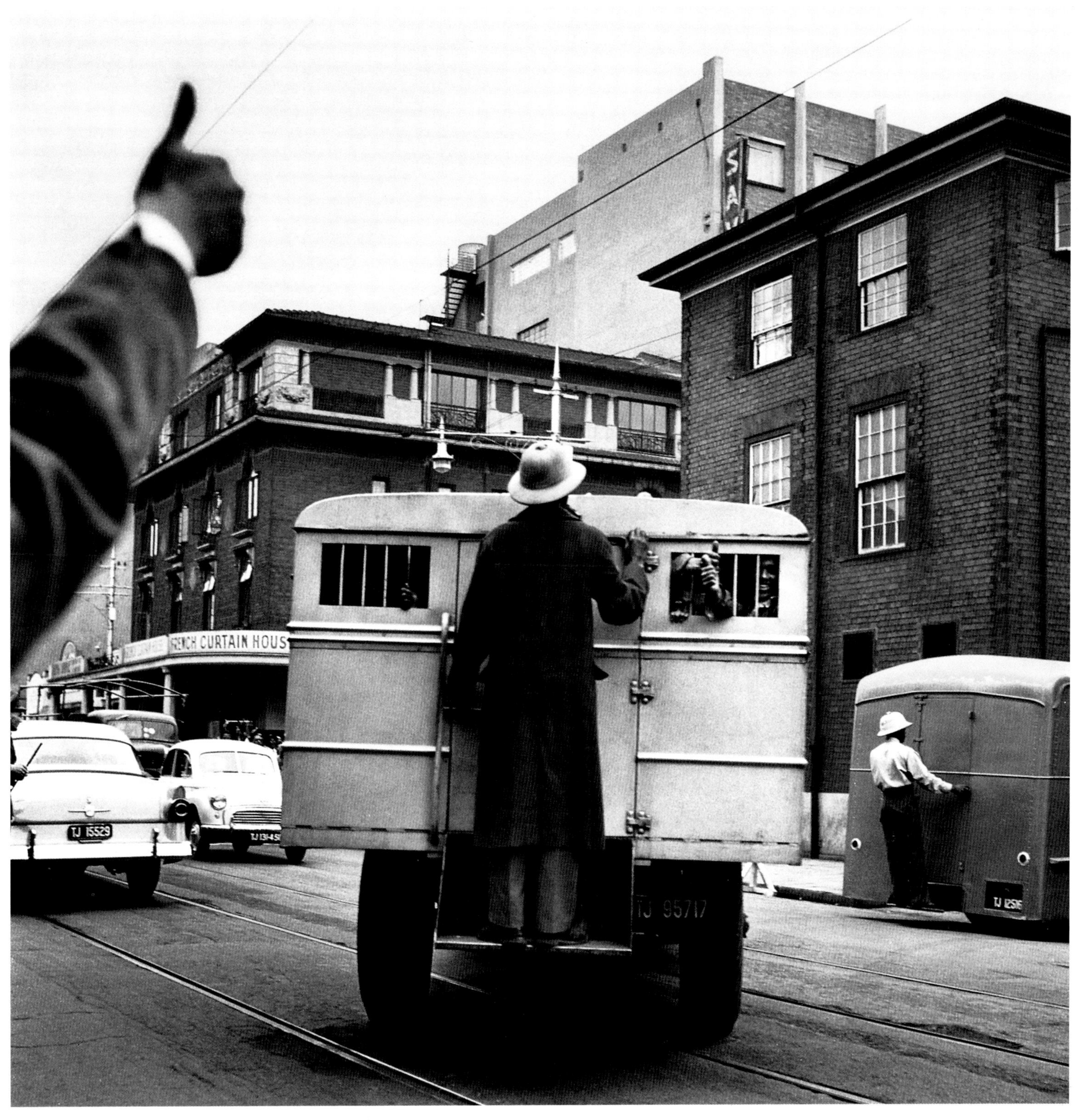

JOHANNESBURG 1956
At dawn on 5 December the SA Police swooped
on 156 political leaders throughout the country,
arresting them on charges of high treason. The
Treason Trial finally collapsed four and a half
years later and the defendants were acquitted of
all charges.

JÜRGEN SCHADEBERG

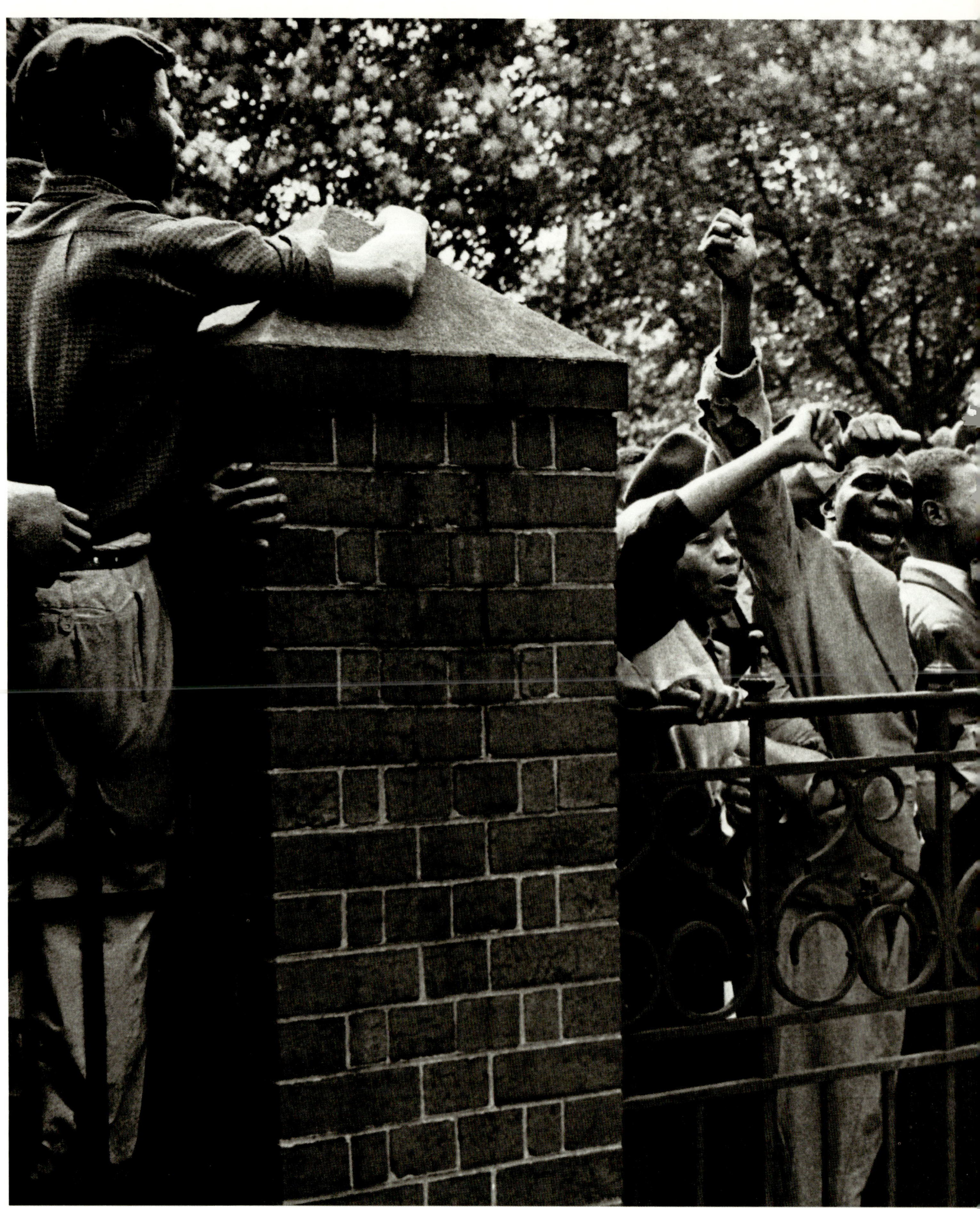

JOHANNESBURG DECEMBER 1956. Treason Trial. The crowd went mad and cheered as the accused arrived at the courthouse in prison vans.   JÜRGEN SCHADEBERG

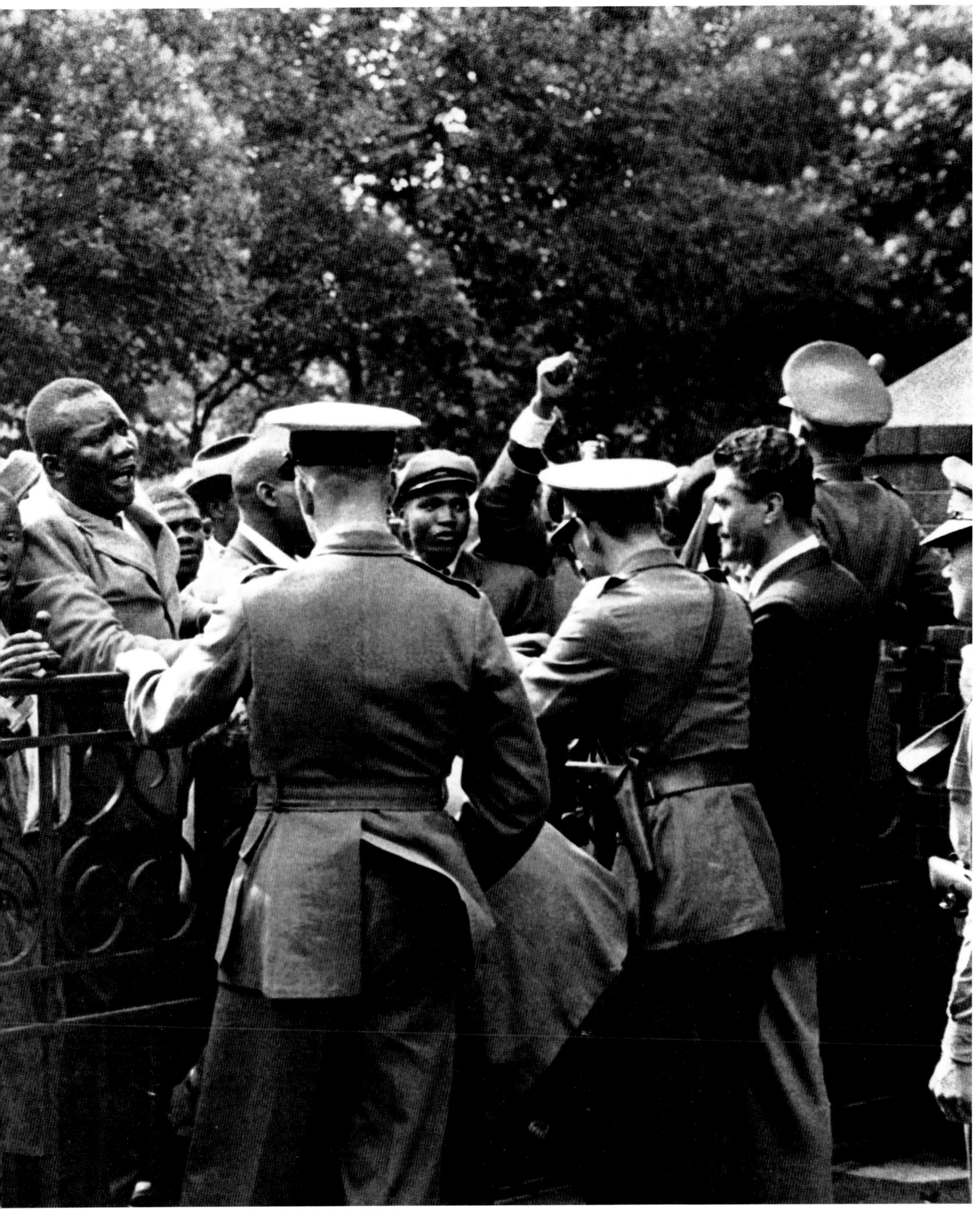

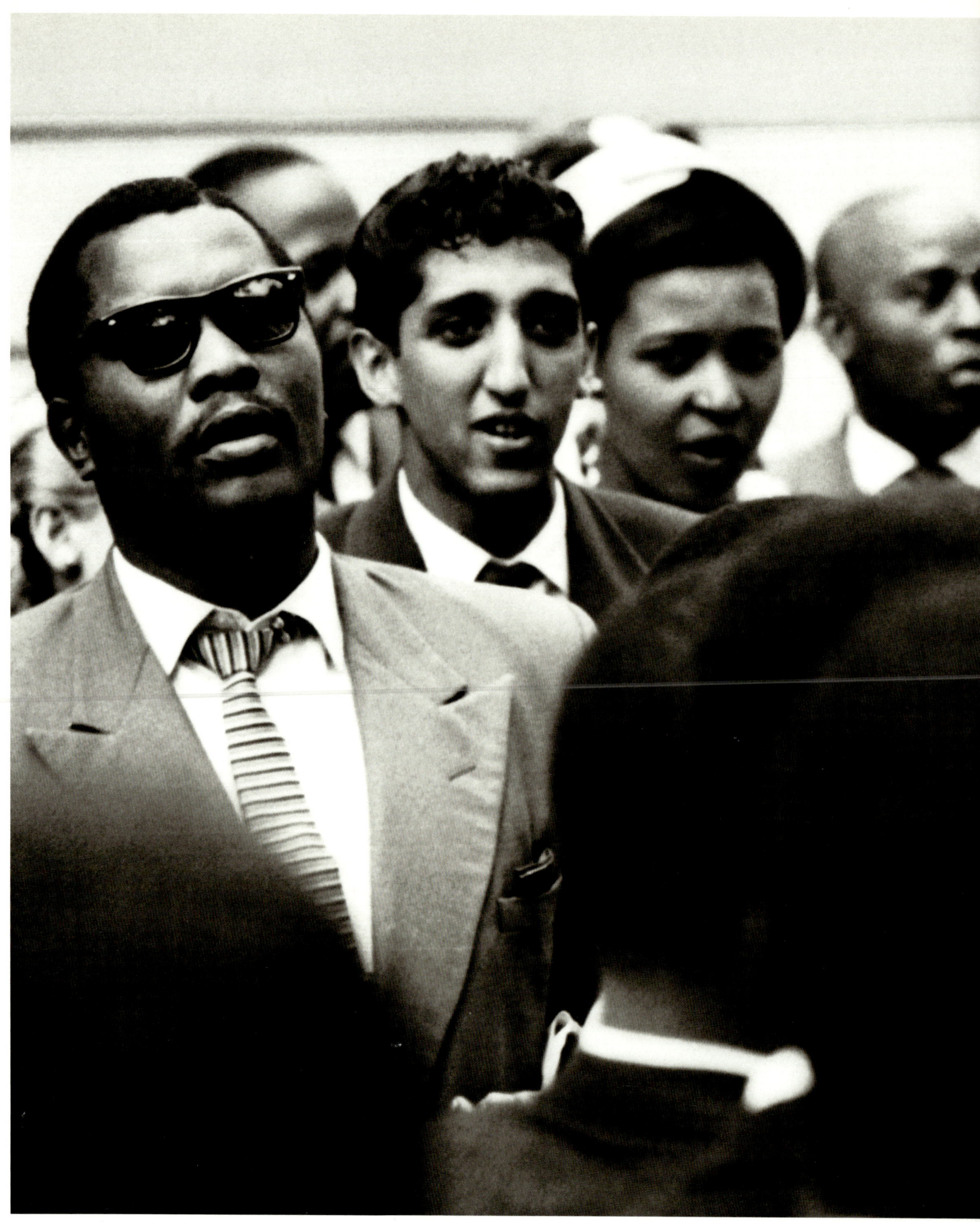

PRETORIA 1958. Treason Trial. Aziz Pahad (second from left), Winnie and Nelson Mandela singing **Nkosi Sikele Africa** outside the court.   PETER MAGUBANE

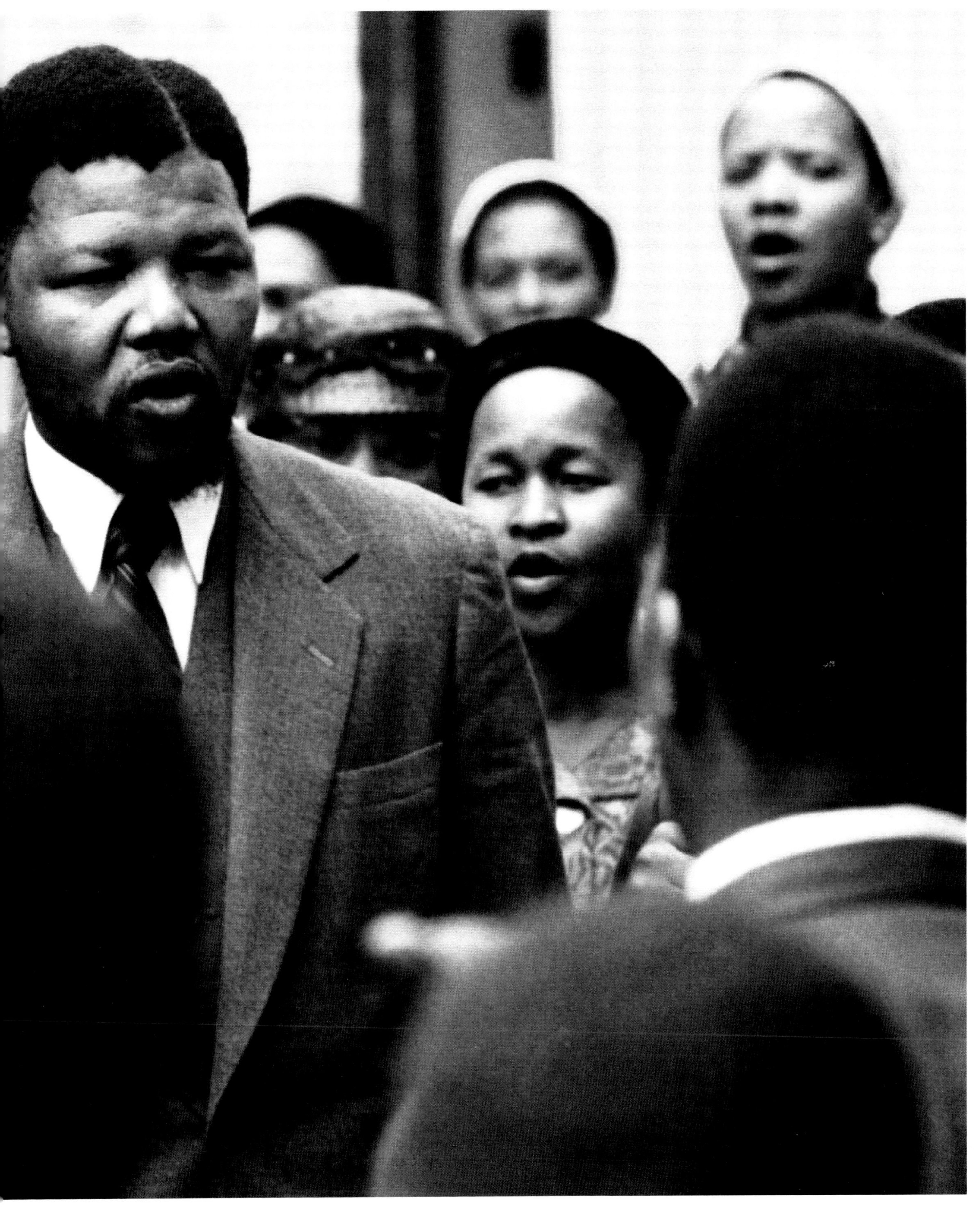

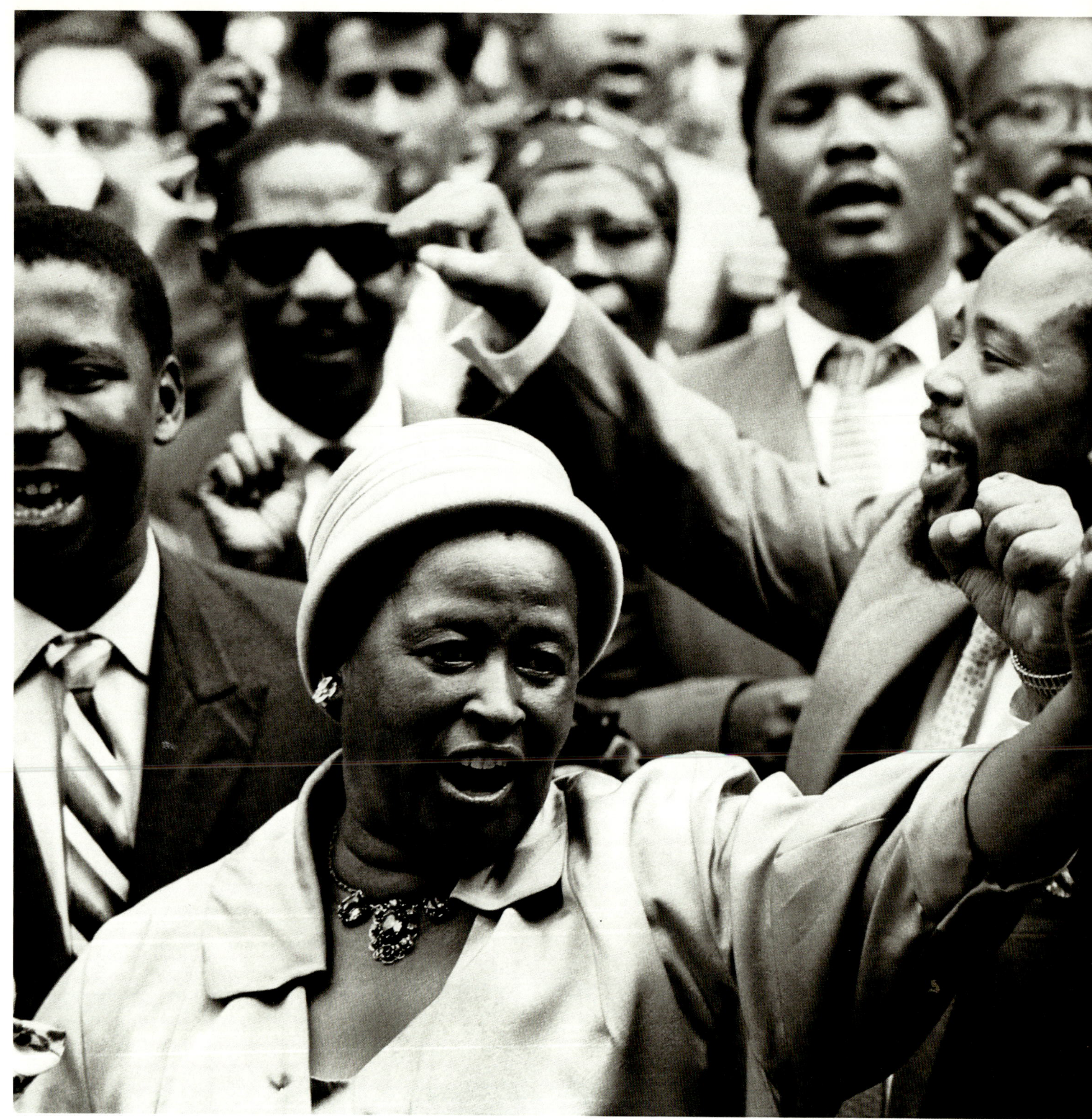

PRETORIA 1958
It's finally over and Robert Resha makes the
'Africa' salute. The Crown had withdrawn
indictment against all the accused in the Treason
Trial. A few months later, on 19 January 1959,
Nelson Mandela and 29 others were put on trial
again.

PETER MAGUBANE

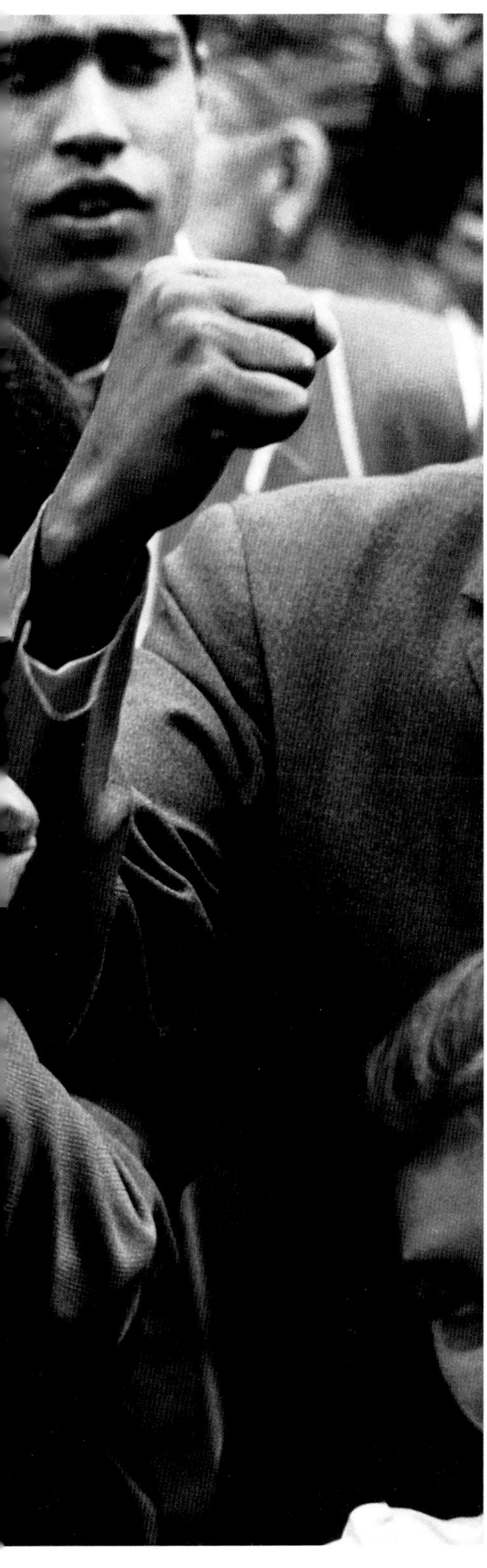

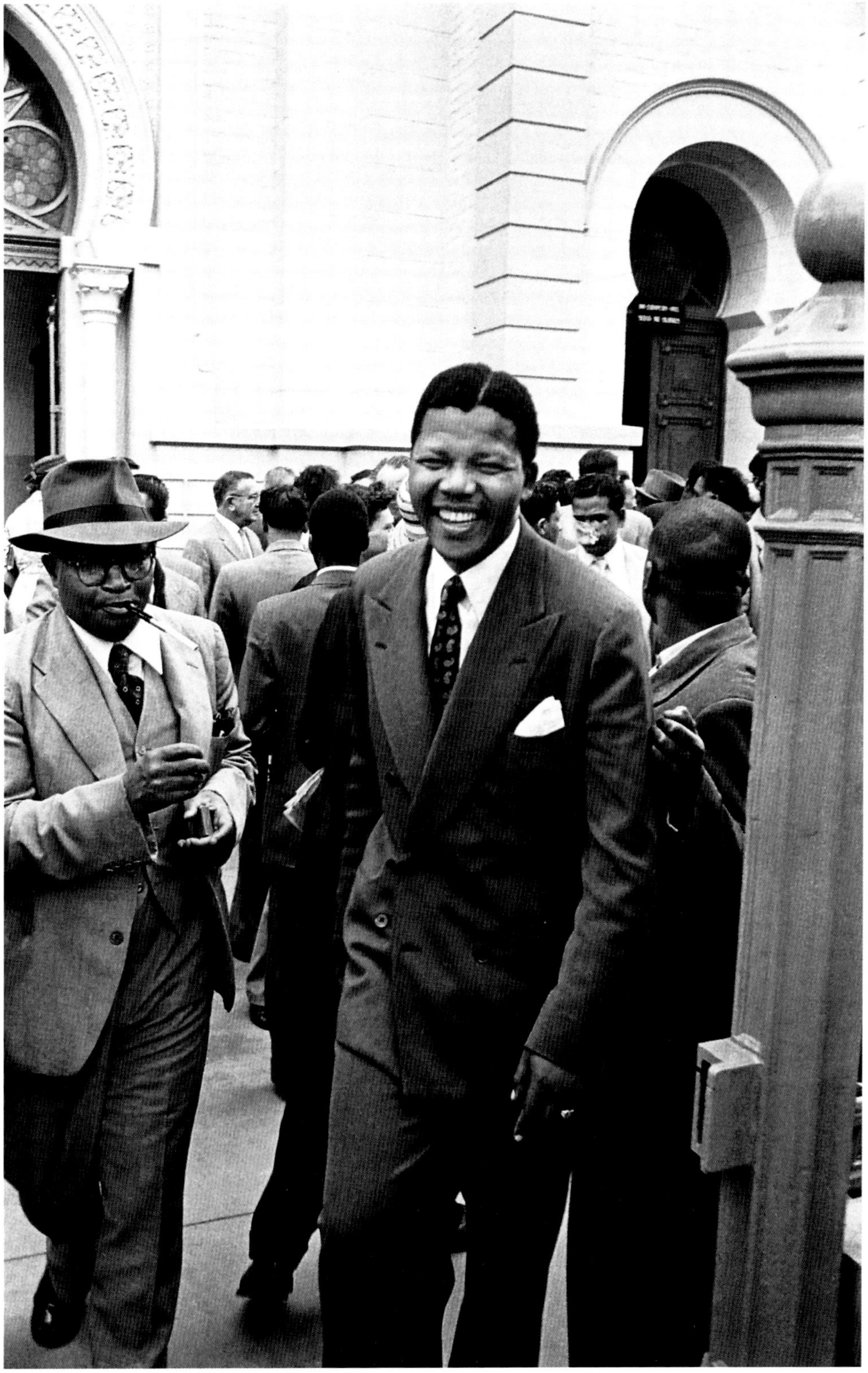

PRETORIA 1958
Moses Kotane (left) and Nelson Mandela leave
the court — a converted synagogue — during
the Treason Trial. It lasted for four and a half
years, causing misery and suffering to hundreds
of the accused and their families. Not one person
was found guilty.

JÜRGEN SCHADEBERG

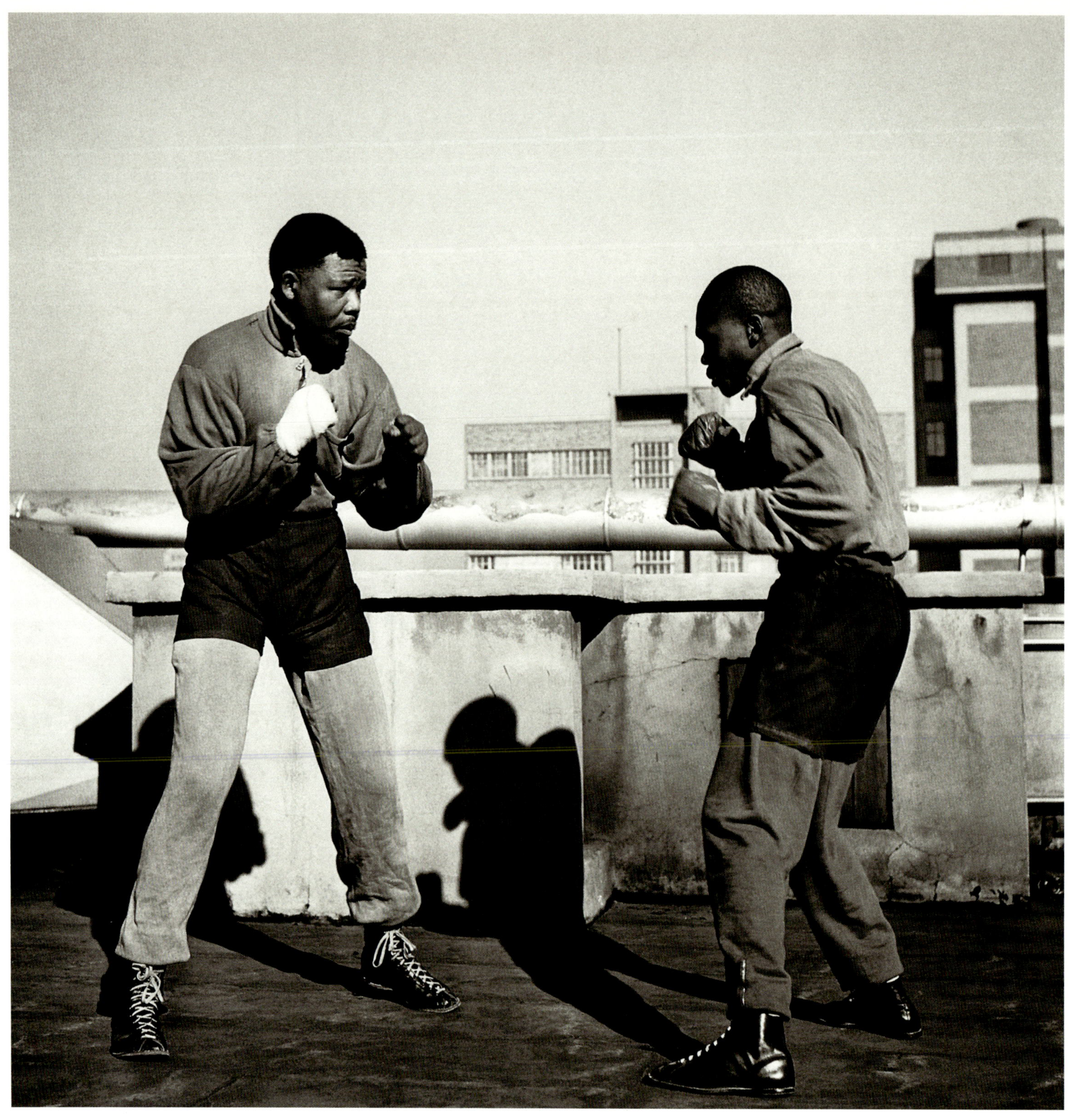

JOHANNESBURG 1956
Nelson Mandela was a keen and enthusiastic
amateur boxer. During the Treason Trial he went
to Gerry Moloi's boxing gym every evening —
sometimes shadow-sparring with the champion
Moloi himself.

BOB GOSANI

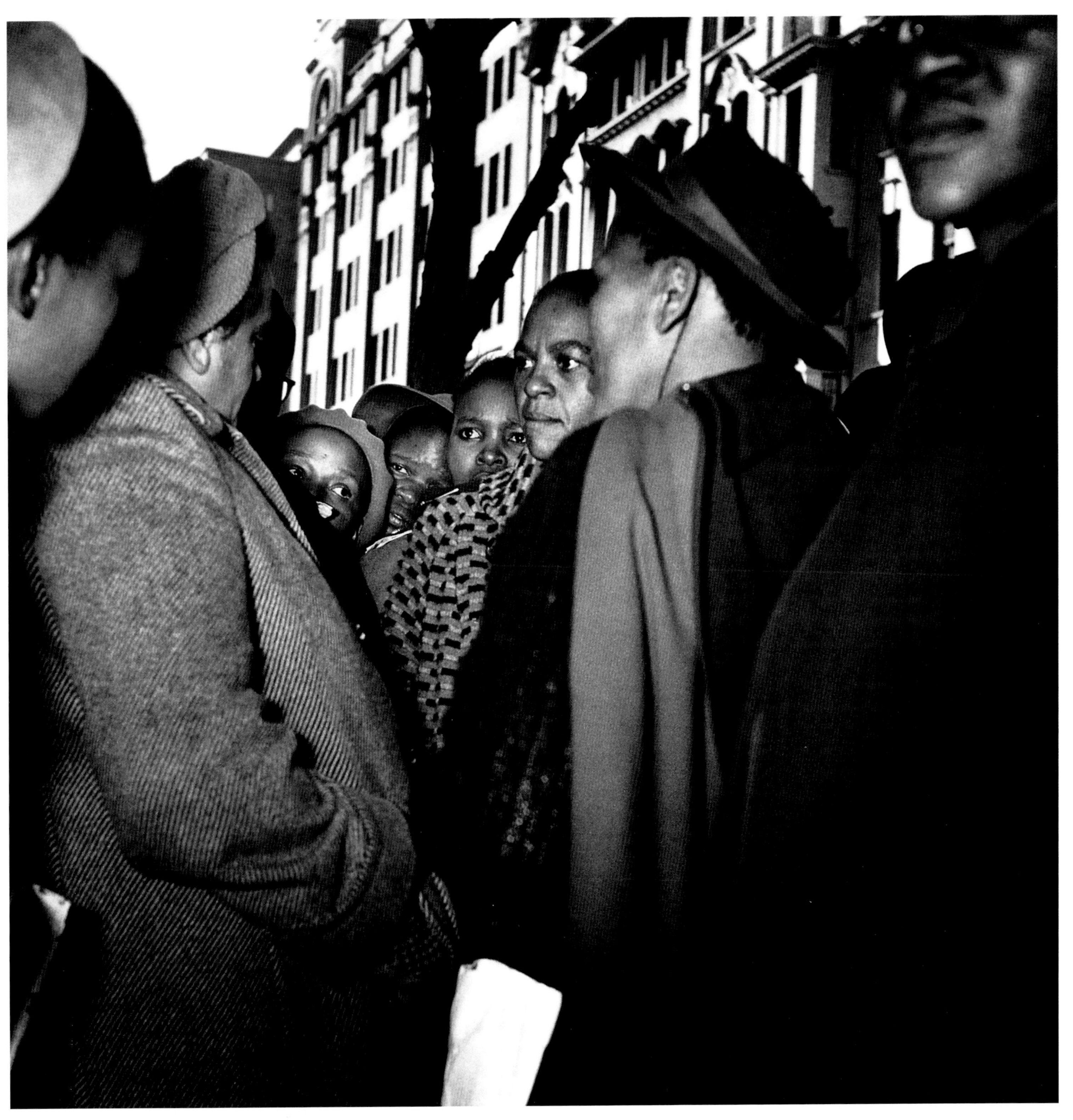

JOHANNESBURG 1958
Voices of non-white nurses rang out loud and
clear when nursing apartheid became law. They
called a conference in Johannesburg and set up
a new all-race group — The Federation of South
African Nurses and Midwives.

BOB GOSANI

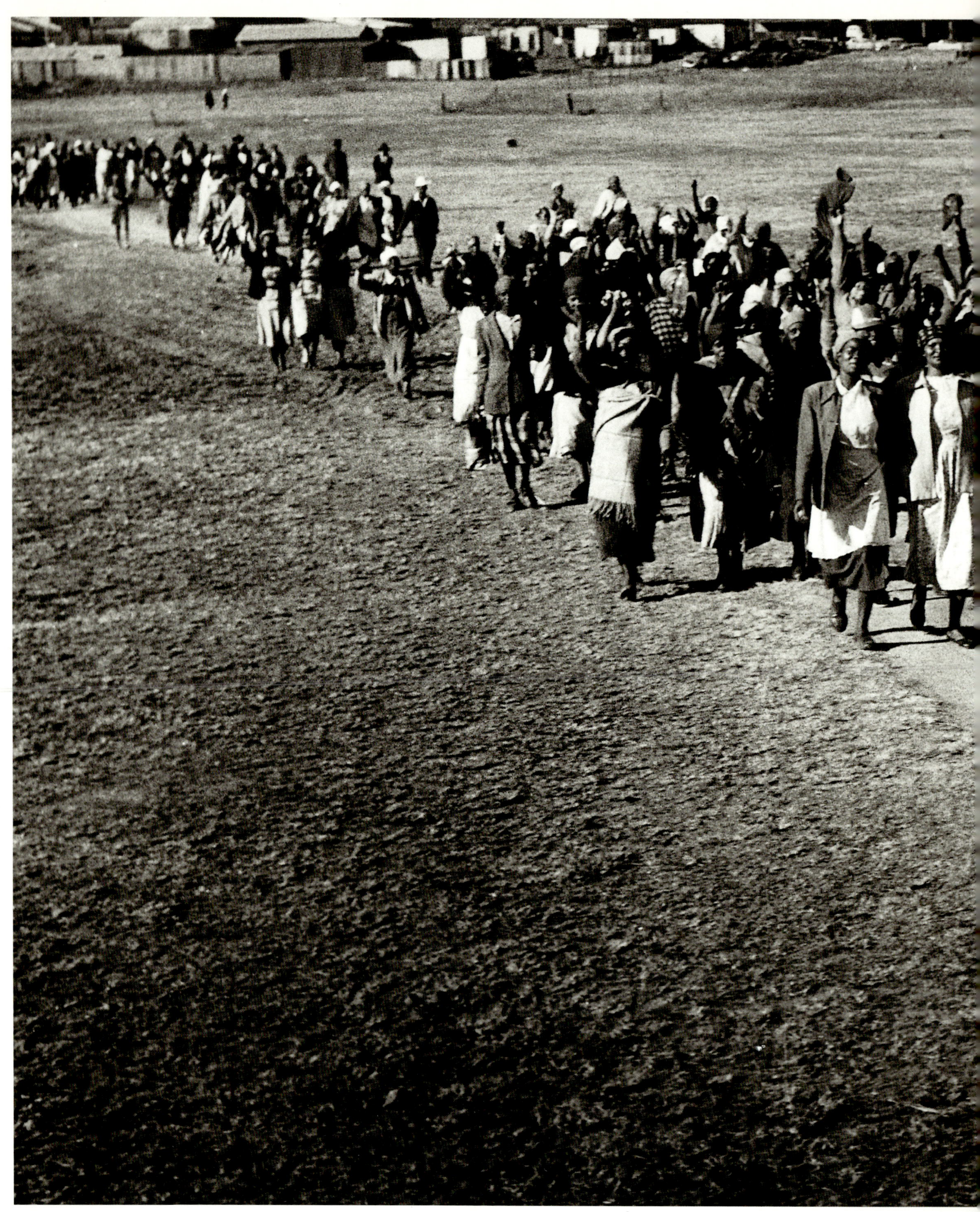

NORTHERN TRANSVAAL 1959. More and more women protest against the discriminating Pass Laws. Throughout the country women collect signatures and hold demonstrations.

PETER MAGUBANE

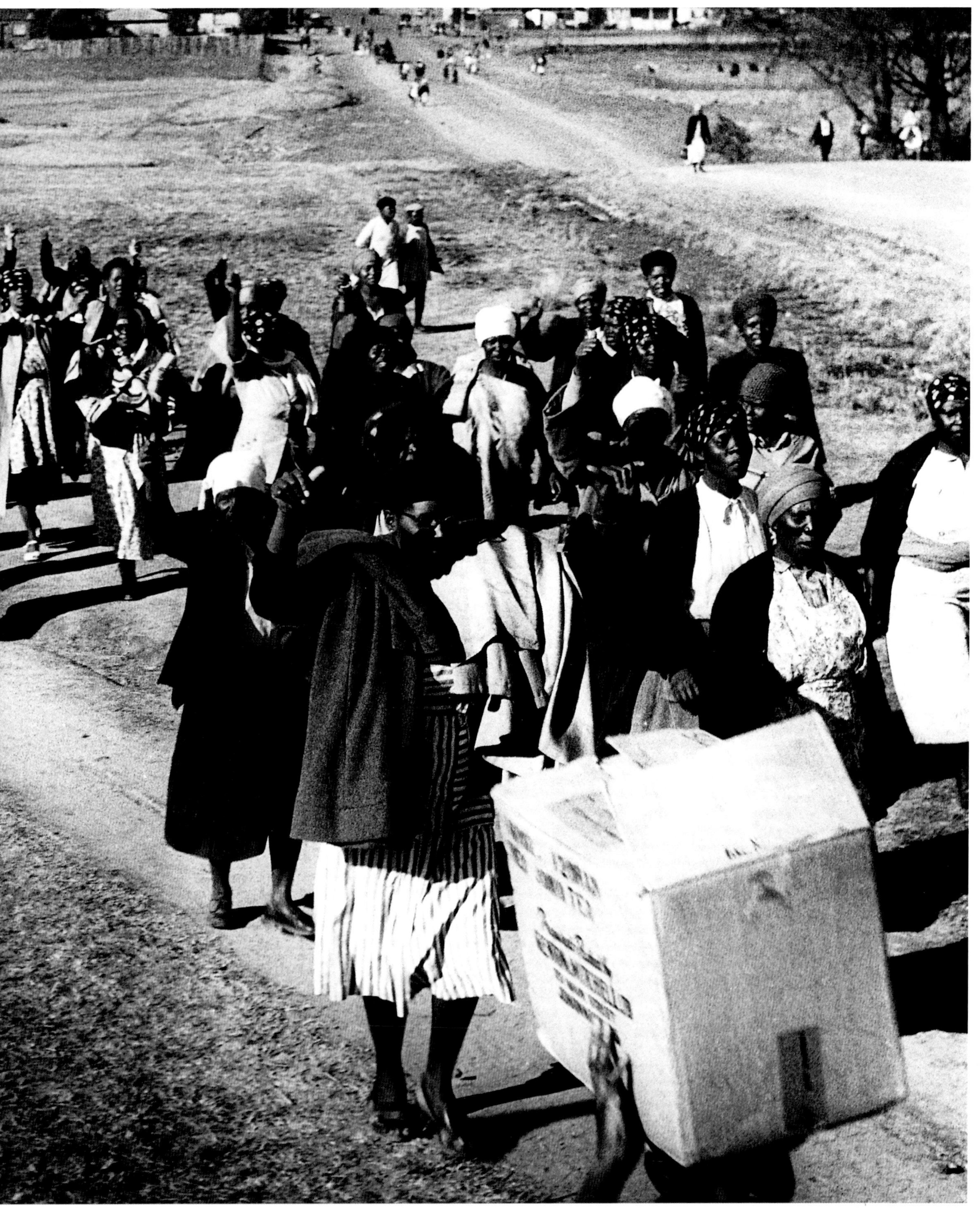

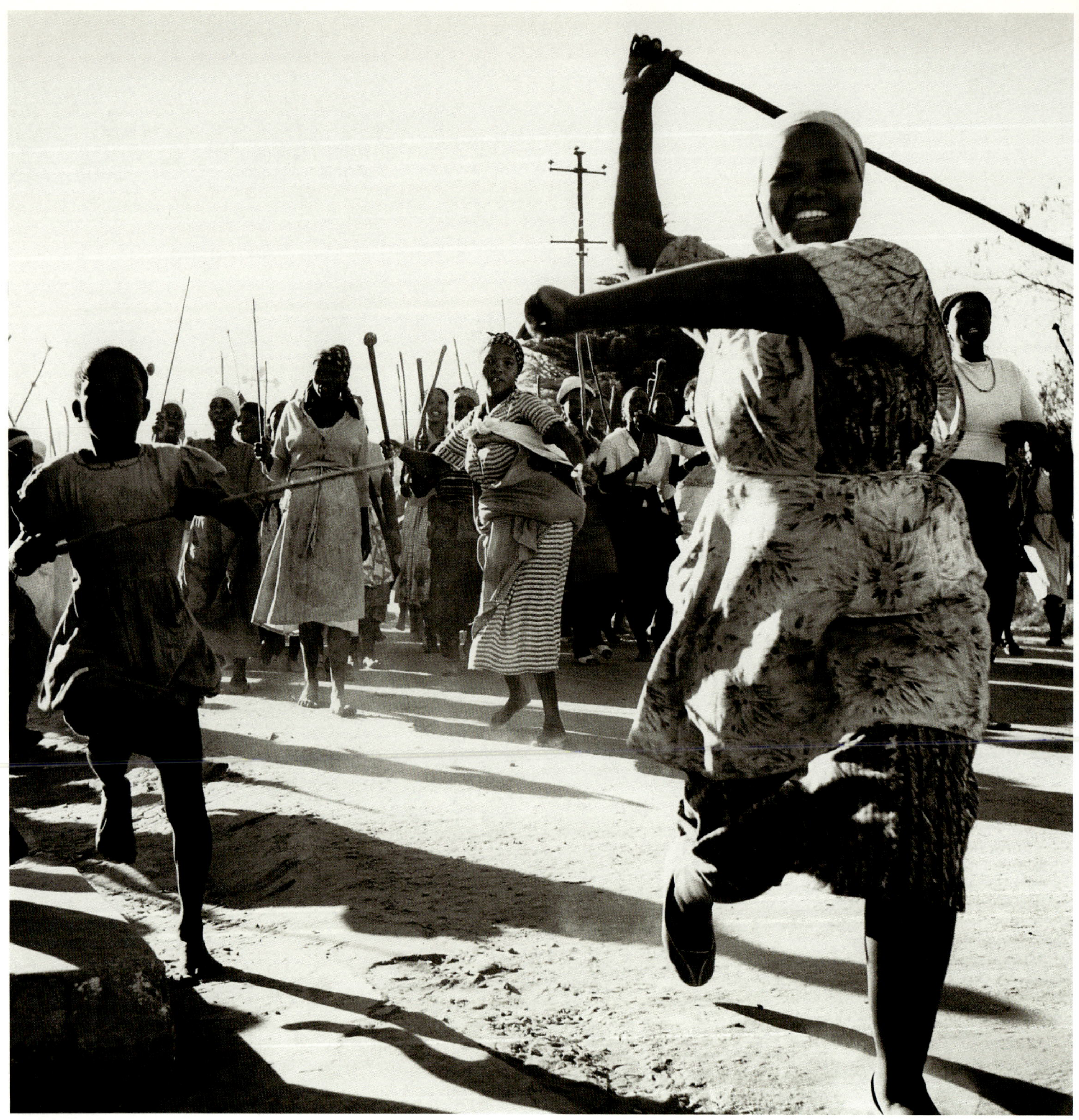

CATO MANOR 1959

Following a mild outbreak of typhoid, steps were taken to clear up the unsanitary conditions. Stills and drums of home-brewed beer were destroyed by the police. This affected a large group of women who brewed traditional beer. These women decided to take action.

GR NAIDOO

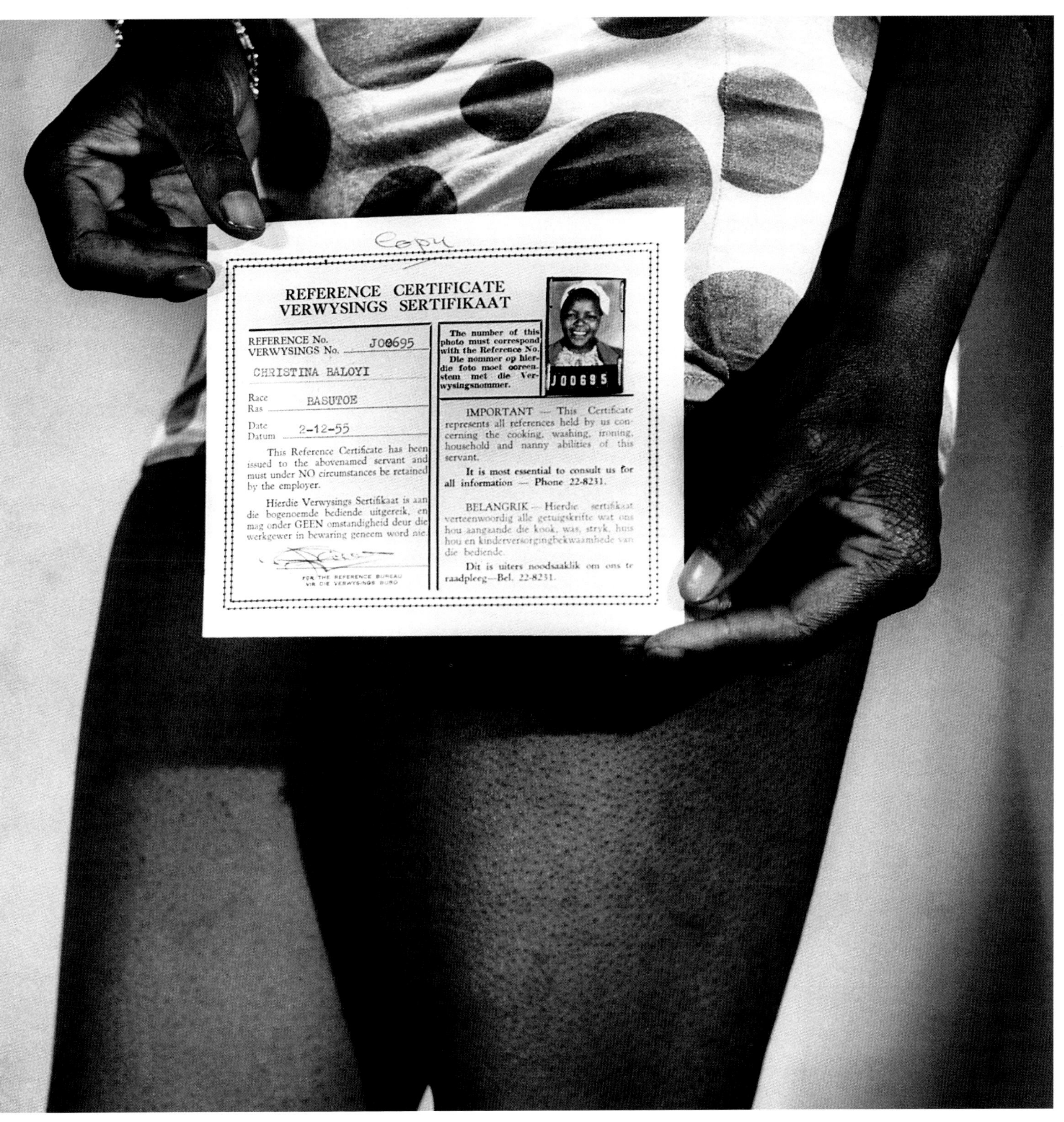

JOHANNESBURG 1956
Women were arrested for vagrancy. Women were
arrested for 'night specials'. Women were
monitored constantly by influx control. Identity
cards, location permits, passbooks — all women
now had to carry these documents at all times.

JÜRGEN SCHADEBERG

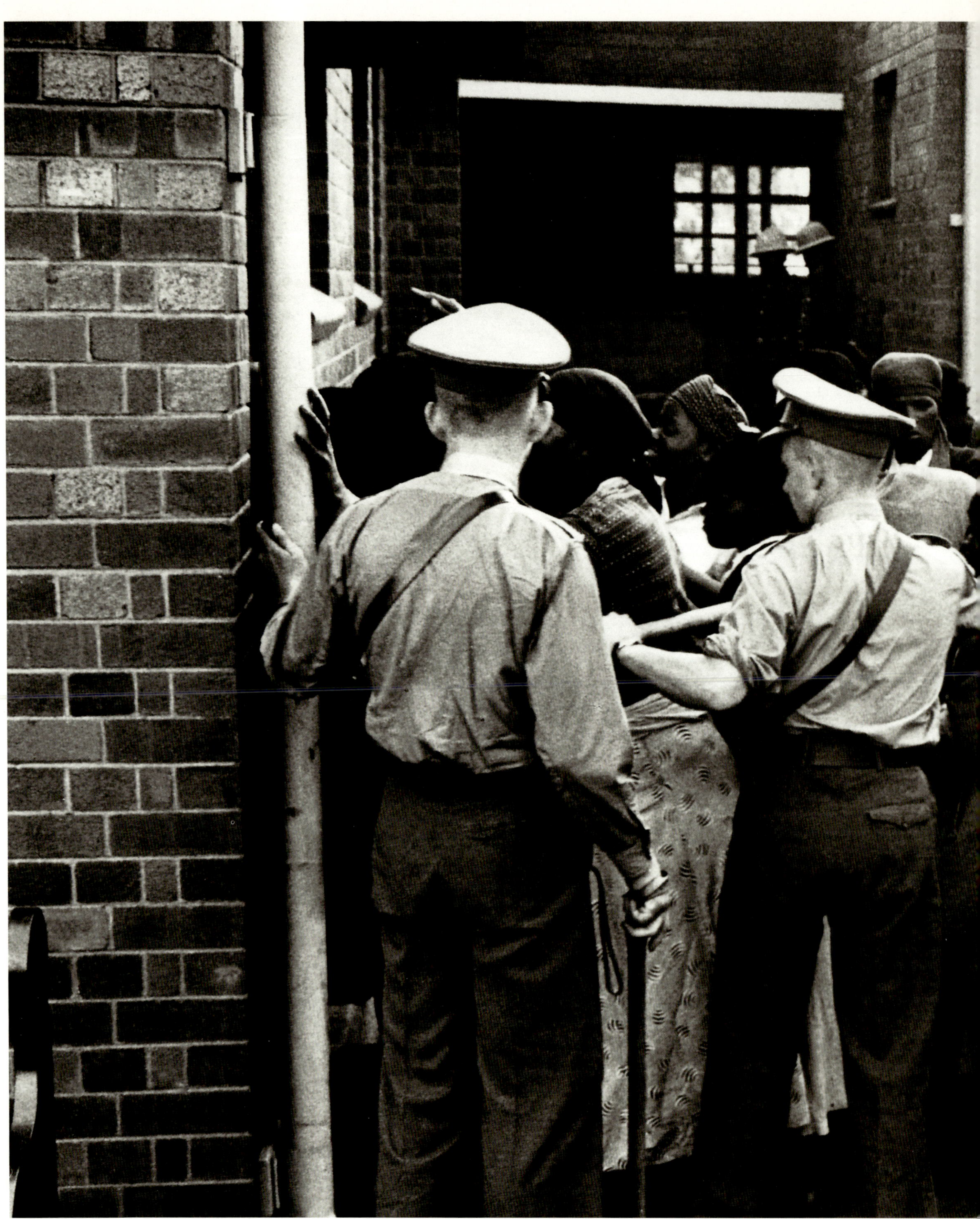

IXOPO 1959. Women from Ixopo marched to put their grievances to the government. They took a white flag to show that they had come in peace... but they never wer

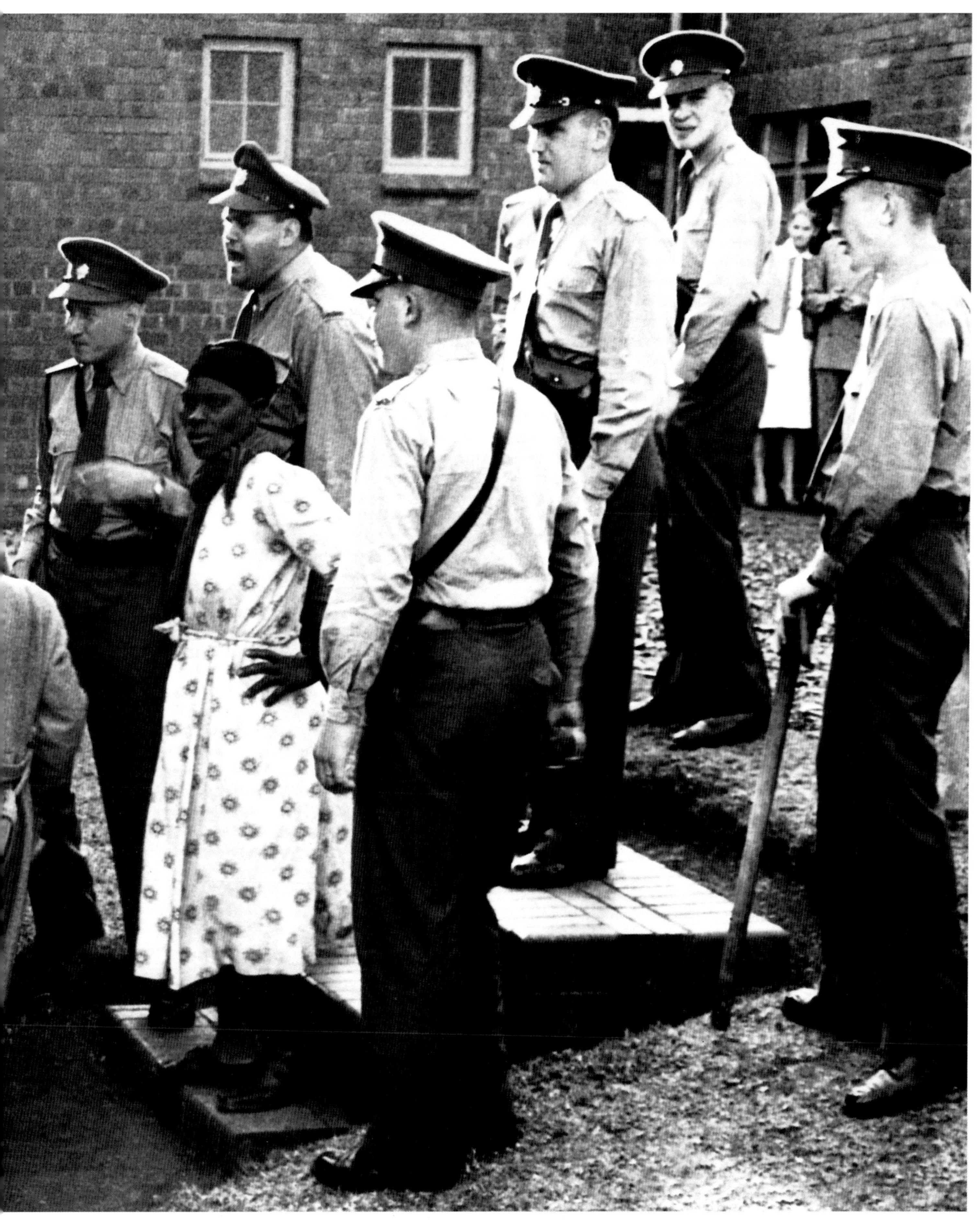

...ome that night. Somebody broke their flag and threw it to the ground. The women ended their march in prayer in jail.   GR NAIDOO

Boxers and Beauties

Joas Maoto the Clown Prince of the ring, alias 'Jumping Jelly Bean'. Born in 1934, he grew up in Alexandra Township, 'no place for people who can't keep on their toes every second of the day. If you just wink for one second, anything can blow up in your face.'

He was known as 'Kangaroo' because of the way he hopped about in the boxing ring — never in one place, always out of his opponent's reach.

Kangaroo walked about with knife and bullet scars. His first left finger was just a small stump, the result of a knife attack! 'I had to have it cut off because of boxing. After it had healed I could not make a fist. It had to come off.'

'Nobody thought I would live at all after I was born. They said I was too tiny to make it. I was a premature baby! I grew up in a rough and tough area in Alexandra Township, the "Dark City".'

'Tiny in body as I was, I just had to force myself to be rough and tough too. The skinny and bow-legged imps like me had to bow down to the commands and wishes of the big-boned bullies. The other fellows' blows gradually instilled vigour into my blood. I developed guts and a will to win, no matter how tough the opposition, I became a bully myself.'

'All this time my mother was fighting heavily to save me from the creepy claws of the underworld and an idea struck her. Boxing!' His mother took Joas by the hand to gym. Within a few months he put on weight and fought in the Alexandra Township amateur championship, winning the title in 1953.

'Kangaroo' took up professional boxing in 1954.

Nat Nakasa
Drum 1957

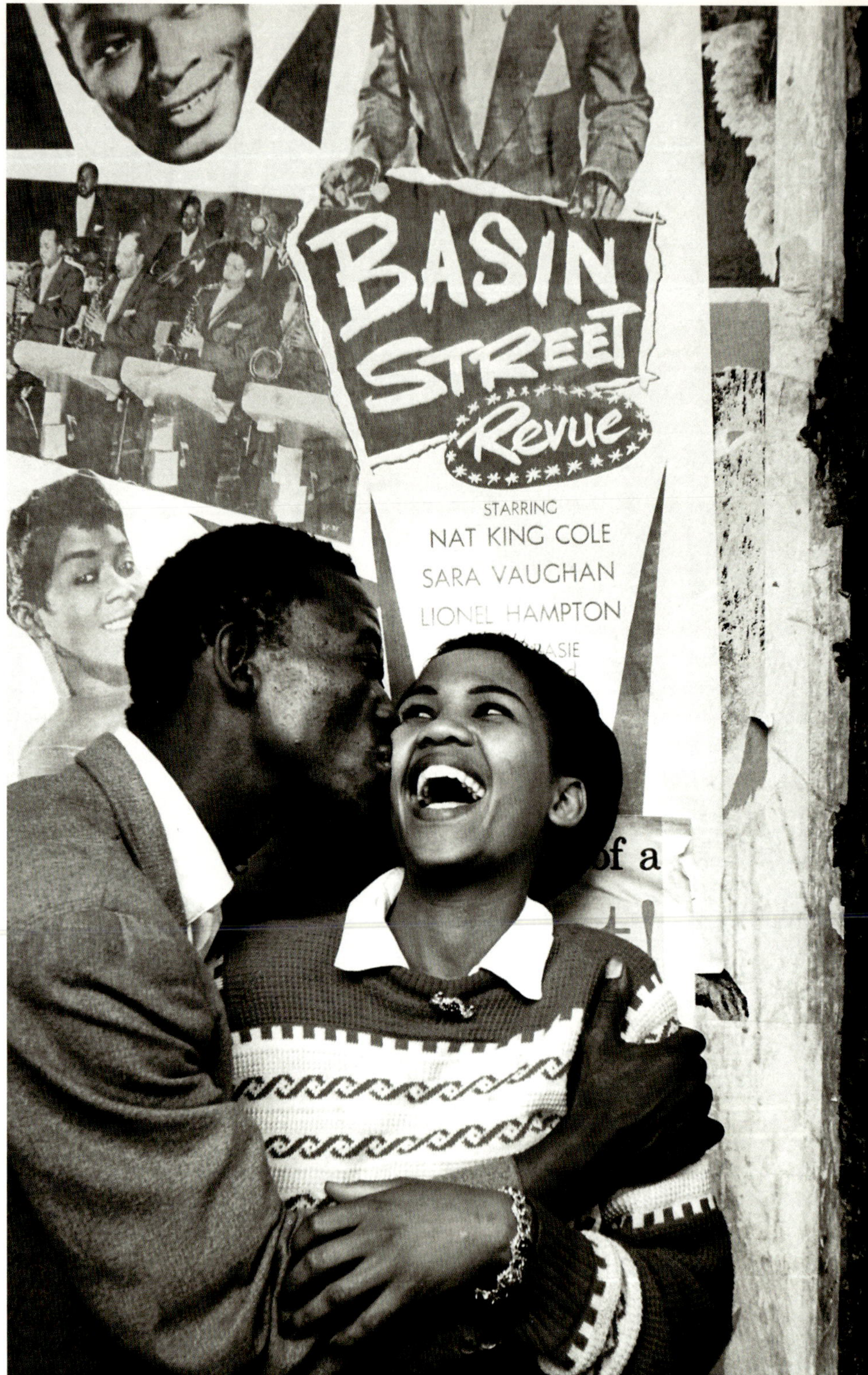

JOHANNESBURG 1959. Dottie Tiyo, former Miss South Africa, a successful actress, a great admirer of the opposite sex. 'I've got more boyfriends than I've got new dresses,' she says.

PETER MAGUBANE

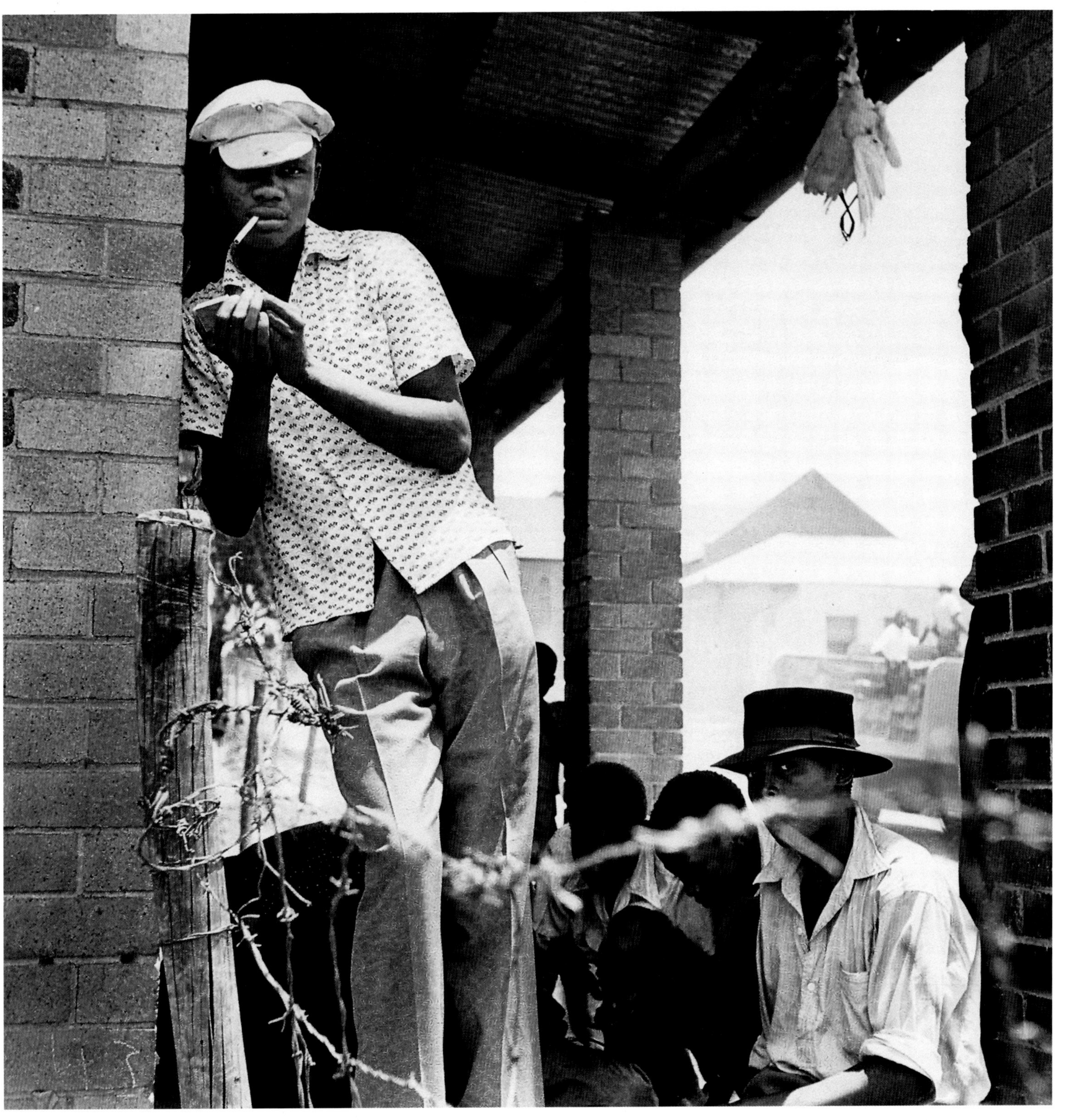

ALEXANDRA TOWNSHIP 1957
'Jumping Jelly Bean', Joas 'Kangaroo' Maoto,
Welterweight Champ, grew up in Alexandra
Township. Joas resembled a kangaroo when he
jumped around the ring... and the crowds
shouted 'Hula hoop' and 'Kangaroo' jumped about
like popcorn.

PETER MAGUBANE

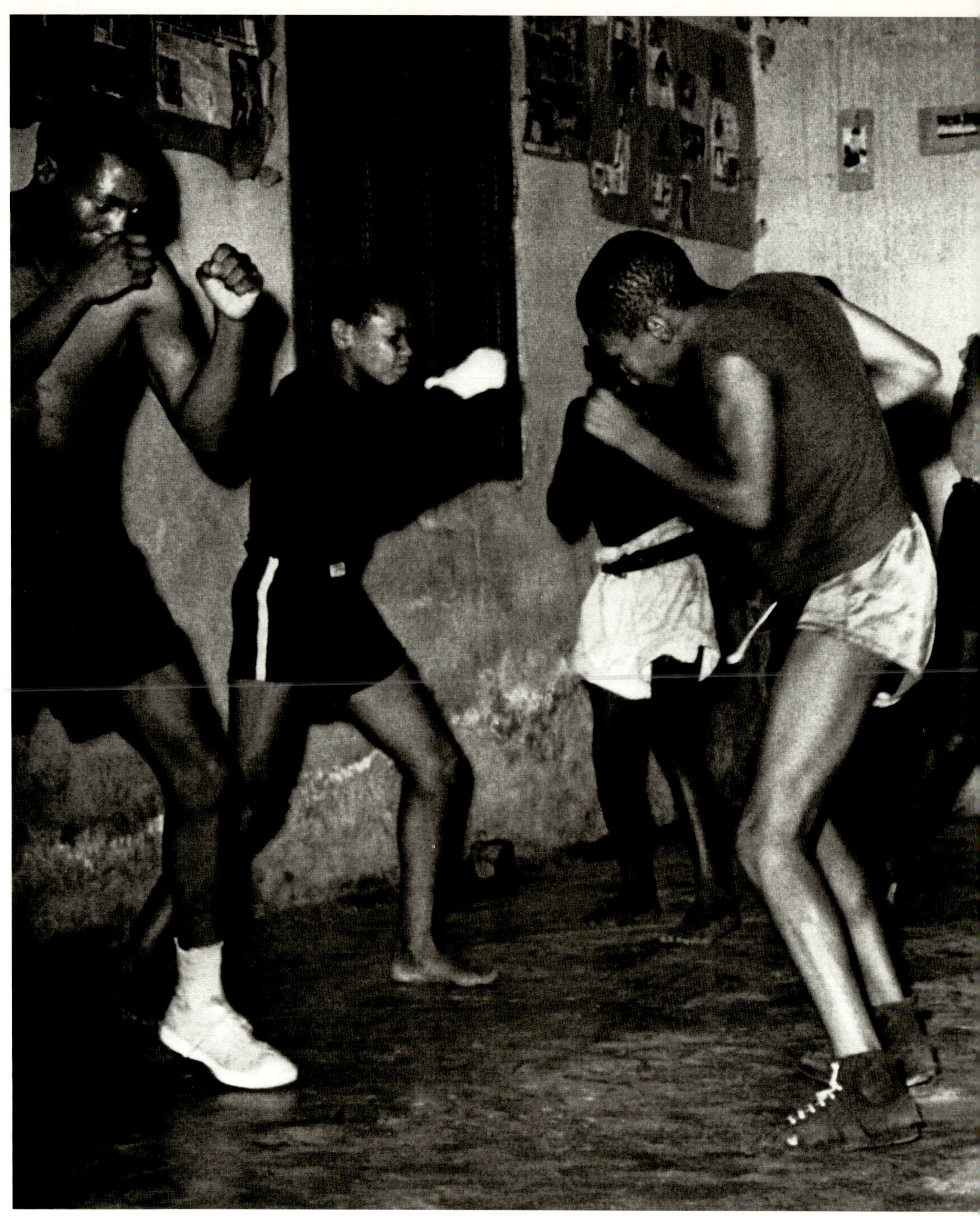

SOPHIATOWN 1954. The boxing world offered a chance to break away from slum life for these boys ... for the girls it was the world of beauty queens.

JÜRGEN SCHADEBERG

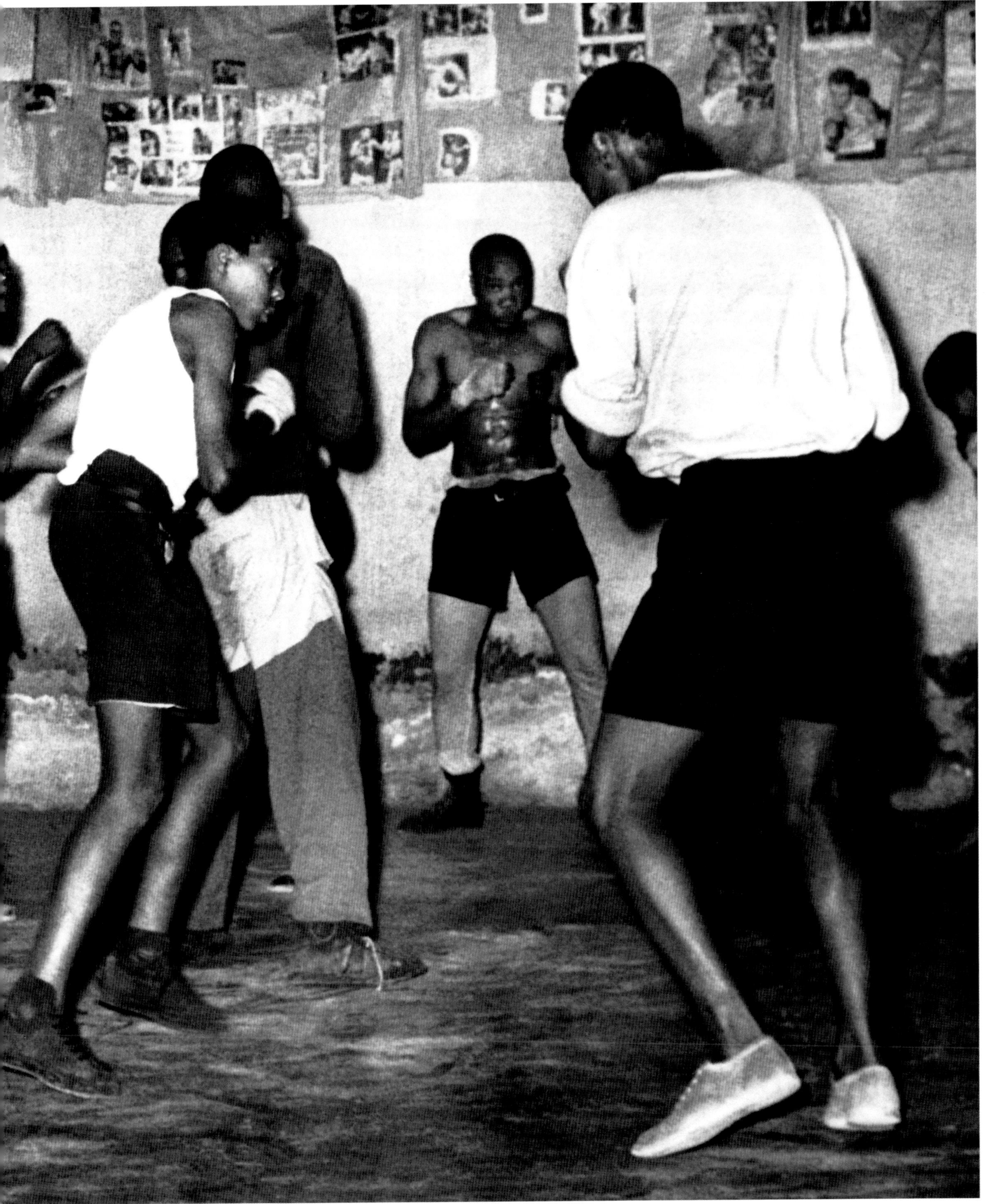

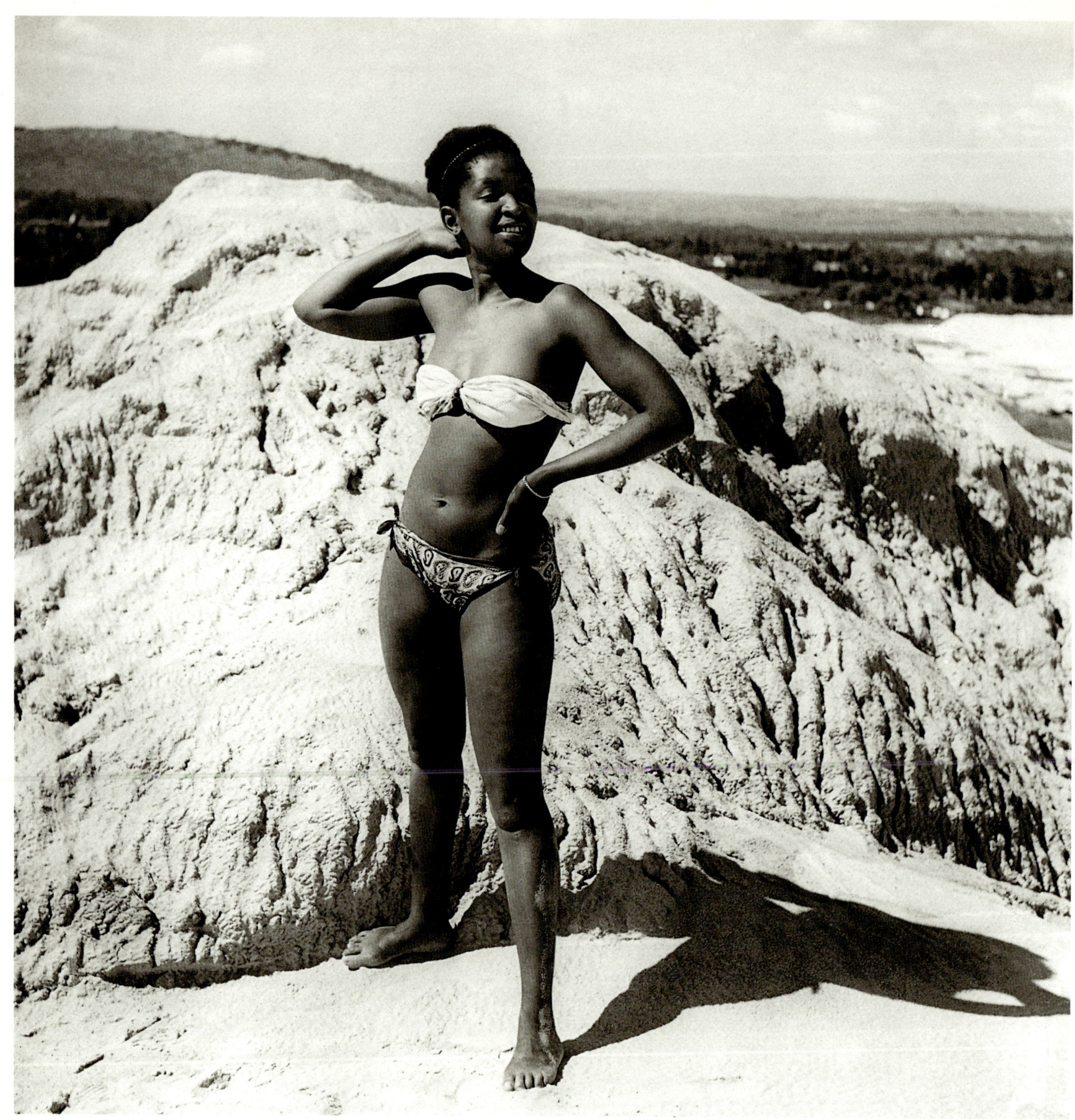

JOHANNESBURG 1952
Blues singer and film star Dolly Rathebe posing
on a mine dump for a cover picture. Dolly and
Jürgen, (the photographer) were picked up by the
police, who suspected them of contravening the
Immorality Act. The charges were later dropped.

JÜRGEN SCHADEBERG

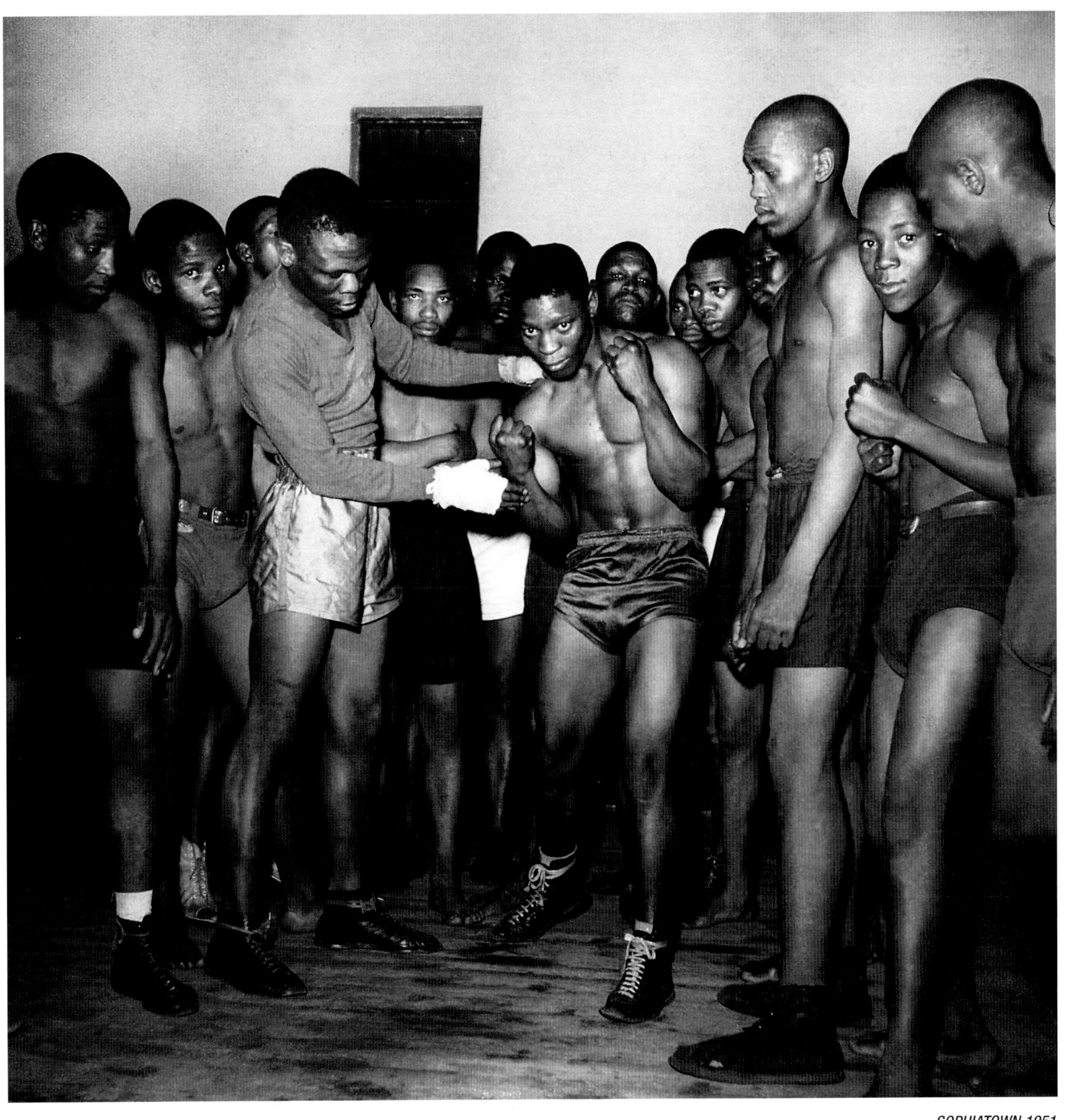

SOPHIATOWN 1951
So many aspirant world champions.

JÜRGEN SCHADEBERG

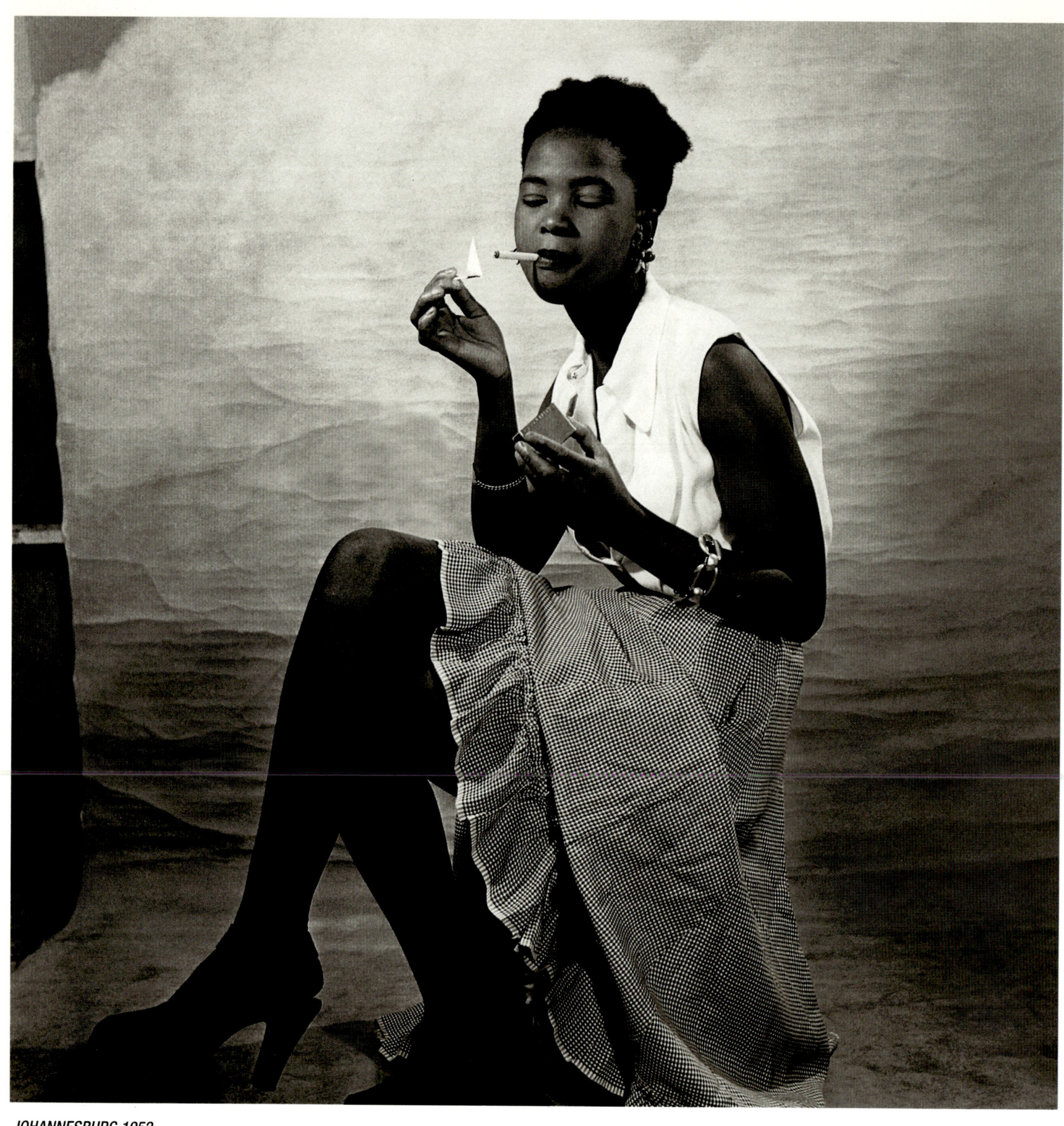

JOHANNESBURG 1952
A smoke break between poses during a photo
*session for a **Drum** cover.*

JÜRGEN SCHADEBERG

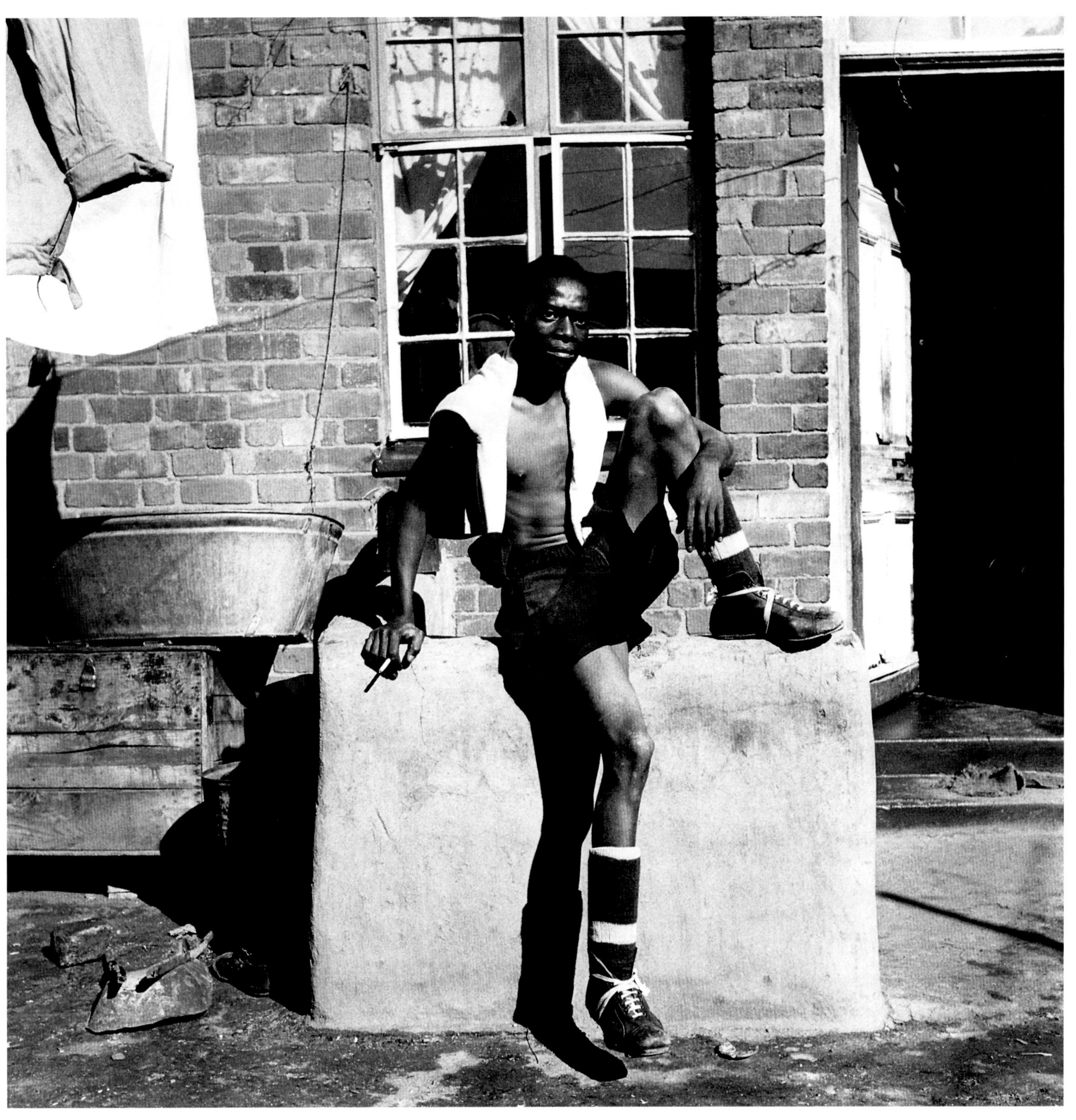

ALEXANDRA TOWNSHIP 1953
Peter Mavuso, the professor of Alexandra Soccer.
When this spectacular player swayed hither and
thither into action, dazzling his opponents, off
balancing this way and that, tumbling, only to rise
again, the crowd shouted 'Professor! ... my Boy!'

BOB GOSANI

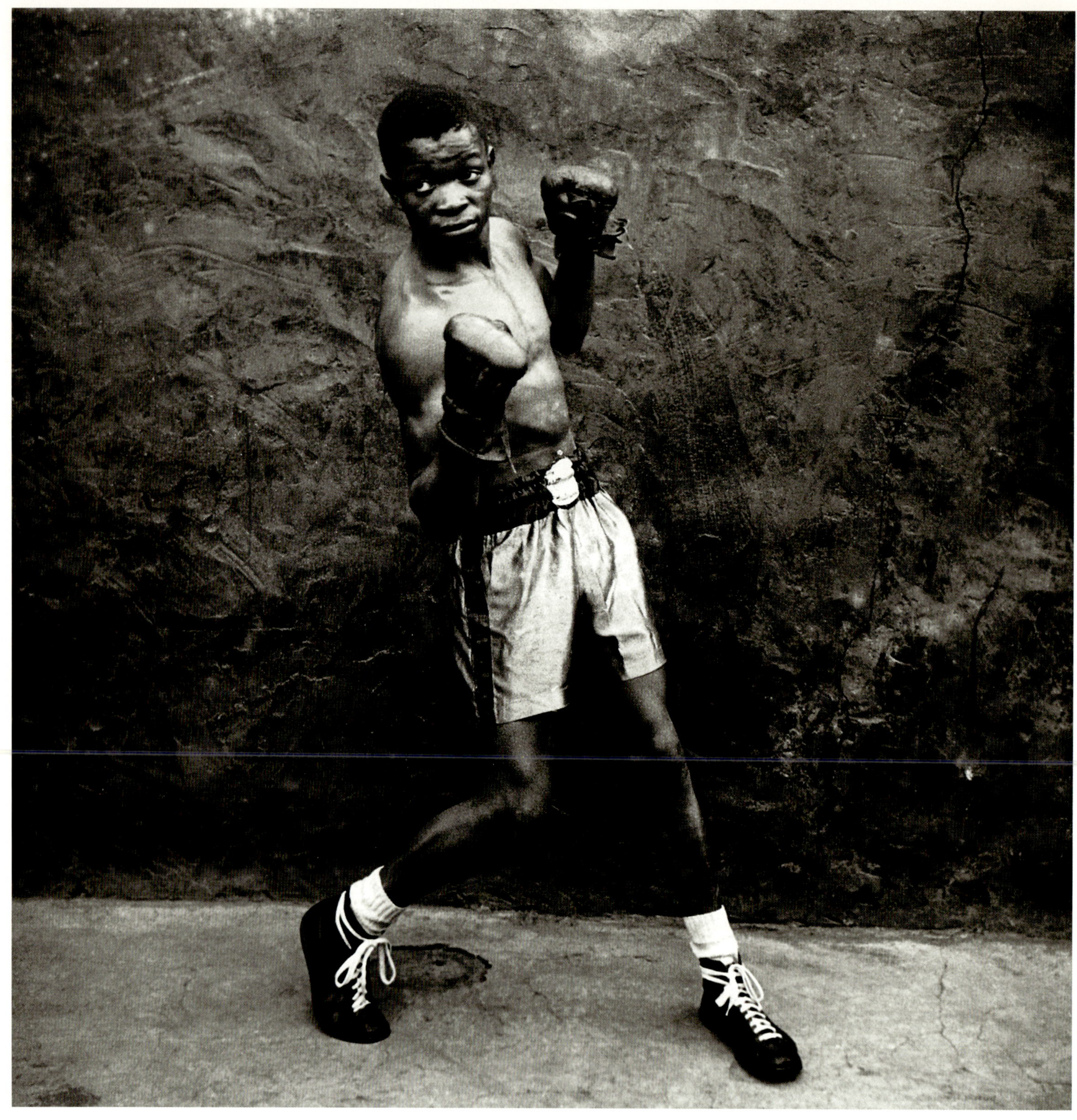

ALEXANDRA 1952
Boxers get big money. Yeah, sure, about one in a million of them. But for the others Nix — it isn't true. What about the small fry who really keep boxing on the go and at the same time make it possible for the giants to collect? The small man is in the majority. He sticks in the game hoping that one day he will hit the jackpot. But out of the whole breed only two out of ten make it. Now take a boxer fighting for a £7 10s split, like featherweight Martin Tsotesi. After winning the fight he got his 60% — £4 5s. Twenty-five percent of that went into his manager's pocket, leaving him with a cool £3 2s5d. So they call him the 'small-time £4-a-nighter'. Looks tough, hey?

BOB GOSANI

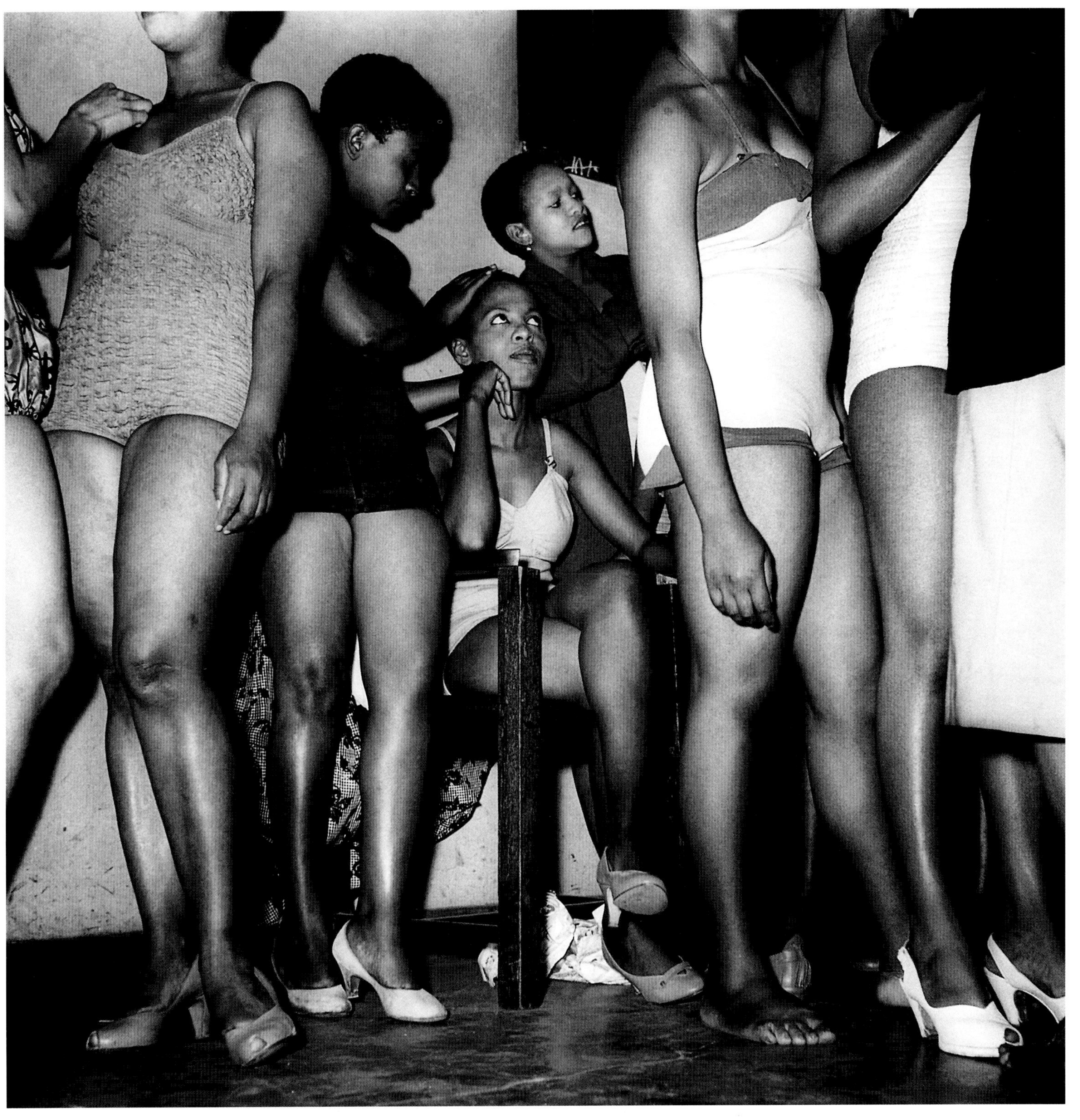

JOHANNESBURG 1957
Anxious and excited, they're making a bid for the
'Big Time', and the hundreds of pounds in prizes
that will go to the winners of the finals. The
wolves in the smoke-filled darkness of the hall
howl 'keep her on, we haven't had a good look
yet,' as a young girl moves uneasily under the
stage lights.

JÜRGEN SCHADEBERG

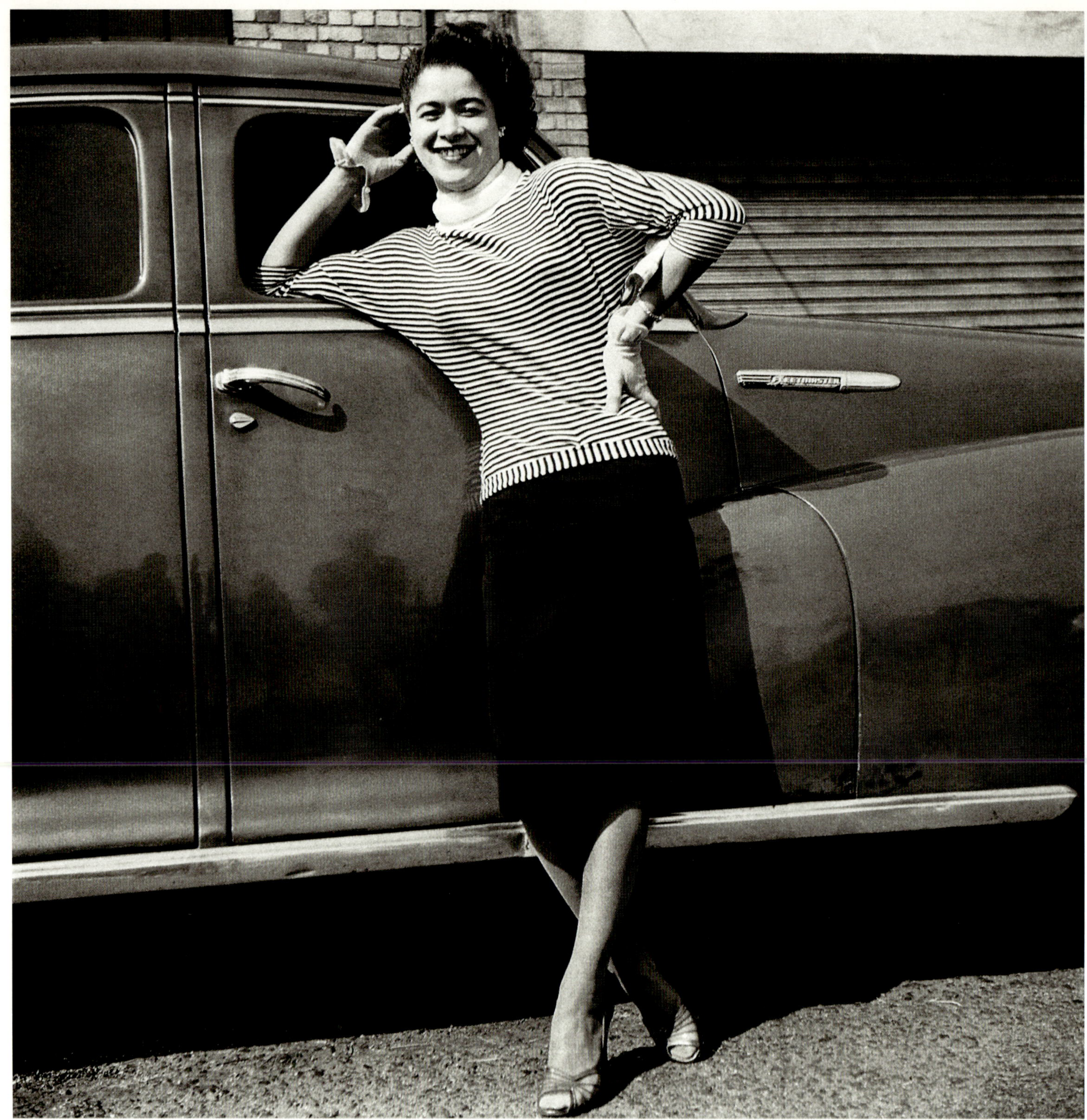

JOHANNESBURG 1957
*Selma Kolae, beauty queen, model and **Drum** cover girl.*
Some of her coloured friends say its a terrible thing for
a coloured girl to appear in a 'Kaffir' magazine... One
day a couple of coloured blokes wanted to kiss her in
the street. But when she wouldn't play they said: 'Au, let
her alone, she's that girl who appears in the Kaffir
*magazine, **Drum**.'*

BOB GOSANI

96

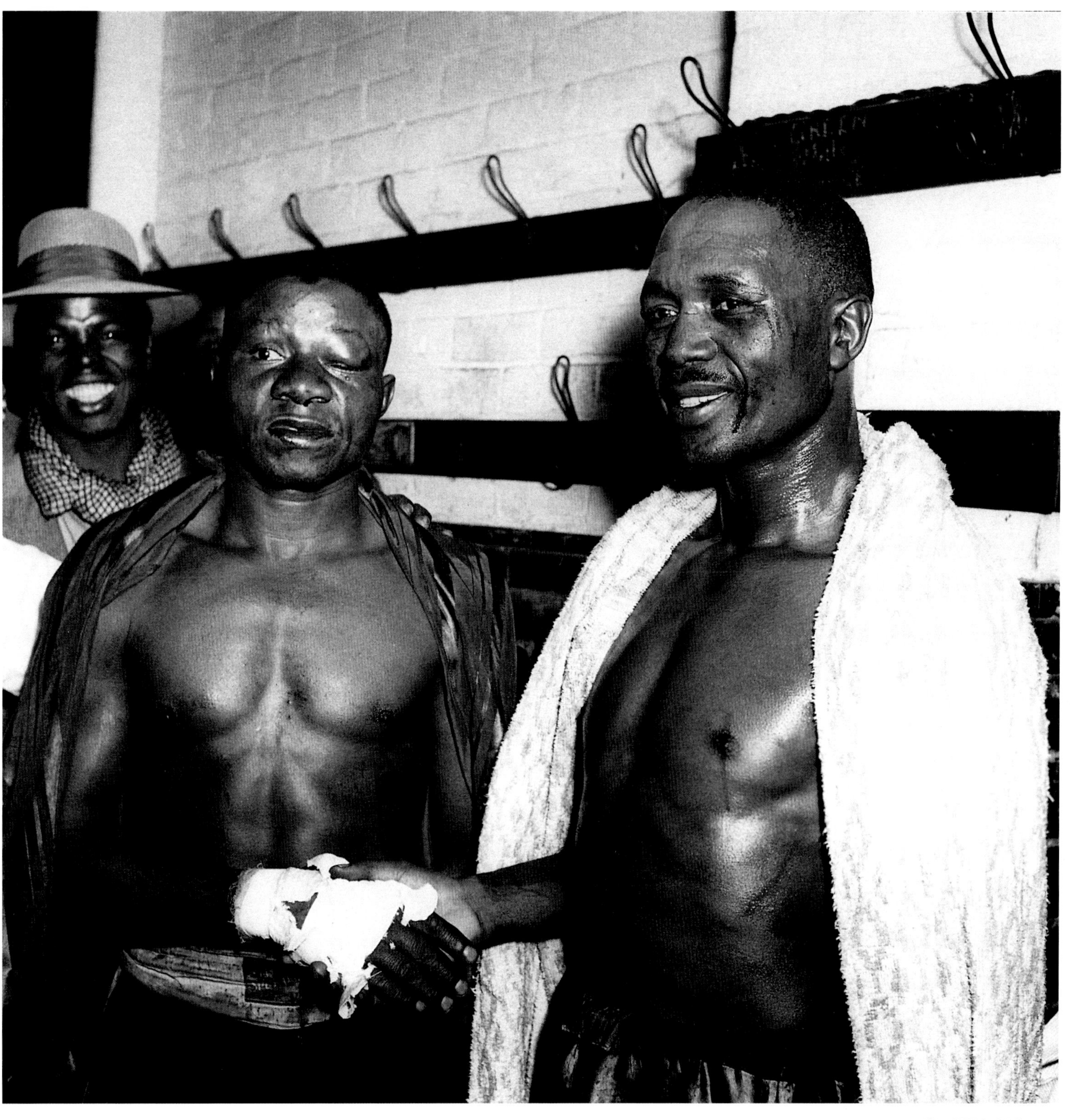

JOHANNESBURG 1953
Johannes 'Jolting Joe' Masiko's (right) first fight, after his
return from England, against Julius 'Guts' Caesar over
twelve rounds in Johannesburg. Jolting Joe, South African
Middleweight Champion, beat Guts on points and left him
with a blue eye.

BOB GOSANI

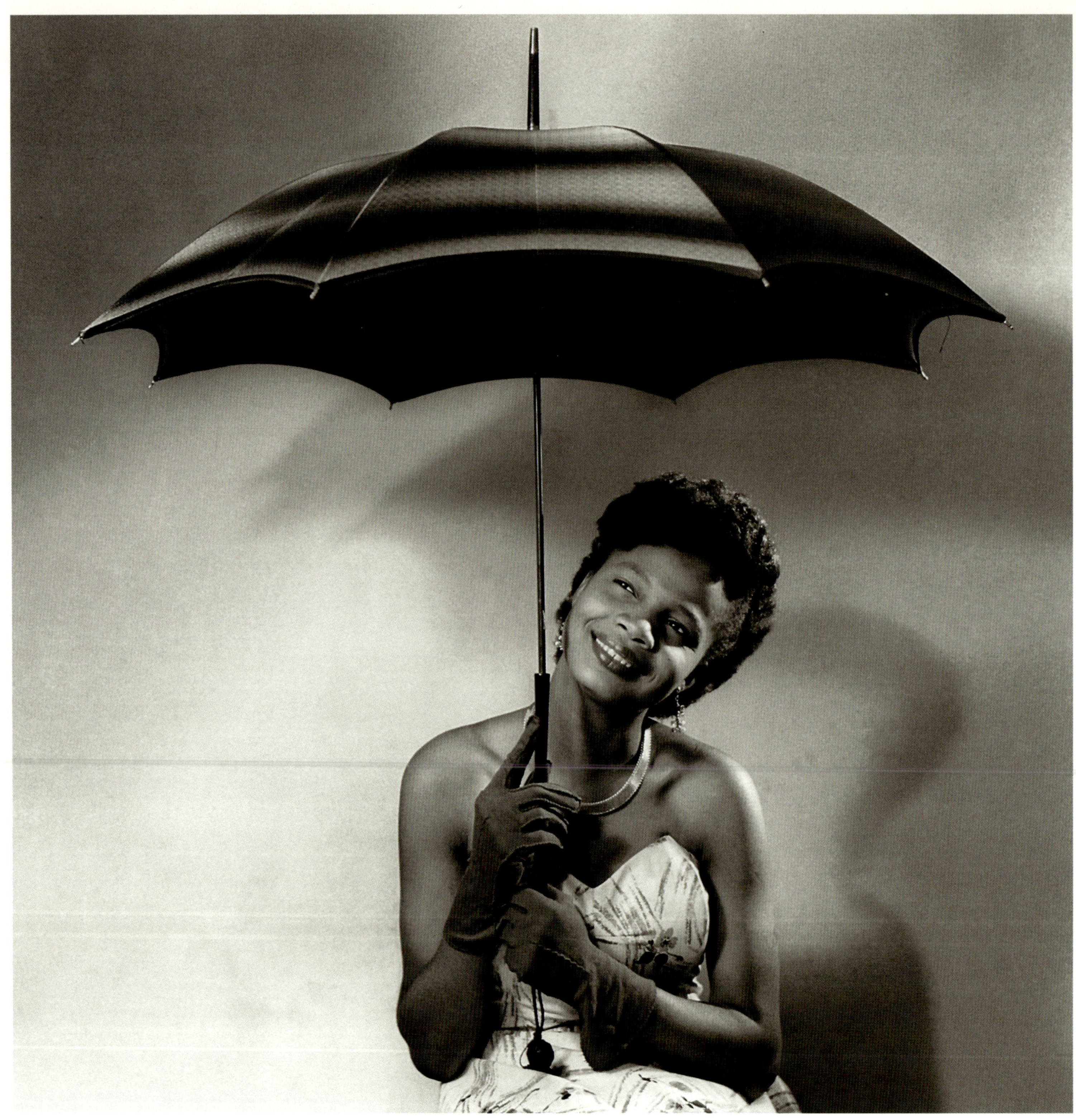

JOHANNESBURG 1954
Imelda Nicol just blew into the office the other
day... the editorial staff stood agape with wonder.
Then our beauty scout burst into life. He seized
her and dragged her into the studio. Such beauty,
such form, such personality.

JÜRGEN SCHADEBERG

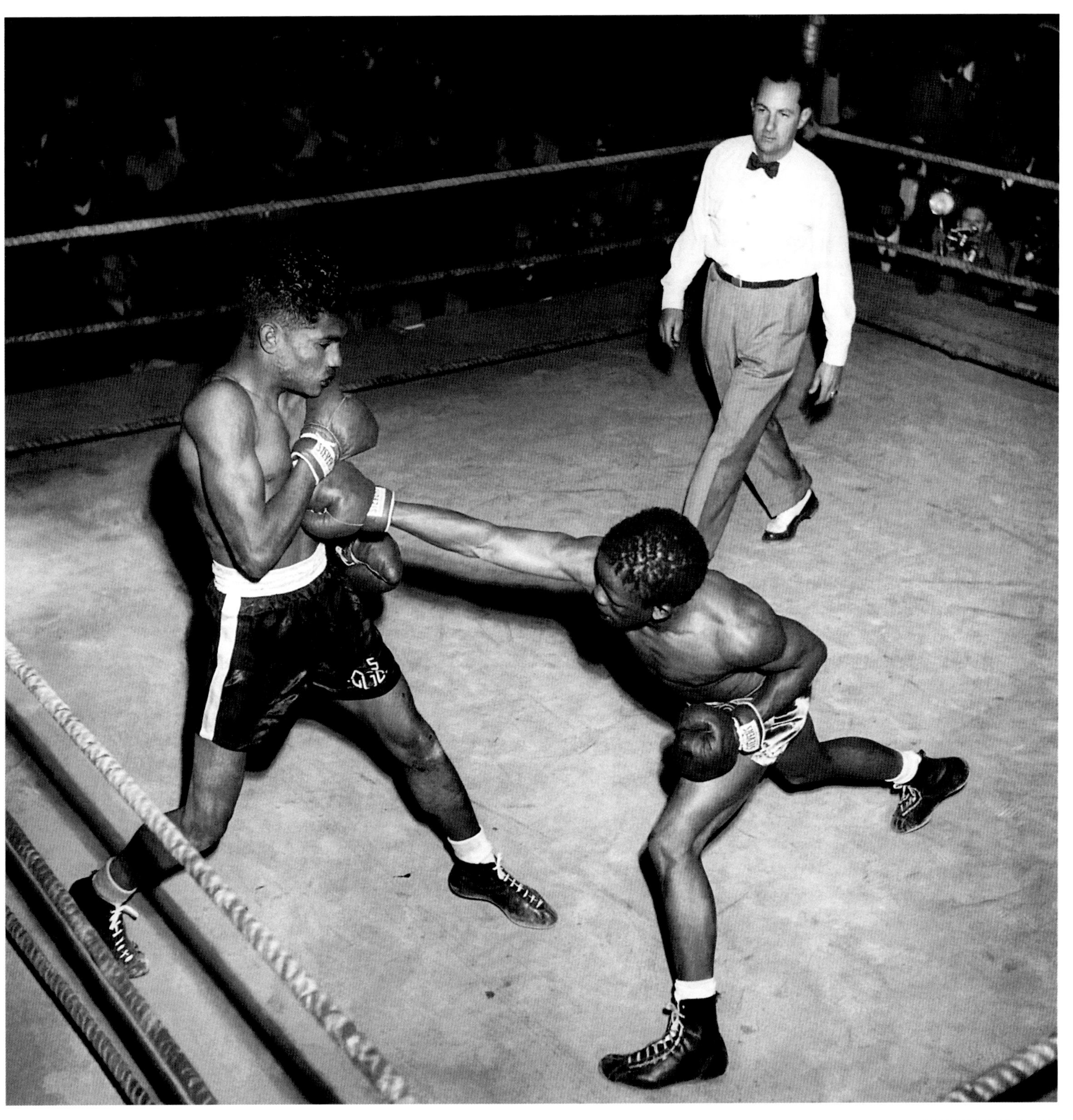

JOHANNESBURG 1952
Jake Tuli, Empire Flyweight Champ. In May 1952
Jake throws a straight right to Shaik Osman's
body, defending his South African Bantamweight
title. Then, on 8 September 1952, Jake beat the
Empire Flyweight Champion, Teddy Gardner, in
England. He gave the Britisher such a going-over
that Gardner gave up in the 12th round.

JÜRGEN SCHADEBERG

Jazzin' the Blues

Samuel Tutu who always practiced the accordion on the train, he told me: 'Boy, I was the lion of the keyboard until one helluva boy came and grabbed the crown right out of my hands. He was Meekley "Fingertips" Matshikiza. I was playing at a dance when Meekley walked in. He played after me and the next morning I took the first train and quit East London for Johannesburg.'

Meekley Matshikiza, my eldest brother, is now a retired musician in Queenstown. He has seven sons who all play the piano like nobody's business.

Maybe if they were around in the early 1930s, they'd have been house pianists around the famous joints like the 'African Hall' in Doornfontein or the 'Ebenezer Hall' in Ferreirastown and other houses where the people were taking to ballroom dancing.

Nobadula Hall Memories. I remember scampering through the back door in 1938. I was a member of a concert party with RT Caluza, touring the Union. A shot was fired and I remember seeing a dagger in the air. The little boy that was me made straight for the door.

Also the night at the Bantu Sports Club when Snowy Radebe was singing. I had heard great singers — Rhoda Bhengu, Faith Caluza, Marie Dube, Linda Nkosi and numerous polished, trained voices. I loved these women. I loved singers. I loved Rhoda Bhengu, and she became my adopted mother at school.

But when I heard Snowy at the Bantu Sports Club I had never before heard a voice of such great power, range, beauty and sheer magnificence. Something hit me, and I knew it was love. I loved Snowy. The kind of love when a little boy loves a big girl and is shy but wants to tell her. I didn't know what it was. They told me it was 'calf-love'. Love of something magnificent and out of reach. Really, we all loved her music.

I loved the dingy lights of the club house. The smell of roast meat from the kitchen behind the stage. The people muttering through tobacco smoke and rhythm pounding through my head. I loved the powerful piano tones of Samuel Tutu and I stood in a haze. Snowy's soprano, Tutu's piano, roast meat and jazz overpowered me and I fainted over the piano. Singer Ezekiel Mogale carried me out of the hall and poured cold water over my face. Voices were saying: 'The little boy is overpowered by the music.'

Todd Matshikiza
Africa 1954

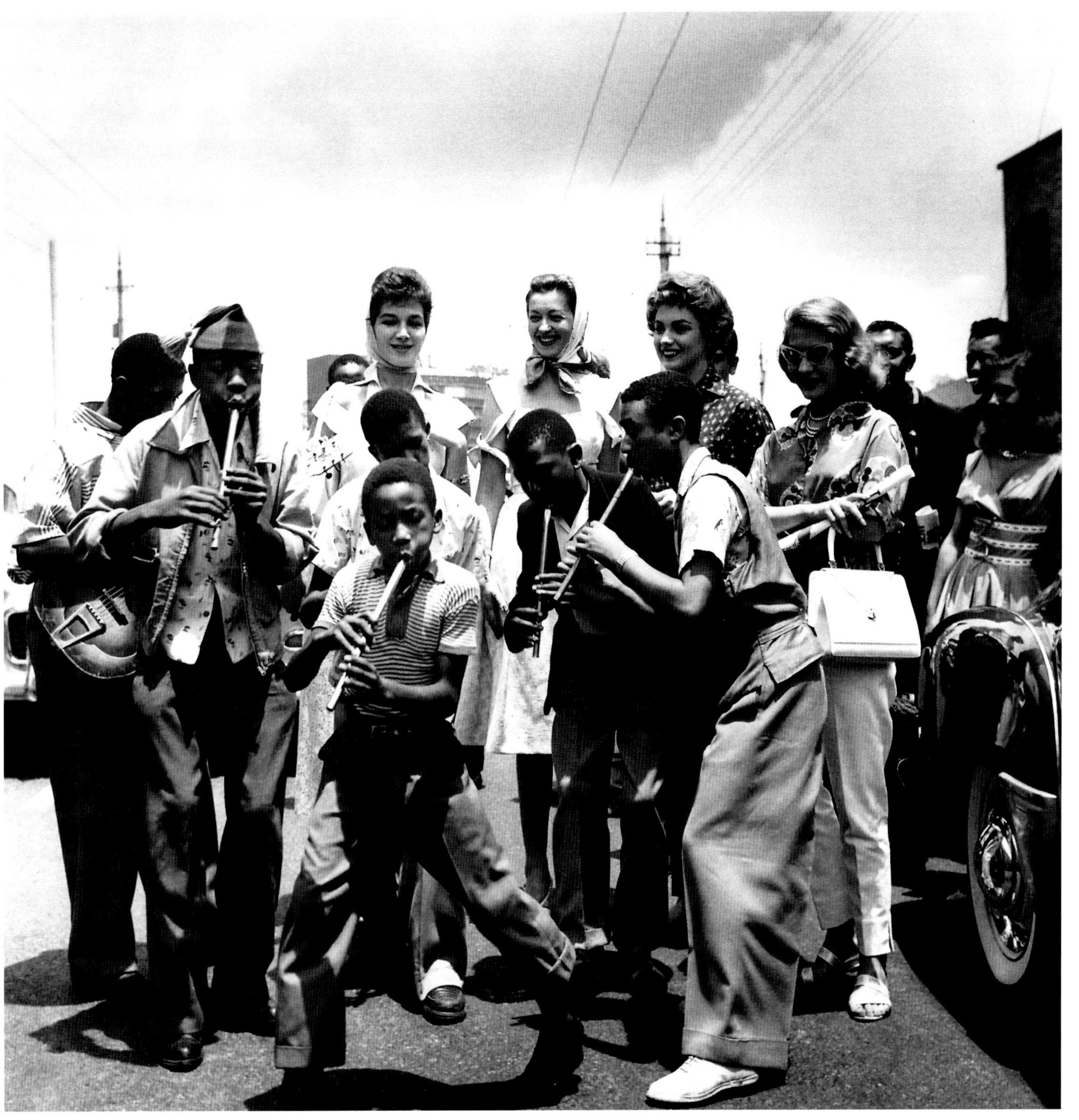

JOHANNESBURG 1953
'Wow! These boys have talent in their fingers'. Go along to a white suburb any evening and you'll hear
those flutes going. The black guys in these suburbs depend upon the flute and the guitar for most of their
fun. Under the dark shades in the cool avenues they gather and blow their whistles, guitars strumming
along. They've got a lot to learn, but not about enthusiasm. Yes, this is the boom of the penny whistle — it
costs about eight shillings!

JÜRGEN SCHADEBERG

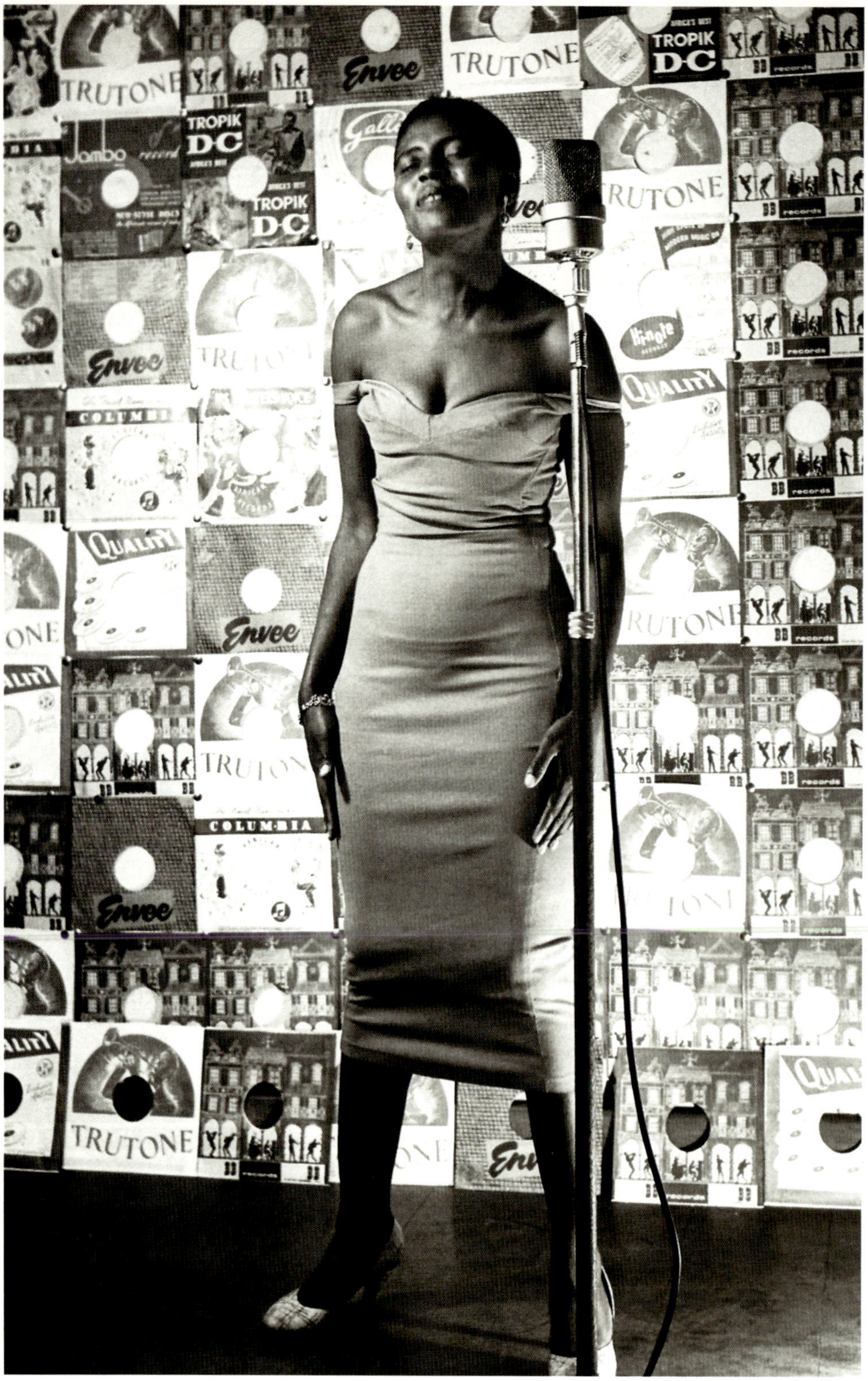

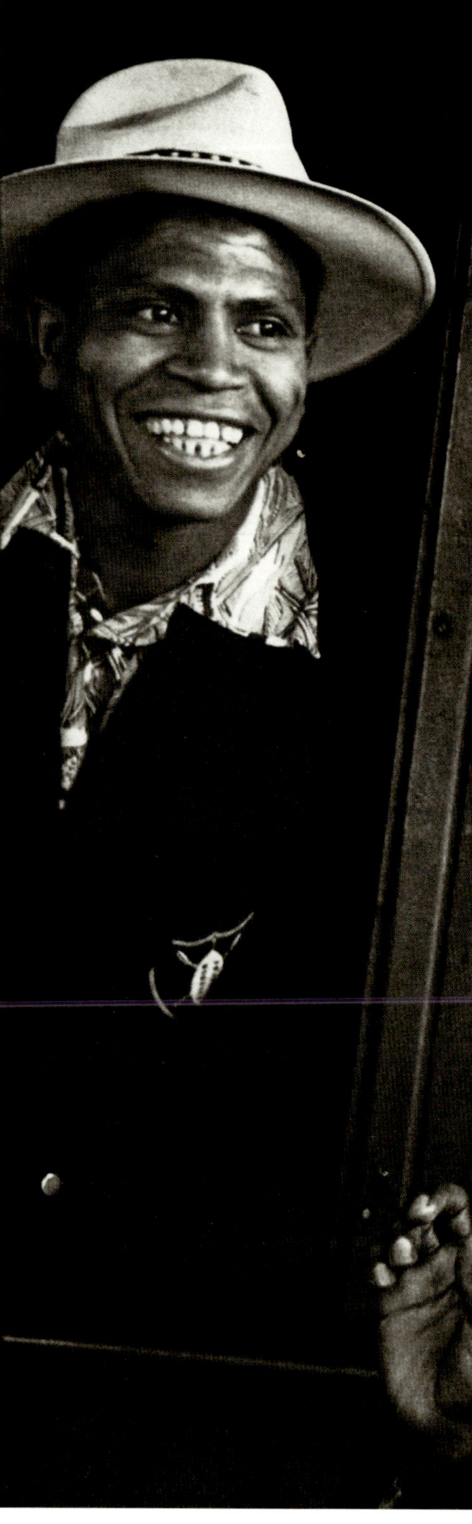

JOHANNESBURG 1955
Miriam Makeba.
One night, when singing at a charity show in Johannesburg, Nathan Mdledle, leader of the Manhattan Brothers, came up to Miriam and said 'I like the way you carry a tune', and he asked her to join his company. Soon after she joined them she made a disc of Mackay Davashe's **Lakutshon Ilanga**. *It was later translated into English as* **Lovely Lies**. *Miriam never looked back. In 1957 she teamed up with the African Jazz Group and met her first husband Sonny Pillay.*

JÜRGEN SCHADEBERG

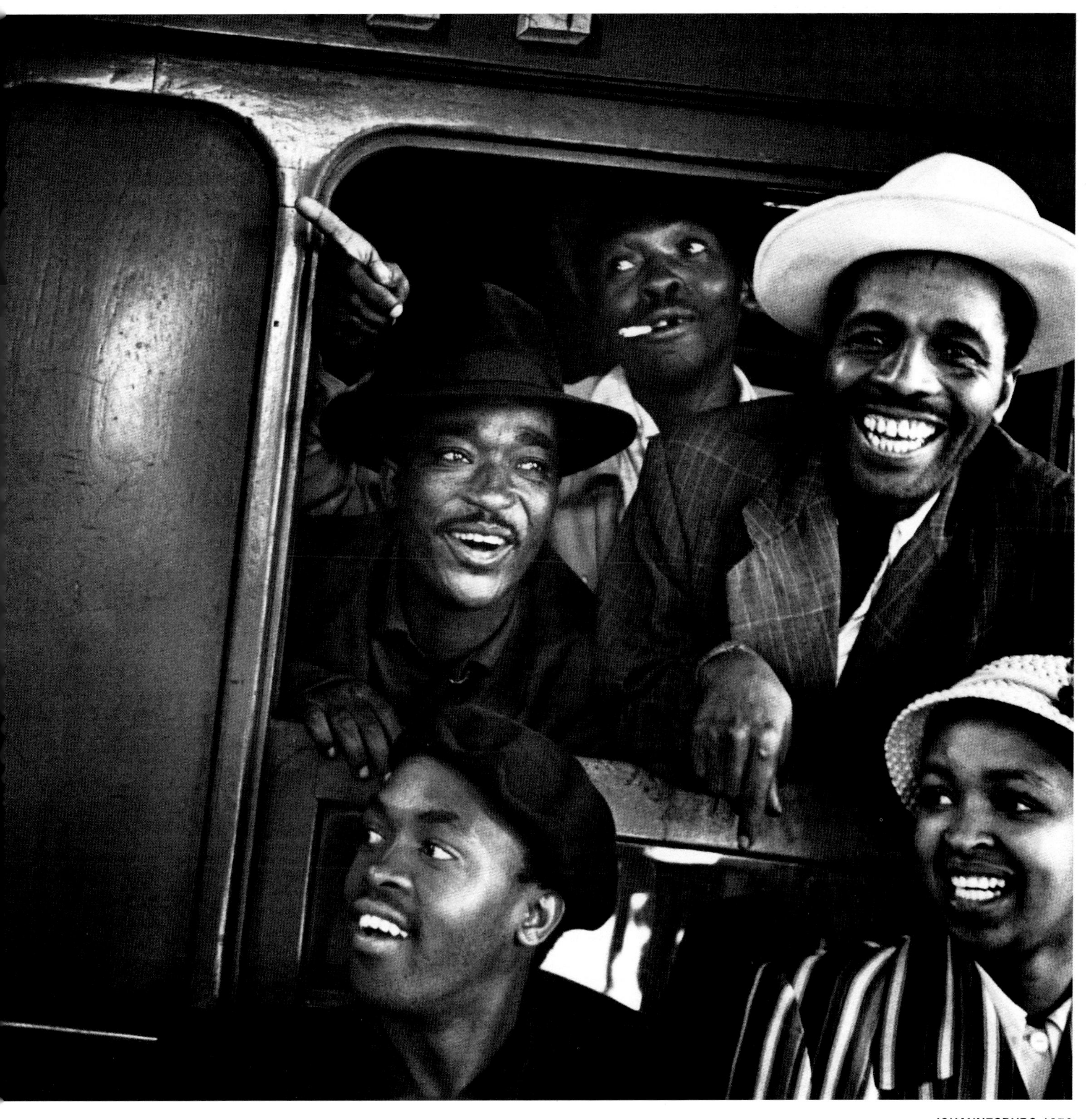

Leaving Johannesburg on the 'Jazz Train' to Durban. The African
Jazz Parade troop swung their way to the coast and the 'banana
city' went crazy! They travelled throughout South Africa, singing,
dancing and jazzing to packed houses — their tunes **Black
Magic, Skokiaan** and **The Sunny Side of the Street**. Dolly
Rathebe on the right.

BOB GOSANI

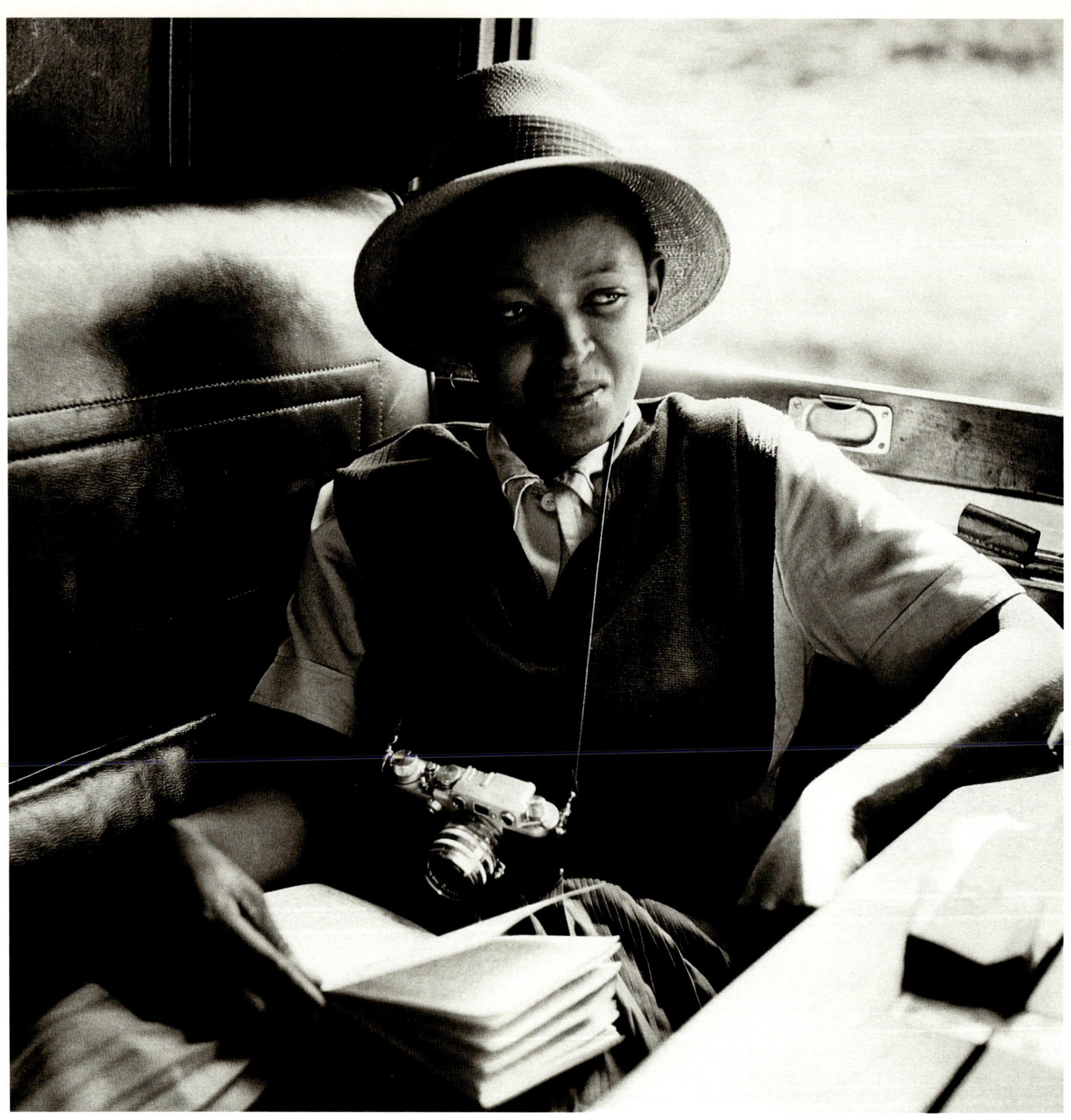

JOHANNESBURG — DURBAN
Blues singer Dolly Rathebe on the 'Jazz Train' touring South Africa.
Dolly started her career singing and jitterbugging at the old Theatre
of Africa Jazz Hall in Sophiatown. She sang in churches and at
weddings, and thrilled mourners with her singing at the wakes of
dead friends.

BOB GOSANI

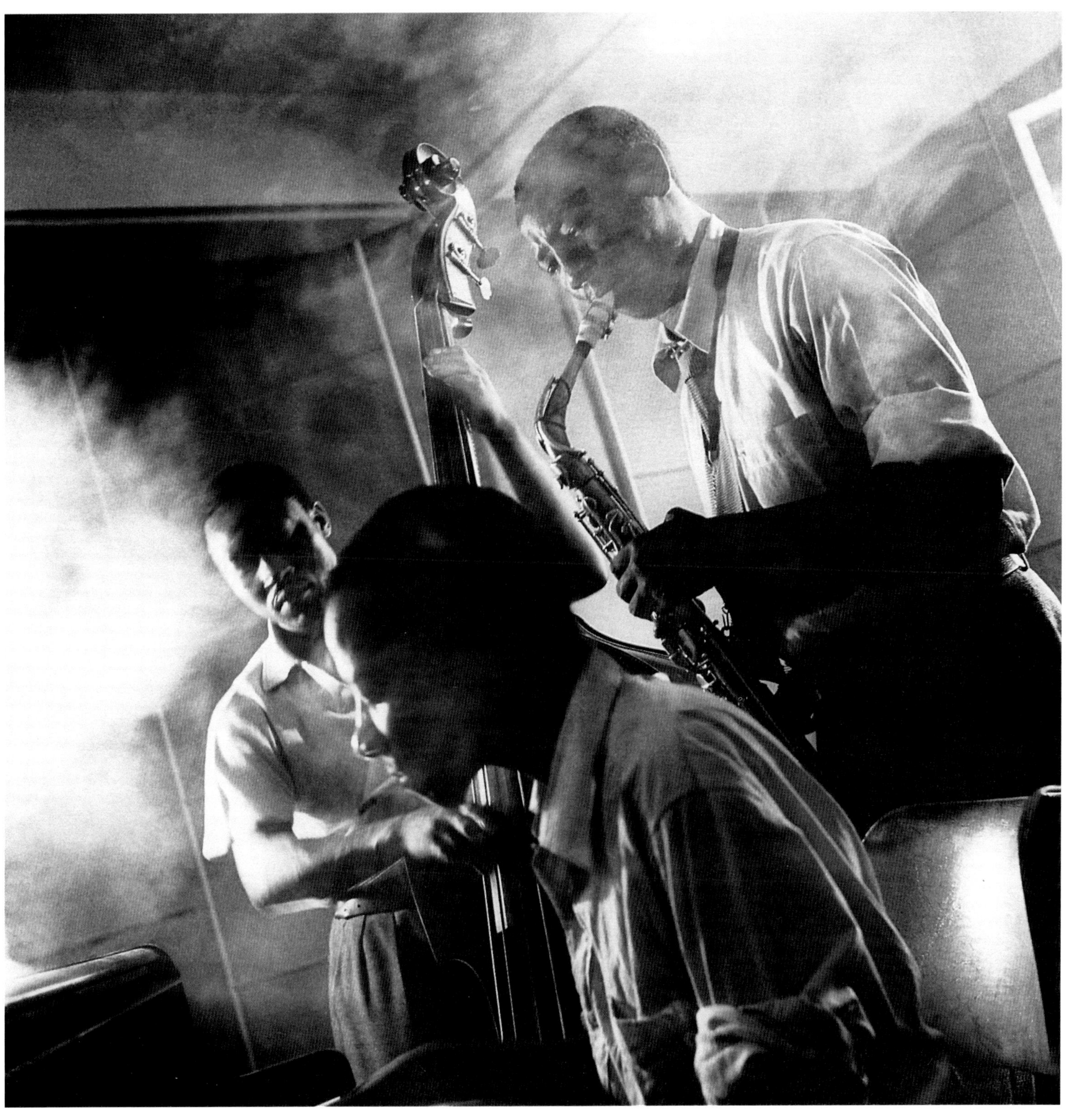

JOHANNESBURG 1953
The three Jazzolomos: Jacob 'Mzala' Lepers (bass) Ben 'Gwigwi' Mrwebi,
(alto sax) Sol 'Beegeepee' Klaaste (piano).
'We three, the Jazzdizzleers be. Non-stop eight to four am, that's what
makes us such dazzling dizzlers in the jazz business. Ragtime, swing, jazz
bop. An occasional gunshot whizbang 'gainst the wall behind you — till
four am'.

JÜRGEN SCHADEBERG

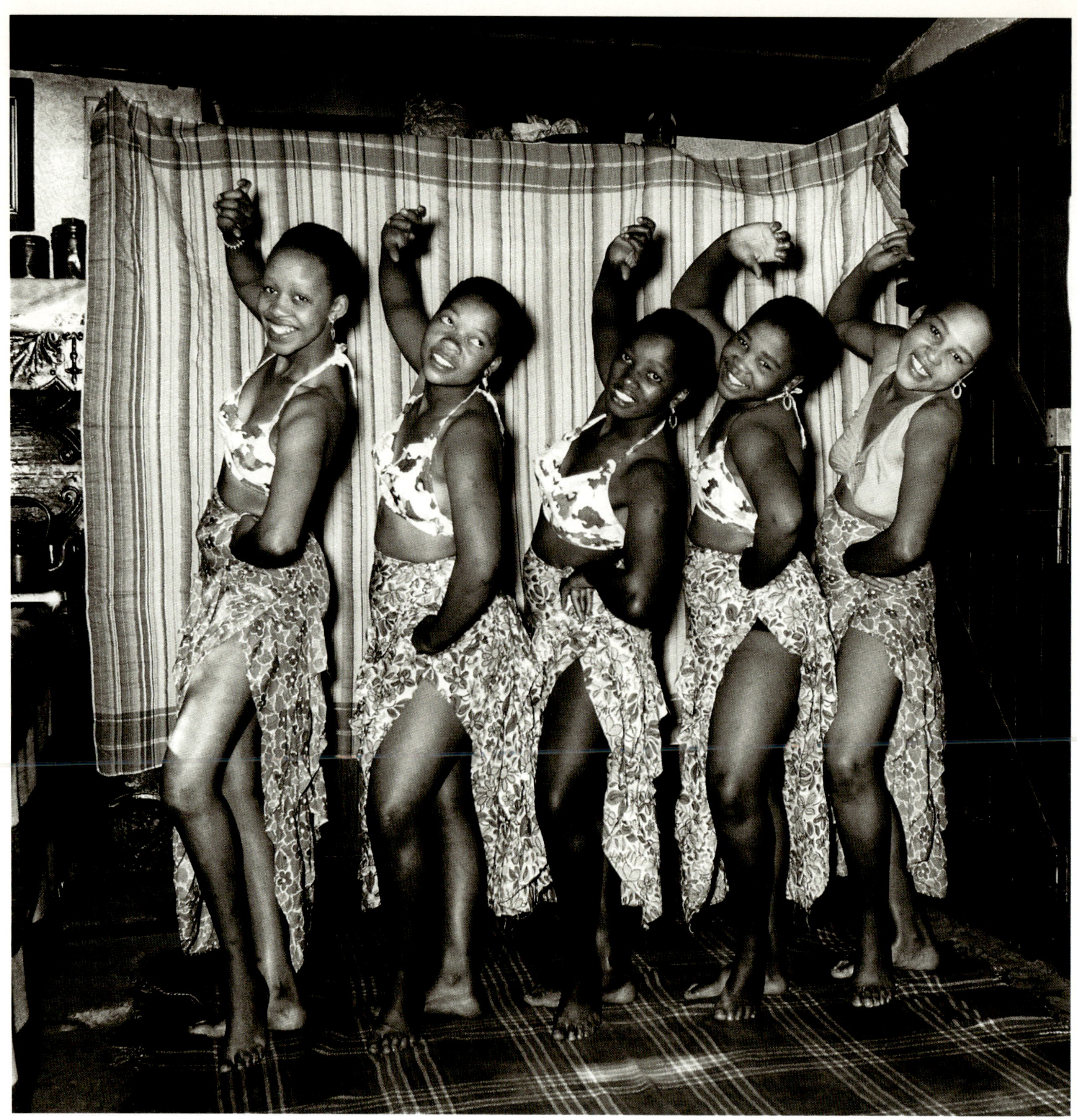

ORLANDO TOWNSHIP 1952
*I like the style of the 'Gay Gaieties' crowd. Pretty. Hard-
working. They go about it quietly. They spare their mouths
and throats for the stage. And they never fail to please you.
And what they haven't got in oomph is still to be got... as
one glance at these sizzling sizzlettes will tell you.*

JÜRGEN SCHADEBERG

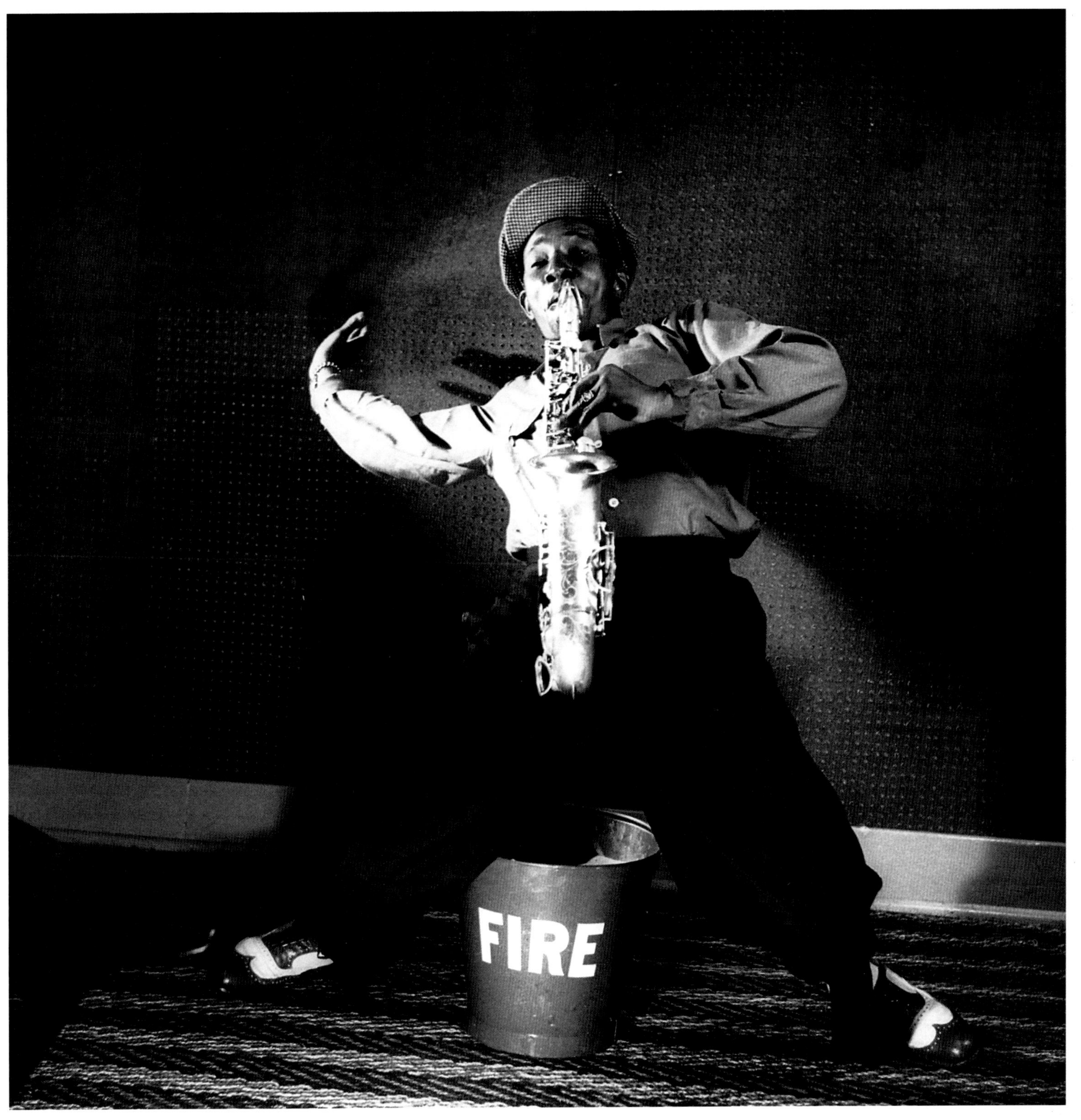

JOHANNESBURG 1952
Benni Benjo 'Gwigza' of Mrwebi, also known as
Gwigwi, clarinet, alto sax player, band leader,
clown and showman. Gwigwi was leader of the
Harlem Swingsters in the 1950s. Name a stage,
he was on it. Name a show, he was in it, playing
his clarinet and his alto sax. He played highbrow
and lowbrow with equal zest.

JÜRGEN SCHADEBERG

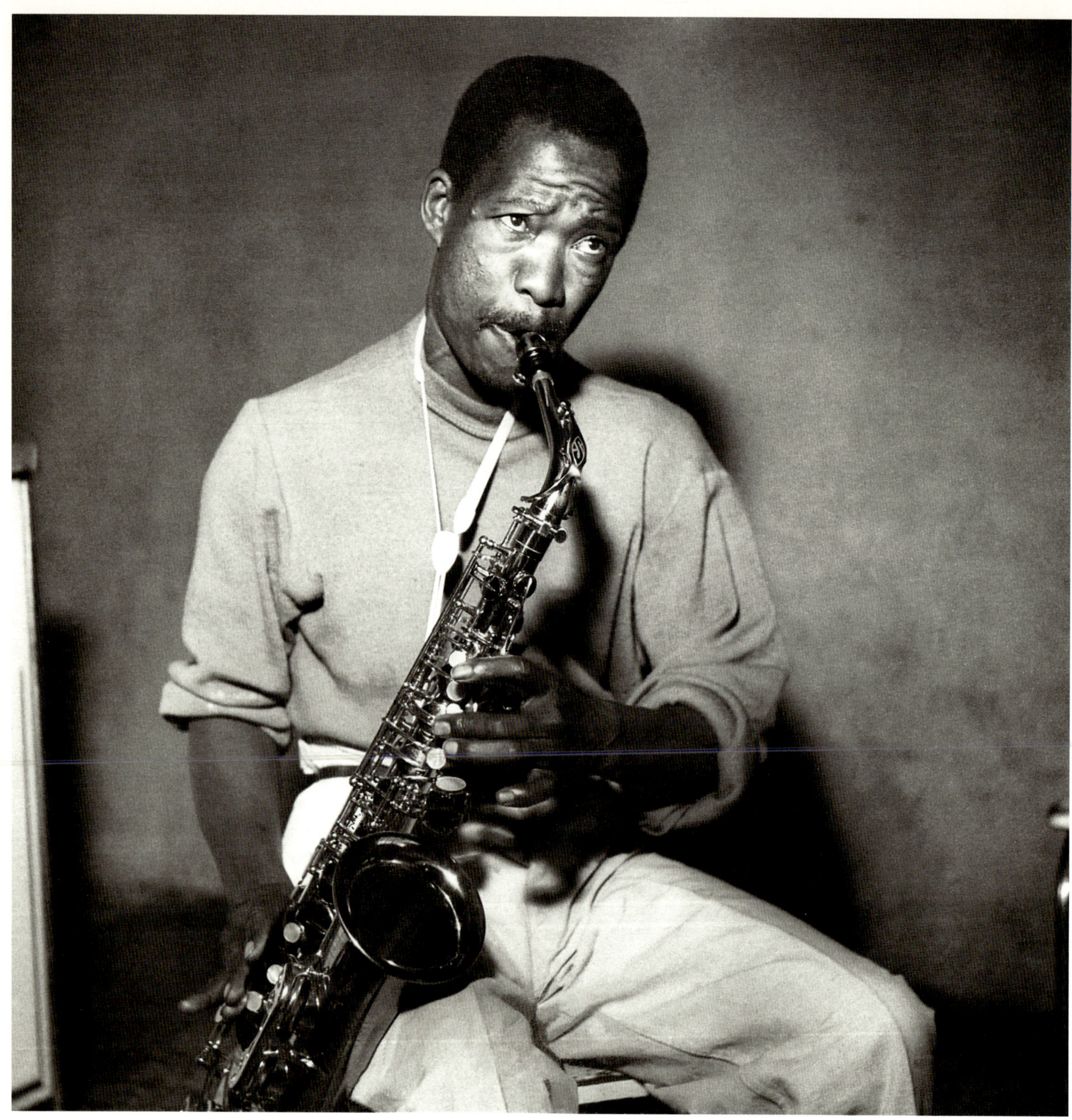

GEORGE GOCH 1952
Kippy 'Morolang' Moeketsi
*Kippy walked out of a Standard five classroom never to return. He started selling
newspapers and worked as a caddy at the golf course. He studied the clarinet and
started to play at dance-halls together with his guitar-playing neighbour General
Duze, Mackay Davashe and others. He refused to play 'Bantu' music or commercial
music. Kippy Moeketsi, all agreed, was a genius of the sax, perhaps the greatest
jazz man to come out of South Africa.*

JÜRGEN SCHADEBERG

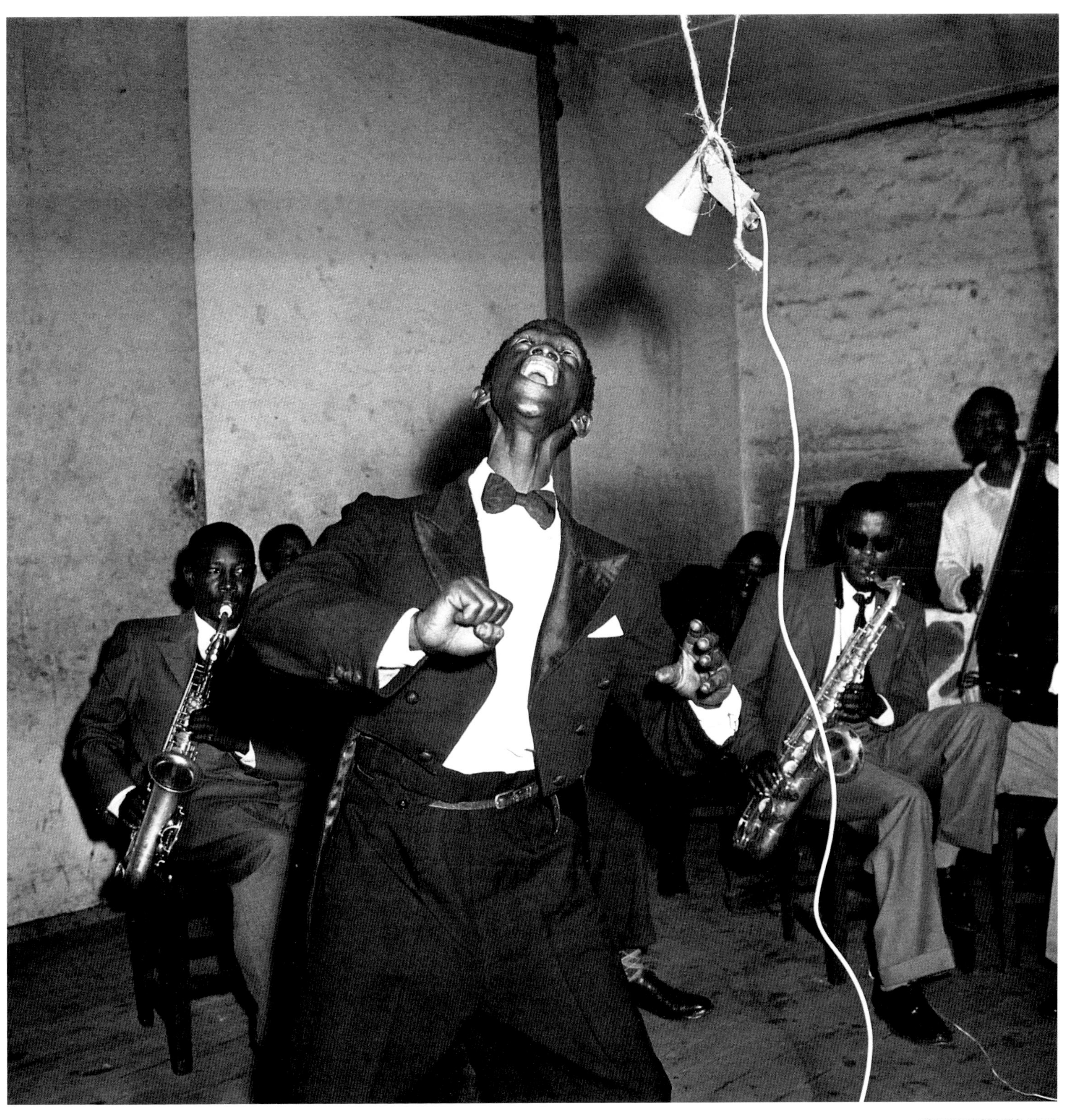

JOHANNESBURG 1955
'Old man river'
Every weekend in most music halls, small or
large, there were talent competitions for the
young and old.

GOPAL NARANSAMY

109

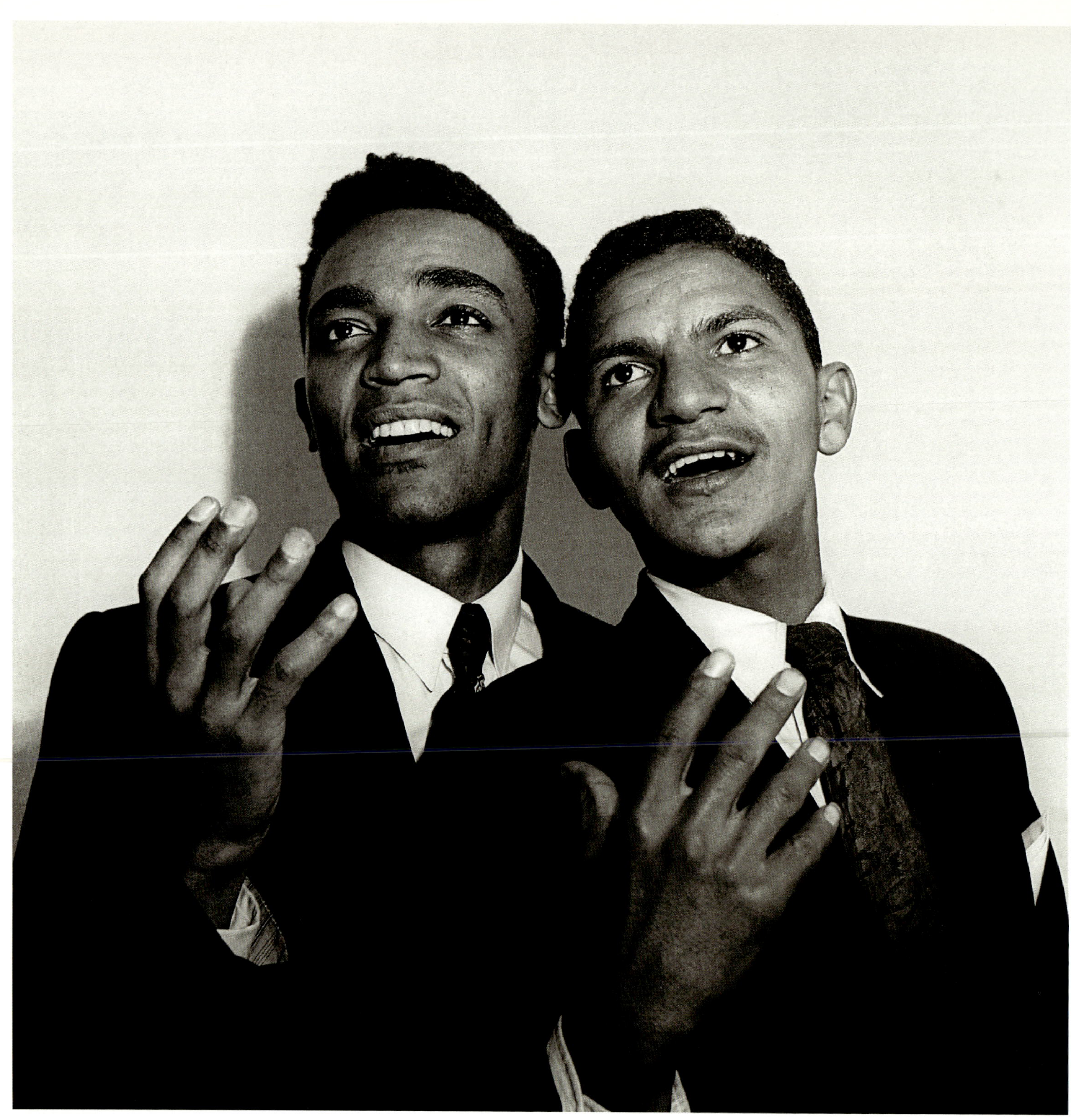

JOHANNESBURG 1957
Billy Birkenstock (left) and Joe Du Prooz, 'The
Duo from the Cape'. Billy later went to England,
singing with the Jack Parnell Orchestra, and
became known as Mr Sensation.

GOPAL NARANSAMY

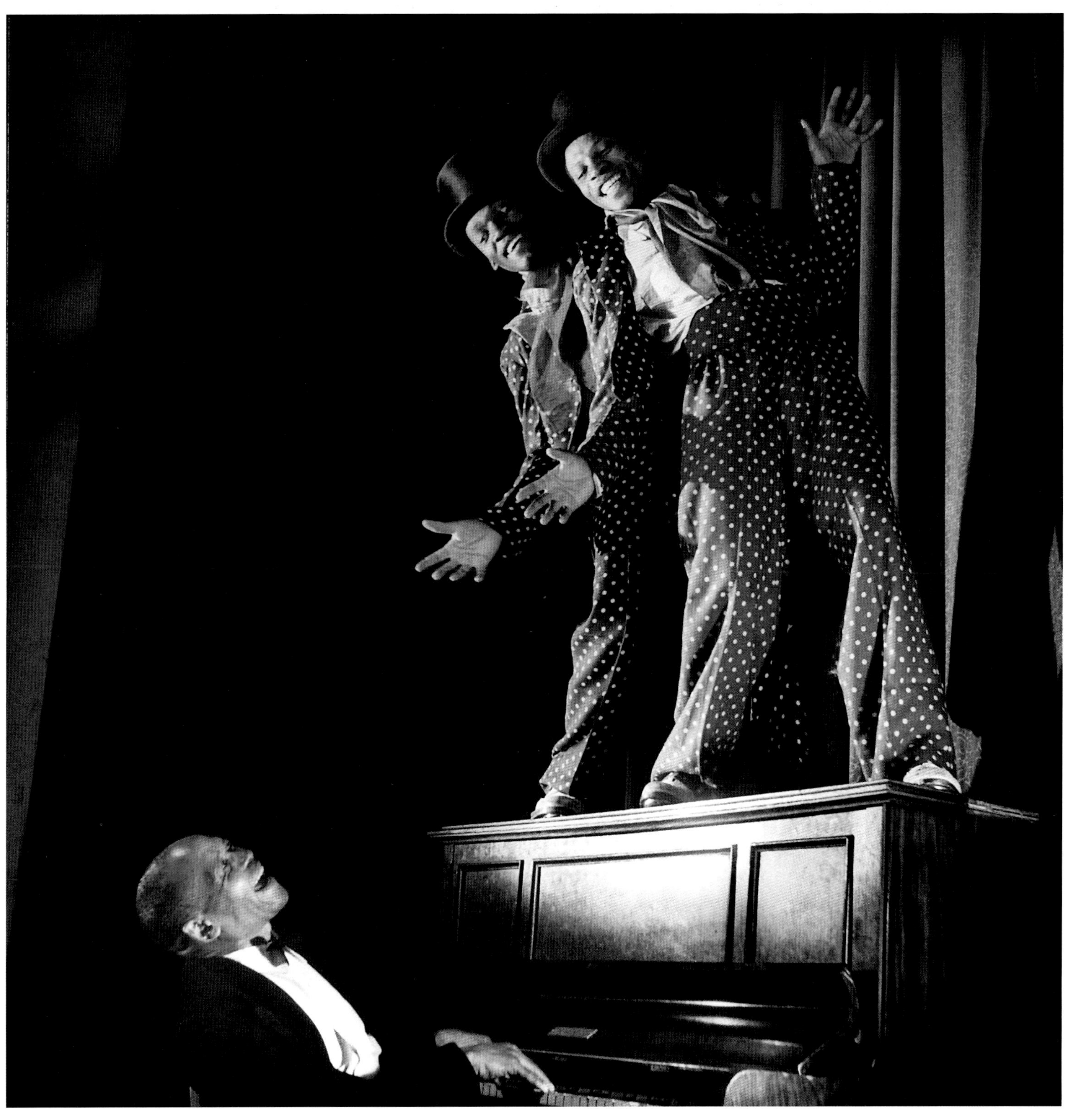

JOHANNESBURG 1951
A show on the piano for the photographer... and
then there was August Msarurgwa from
Zimbabwe. He composed **Skokiaan**. Everybody
went crazy about it. They recorded it and
Louis-Armstrong-Satchmoed it.

JÜRGEN SCHADEBERG

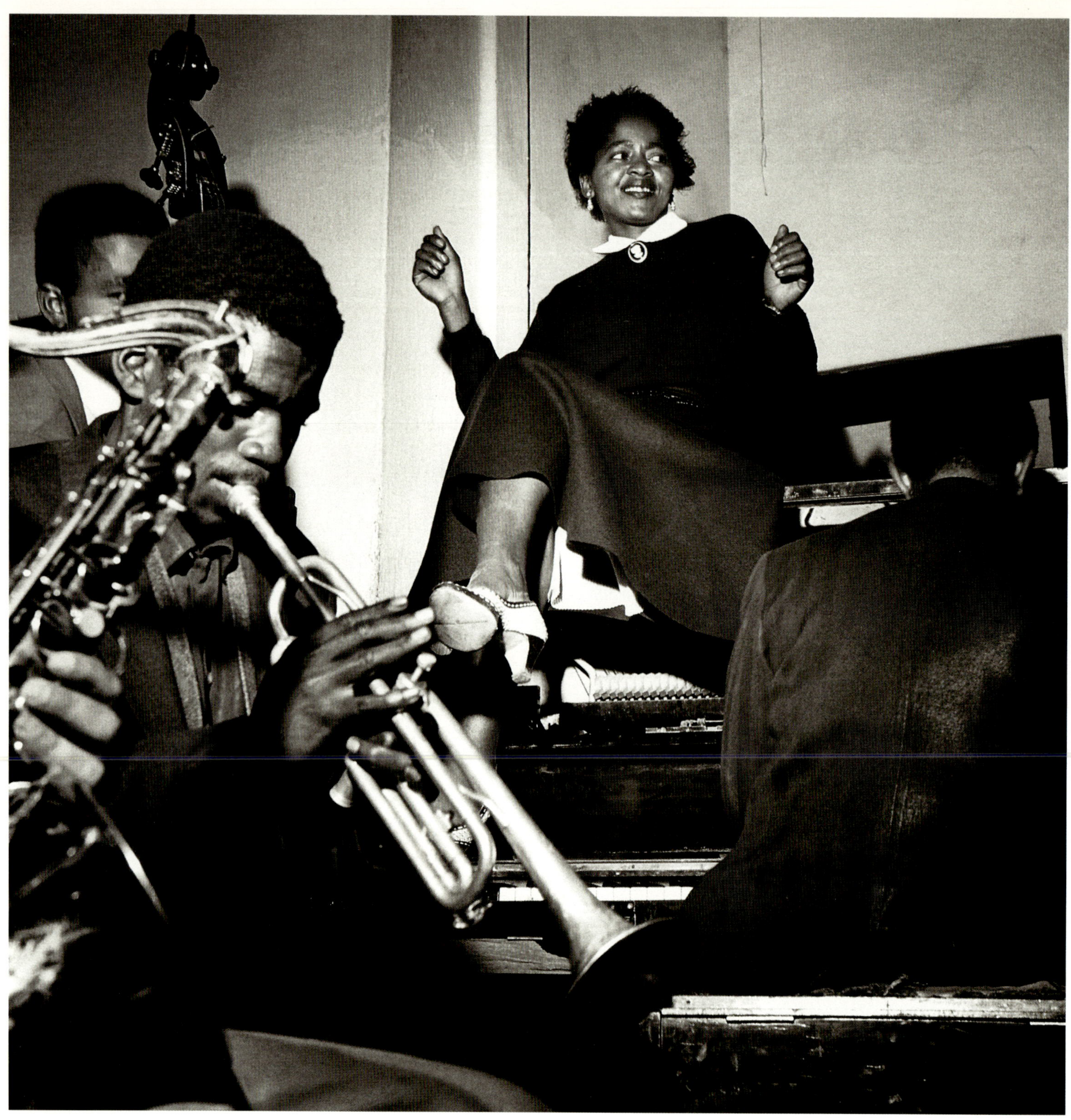

SOPHIATOWN 1952
*A wild jam session. If jazz comes from Africa and rocks America, then it must be darned good. It started with **Mbube**, which they called **Wimoweh**. This was Solomon Linda's music.*

JÜRGEN SCHADEBERG

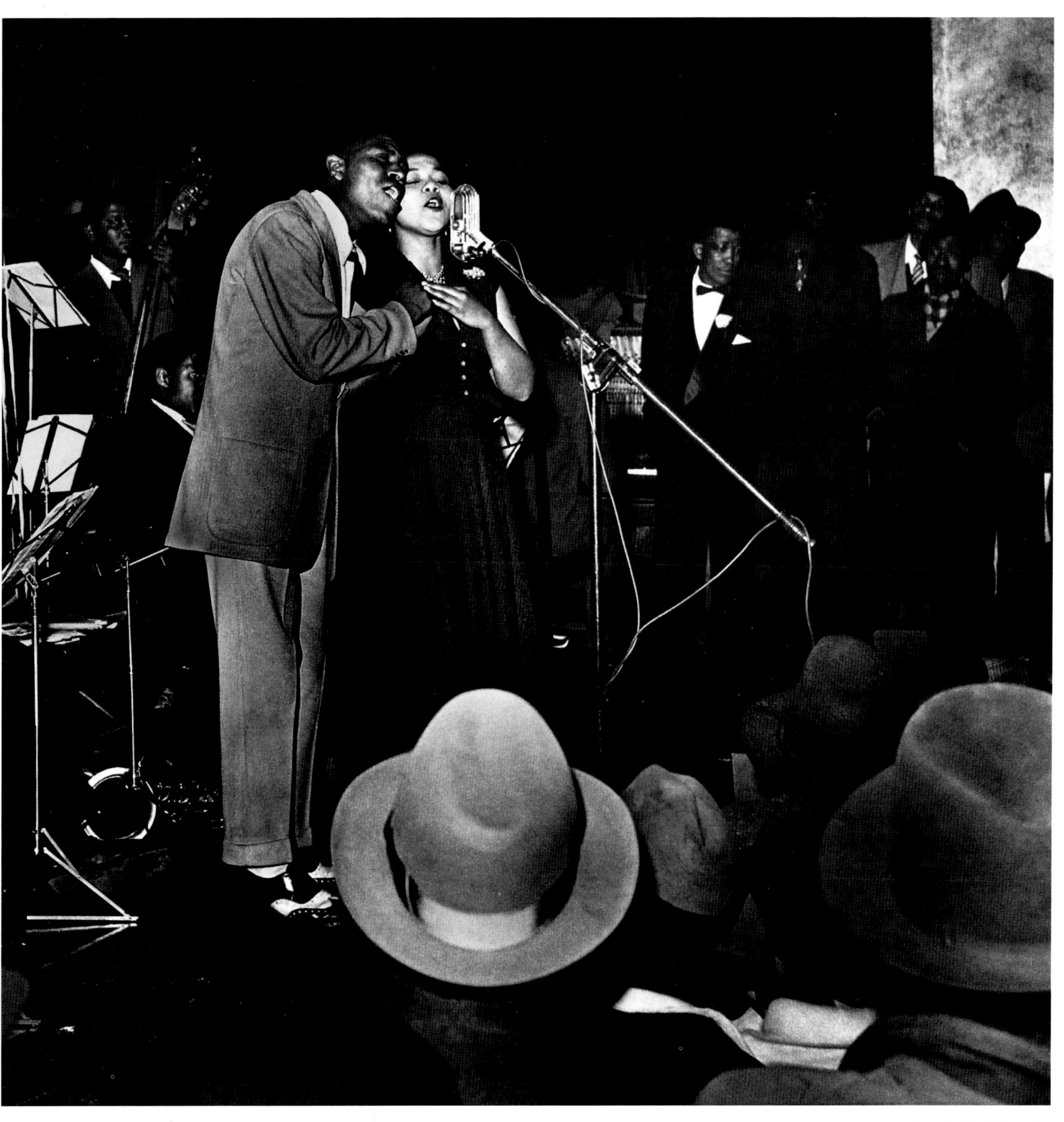

JOHANNESBURG 1957
Louisa Emanuel with Isaac Peterson.
'Confess, confess... why don't you confess?' —
was the song of thcir success.

BOB GOSANI

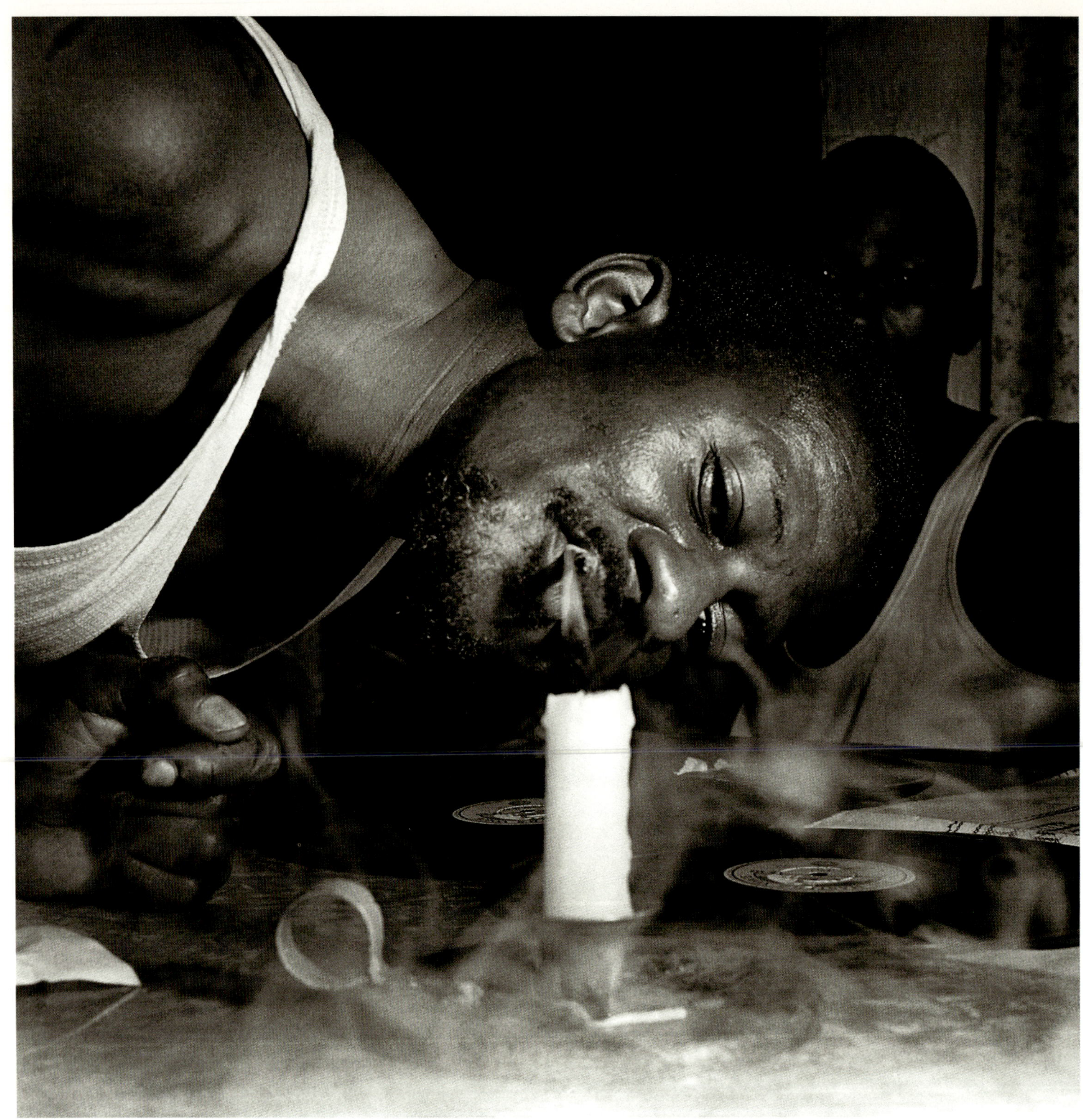

ORLANDO TOWNSHIP 1954
Saxophonist Wilson 'King Force' Silgee — one of
the jazz pioneers of the 1930s. His music made
you stop dead, beat your chest and cry out loud
with the jazz force of his tenor horn. King Force
was the life blood of the great Jazz Maniacs
Orchestra.

BOB GOSANI

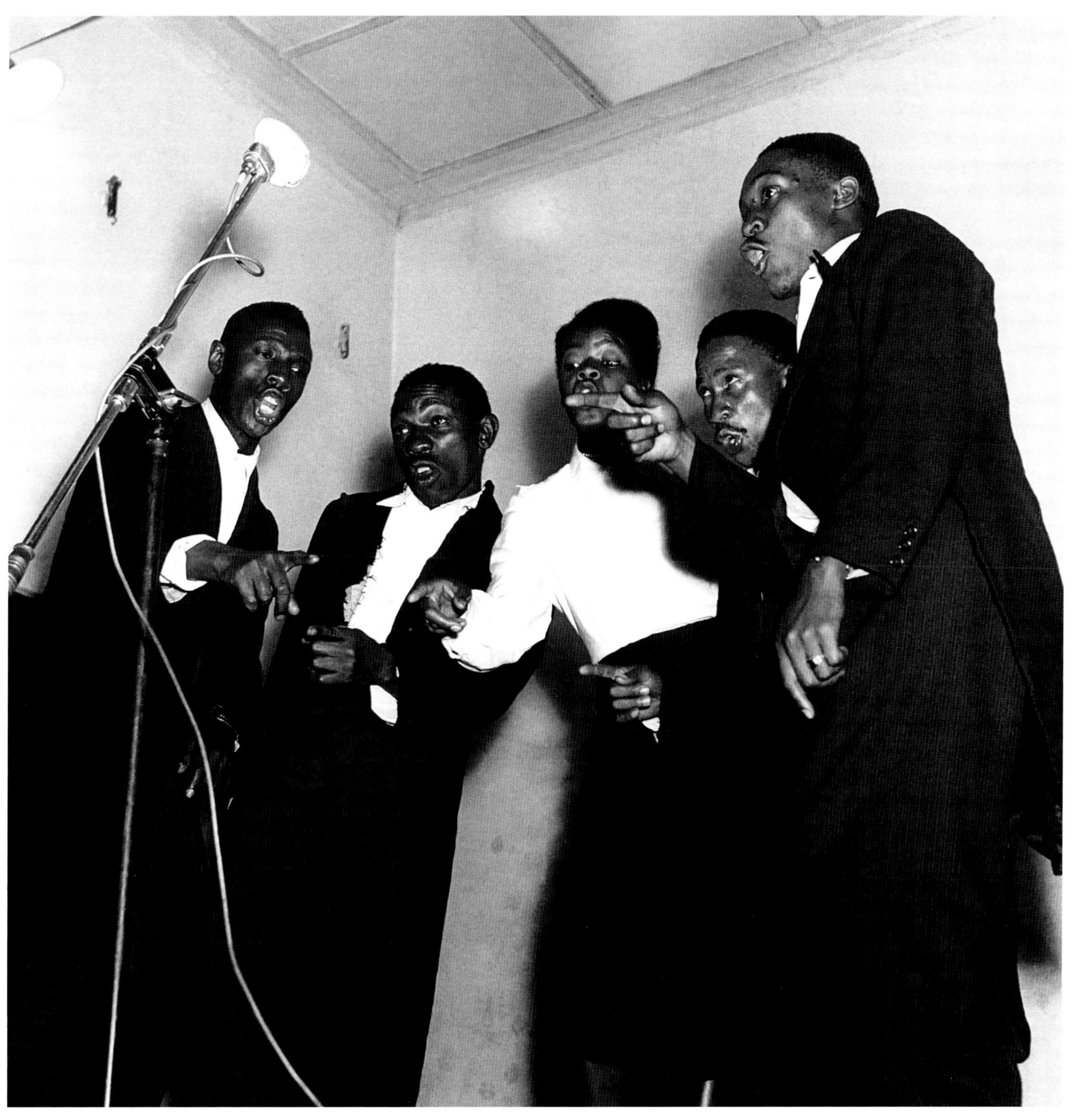

'Ahaha! There's something in the air', sang the Manhattan Brothers, together with 'Blues Queen' Emily Kwenane, Nat 'Dambuza' Mdledle, Rufus Koza, Ronny Sehume and Joe Mogotsi.

In 1934 four boys between the ages of eight and ten years old put their heads together and sang. The infant tones were crude, but there was harmony. They found that they could sing together so they teamed up. The Manhattan Brothers stayed together, shouting the blues, howling the boogie-woogie beat, jamming the jazz idiom, or moaning the sad ballads of love. In 1955 in Johannesburg they celebrated their 21st year in show business. They discovered Miriam Makeba and became stars in the King Kong Jazz Opera.

JÜRGEN SCHADEBERG

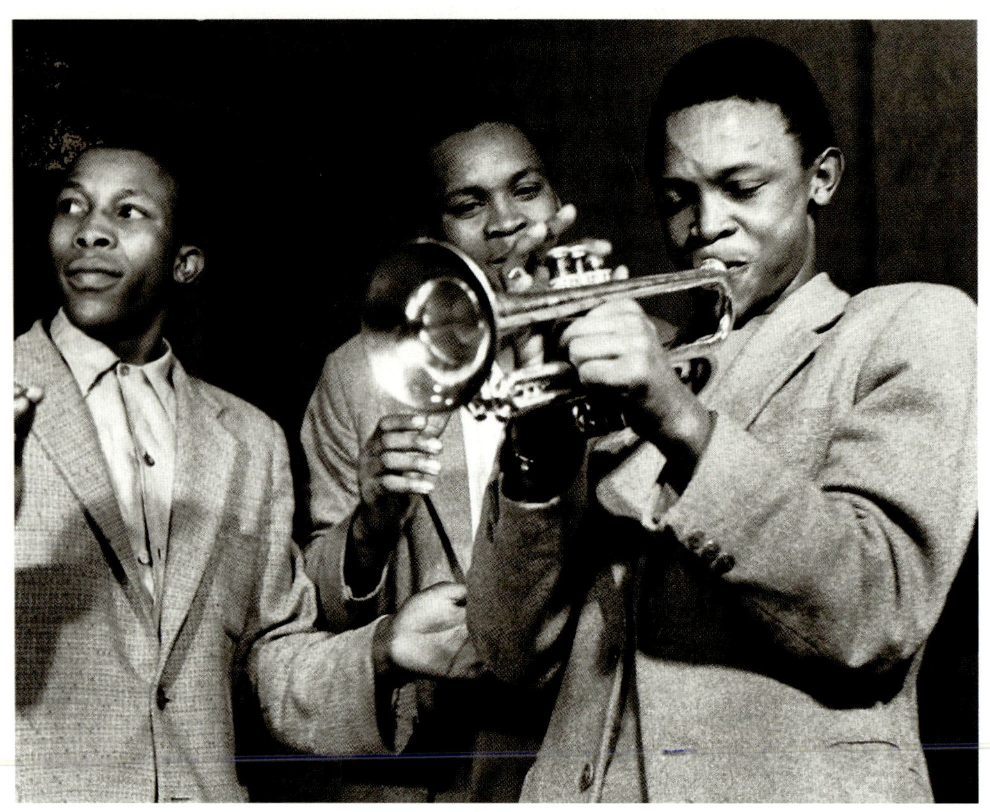
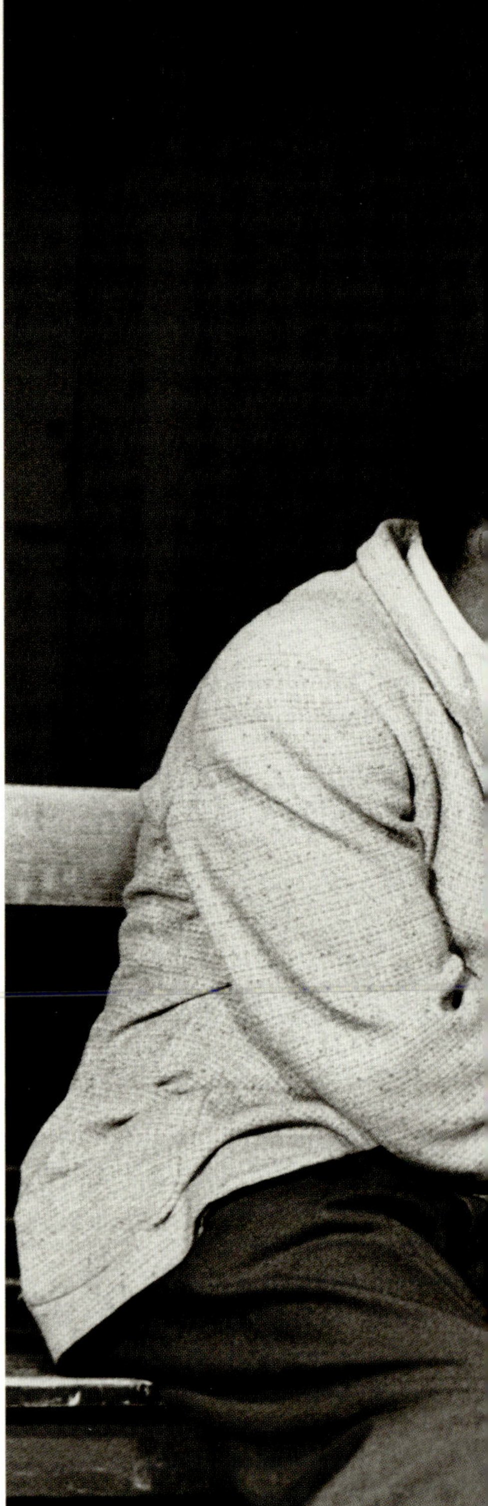

JOHANNESBURG 1954
Father Trevor Huddleston, a strong supporter of African music, organised a trumpet from the famous Satchmo for the young Hugh Masekela.

JÜRGEN SCHADEBERG

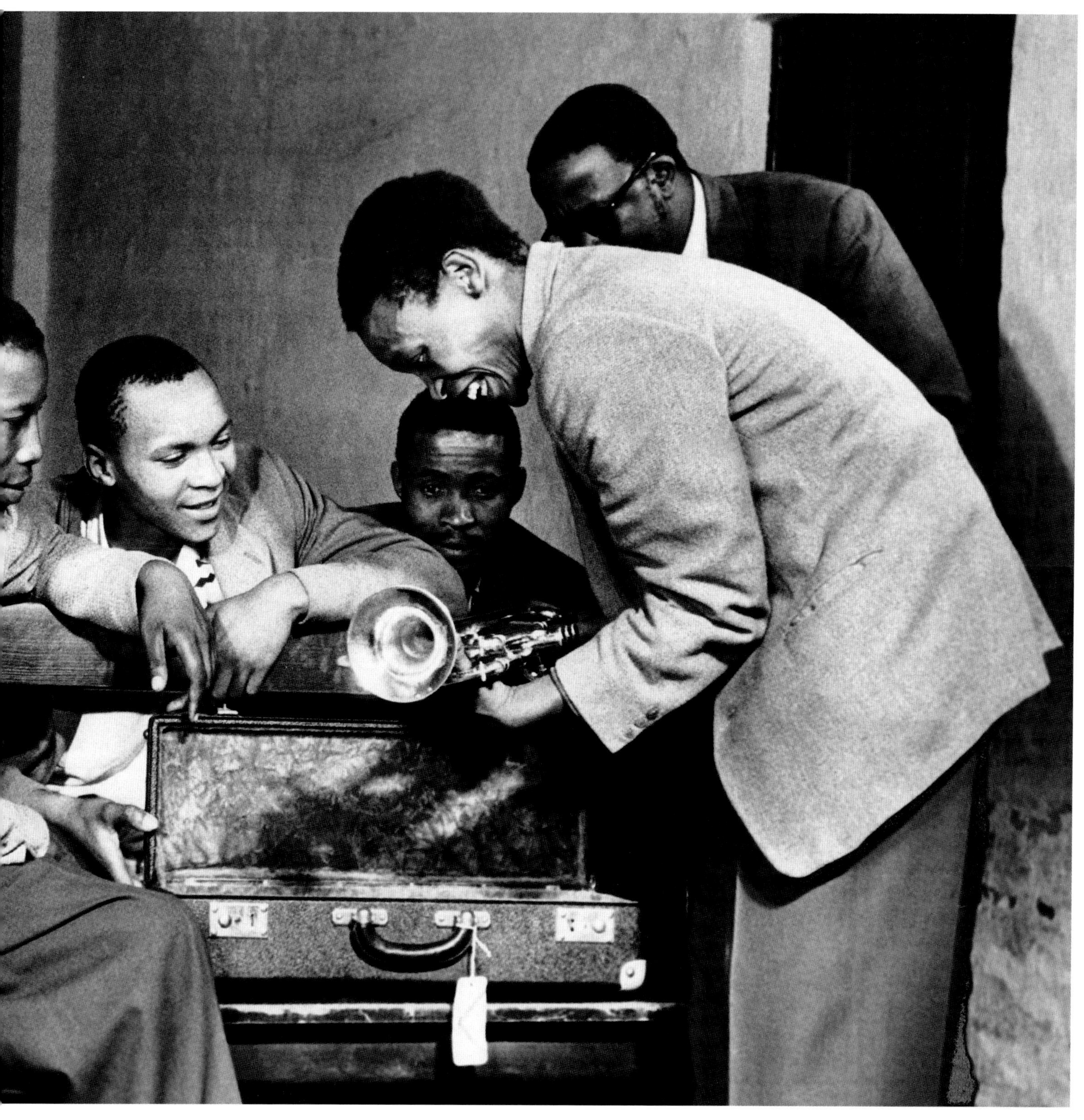

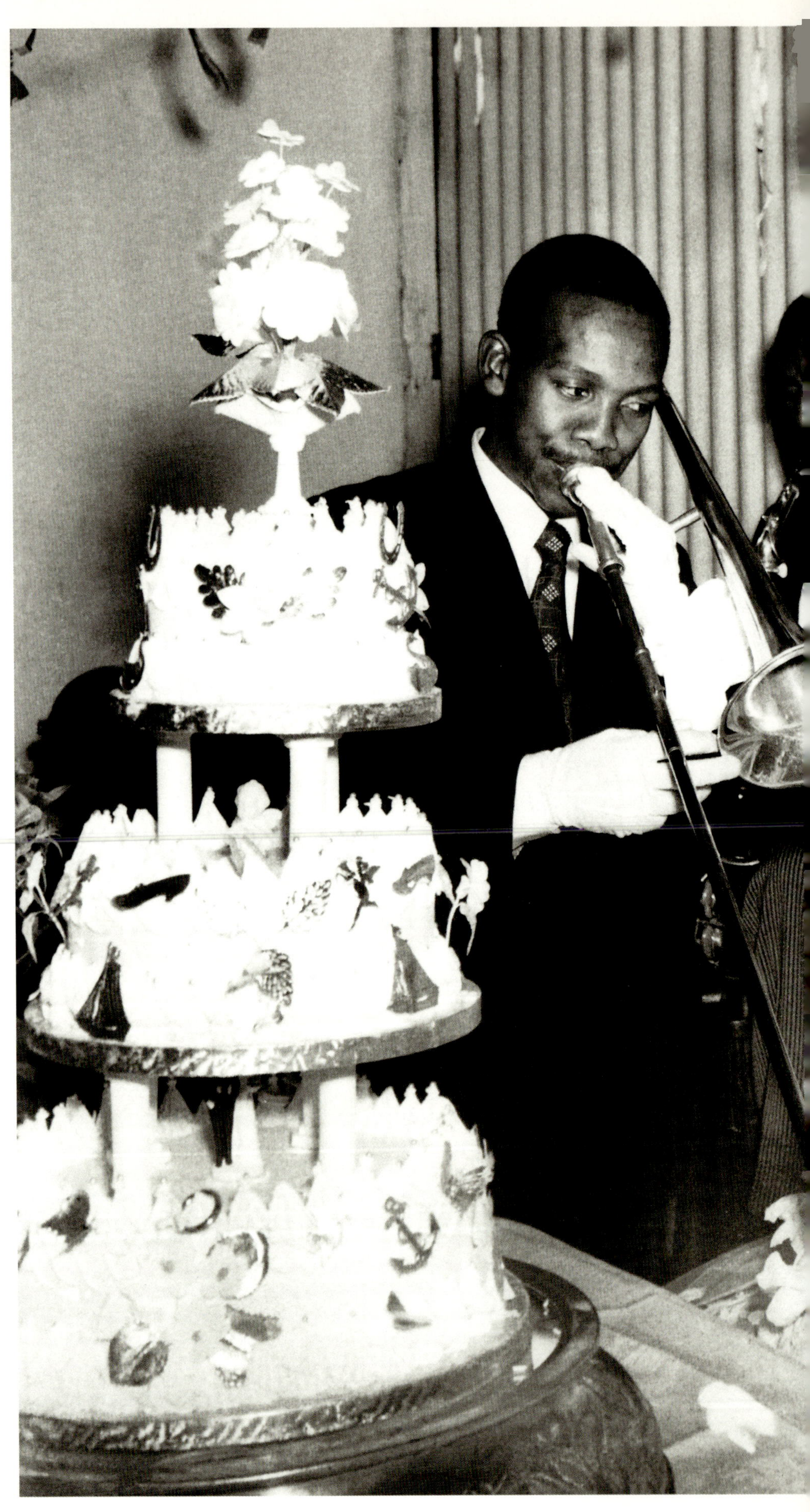

SOPHIATOWN 1956
Wedding Party.
JÜRGEN SCHADEBERG

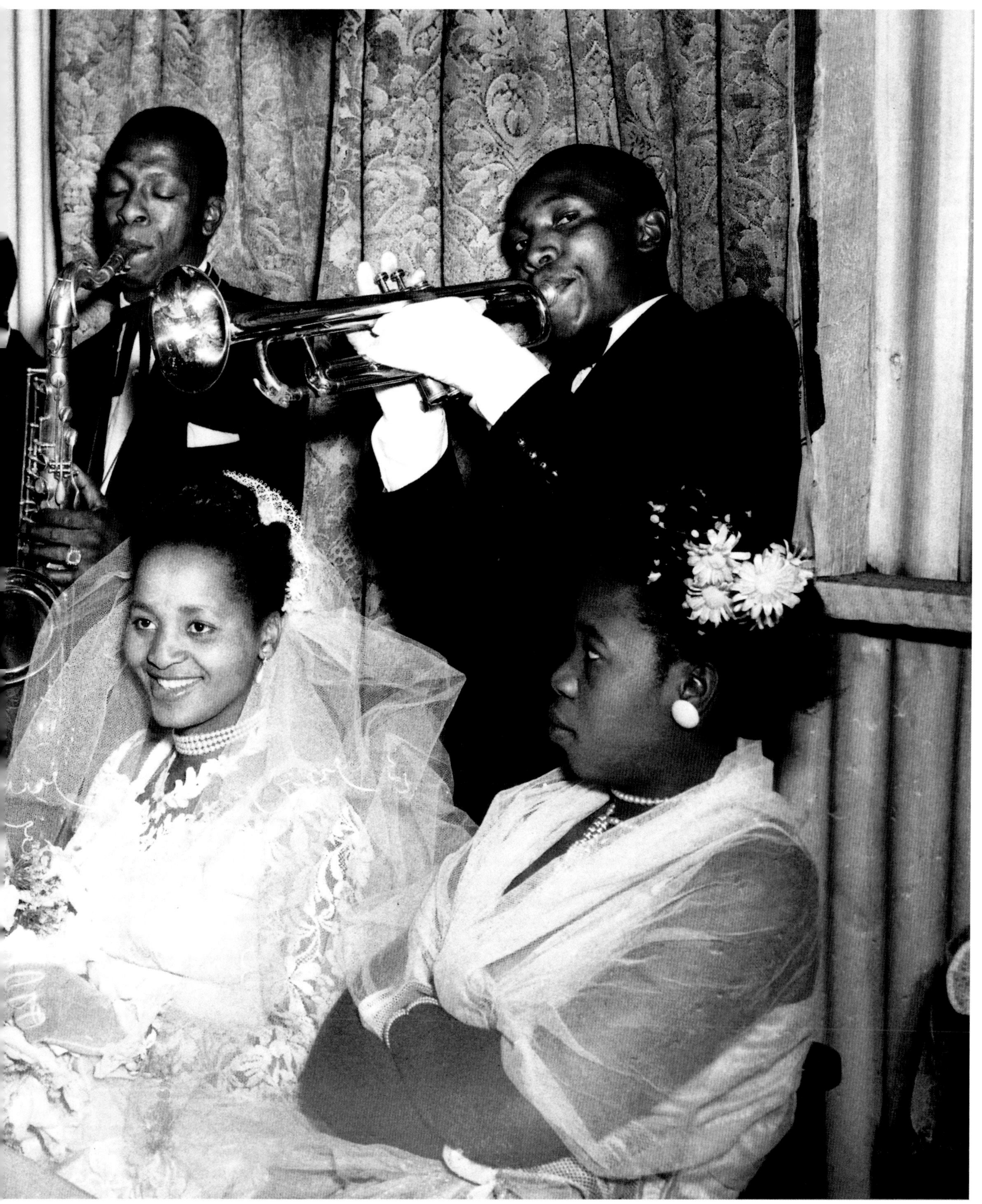

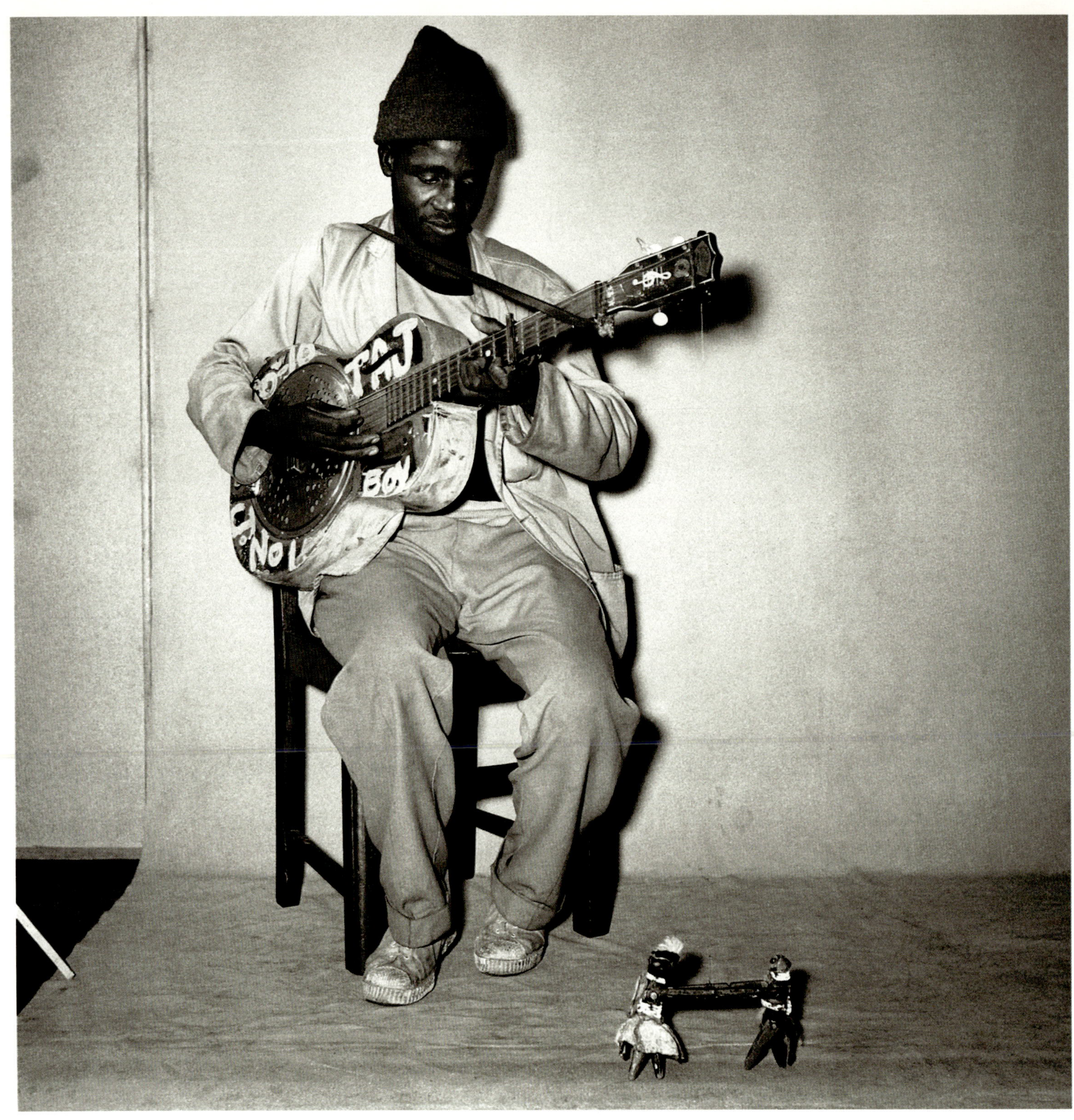

JOHANNESBURG 1954
Street singer Taj Boy No 1
'I guess I been singing since the day I was born — like every baby
when he's crying. Boy dat's a concerto! How I started pluckin' dis
here box of strings is just a simple affair. I made one for myself after
seein' a movie pitcher of Gene Autry and some boys in de prairies. In
no time I was a cowboy right in de middle of de street, without de
prairies....'

JÜRGEN SCHADEBERG

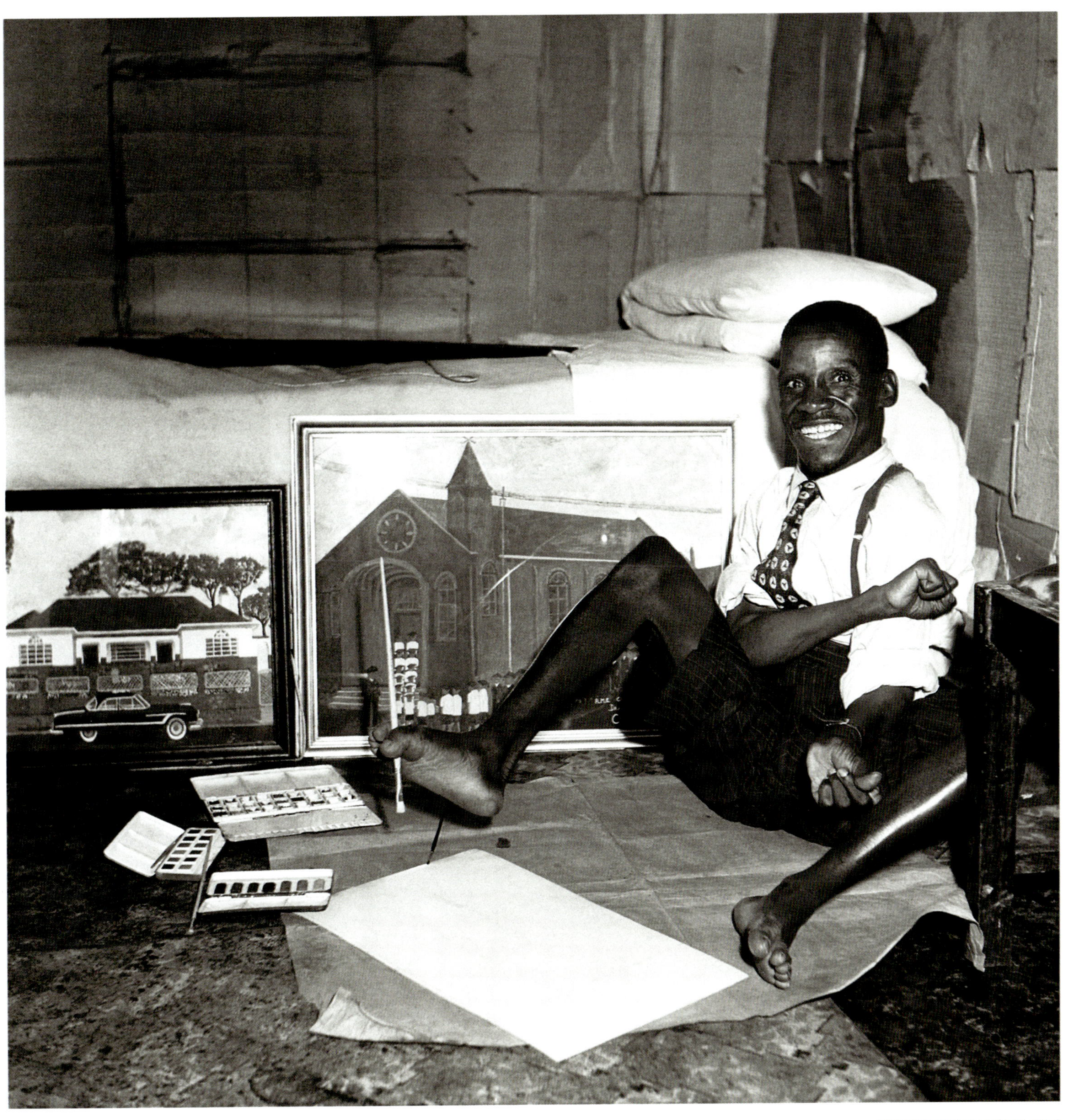

GERMISTON TOWNSHIP 1954
At the age of four months Calvin Lekoane had an illness
which left him almost totally paralysed. At the age of six
he began to use his feet to do things he should have
done with his hands. At the age of fourteen Calvin
started to draw, sliding along the ground. He painted
street scenes, earning his living by selling his paintings.

BOB GOSANI

121

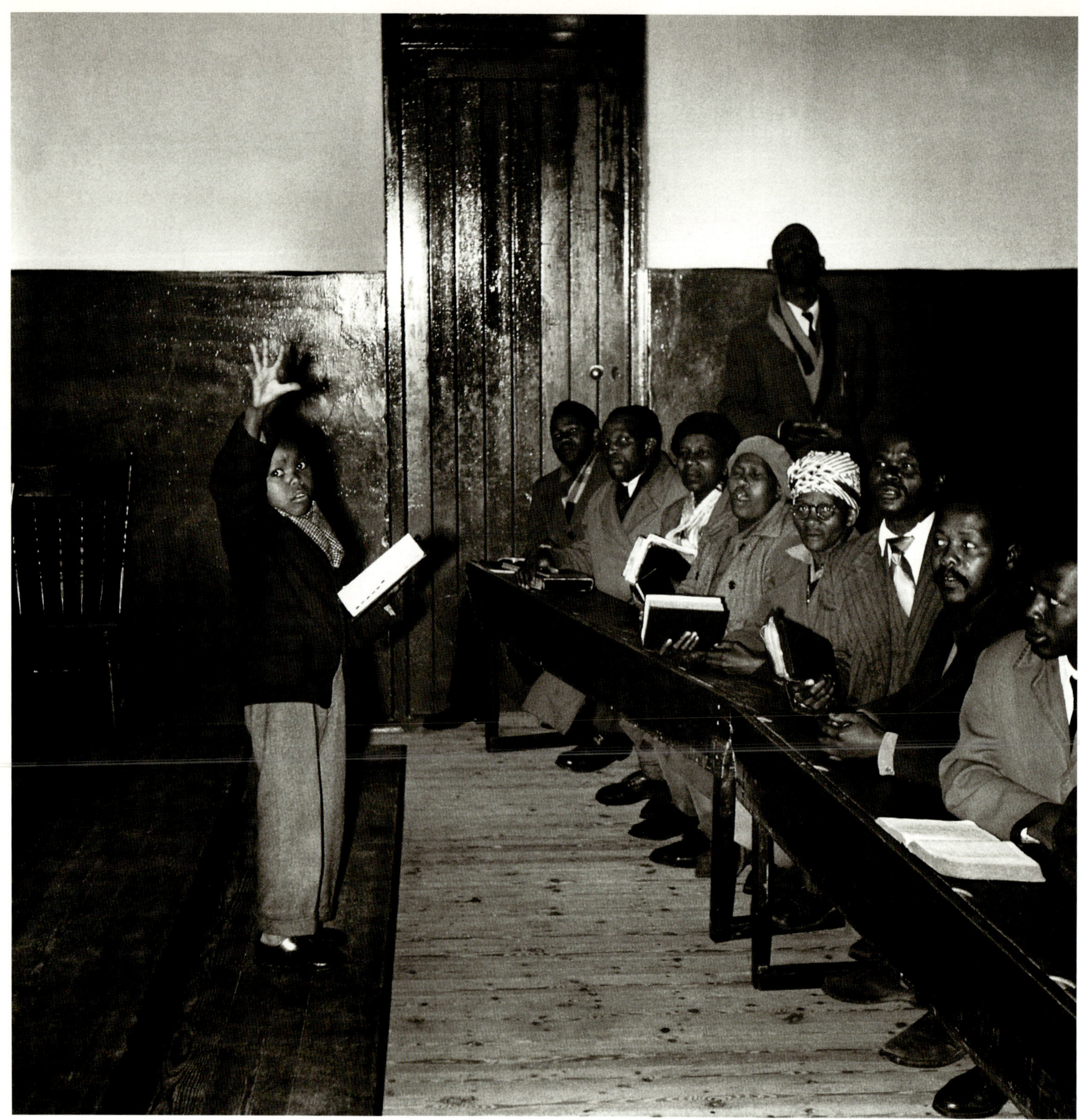

PORT ELIZABETH 1956
Cecil Ndumiso Ntile — nine year old preacher, makes them weep. 'His words hit sinners the hardest and since everyone is a sinner everyone is hit hard'. 'I'm not a preacher, though I preach', says Cecil. 'No prophet either but just a messenger of God, sent to Port Elizabeth to convert the ungodly.'

LIONEL OOSTENDORP

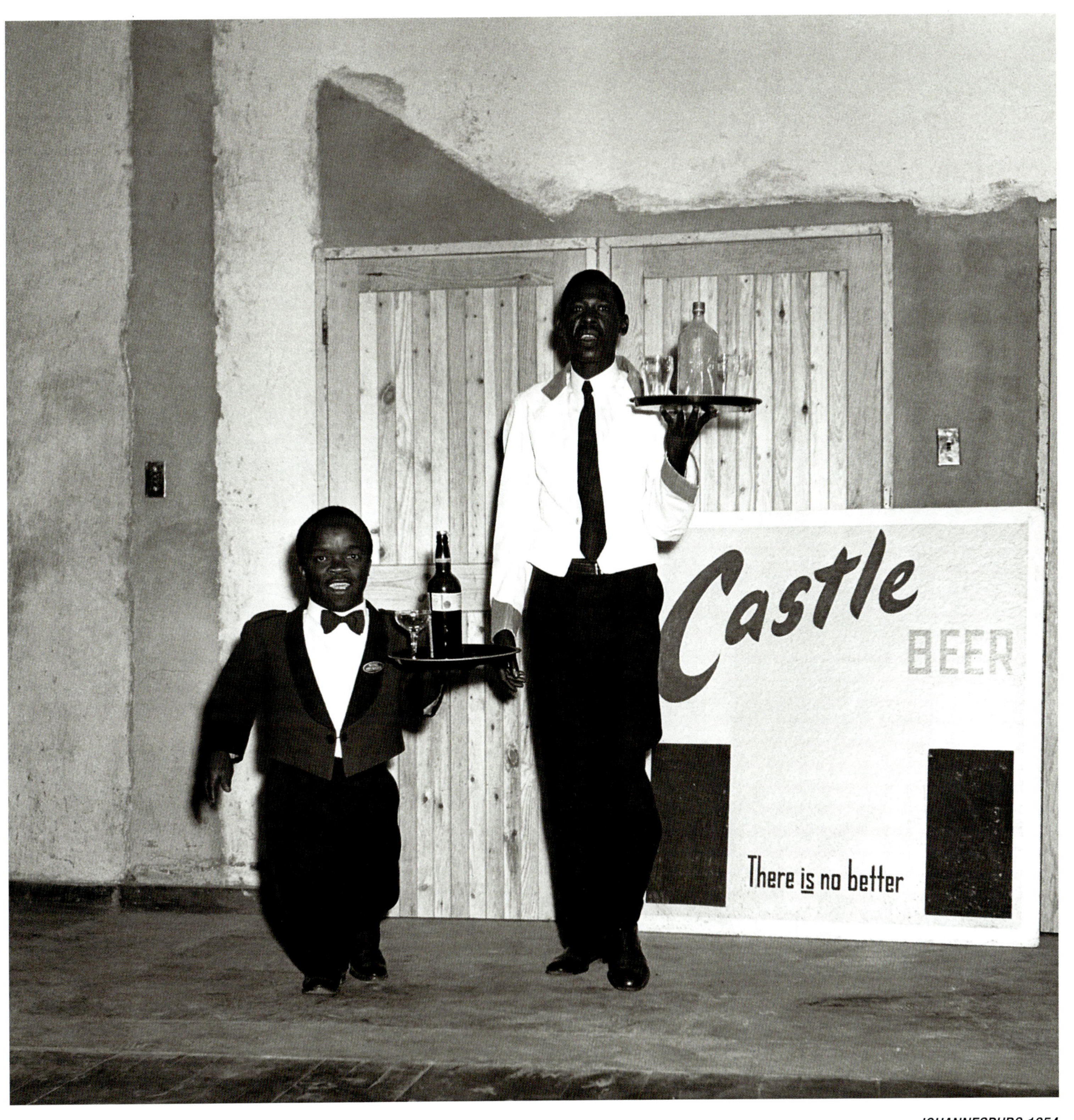

JOHANNESBURG 1954
*Benjamin Mopeli, one of the shortest men in
South Africa. Not that there's far less of him than
in most of us! As you can see he is packed very
densely. This 31-year old pint-size doesn't find
life in the small too odd. 'The only trouble is a
man has to rely completely on tailored clothes!'*

JÜRGEN SCHADEBERG

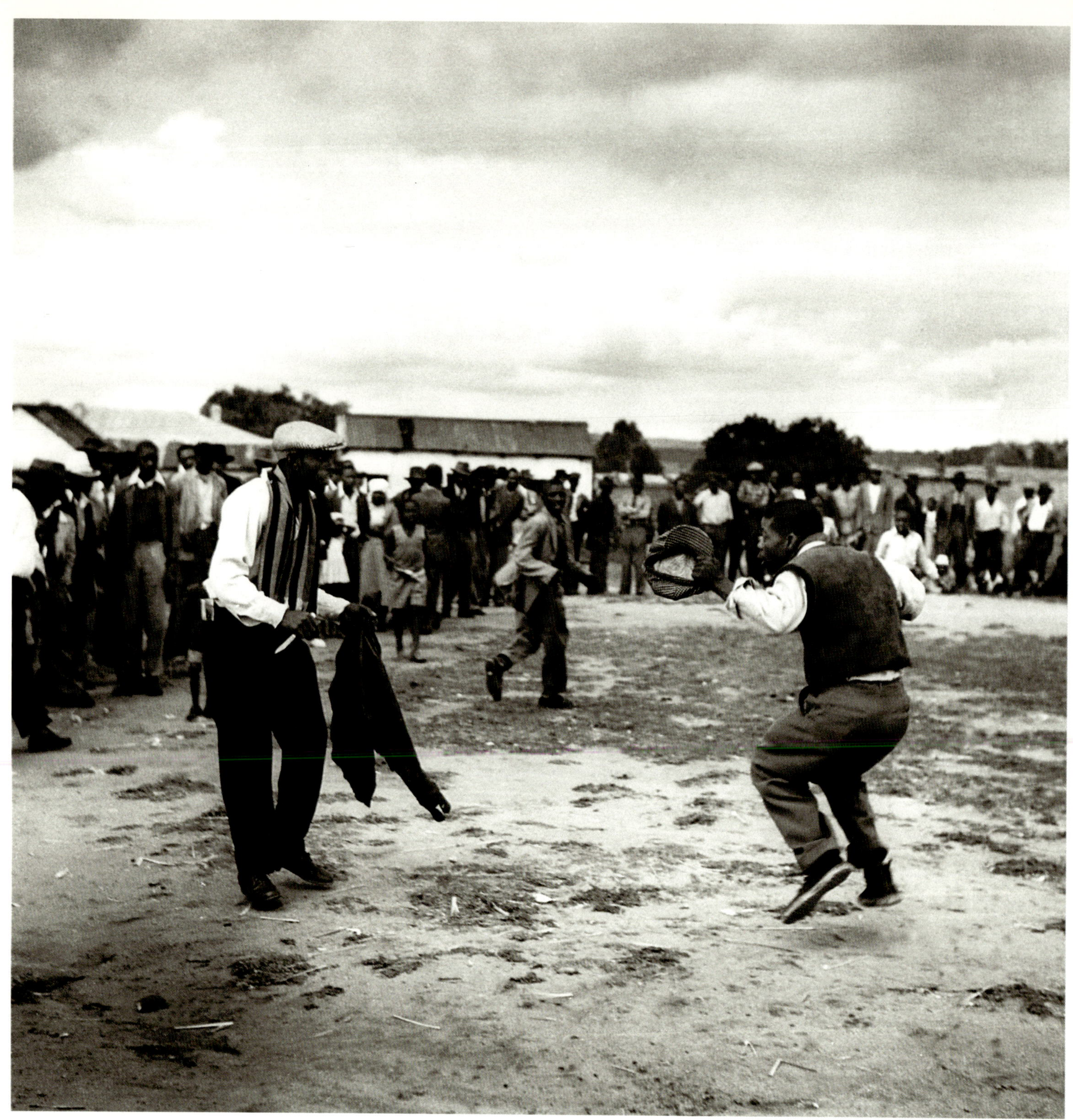

ALEXANDRA TOWNSHIP 1953
Gang warfare between the 'Mau-Mau's' and the
'Spoilers', the 'Americans' and the other gangs...
they start fighting on a Sunday afternoon during
a friendly football match. It starts with a knife
fight and then ends with a hit and run street
battle.

JÜRGEN SCHADEBERG

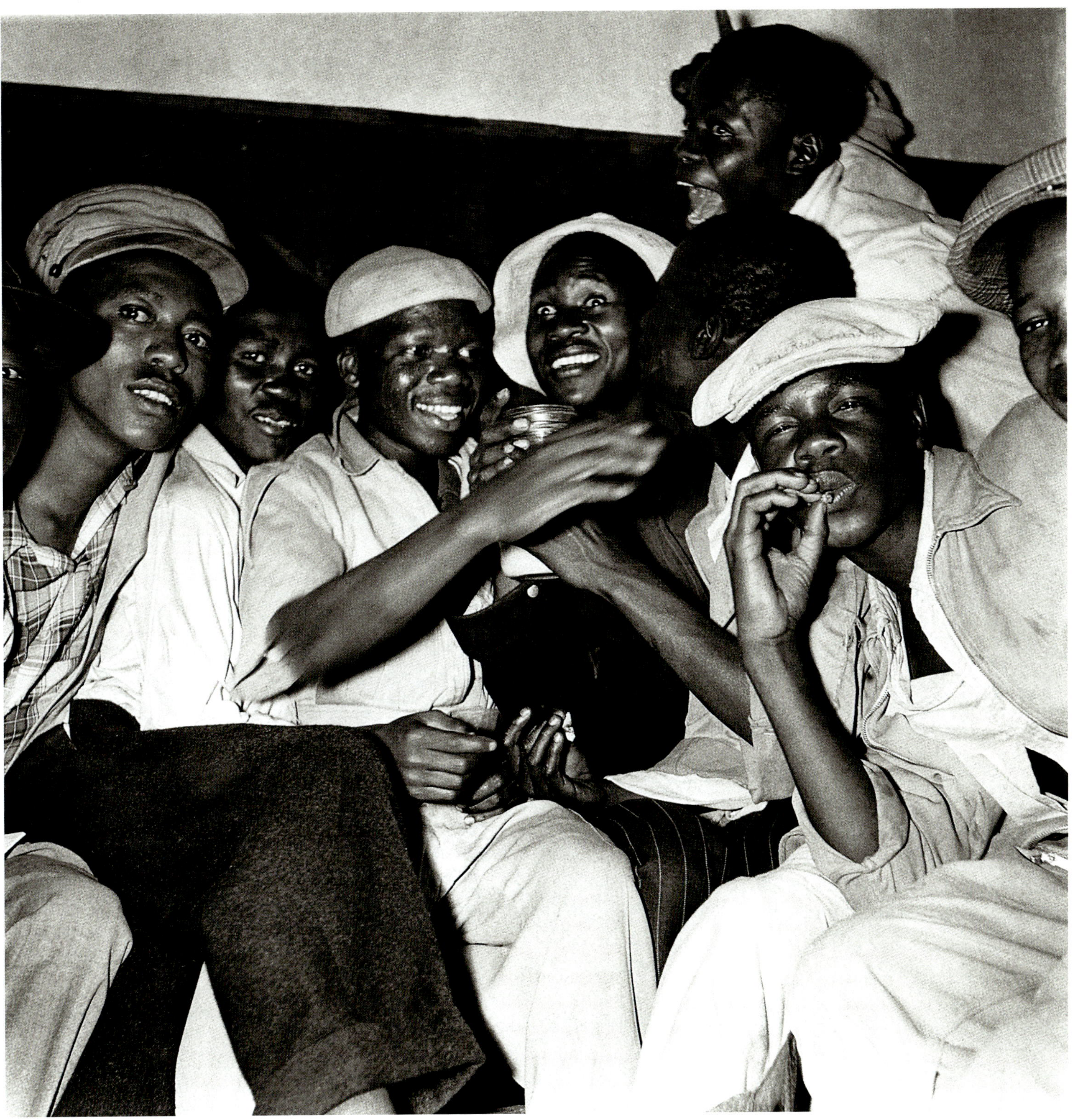

SOPHIATOWN 1954
They call them tsotsis — cool, sharp and fast,
silent movers. Some are pickpockets and cut
throats, hooligans and ruffians, ...others are
sophisticated young men of the new age, witty,
streetwise and smart.

BOB GOSANI

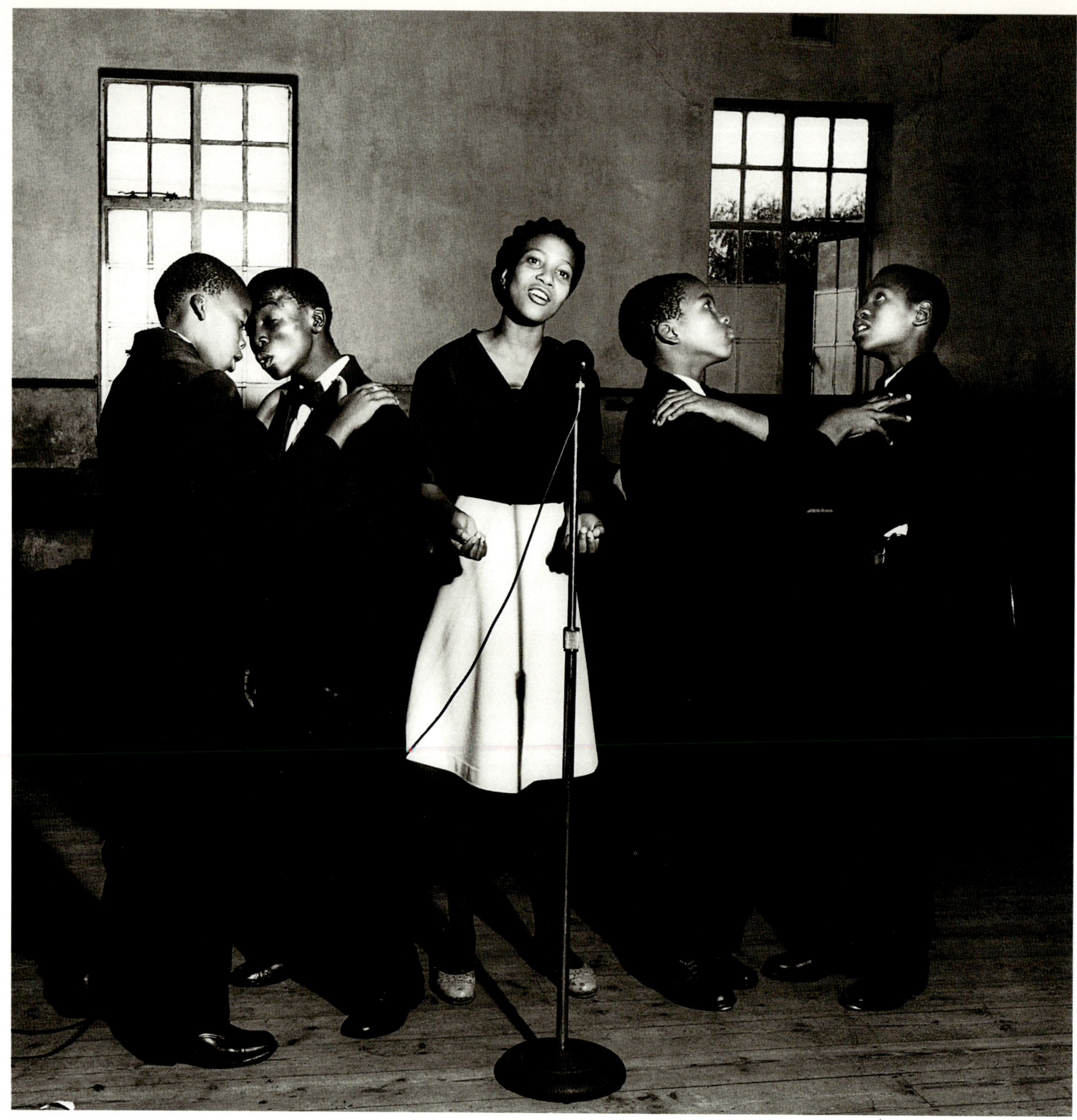

SOPHIATOWN 1954
The 'Midnight Kids' of Western Township. They were
terrific. They had an enterprising leader, a school
teacher, who endeavoured to train them. Audiences
went crazy with excitement, stomping their feet,
shouting and whistling at those ten-years-olds giving it
all they'd got. Such promise, such talent.

JÜRGEN SCHADEBERG

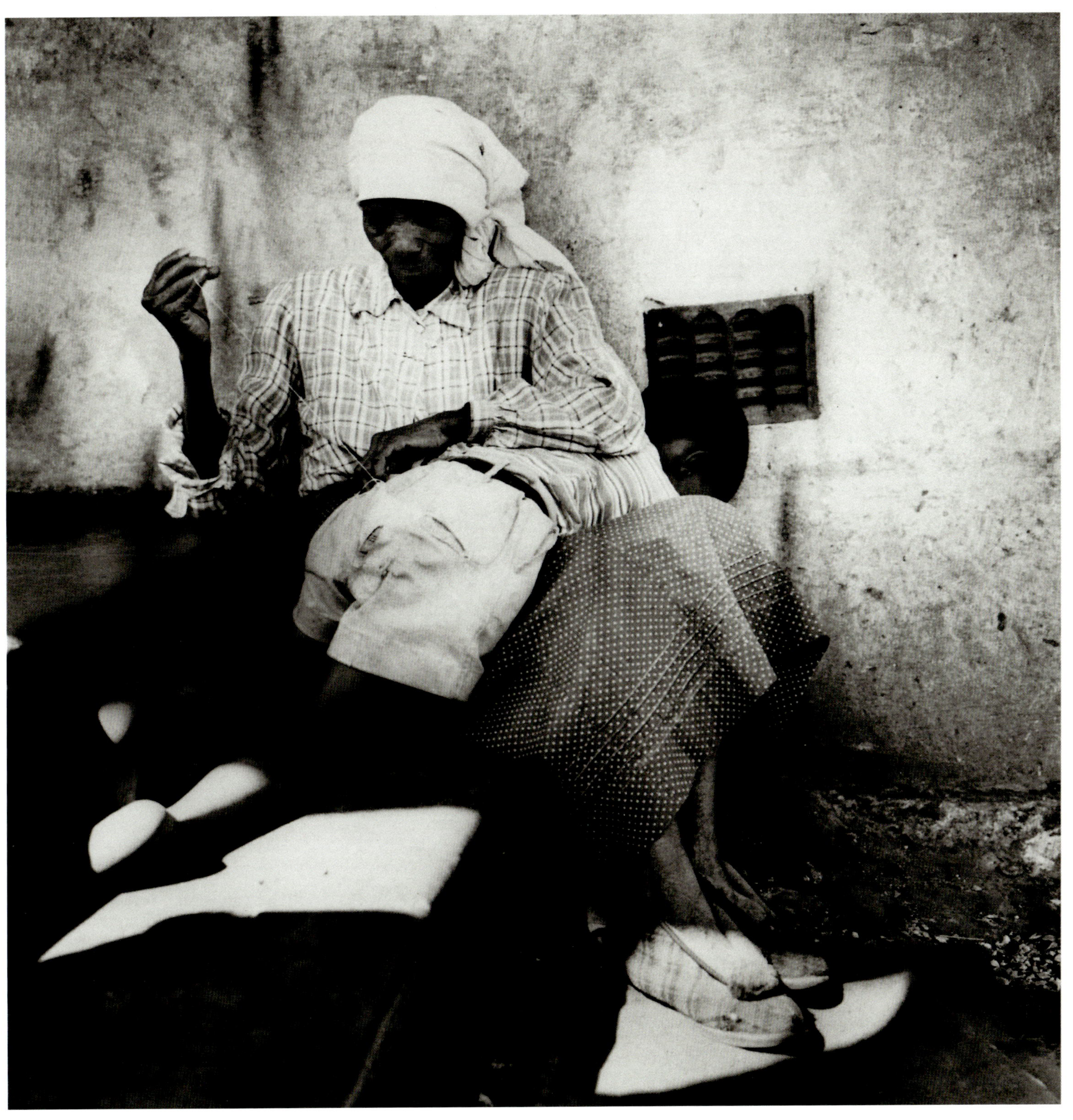

MAMELODI 1955
Grandma is there for the kids. Mother works in
the Golden City as a domestic worker, and father
works on a building site. Both of them only come
home over the weekends.

BOB GOSANI

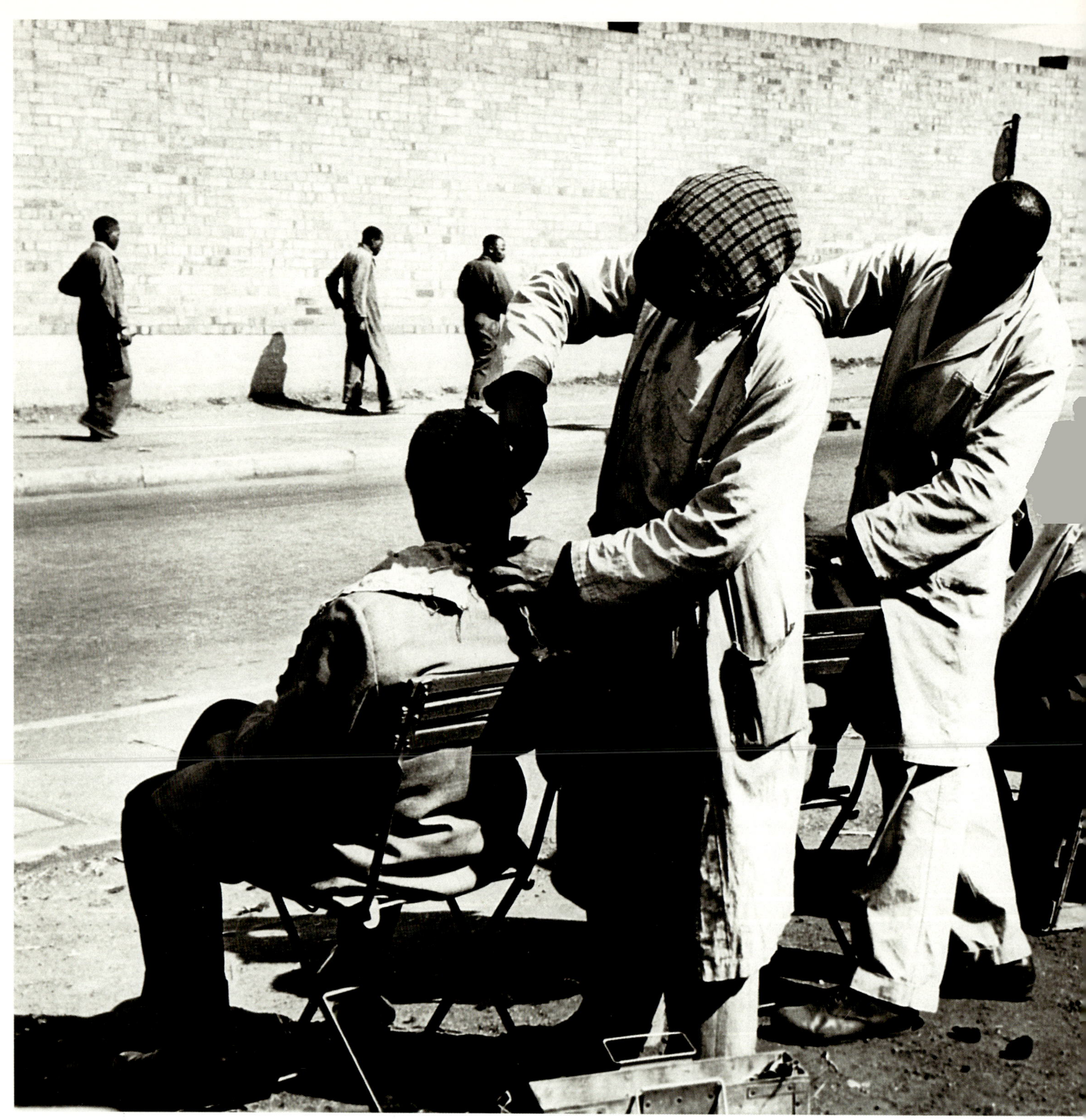

SOPHIATOWN 1958
Haircuts everywhere, anywhere, at bus stops and
terminals, railway stations and at the corners of
Main Street. The latest cut for nine pence.

JÜRGEN SCHADEBERG

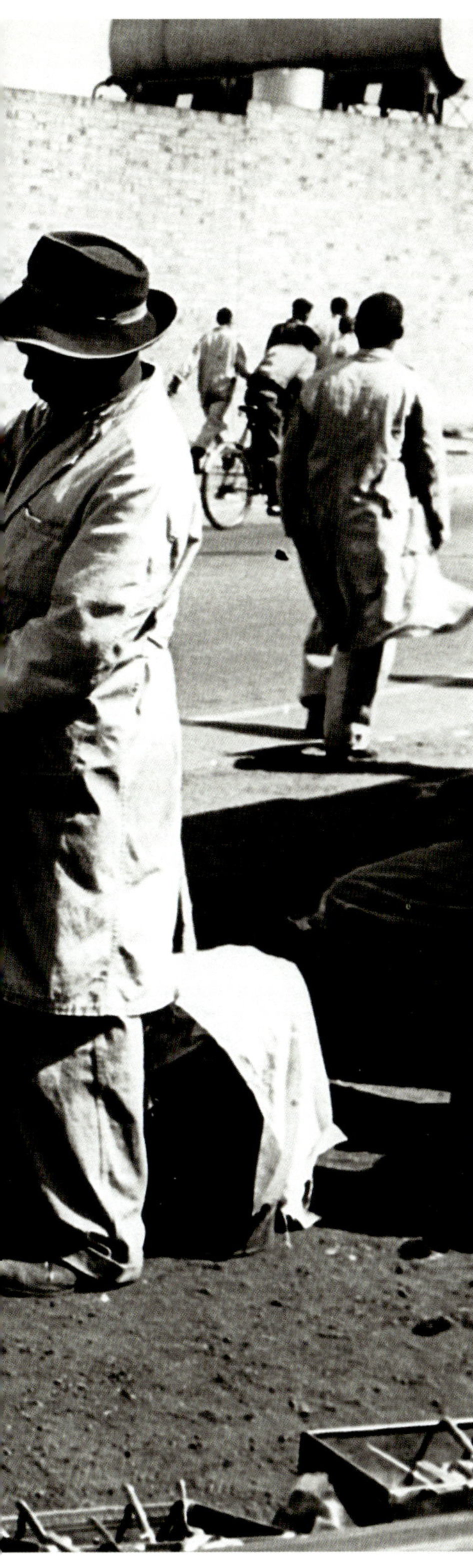

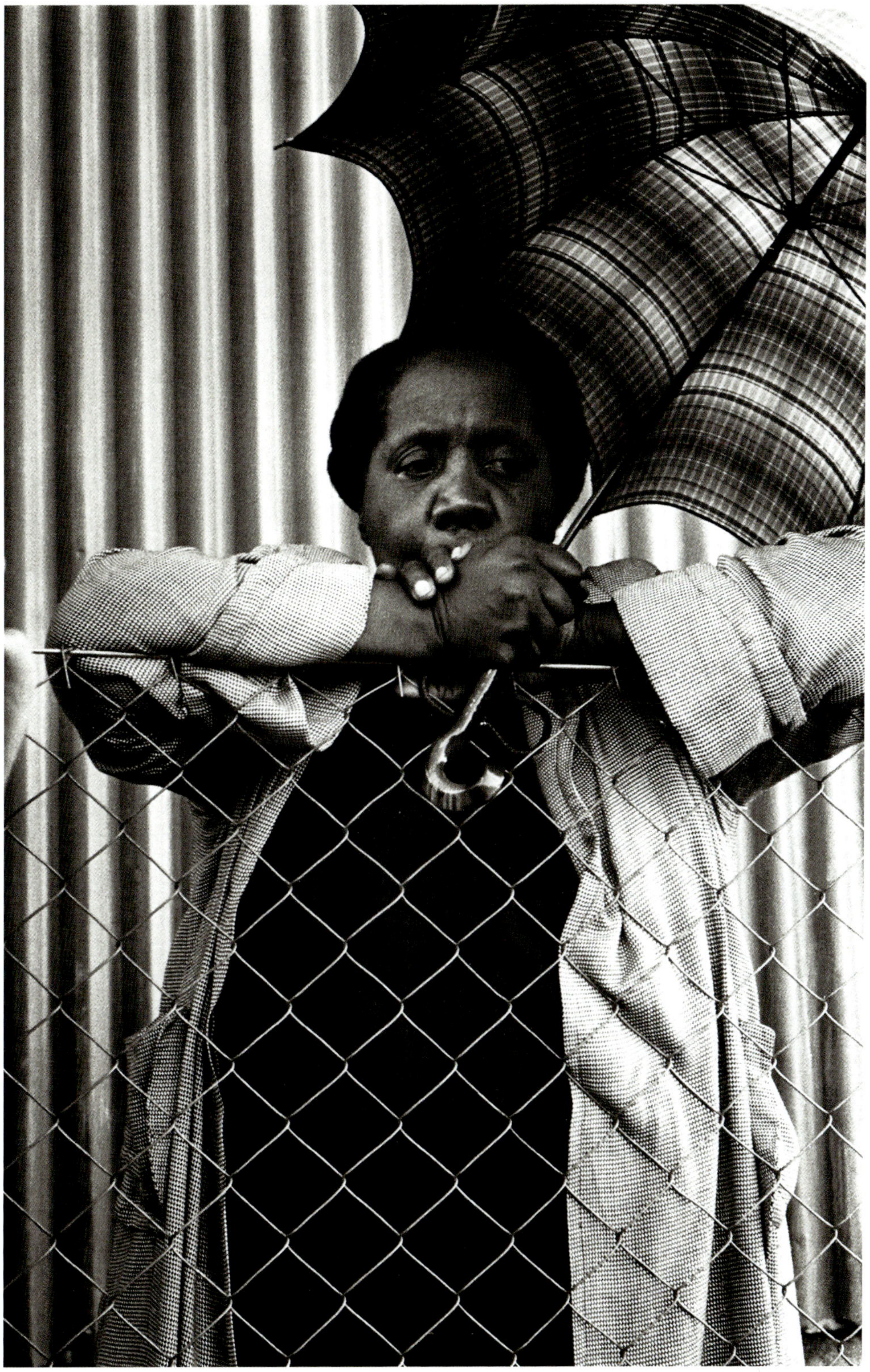

SOPHIATOWN 1957
Aunt Em in 1936. She was on the piano with
Peter Rezant's The Merry Blackbirds. Everybody
loved Emma. During World War II she went to
hundreds of military camps with her husband's
De Pitch Black Follies.

PETER MAGUBANE

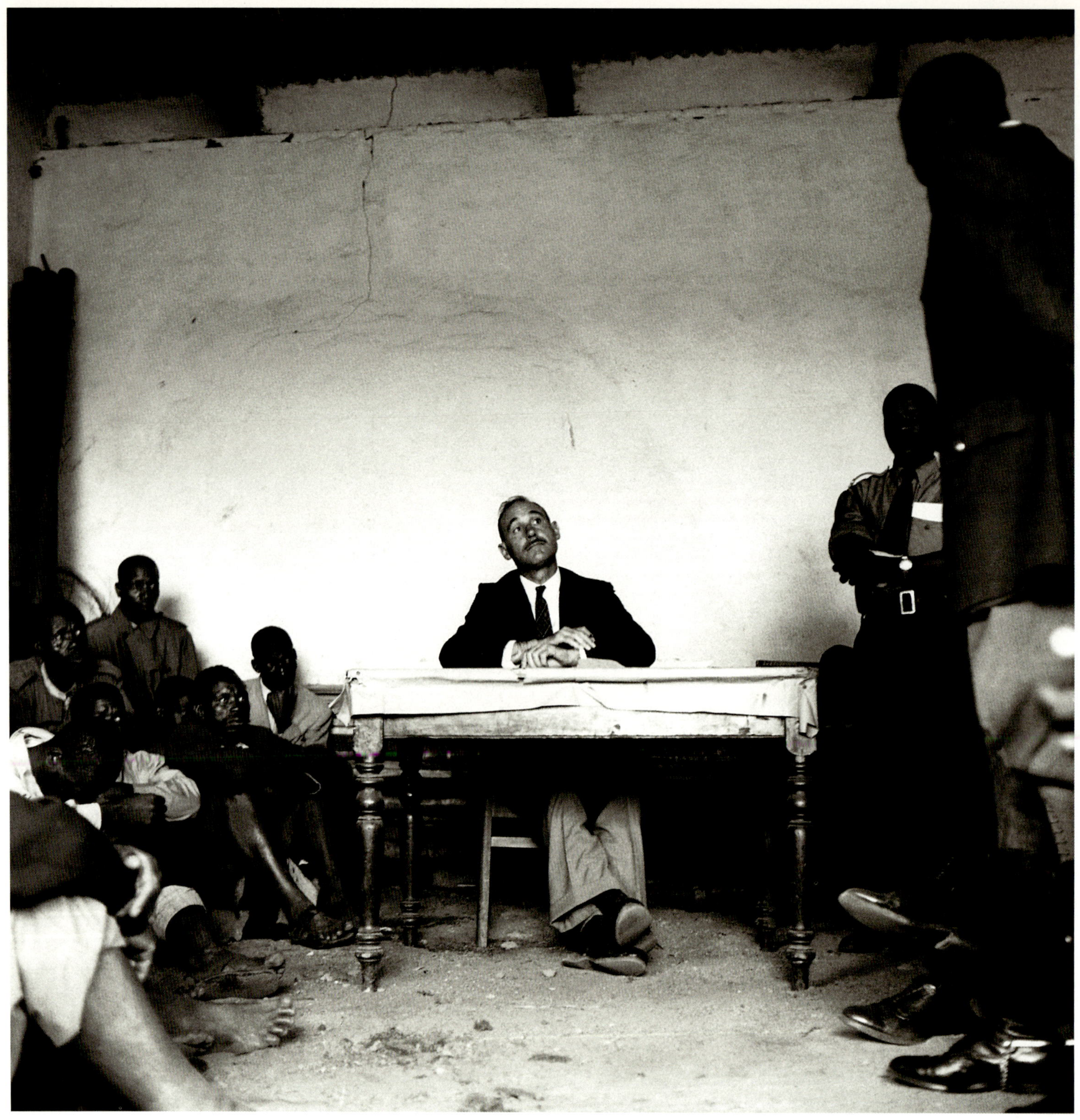

ZULULAND 1957

The magistrate raises his eyes above the documents and plunges them like daggers into hearts of all who watch him. It was common, in the tribal reserves of South Africa, for a white magistrate to hold court in the tiny town of Mtubatuba in Zululand. For example he presided and gave judgement in a major dispute between several Zulu chiefs. There is silence as the magistrate pronounces the sentences which are often harsh. They rankle in the minds of all who are present, and so they sing about it.

RANJITH KALLY

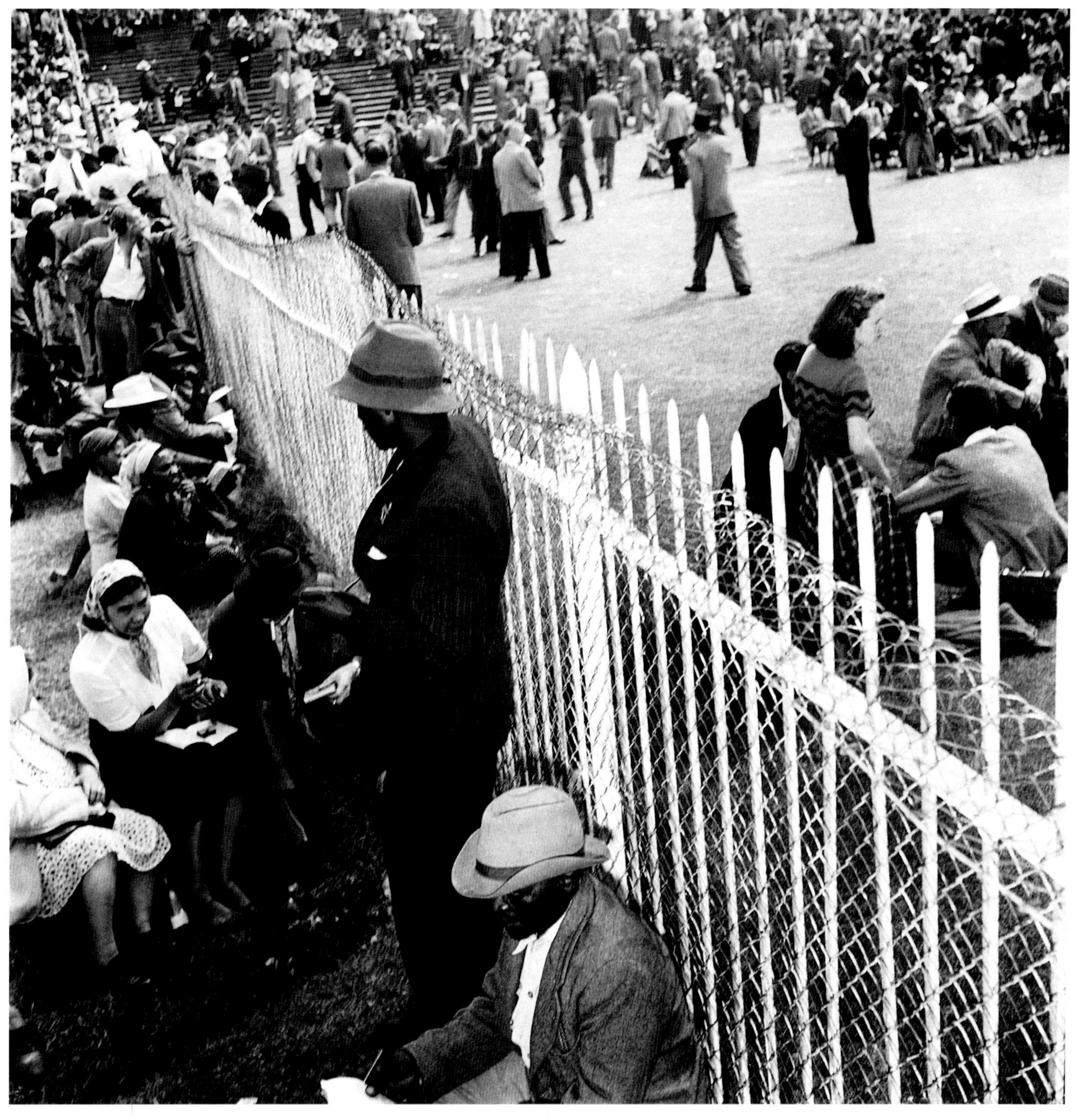

JOHANNESBURG 1953
There is a fence at the races. On one side the whites place their bets. On the other side 'non-whites' put their money on the horses.

JÜRGEN SCHADEBERG

131

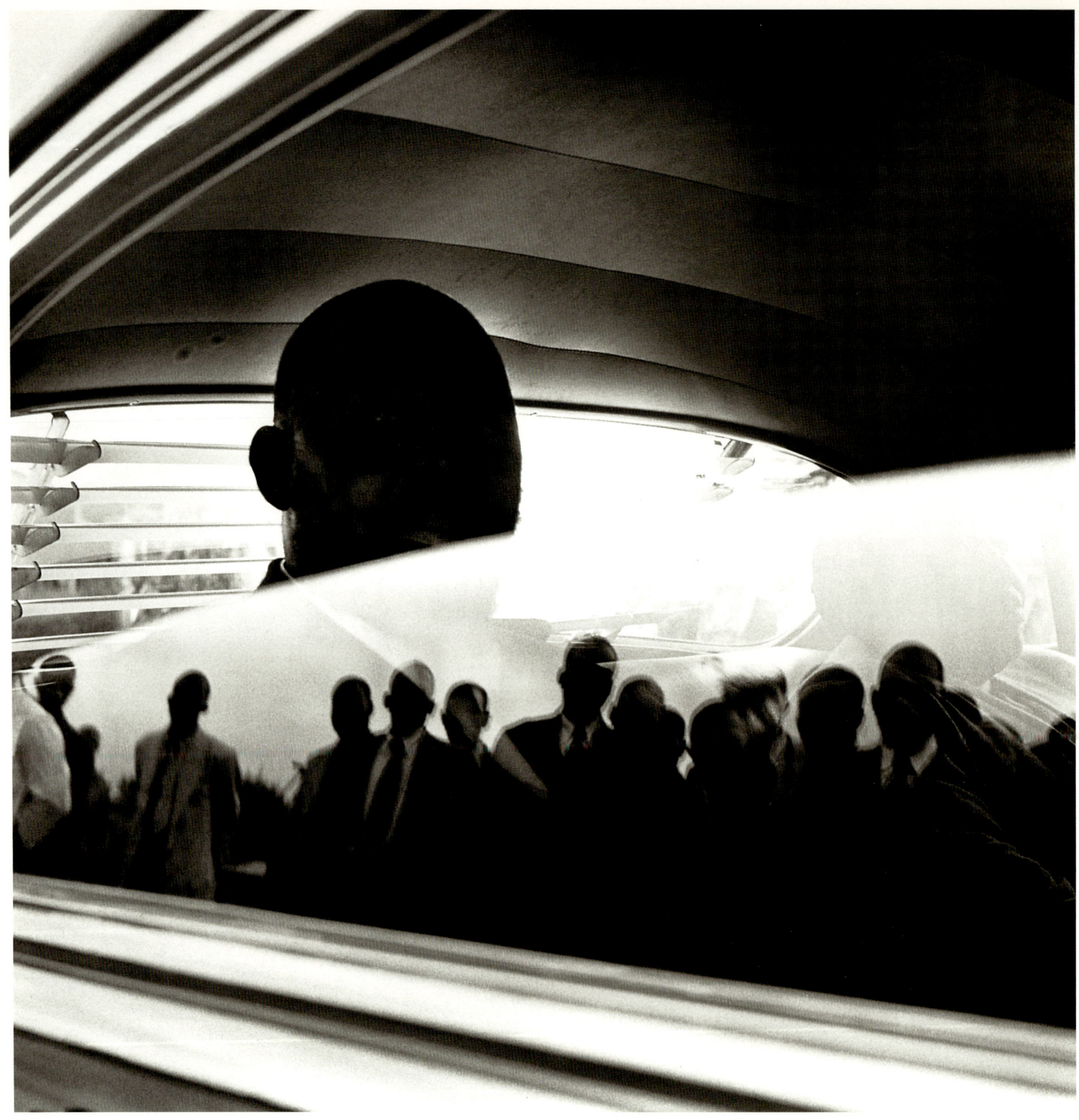

PORT ELIZABETH 1958
The new Messiah, Bishop Limba, arriving in his Buick at a gathering,
welcomes his followers. Limba was a powerful and dominating personality.
He never addressed his people directly but talked to them through a human
transmitter. Church members had to be humble, quiet in their bearing and
had to live clean and healthy lives, be decently dressed, avoid obscene
language and all rowdiness.

BOB GOSANI

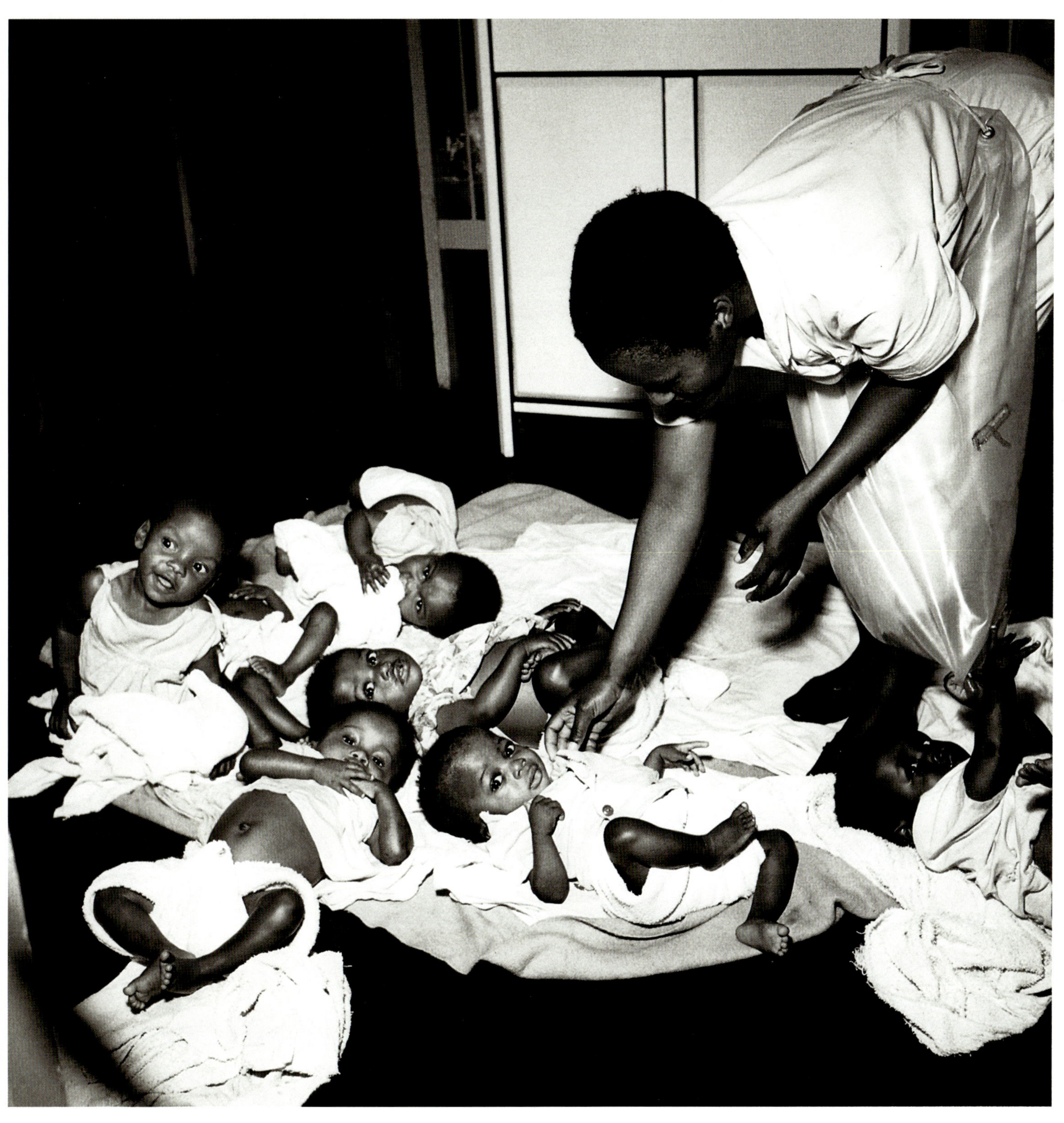

CATO MANOR 1955
Abandoned babies at an orphanage.

GR NAIDOO

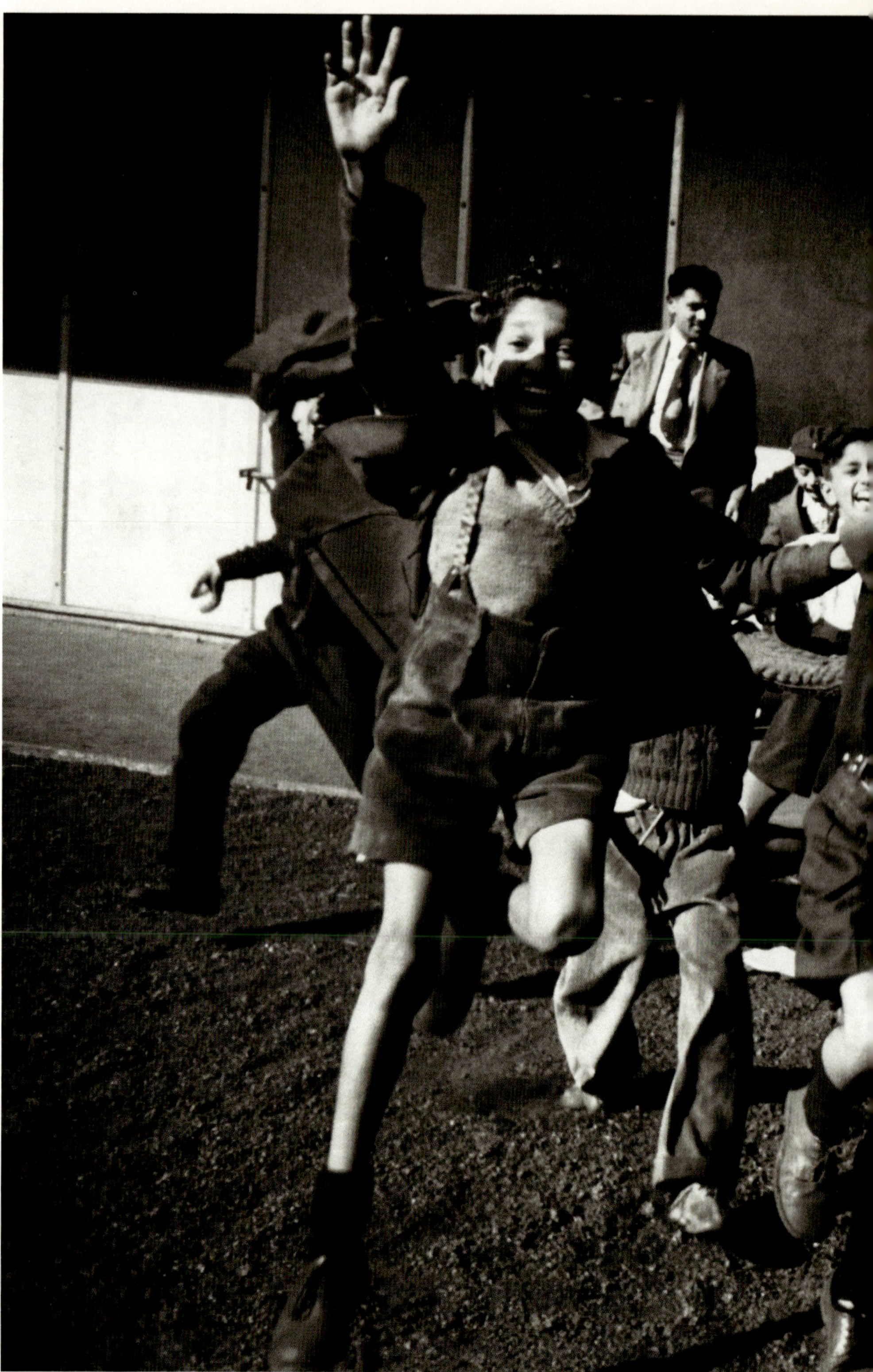

School is out. A Standard six history examination paper at the time posed the following questions: Who is at present (a) the Governor General of SA? (b) the Prime Minister of SA? (c) the Minister of Native Affairs? (d) the Under-Secretary for Bantu Education? (e) the regional Director for Bantu Education in the Transvaal? (f) the Administrator of the Transvaal? Question (2) asked for an outline map showing where each African ethnic group lived.

LIONEL OOSTENDORP

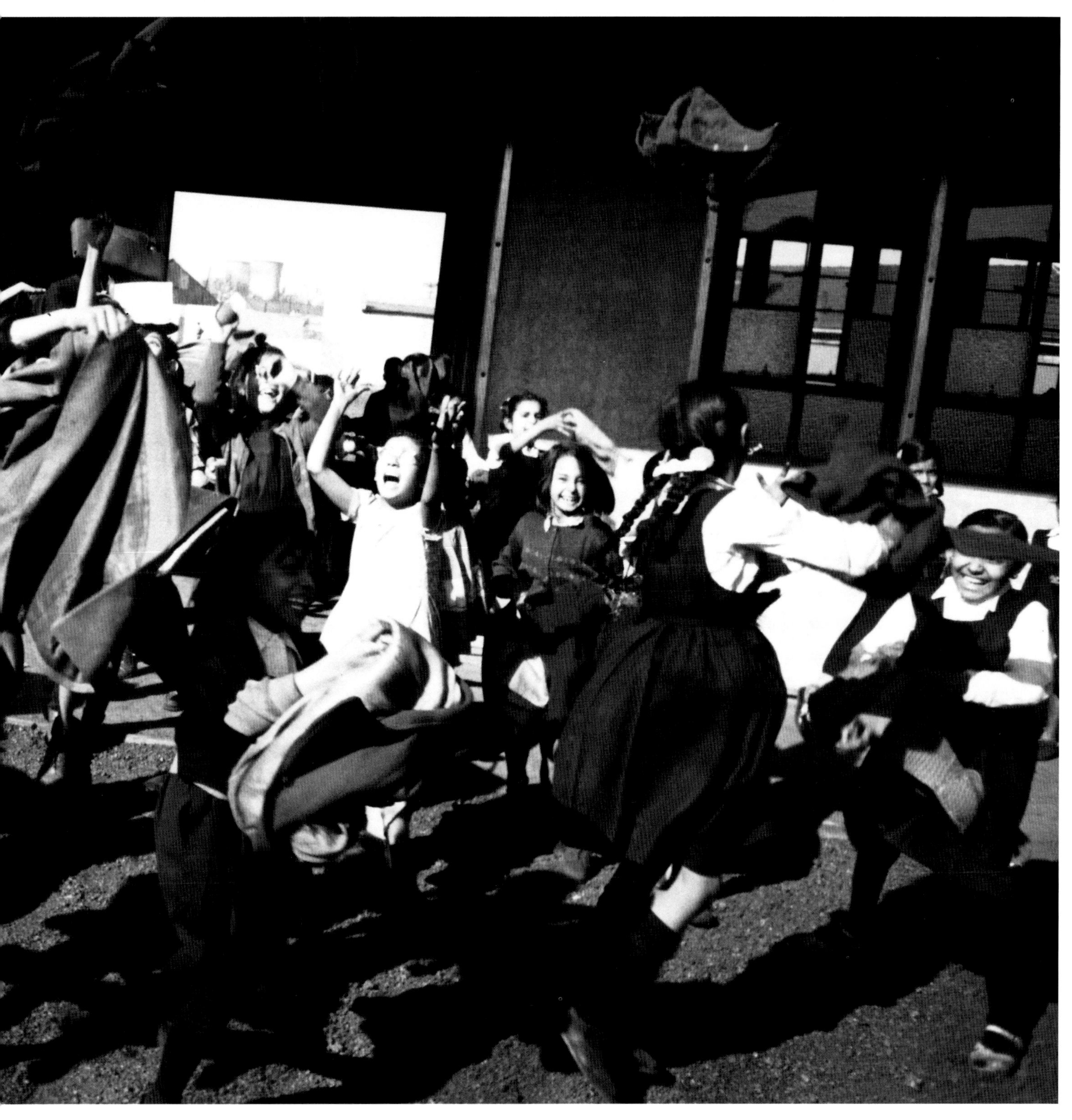

Sophiatown Magic

Somewhere here, and among a thousand more individualist things, is the magic of Sophiatown. It is different and itself. You don't just find your place here, you make it and you find yourself. There's a tang about it. You might now and then have to give way to others making their ways of life by methods not in the book. But you can't be bored. You have the right to listen to the latest jazz records at Ah Sing's over the road. You can walk a coloured girl of an evening down to the Odin Cinema, and no questions asked. You can try out Rhugubar's curry with your bare fingers without embarrassment. All this with no sense of heresy.

But so much has gone — veritable institutions. Fatty of the Thirty-nine Steps. Now that was a great shebeen! It was in a good street. You walked up a flight of steps, the structure looked dingy as if it would crash down with you any moment. You opened a door and walked into a dazzle of bright electric light, contemporary furniture, and massive Fatty. She was a legend. Gay, friendly, coquettish, always ready to sell you a drink. But now that house is flattened. I'm told that in Meadowlands she lost the zest for the game. She has even tried to look for work in town. Ghastly.

Can Themba
'From The House of Truth'

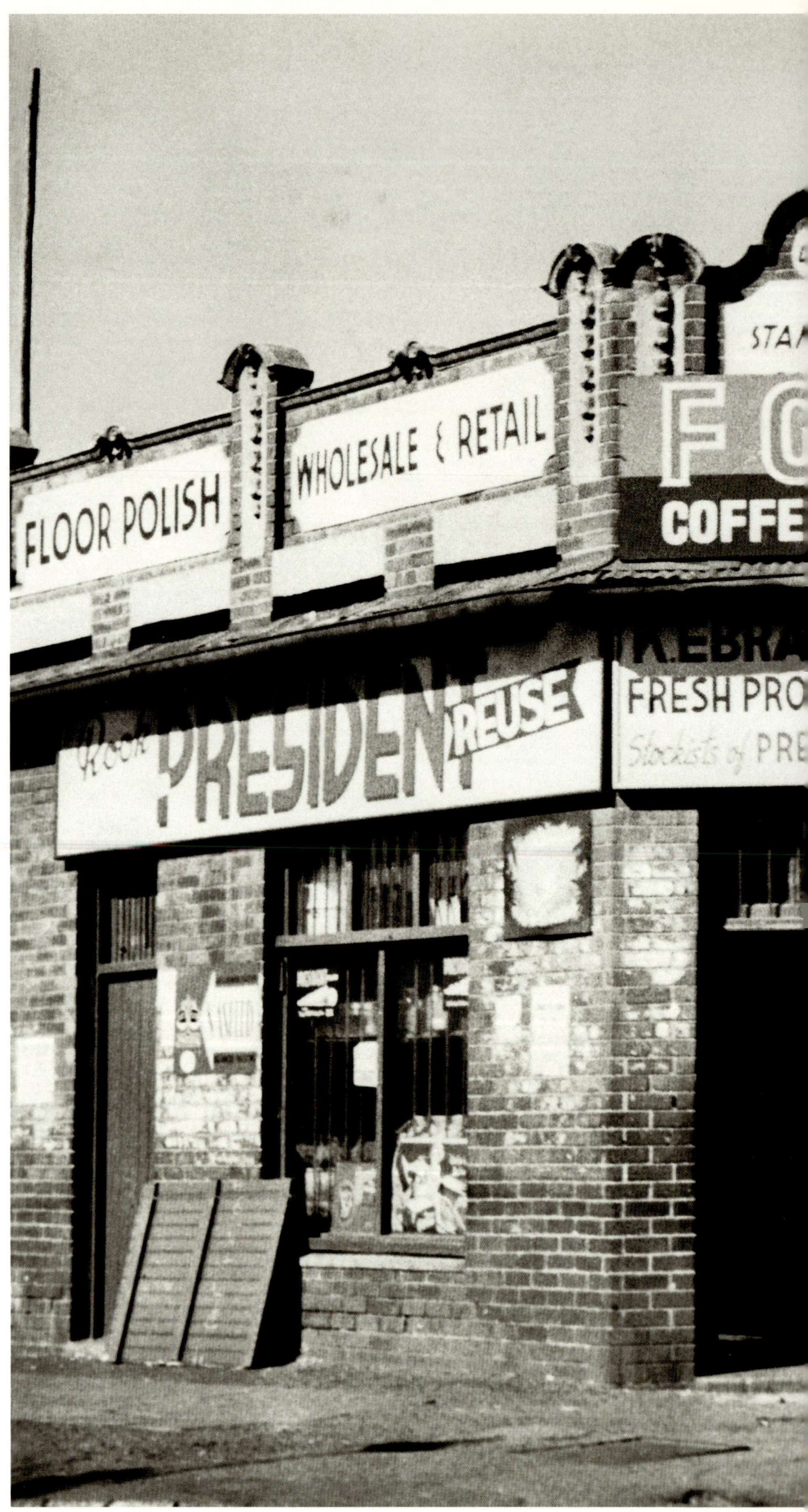

SOPHIATOWN 1956
In 1953 the oldest settlements, Sophiatown and three other townships in the western part of Johannesburg, were declared 'blackspots' by the government. The people living in these 'blackspots', which were surrounded by white suburbs, were scheduled for removal.

BOB GOSANI

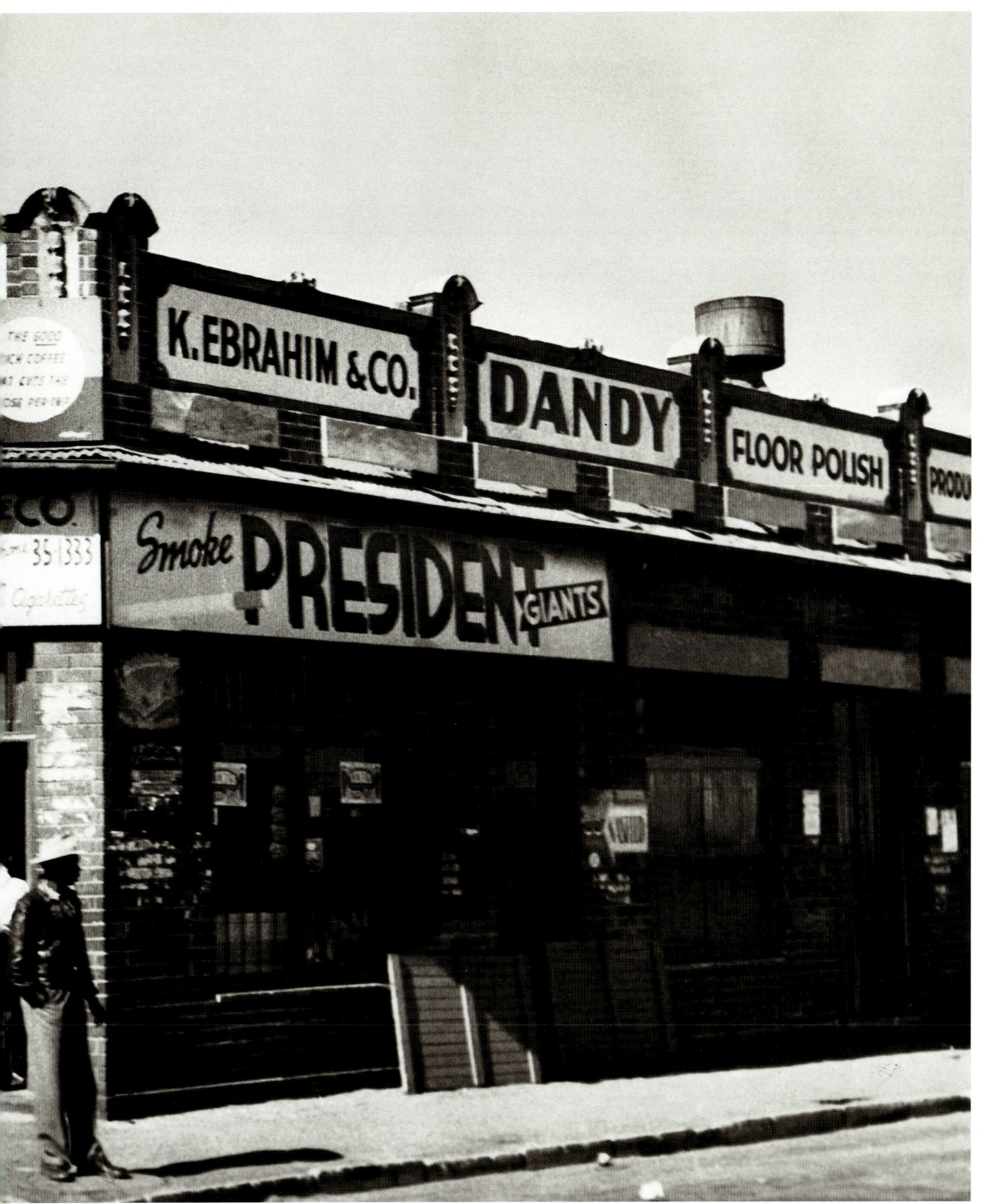

THE GOOD
RICH COFFEE
HAT CUTS THE
OSE PER
K. EBRAHIM & CO.
DANDY
FLOOR POLISH
PRODU
ECO.
35 1333
Cigarettes
Smoke PRESIDENT GIANTS

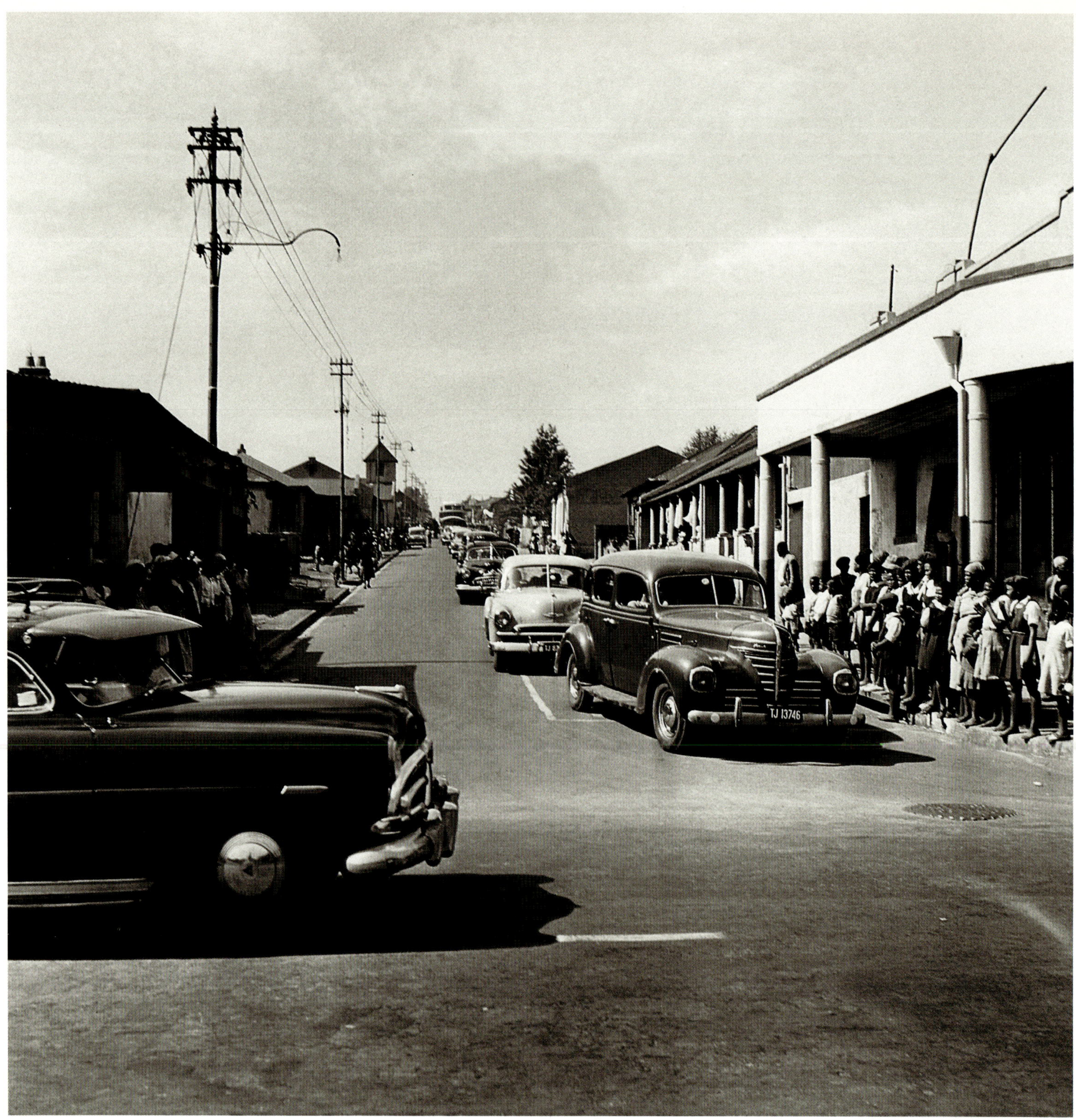

SOPHIATOWN 1953
Sophiatown was different from other black
townships in South Africa. People didn't have to
get permission to live there and people of all
racial backgrounds could buy and own property
there. Despite poverty, squalour and violence,
Sophiatown was exuberant and alive.

JÜRGEN SCHADEBERG

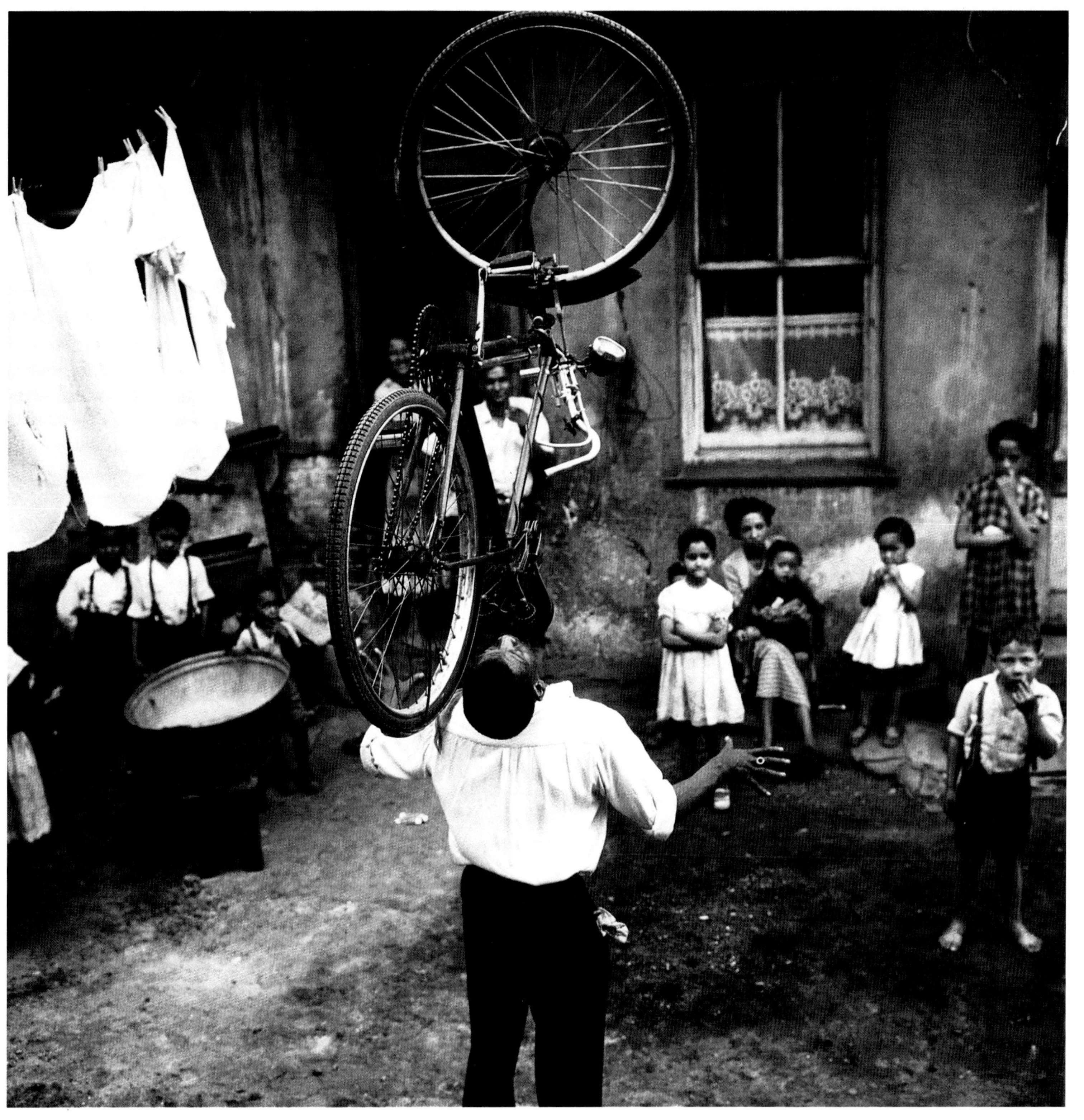

SOPHIATOWN 1955
Writers, musicians, politicians and journalists live
side by side with the gangsters, shebeen queens
and black and white 'Bohemians' in Sophiatown.
There was the boxer, Ezekiel Dlamini, hero of the
jazz opera **King Kong**. There was the blues singer
Dolly Rathebe and of course **Drum** editor Can
Themba and writer 'Bloke' Modisane, among others.

JÜRGEN SCHADEBERG

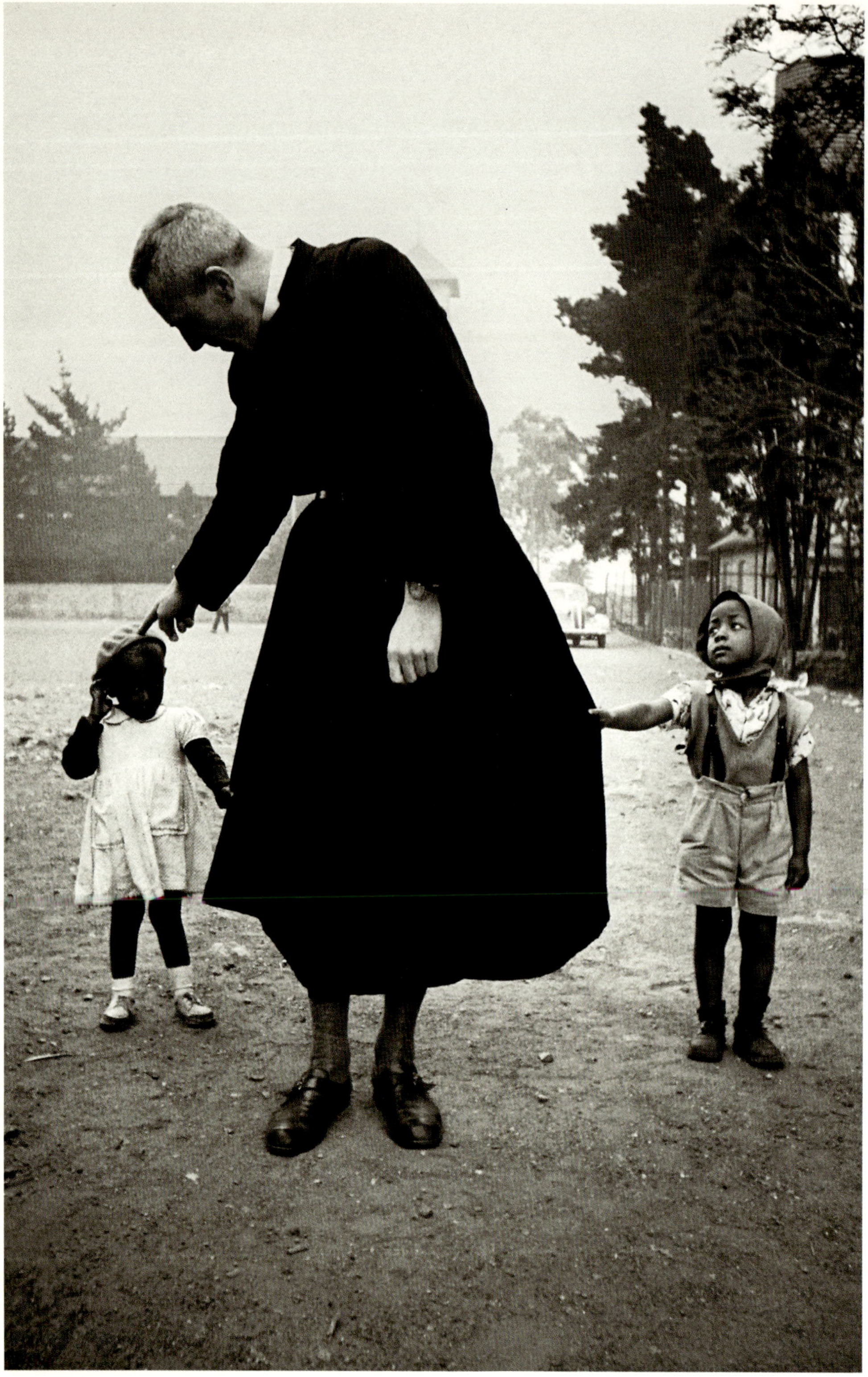

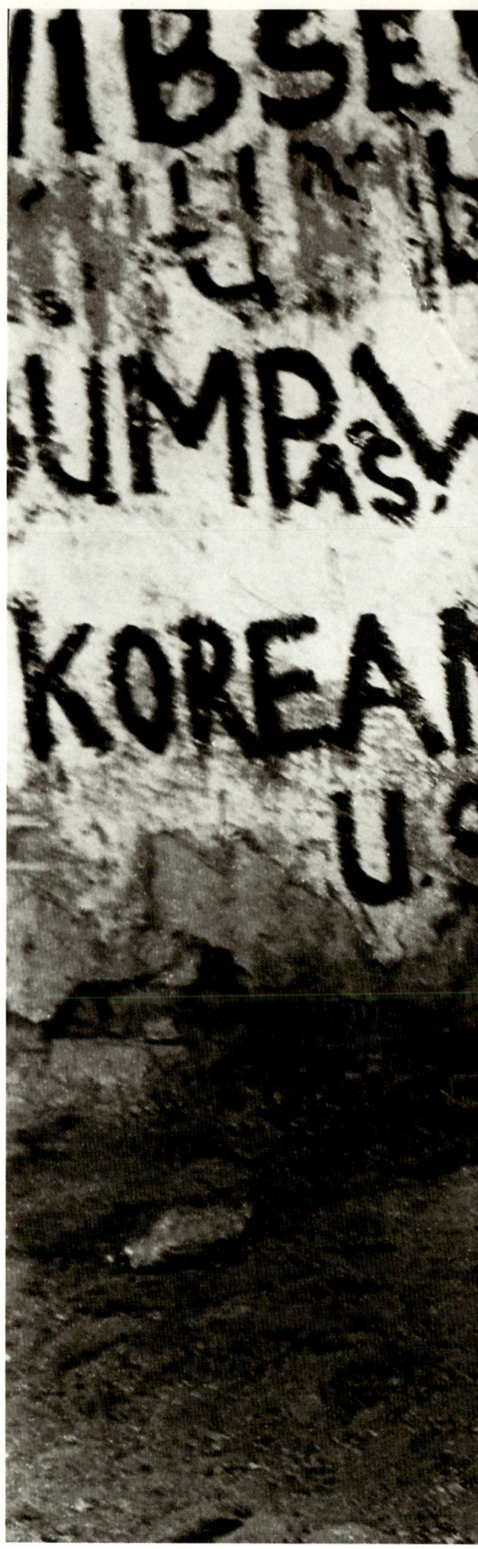

A Tickey

Early one morning I went to the home of seven year-old Patience Bothile, whose family had been forcibly removed from Sophiatown to Orlando East. I caught her just as she was getting up, preparing for the day, a bitterly cold one. She was in a flannel petticoat. She slipped on a flimsy dress and carried a little bath tub to the tap attached to the lavatory. She got cold water and started to wash.

Inside the kitchen was a stove fire, and nearby two young boys were tinkering with a pressure stove, which flared and faded now and then. It was obvious

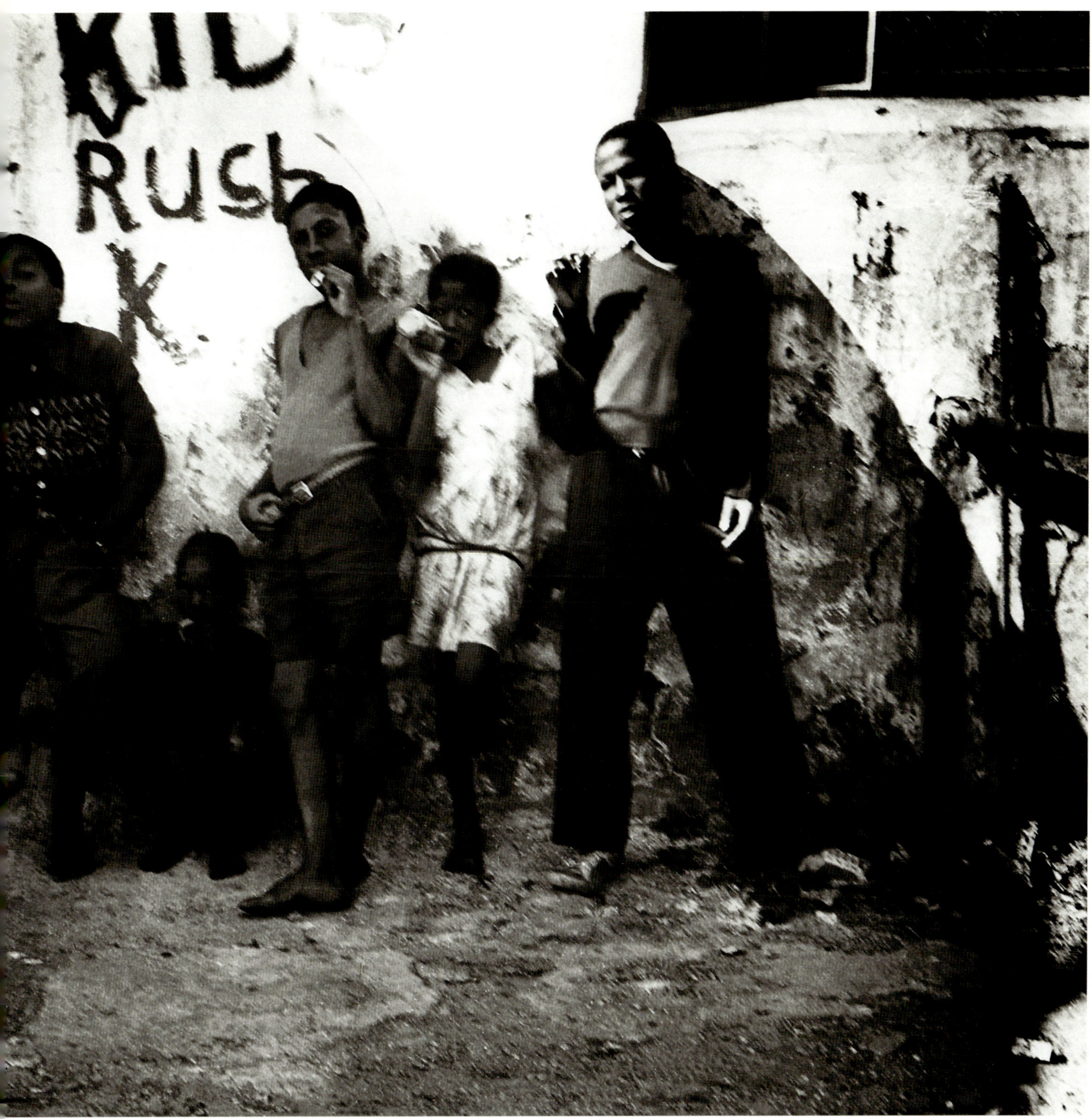

that there wouldn't be tea for little Patience.

By now she was shivering, blowing her warm breath into her cupped hands. She got into her smart gym dress, white shirt, and battered shoes. She took her school case, and, with all the patience in the world, ran off to school.

She has a sweet face, dulled by the cold and the hunger fluttering inside her. I knew what just a cup of hot broth, a slice of bread with peanut butter could do. for this dear child. I'm told it would cost just a tickey. Somebody's got to find that blasted tickey!

Can Themba, 'Journalism'

(A tickey was a three penny coin)

141

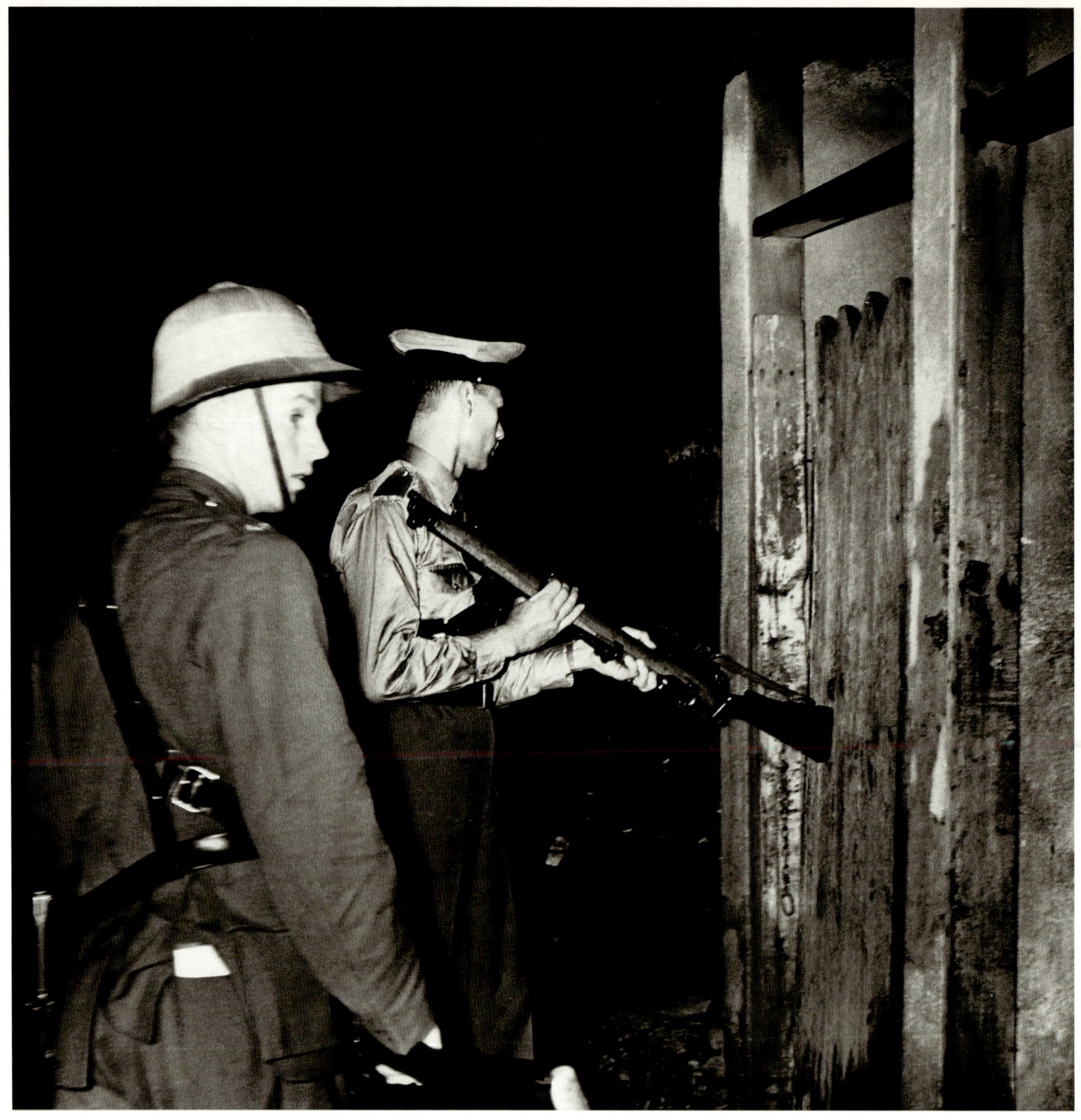

SOPHIATOWN 1955
The 12 February 1955 was the day the Sophiatown removals were due to start. The ANC had called on 5 000 volunteers to mobilise around the slogan of defiance 'Asi hambi — we won't go!' and a stay-away was planned for the first removal day. But, on 10 February, two days ahead of schedule, eighty lorries and 2 000 armed police moved into Sophiatown and began to move the people out of homes they had occupied for generations.

JÜRGEN SCHADEBERG

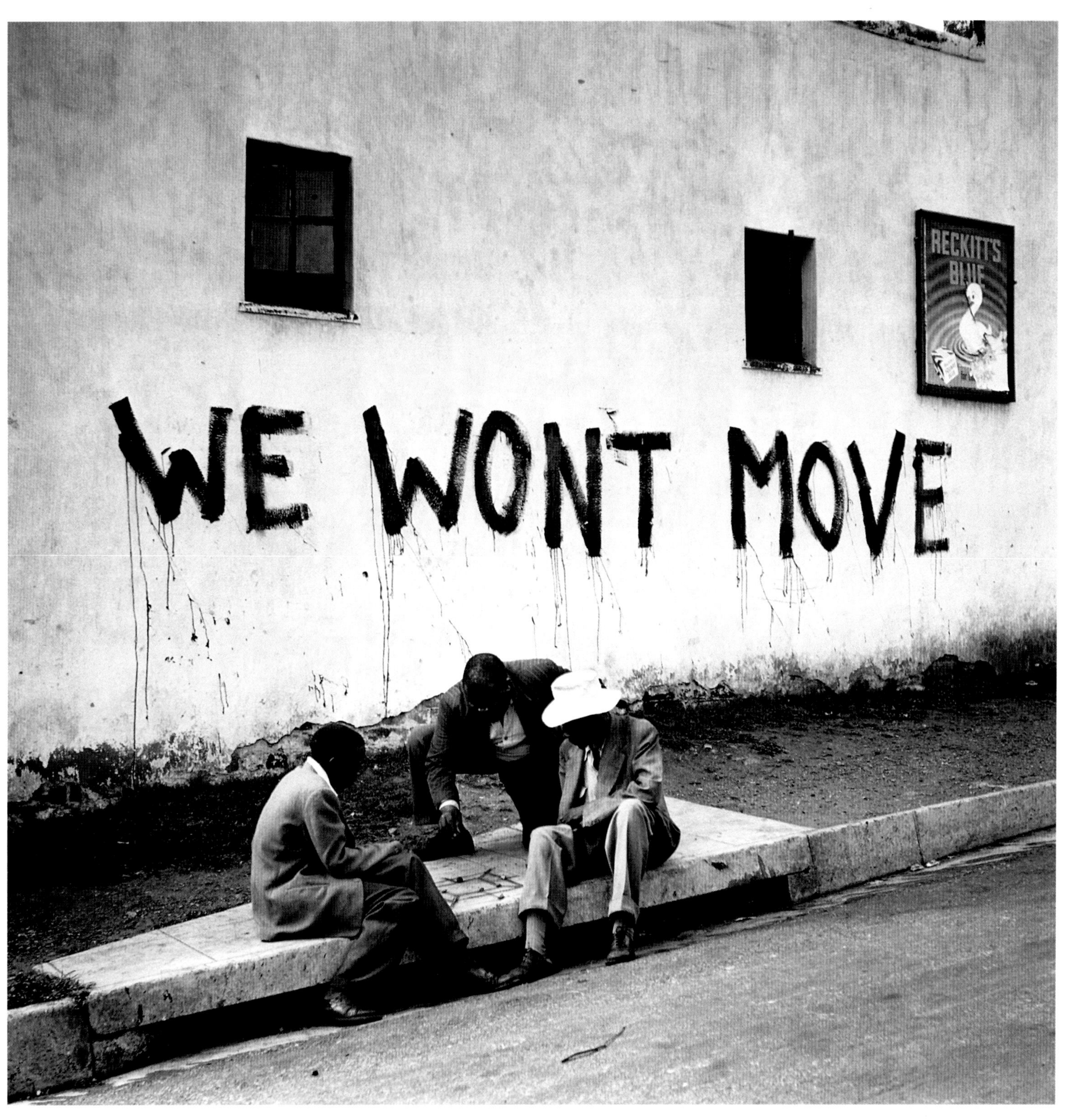

SOPHIATOWN 1955
The people said 'We won't move!' and when the
police arrived that first day people banged and
tapped with stones and iron bars against the
lamposts, and Sophiatown echoed in defiance.

JÜRGEN SCHADEBERG

It's a Tough, Jazzy, Dreadful Season

In my Sophiatown, Christmas insinuates itself on and from 16 December. I become rattled by the constant crack of fireworks. I jump and rush out to see if anybody I know has not been shot. Women scream every night.

I have enough worries of my own. I begin to worry about what the children at home are going to wear; a new suit for each of the two boys, a dress for the little girl. Shoes, socks, hats, shirts and maybe toys. There must be a chicken or turkey and perhaps a bottle or two of brandy.

Christmas Eve, which is also pay-day, I come home laden with gifts, but before I get home I meet a group of people in comic dress singing jazz or pop songs they have made up for the season. Women's bodies bulge disturbingly in men's attire, and men with painted faces and lips, wearing short dresses, walk with an awkward sway. I follow them aimlessly, lured by their song and frolic. I follow them along dirty, twisting streets and through smelly backyards, walking into pools of stagnant water. I find myself miles from home and tappet back to find friends waiting for me.

'Happy Christmas!' they shout, shaking my hand. I'm expected to offer drinks, but past 'dry' Christmases have taught me my lesson and five minutes later they drift out. I can't afford to give everybody a drink. Then the girls walk in. They are lovely, they are happy and distracting, as only African girls can be. I find myself putting a bottle on the table. Jazz trumpets blare in the background as we drink and dance round and round in the room until I collapse.

Then it is Christmas morning. My head is heavy, my tongue is bitter and my body is numb. The streets become swarmed with merrymakers carrying drinks, because nobody gets arrested on Christmas. Girls wearing trousers shout: 'Happy!' Cars speed wildly along the narrow streets, forcing us into the gutters. The filth from the gutter is laughed off. Somewhere along the way we find a little girl's body on the side of the gutter. She was unlucky.

We meet other groups, exchange drinks and greetings. We go up one street and witness a fight. Four hoodlums are stabbing one man. He tries to break away from them and run for it, but they stay with him, their blades sinking into his body until he falls. One of four 'heroes' kicks the fallen man in the face, and they walk off brandishing their blades and threatening to stab anybody who gets in their way. The sight of a man dying always fills me with horror. I get our group to walk off.

Somewhere on our way a woman screams and complains that a certain man wants to drag her away by force. We turn round to face the man and find ourselves confronted by a hostile gang of armed thugs. The girls scream and rush in all directions. Some of us get stabbed. Then I walk home. Dejected.

Ambulances stream past with frightful regularity. The groups become fewer, the wails of women long and frequent, and I shut my door and feel sorry for the race of man and for being part of it. The greatest killer in the locations is the season of Christmas, and the one day I dread to look at the newspapers is the day after Christmas.

But in my mind I know there should be a Christmas away from the crowded streets, the smelling gutters and the killing animals who cannot be happy without causing misery. It will be full of good cheer. Perhaps I am a dreamer. If so, then I never want to wake and find myself with the Christmases I know.

William 'Bloke' Modisane
Drum, December 1955.

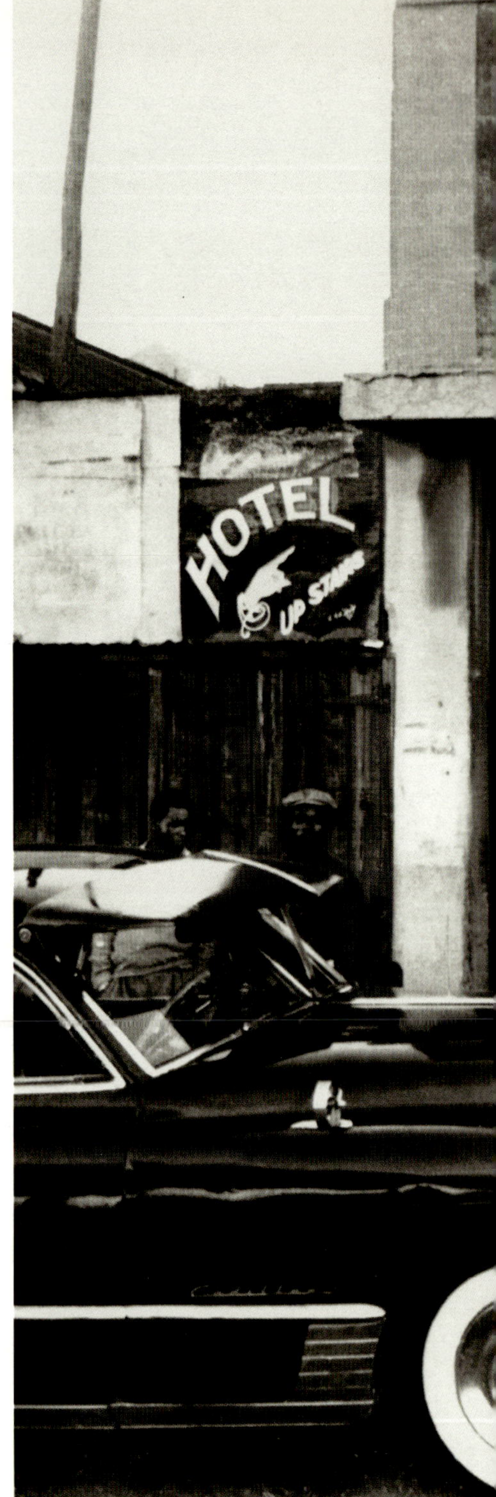

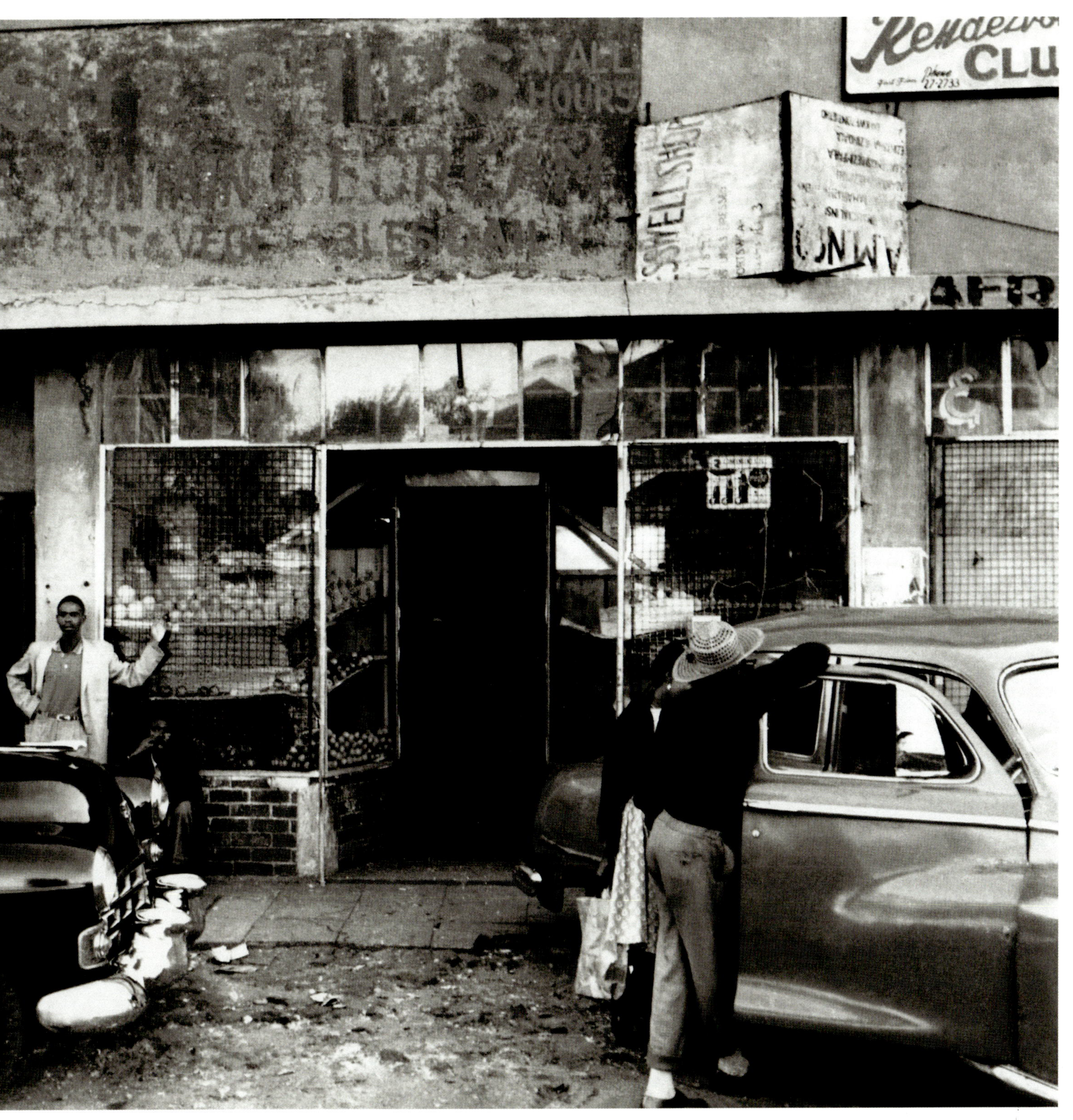

SOPHIATOWN 1957
'Sophiatown, my beloved Sophiatown, the centre
of the metropolis'... but still as some streets
disappeared, as people moved in pockets, life
went on as before.

JÜRGEN SCHADEBERG

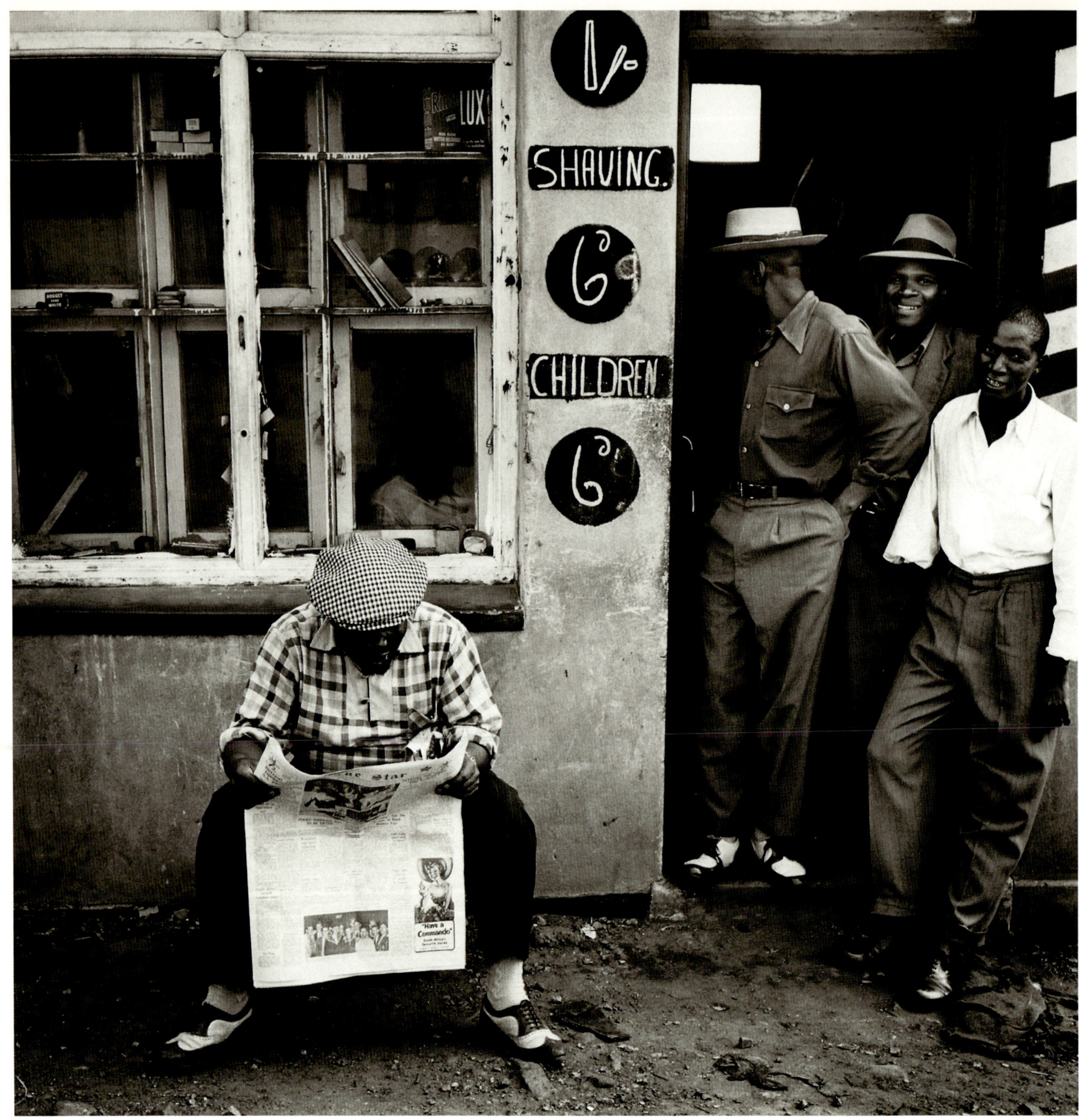

SOPHIATOWN 1959
The city within a city, the 'Gay Paris' of
Johannesburg, the notorious Casbah Gang den,
the most shebeenist of all. Sophiatown is now
breathing for the last time.

JÜRGEN SCHADEBERG

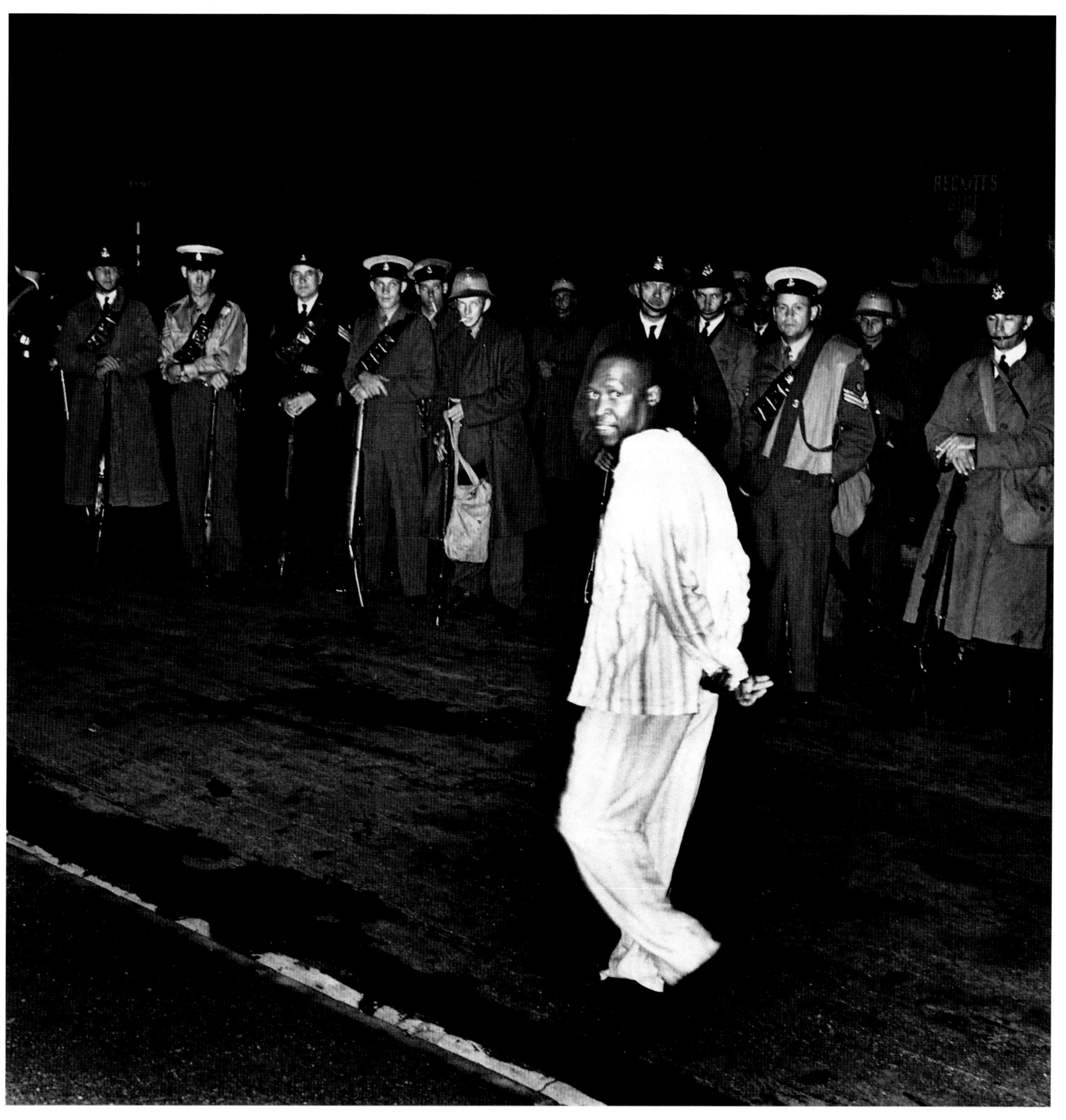

SOPHIATOWN 1955
It took 2 000 armed police and army reinforcements to move the first 100 African families and their belongings to Meadowlands.

JÜRGEN SCHADEBERG

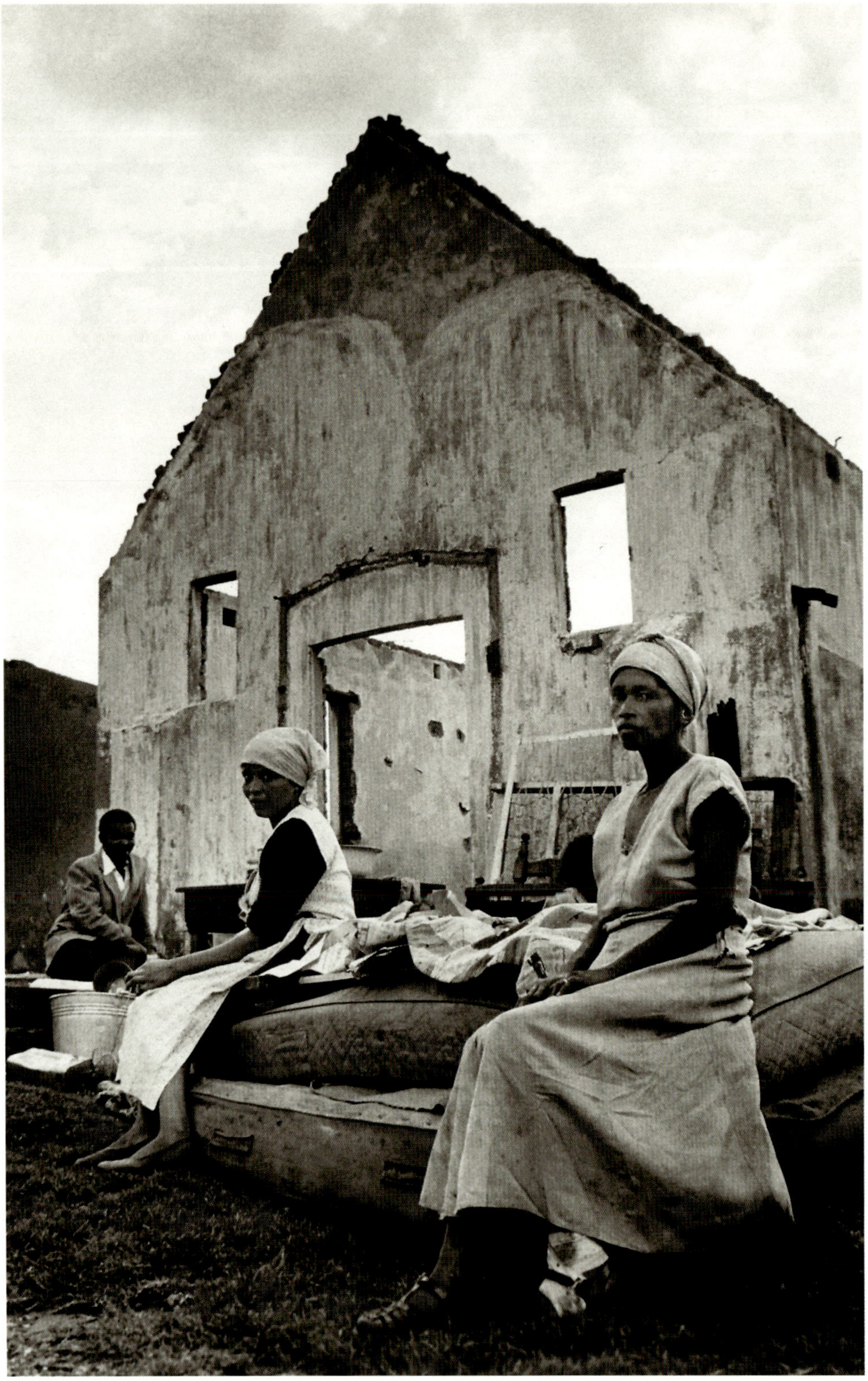

SOPHIATOWN 1959
Waiting for the trucks, their home has been demolished and they are ready to be moved to the matchbox houses in Meadowlands.

JÜRGEN SCHADEBERG

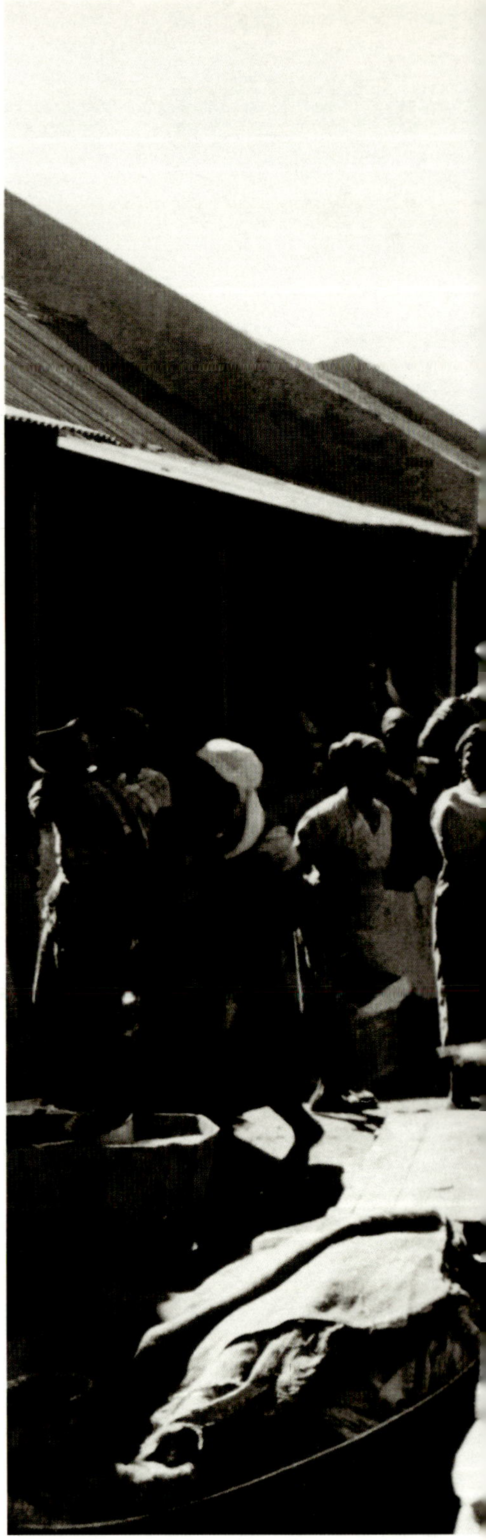

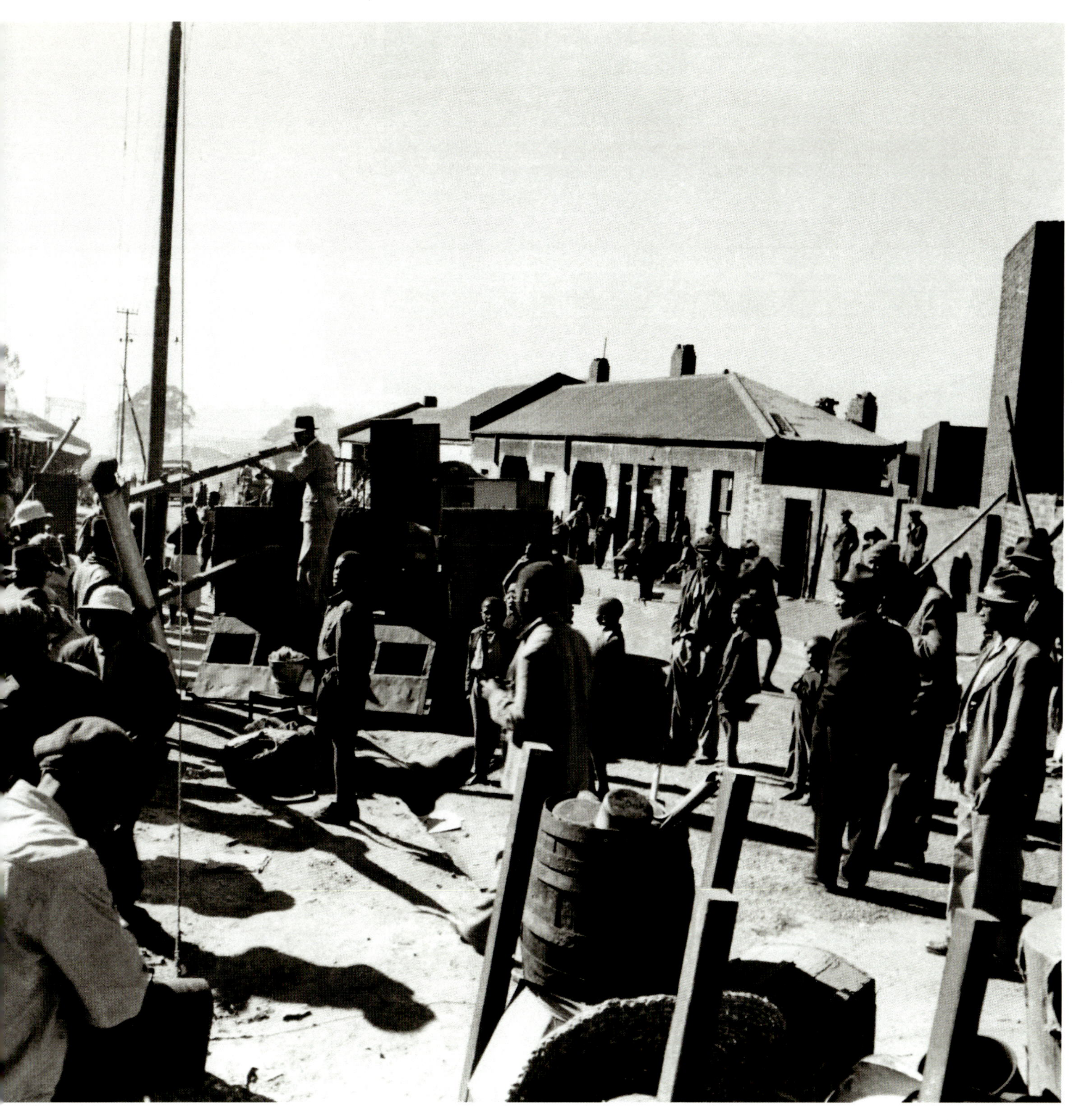

SOPHIATOWN 1959
All their belongings are piled onto the Army
trucks. Soon afterwards their houses were
bulldozed flat.

PETER MAGUBANE

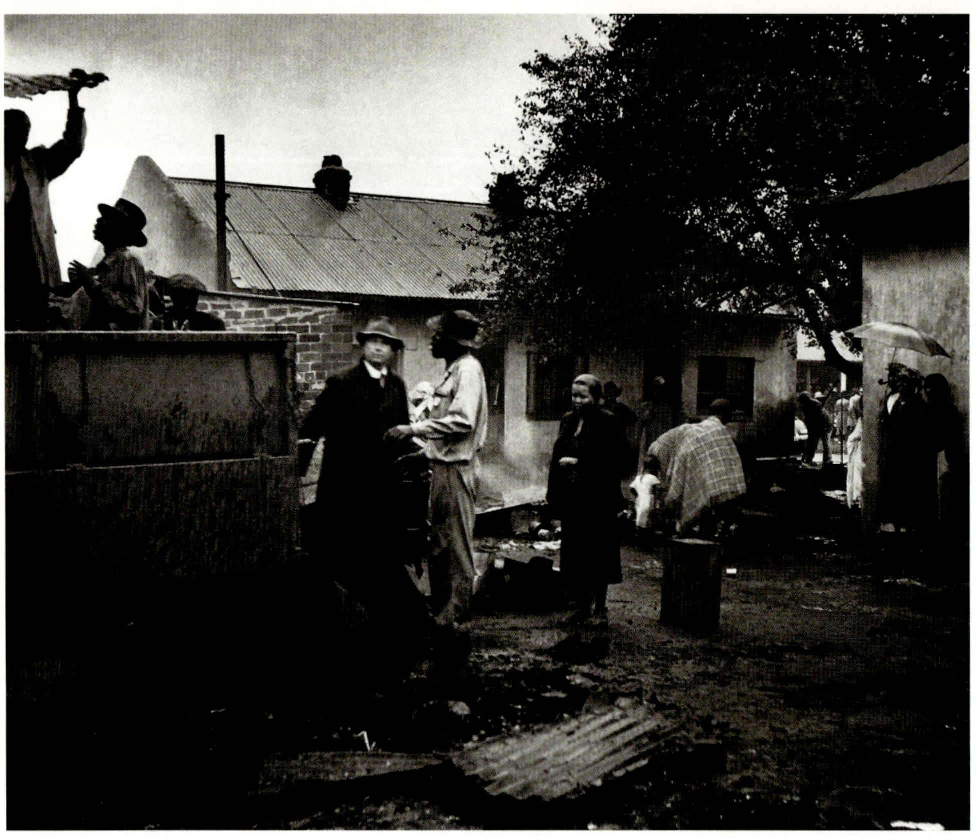

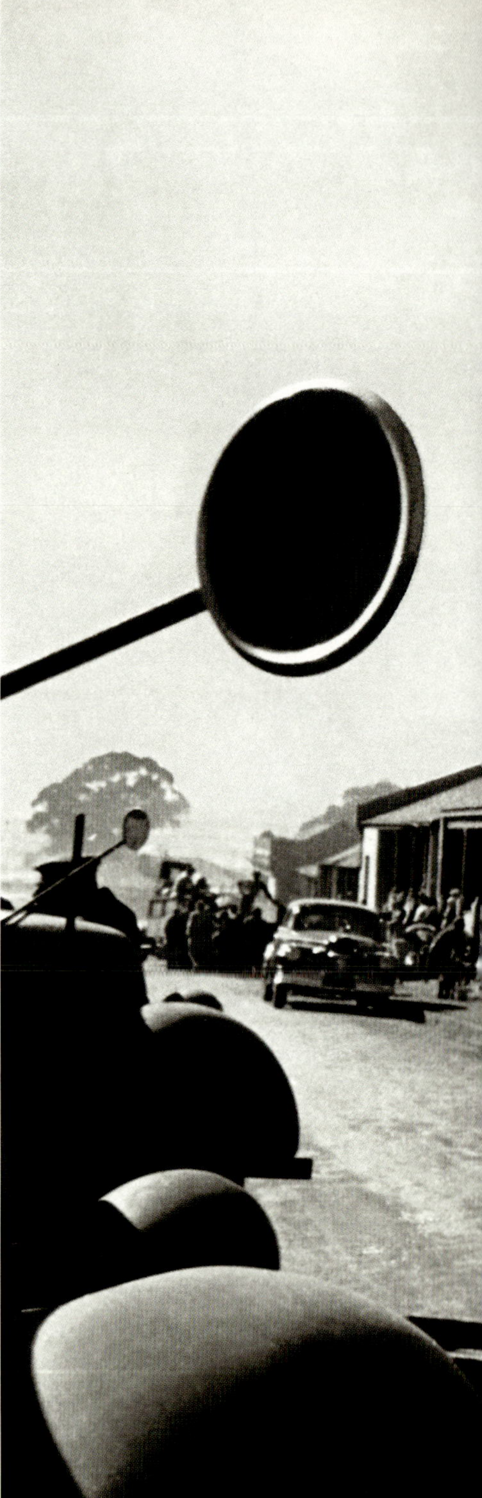

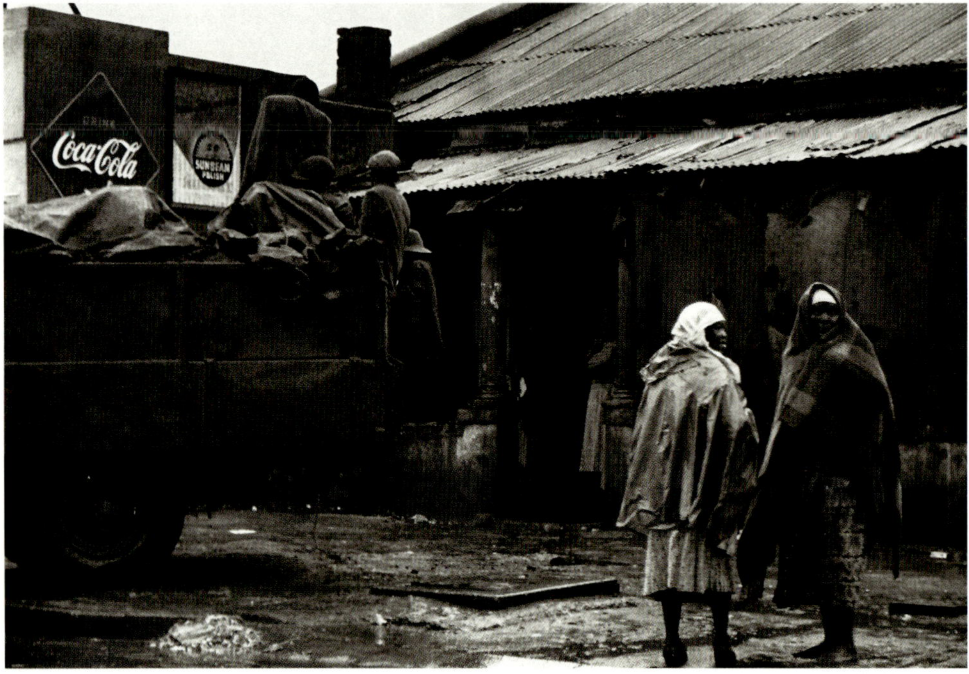

SOPHIATOWN 1959
*In sunshine and rainstorms the people and their
belongings were moved. And after the people had
gone, the demolition squads moved in.*

BOB GOSANI (left)

PETER MAGUBANE (below and right)

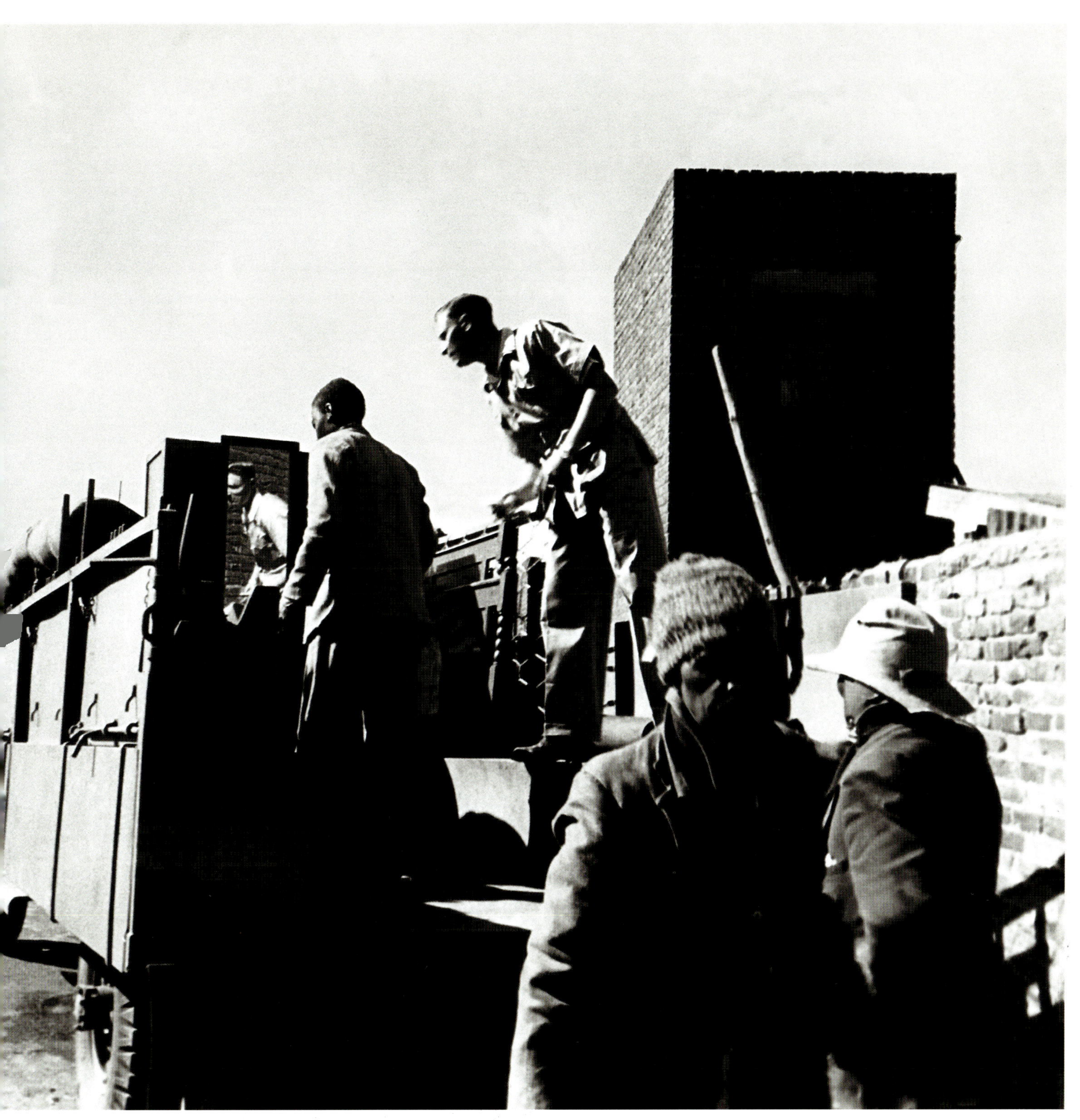

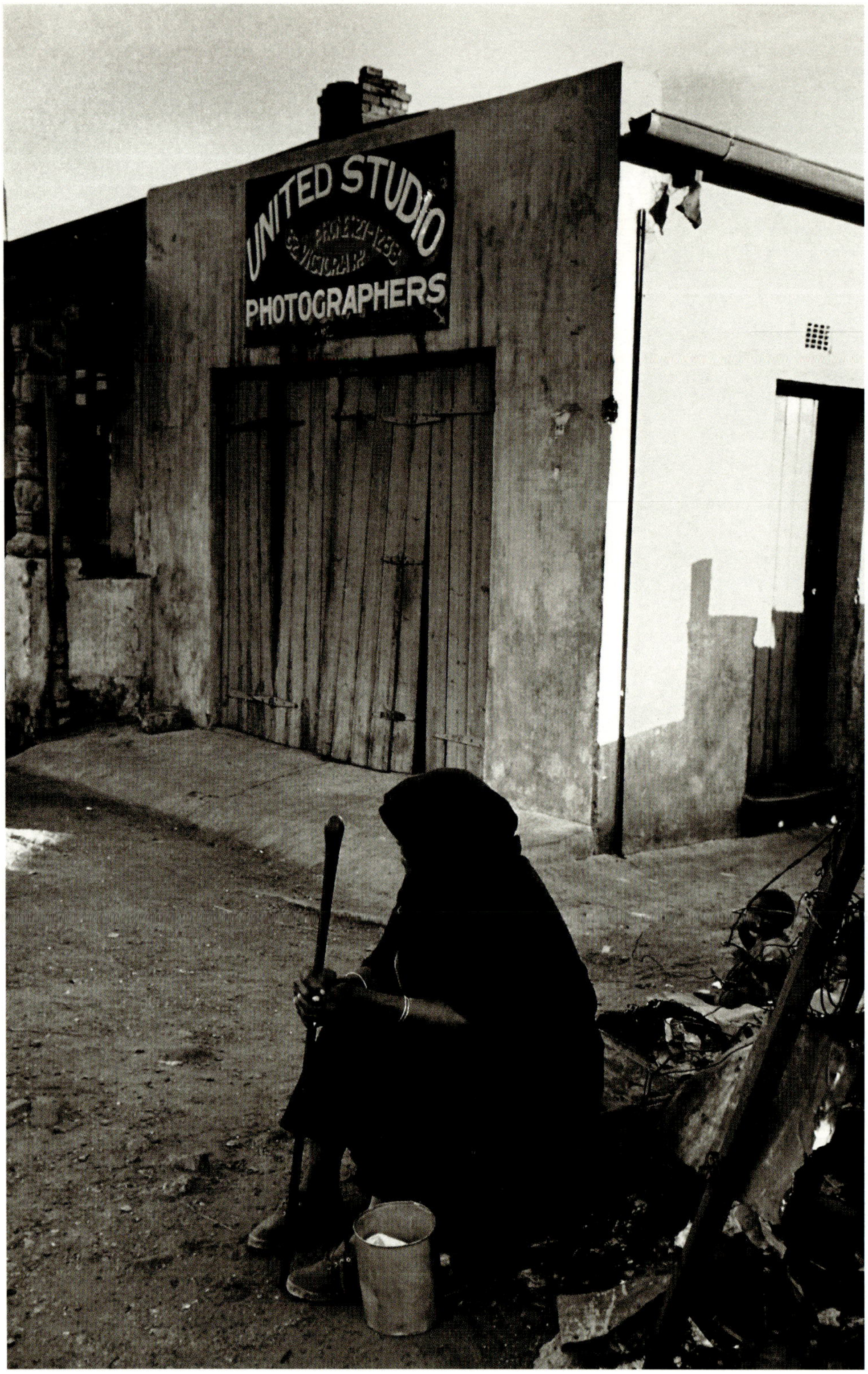

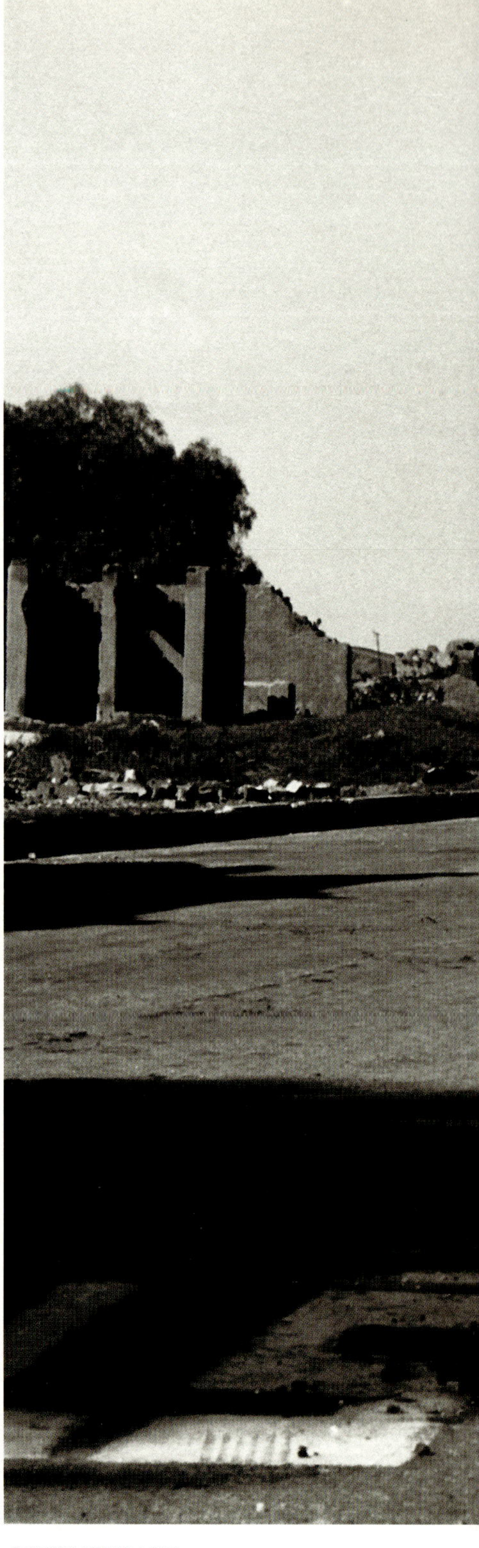

SOPHIATOWN 1959
By 1959 most of the houses in Sophiatown had disappeared. Big machines and men with picks beat down the last walls of Sof'town. Take a last look and say goodbye.

JÜRGEN SCHADEBERG

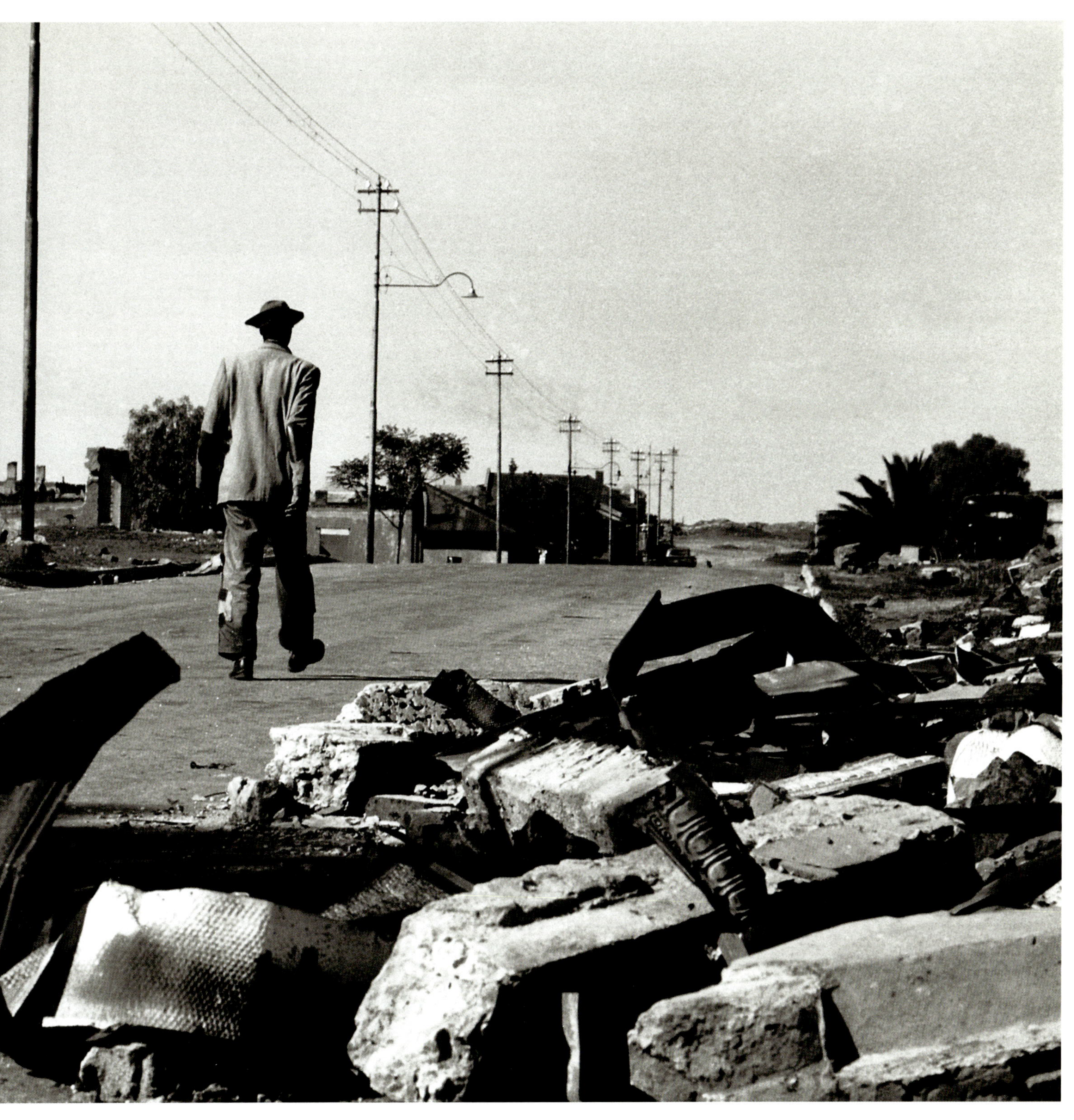

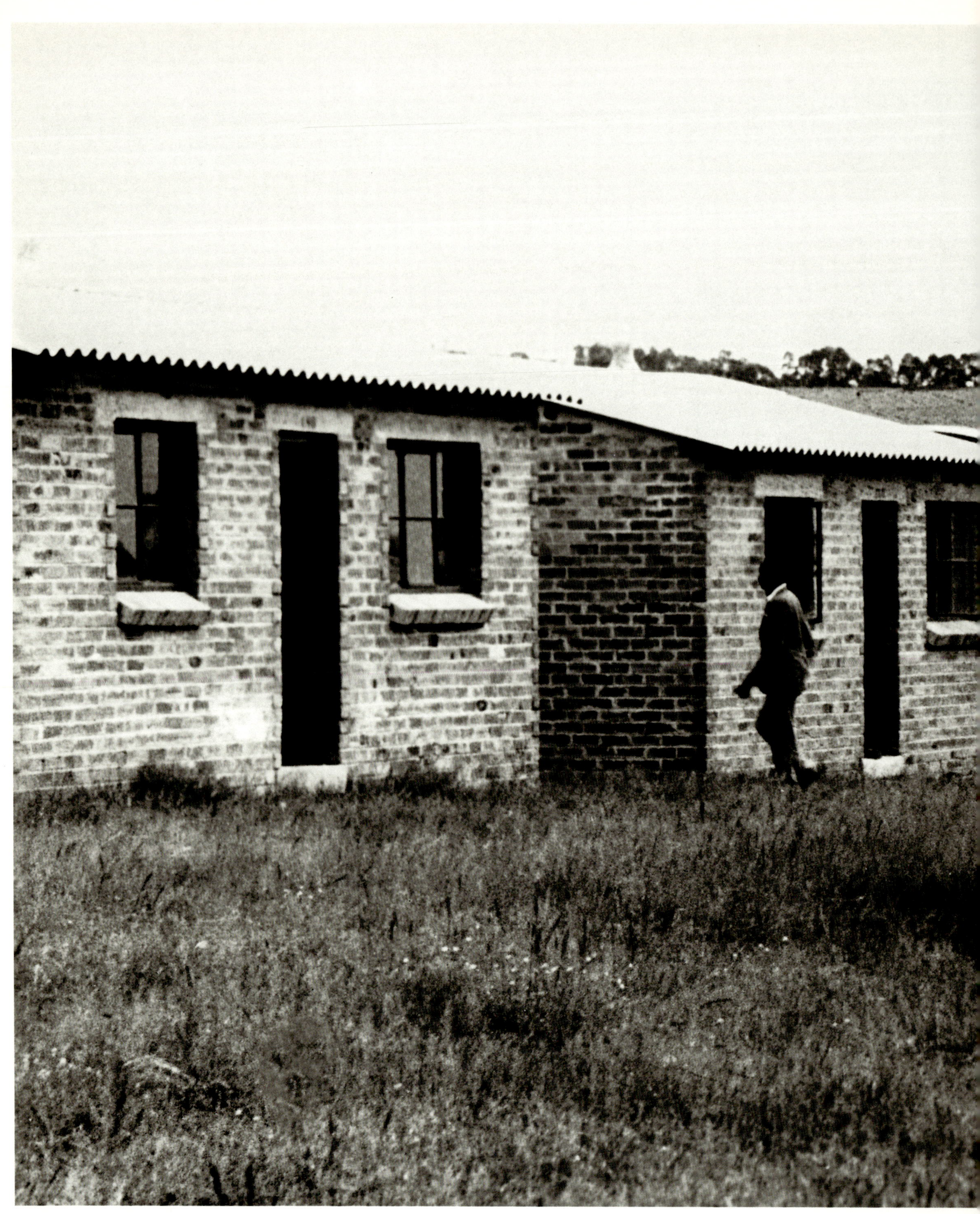

MEADOWLANDS 1959 *The families from Sophiatown ended up in these small matchbox houses, and they were four times further from their places of work than before.*

BOB GOSANI

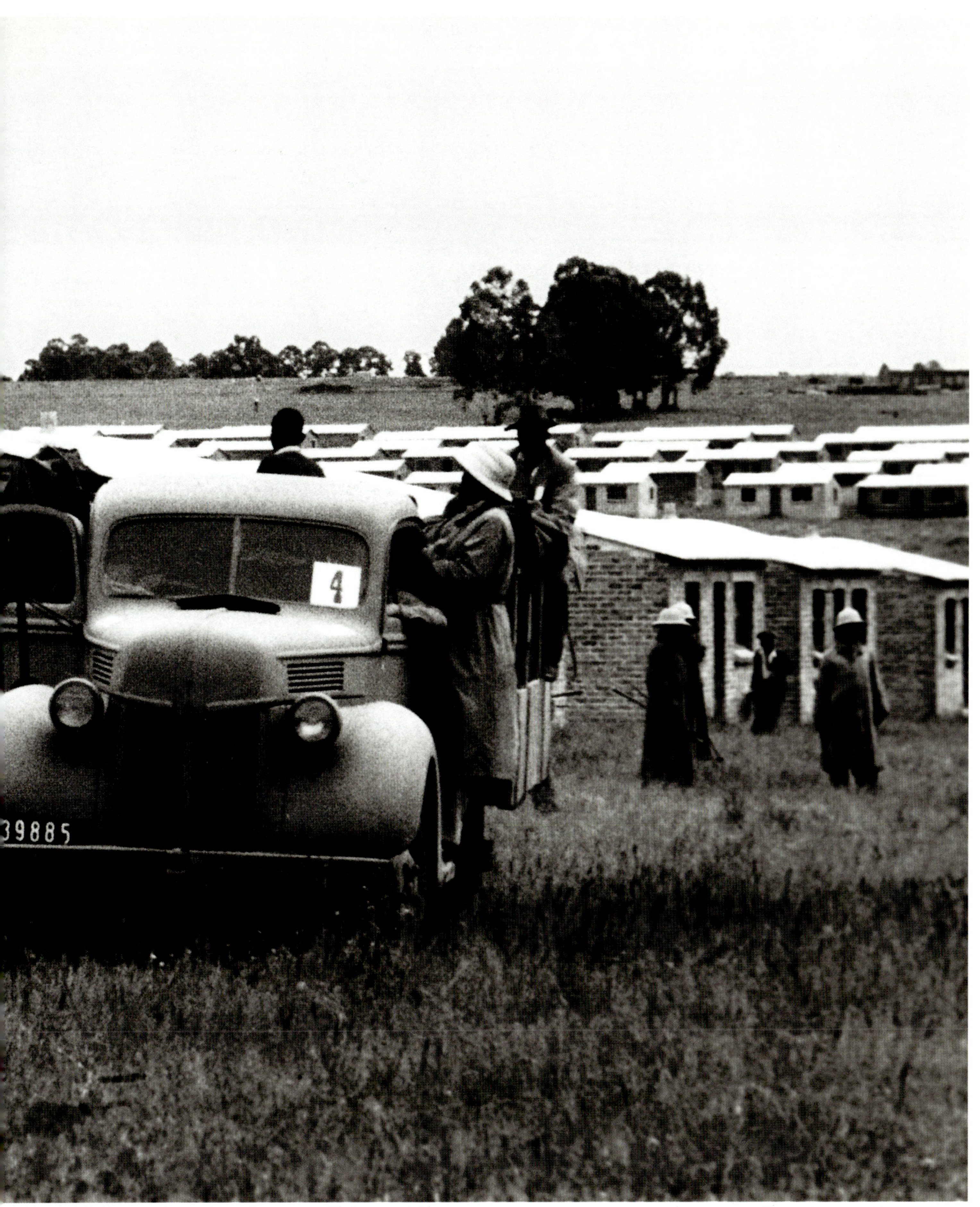

A Who's Who of the 1950s

YUSUF DADOO: Born in Krugersdorp, in 1909. His father sent him to High School in India and later to study medicine in London. There he became involved in fighting for the independence of India. In 1936, he returned to South Africa where he became President of the South African Indian Congress. Dadoo participated in the 1952 Defiance Campaign. He was arrested several times because he proclaimed himself a communist. Officially, he practiced as a medical doctor and in 1960, after Sharpeville, escaped to Botswana and then moved with his family to England. In 1972, Yusuf Dadoo became the leader of the Communist Party of South Africa. He remained as leader until his death on 19 September 1983.

MANILAL GANDHI: Born in India in 1892. He was the second son of Mahatma Gandhi. He came to South Africa with his mother and brothers when he was still a young boy. Manilal Gandhi never managed to move out of his famous fathers' shadow. The young Ghandi strove to imitate his fathers' way of thinking and living, but in the process was often misunderstood by political leaders of the resistance movements. Some thought that he was politically immature and that his emphasis on individualism would achieve nothing in the context of South African politics. Manilal was deeply religious, and his intense personal desire for justice and peace was founded in his vital religious faith. He died in 1956.

ROBERT 'BOB' GOSANI: Was born in 1934. In 1952 he started working as an apprentice photographer in the darkroom at *Drum*. Gosani soon became recognised as one of the top photographers of the 1950s. After a serious motorcar accident in 1957, where he lost a lung, he worked as a freelance photographer. He died in August, 1972.

HELEN JOSEPH: Born in England in 1906. Soon after she came out to South Africa she became very involved in the anti-apartheid struggle. She was one of the founding members of the Congress of Democrats and for a time was its Vice President. In 1954 she was also one of the founding members of the Federation of South African Women, the organisation which led the world-famous march of 20 000 women to the Union Buildings in 1956. The women were protesting the extension of passes to African women. In 1956 Helen Joseph was one of the accused in the Treason Trial. She, together with all the other accused, was acquitted in March 1961. In the 1960s and 1970s, she was continuously banned and placed under house arrest. In 1986, at the age of 81 she published her autobiography entitled *Side by Side*, which was banned in South Africa for many years. She died in December 1992.

ALBERT LUTHULI: Was born in 1898, and was the son of a minister. The family lived in what was then Southern Rhodesia at the Solisisia Mission station. In 1920, Albert Luthuli became a teacher at Adams College. For two years he was the leader of the Teachers Union in Natal. He campaigned tirelessly for better wages for teachers. In 1936, he became an elder of the Groutville Mission which was situated in the midst of Natal's sugar cane industry. Luthuli became aware of the conditions under which sugar cane workers worked and began to fight for their rights. In 1945, Albert Luthuli became a member of the ANC. By 1951 he had become leader of the Natal branch. In 1952, he was elected National President of the ANC and retained this position untill 1960. In that year he was banned from holding office in his organisation and from meeting with more than two people at a time. But the international community recognised his efforts towards peace, and he was awarded the Nobel Peace Prize in 1961. In 1962, the University of Glasgow offered Luthuli the position of Rector, but the South African authorities denied him a passport. Still banned from public gatherings, Chief Luthuli spent his last years as a small farmer. In 1967, Chief Luthuli, his eyesight and hearing failing, crossed the Umvoti River railway bridge where he was struck down by a goods train. He died from the injuries sustained.

ARTHUR MAIMANE: Born in Pietersburg, in 1932. In 1951, he joined *Drum* where he became a sports writer and entertainment columnist. He wrote a series of fast moving detective stories, in a Peter Cheney style, which were published in *Africa* and *Drum*. Later he became news editor for *The Golden City Post*. In 1958, he went to Ghana where he worked as *Drum* correspondent. Later he moved into radio work. In 1961, Arthur Maimane went to London where he worked for British Television, first for the BBC and later in 1973, as producer for an independent news station, ITN. In 1990, Arthur Maimane returned to South Africa to work for the *Weekly Mail* and in 1994 he became managing editor of *The Star*.

MIRIAM MAKEBA: Known as the 'Girl with the smile in her voice', Miriam Makeba was born in Jeppe on 4 March 1932. Her father, a teacher, died when she was seven years old and Miriam's sangoma mother sent her to live with her grandmother in Pretoria. There she sang in the choir at the Methodist school. However, there wasn't enough money to keep Miriam at school, and eventually she was forced to leave. She managed to find work as a domestic servant. In 1952, she first started singing on stage when she joined the Cuban Brothers. In 1954, she sang with the Manhattan Brothers. In 1957, she teamed up with the African Jazz Group, and met her first husband Sonny Pillay. In 1958, Miriam joined the jazz opera *King Kong* and then left South Africa. In London, she was discovered by Harry Belafonte, who groomed her, transforming her from a retiring Xhosa girl into the refined cosmopolitan lady of song who became world famous for her *Click Song, Mbube* and *Kilimanjaro*. While in New York she married Hugh Masekela. In 1969, Miriam married for the third time — civil rights campaigner, Stokely Carmichael. They settled in Conakry in Guinea. In 1990, she returned to South Africa for the first time since her exile, and since then has been commuting between Europe and South Africa.

NELSON ROLIHLAHLA MANDELA: Was born in Qunu, Transkei, in 1918. He was the son of a Xhosa Chief. He studied law at Fort Hare University and the University of the Witwatersrand in Johannesburg. In 1952, together with Oliver Tambo, he started his own law practice in Johannesburg. In 1944, together with a number of younger members of the ANC, he started the ANC Youth League. The Youth League argued for more radical and direct action against the laws which oppressed black people. They believed the ANC's policy of protest through petitions and legal channels had not achieved anything for black people. Mandela became Youth League president in 1950. In 1952, he was the main organiser for the Defiance Campaign where scores of people went to jail for defying what they believed to be unjust laws. In 1956, Mandela was one of the main accused in the famous Treason Trial. He was acquitted in 1961. After the Sharpeville massacre during a pass protest in 1960, and the banning of the ANC and PAC, Nelson Mandela went underground. Although he was wanted by the South African police, he continued to give interviews to the press and make appearances at meetings. In 1962, Mandela was involved in the formation of the military wing of the ANC 'Umkhonto we Sizwe' (Spear of the Nation). In the same year, he left South Africa and visited Ethiopia. In Addis Ababa, Mandela addressed a conference of the Pan Africanist movement. He later visited Algiers and London. There he met Hugh Gaitskil, and sought aid,

arms and money for the ANC. On 5 August Nelson Mandela was arrested in Howick, Natal, posing as a chauffeur. He was tried in a Johannesburg court and was found guilty of leaving the country without a passport and causing incitement to strike. He was sentenced to five years imprisonment on Robben Island. In 1964, at the Rivonia Treason Trial, Mandela and seven others were sentenced to life imprisonment on Robben Island. Mandela was finally released from prison in February 1990. In April 1994, he was elected as the first black president in the first democratic election in the history of South Africa.

HUGH MASEKELA: Born in Witbank in 1939. When he was fourteen, he saw a film called 'Young man with a Horn'. This inspired him to learn to play the trumpet. He first played in the Huddleston Jazz Band founded by Father Trevor Huddleston. Huddleston, impressed by the young Masekela's playing, organised a special trumpet for him from Louis Armstrong. In the early 1950s, together with Jonas Gwangwa, Masekela formed The Merry Makers of Springs. In 1959, he played with Dollar Brand in a group called Jazz Epistoles. Eventually he left South Africa. Masekela studied at the Royal Academy of Music in London, and then went to America, where he made recordings and went on many tours. One of his greatest successes was in 1967 — a song called *Grazing in the Grass*. In 1980, he returned to Southern Africa, first to Zimbabwe and then later to Botswana. In 1986 he founded the 'Botswana International School of Music', a non-commercial institute to support African musicians. In the early 1990s Masekela returned to South Africa to live.

ZACHARIAH KEODIRELANG MATTHEWS: Was born in Kimberley in 1902. His father worked as a labourer on the diamond mines and in later years owned a cafe. ZK, as he was known, supported himself during his high school years by working as a waiter. He

became the first black person to receive a BA degree in South Africa — this he obtained from Fort Hare University. He obtained a teaching post at Adam's College in Natal. While teaching, ZK studied law, and after receiving his law degree, he practiced as a attorney. He then got his MA from Yale University in the United States of America. He undertook further studies at the London School of Economics, and was then offered a post at Fort Hare University in Economics and Social Anthropology. In 1945 he was appointed Professor of African Studies at Fort Hare University. Matthews had been an active member of the ANC since 1940. He became a recognised leader and was asked to give evidence before the United Nations hearings on apartheid. When he returned to South Africa in 1952, his passport was withdrawn by the South African authorities. He was also, in 1956, among those arrested and charged with treason. Together with his co-accused, he was acquitted in 1961. In 1962, ZK left South Africa to take up a post as Secretary of Africa on the World Council of Churches in Geneva. Later he was appointed Botswana's Ambassador to the United States and permanent representative at the United Nations. In 1967, he received a Honorary Doctorate of Law degree from the Franklin and Marshall College in Pennsylvania. He died in Washington in 1968.

KIPPY MOEKETSI: Born in Sophiatown in 1926. He left school at an early age and went to live in the George Goch hostel in Johannesburg. He sold newspapers and also worked as a golf caddy. In the late 1940s, he learned to play the clarinet. He wanted to make 'Jazz Music', not 'Bantu Music' and certainly nothing commercial. Then he formed South Africa's first 'saxtet' with General Duze and Mackay Davashe. By the early 1950s Moeketsi had become an institution in the South African jazz scene and was known as a genius with the saxophone. In 1960, he joined the

King Kong Jazz Opera and went with this production to London. Back in South Africa he made records and played in small clubs. For many, Kippy Moeketsi was the most profoundly influential and most important jazz musician South Africa has ever known. He died on 27 April 1983.

CASEY MOTSISI: Born in 1933 in Western Native Township. He went to school with Stanley Motjuwadi, who later became editor of *Drum*. During their high school years, Stanley and Casey earned their pocket money by selling sweets on trains. An important influence on Casey at this time was his English teacher, Can Themba. After they matriculated, both Stan and Casey went to 'Normal College' in Pretoria, where they co-edited a student magazine. When Can Themba became the editor of *Drum's* sister magazine *Africa*, Can employed Casey as assistant editor. Soon, Casey began to write his own column for *Drum*. His columns were first headed 'Bugs' and later 'On the Beat' — and he wrote about Johannesburg township and shebeen life. For over twenty years, Casey's pen recorded the humour, pathos and irony of contemporary township life. He died in 1977.

PETER MAGUBANE: Was born in Frededorp in 1932. He left high school after four years and in 1955 joined *Drum* as a driver and messenger. After going on assignments with reporters and photographers, he soon began to carry a camera. Within a few years, he became a top photographer at *Drum*. In the early 1960s Magubane worked for the *Rand Daily Mail*. In 1963, he had his first photographic exhibition in Johannesburg. In the late 1960s, Magubane was banned, and then subsequently arrested. He spent 586 days in prison, including ninety eight days in solitary confinement. His subsequent banning order ran for five years and one of its provisions was that he was not allowed to take photographs. Peter Magubane has won numerous international prizes for his photographs and has published many books of his photographic works.

LILLIAN NGOYI: Was born in Pretoria in 1911. Her mother worked as a washer woman in white households and her father was a miner in the Eastern Transvaal. Lillian went to the Kilnerton Training Institute to train as a teacher but had to leave after the first year due to lack of funds. She then went to City Deep Mine hospital to train as a nurse. In 1952, she participated in the Defiance Campaign. Ngoyi became very involved in women's issues in the ANC and soon became Vice President of the Women's League. She was also soon to become the leader of the Federation of South African Women, and led the famous anti pass march to Pretoria in 1956. Lillian Ngoyi was the first African woman member to be on the Transvaal and National Executive of the ANC. In 1954, she became the treasurer of the South African non-European Council of Trade Unions. Ngoyi was one of those charged with treason in the 1956 Treason Trial. Soon after her acquittal in 1961 she was banned. The banning order, from 1962 to 1972, prevented her from finding proper work and she was forced to make a living by taking in sewing jobs. In 1956, she was elected president of the ANC Woman's League and remained so until her death in 1980.

NATHANIEL NDANZANA NAKASA: Born in Durban in 1937. He started his journalistic career on the newspaper *Llanga Lase Natal*. In 1955, he joined *Drum* in Johannesburg. He found many of the themes for his stories amongst the intellectuals of Hillbrow. With the help of Nadine Gordimer he started a literary magazine called *The Classic* and was the first black writer to be given a weekly column on the Johannesburg newspaper *The Rand Daily Mail*. Nakasa's style was highly personal, he presented a most enticing picture of the reality of daily life. Nakasa was awarded a scholarship to Harvard University, but the South African authorities refused to issue him with a passport. After serious consideration he decided to leave South Africa and live in exile. He went to the United States on an exit permit (valid for one exit only) which prevented him from ever returning to South Africa. After a year at Harvard he wrote extensively for newspapers and magazines. He appeared on television in the programme 'The fruit of the fear' and 'The critic of apartheid'. He was also commissioned to write the biography of Miriam Makeba. But Nakasa was depressed and homesick. In New York, early on the morning of 14 July 1965, he plunged seven storeys to his death.

HENRY NXUMALO: Was born in Port Shepstone, Natal in 1918. Henry's father Lazarus and his mother Josephine had seven children. Henry was the eldest. Henry left school at the age of sixteen and went to Durban where he worked as a kitchen boy. He trekked to Johannesburg where he found work in a boilermakers shop. In his spare time he began to write poetry, some of which was published by *Bantu World*. This newspaper then employed him as a messenger, and after three years he had risen to become the sports editor. He joined the army during the war and then returned to *Bantu World*. At that time he also wrote a regular column for the *Pittsburgh Courier*. Henry joined *Drum* as a sports editor in 1951 and soon became known as 'Mr Drum' for his investigative journalism. One of his more famous stories involved him signing up as a labourer on the scandalous Bethal potato farms. He then created a minor offense in order to be arrested, so that he could investigate the Fort Prison. In 1957, while researching a story about abortions, Henry was murdered.

DOLLY RATHEBE: Born in 1928 and grew up in Sophiatown. She started her career by singing at church, weddings and wakes. Wakes in Sophiatown were a social institution to which everyone went even if you didn't know the dearly departed. She then became a big local star when she landed a lead singing role in *Jim Comes to Jo'burg*. By 1956, Dolly was a well loved member of the 'African Jazz and Variety' theatre show. Dolly Rathebe made many records and amongst her most popular songs were *Umbombele, Kea Kea Lebone* and *Kiddies Blues*. Since the early 1990s she has sung with The Elite Swingsters and has travelled to Europe. She has also acted in a number of television dramas and feature films.

WALTER SISULU: Born in Ngcobo, Transkei, in 1913. His family was very poor and he was not able to complete his schooling. He went to Johannesburg as a teenager in order to find work. There he worked as a miner. In the 1930s, Walter became active in the cultural society at the Bantu Men's Social Club. He sang in church choirs and generally set about improving his education. He also became active in the rehabilitation of juvenile delinquents. At that time he worked in a bakery, where he proceeded to organise the workers. This, of course led to him being fired unconditionally and he started a news agency, a printing works and newspaper. In 1940, he joined the ANC and after nine years became its general secretary. He also became very involved in the ANC's Youth League. In 1953, he represented the ANC Youth League on a visit to the Soviet Union. From 1956 to 1961, he was one of the accused in the Treason Trial, and was acquitted in 1961. In 1961, he organised a general strike and was put under house arrest. He then went underground. In 1963, together with other ANC leaders, he was arrested at Lilliesleaf farm in Rivonia, and in 1964 was sentenced to life imprisonment on Robben Island. In 1989 Walter Sisulu was finally released from prison. In 1994 he was still active as Vice President of the ANC and as a member of Parliament.

OLIVER TAMBO: Born in Bizana, Pondoland in 1917, where he was educated at a mission station until he was sixteen years old. He then went to Fort Hare University and did a correspondence course in law. In the early 1940s, Tambo joined the ANC. In 1944, together with others he formed the ANC Youth League. In 1952, Tambo opened a law practice in Johannesburg together with Nelson Mandela. In the same year he became general secretary of the ANC. Oliver Tambo married a nurse, Adelaide, from Sharpeville, and together they had three children. From 1956 to 1961 Tambo was one of the accused in the Treason Trial. He was acquitted in 1961. After the ANC was banned in 1960, Oliver Tambo went to live in London. He was central to building up the organisation in exile and in 1967 he was elected president of the ANC. In 1989 he suffered a stroke in Harare in Zimbabwe. In December 1990, for the first time since he went into exile, he returned to South Africa, where he died in 1993.

DORSAY CAN THEMBA: Born in Pretoria in 1924. He was awarded the Mendi Scholarship to study at Fort Hare University. He then went to the Western Native Bantu School, where he taught English and studied for a degree in Political Philosophy. In 1952, Can Themba won a *Drum* short story competition. He quit teaching and joined *Drum* publications to edit a new magazine called *Africa*. He later became assistant editor of *Drum*. Can was well known in Sophiatown, where he called his home 'The House of Truth'. There all were made welcome. He continued to write and published a number of short stories. In 1962 he moved to Swaziland where he practiced as a teacher. In 1967 he died of a coronary thrombosis.

Chronology
1948 - 1960

1948

❑ 26 May. The Afrikaner National Party won the parliamentary elections. The party fought the election under the slogan 'Apartheid'. Until this period, the British colonial power and the government it controlled had established laws which favoured the white economy and population. After the election these same laws became far more restrictive and detailed. Apartheid ideology was based on racist motives.

❑ 3 June. DF Malan became Prime Minister and formed his government.

1949

❑ The African National Congress elected a new leadership, which involved the radical 'Youth League' branch which had elected Nelson Mandela and Oliver Tambo. The 1912-formed organisation retained its non-violent policy but moved away from the strategy of petitioning and begging for their political rights. From then on it created pressure by mobilising the masses.

❑ The Prohibition of Mixed Marriages Act became law and prohibited interracial marriages between whites and non-whites.

1950

❑ Hendrik F Verwoerd, the chief architect of apartheid theory became Minister of Native Affairs.

❑ The introduction of the Population Registration Act. This act enabled the government to classify people on the basis of race, from birth.

❑ The Suppression of Communism Act. This act outlawed anything to do with communism, which the government believed was the basis on which there were many attempts to undermine the state and the government. This act allowed for the banning of persons, organisations, political activity, and included a provision for house arrests.

❑ Introduction of the Group Areas Act, which opened the way for forced removals and the separation of different racial groups into their own suburbs and townships.

❑ Banning of the South African Communist Party. The party was one of the most important supporters of the South African Indian Congress and later the ANC. From then on, the South African Communist Party operated underground.

1951

❑ March, Cape Town. The first issue of *African Drum* was published. Later, the editorial moved to Johannesburg and Anthony Sampson became editor.

1952

❑ The Native Laws Amendment Act was passed It restricted and controlled the movement of blacks into the city even further, and without work blacks were not permitted to remain in the city for longer than seventy two hours. Only males had to carry passes at all times, which allowed them to stay in one district only. But it was made public knowledge that women would soon have to carry passes.

❑ April. The Defiance Campaign began, organised by the ANC and the South African Indian Congress. Using the principles of Mahatma Gandhi, thousands of volunteers deliberately broke apartheid laws and were arrested.

1953

❑ The Separate Amenities Act was introduced, whereby all public facilities were separated — libraries, hotels, sports facilities, bars, education and transport etc.

❑ The Bantu Education Act was also introduced. This act meant that the government controlled the education of blacks in all schools and the state took over a large number of private schools.

1954

❑ The Industrial Conciliation Amendment Act reserved more work places for whites only. The white working class, most of whom had inferior education, benefitted from this law.

1955

❑ February. The forced removals of the residents of Sophiatown began. It took four years to remove these people from the 'Paris' of Johannesburg to various areas of what was to become Soweto.

❑ 26 June. At 'The Congress of the People' in Kliptown, 3000 delegates met. They came from a variety of organisations and groups which included the ANC, the South African Indian Congress, The Coloured Peoples Congress and the Congress of Democrats. They drafted the Freedom Charter, a document which later became the programme of the ANC, and which proposed a multi-racial, and equal society in a democratic South Africa.

❑ 28 September. Throughout South Africa the police raided offices of opposition organisations. Large numbers of documents were seized and confiscated.

❑ The Thomlinson Commission report was published. The report became the blueprint for the politics of Separate Development, which later formed the basis of Homeland Policy.

1956

❑ 9 August. 20 000 women of all racial groups, under the leadership of Lillian Ngoyi and Helen Joseph, marched to Pretoria. They presented a petition to the government protesting against the issuing of passes to women.

1957

❑ January. Nation-wide price rise of bus fares. A month-long bus boycott began. Lifts were organised from the townships to cities and places of work. Many people walked to work.

❑ The city centres were declared 'white areas'. In general, Indian businesses had most to lose with this law.

1958

❑ HF Verwoerd became Prime Minister.

❑ 26 June. A three-day National Strike began.

1959

❑ Under the leadership of Robert Sebokwe, a splinter group of the ANC called the Pan Africanist Congress broke away. This group argued that the ANC was not militant enough because of its association with whites and Indians, which did not help the liberation of blacks.

❑ White Universities were closed to black students.

1960

❑ 21 March. The PAC organised a national demonstration against pass laws. The police opened fire on demonstrators in Sharpeville and a total of sixty seven people were killed and 186 wounded. The majority were shot in the back.

❑ Throughout South Africa, protest began against the massacre at Sharpeville. Protest strikes followed and the government declared a State of Emergency.

❑ 8 April. The ANC and PAC, under the Unlawful Organisation Act, were declared unlawful and banned.